Poetic Dialogues

Poetic Dialogues

Sandra Buechler

International Psychoanalytic Books (IPBooks)
New York • http://www.IPBooks.net

Poetic Dialogues

Published by International Psychoanalytic Books (IPBooks)
Queens, NY
Online at www.IPBooks.net

Book cover design by Kathy Kovacic
Book design and formatting services by Noel S. Morado

ISBN: 978-1-956864-05-2

For Griffin, Phoebe, Isaac, Eva, their parents, and George

Contents

CONTENTS

Acknowledgments

Poetic Dialogues wouldn't have come into being without the tireless dedication of Tamar Schwartz at IPBooks. I will always be grateful to her.

This book rests on the premise that poets sometimes tell us what we already knew but had not yet thought. They give us words for our sorrow, joy, shame and rage. Sometimes they relieve our loneliness by demonstrating that someone else, the poet, must have felt as we feel, in order to name our experiences so accurately.

To write it, I had to trust my intuition that juxtaposing lines from poems I love could bring out their meanings more fully. In other words, I had to trust the power of my own associative process. For nurturing this faith, I thank the members of my peer group, Mark Blechner, Richard Gartner, John O'Leary, Annie Rosen, and Robert Watson, and my teachers, colleagues, and friends at the William Alanson White Institute.

Poetry is often the most honest expression of what it means to me to be alive. For inspiring a craving to communicate this, I thank Eric, Zoe, Michelle, Nick, their children, and, always, George.

1.

The Power of Poetry
to Evoke Emotions

"...overnight we could be orphaned
& the world become a hell we'd crawl inside..."
Flynn, N, "Sudden." In: *The Art of Losing: Poems of Grief and Healing*,
2010, ed. K. Young. NY, Bloomsbury, USA, p. 26.

———

A similar sense of fragility is conveyed by N.S. Nye (1995) in the poem "The Art of Disappearing" (In Moyers, 1995, p. 323) in which our lives are likened to leaves which can tumble down at any point. The poet challenges us to hold onto the feeling of being a leaf as we decide what to do with our time.

I came back to these quotes a few weeks into the Covid 19 crisis of 2020. They seemed almost too apt to bear, as I struggled with quarantine's privations and uncertainties. And yet reading them was also comforting, because, implicitly, they said someone (the poets) understood and even found words for an all-encompassing nightmare. I was still terribly worried but less lonely.

What gave these lines the power to affect me this way? We could imagine the fact that these are lines from poems is not relevant, and if they were written as lines of prose they would have the same impact. That may be so, but I think it is unlikely that they *would* be written in prose. At least for me, poets are the ones who most often "nail" what it is like to be human. Many

1

do it so economically that they startle me into consciousness of something I almost, but not quite, already knew.

Poetry marries its ideas with its rhythms. Its impact is a product of both, as well as other factors. Edward Hirsch (1999, p. 6) describes how readers complete the poem, bringing their own life experience to it. He declares that "You are reading poetry—I mean really reading it–when you feel encountered and changed by a poem, when you feel its seismic vibrations, the sounding of your depths." Hirsch goes on to write about the hypnotic effect of the rhythms and alliteration in some poems. Being impacted on several levels at once is very familiar to me, from my experiences as a psychoanalyst. I have always believed that there is an exponentially greater effect of any experience that simultaneously moves our minds and hearts, and reaches our conscious and non-conscious selves. For example, the power of many analytic interpretations stems from their content as well as the way analyst and patient are living out the (transferential) meaning of the content (even before that transferential level is made conscious). That is, if I am the analyst, and I interpret something in the patient's behavior as "passive," the power in the interpretation will be much greater if the patient and I are living out something about the dimension of passivity/activity as we speak. And that power is further enhanced when all the levels get interpreted (eventually). Experiences on several levels at once have dimensionality, or, as some of my supervisors would say, "legs." I think good poetry has legs.

Poetry lives on many thresholds–between ideas and feelings, known and unknown, poet and reader, poet and other poets, poet and other observers of human beings. Its status as a permanent visitor allows it to speak with more than one accent. Put another way, it does not owe its total allegiance to reason, or rules, or pure emotions, or any one realm. It straddles them all.

Just as an outsider (to a culture, or a family, or a profession) can sometimes see what insiders fail to register, so poetry notices what others miss. It sees the stars in ways that might not occur to the astronomer, and it sees human beings in ways that might not occur to other students of human behavior.

In this first section I reflect on how I understand poetry to work, and why some poems make me feel found. In a subsequent section I explore how some poems capture particular emotions, and how they might foster our emotional balance. In the next, I listen as two or more poets speak to each other (at least, in my imagination). Then I create a dialogue between some lines from Shakespeare's plays and poetry written well after his time.

Throughout, I make an effort to juxtapose poems with other poems or lines from other forms of literature. I believe meaning is born in dialogue. Of course each of the poems I cite has meaning on its own, but it is my belief that new meanings emerge when they converse. Poems are living beings and, like their creators, they change with new partners. As the poet and critic Edward Hirsch (1999) put it:

> We make meaning together, we wrestle with what we read and talk back to it, we become more fully ourselves in the process. We activate the poem inside us by engaging it as deeply as possible, by bringing our lives to it, our associational memories, our past histories our vocabularies, by letting its verbal magic infiltrate our bodies, its ideas seep into our minds, by discovering its pattern emerging, by entering the echo chamber which is the history of poetry, and most of all, by listening and paying attention. *Attentiveness is the natural prayer of the soul.*
>
> (p. 260, italics in original).

What is unusual about poetry that equips it to communicate emotion?

1. It is, very often, a search for a truth. Bill Moyers put it simply (1995, xiv) "Poetry is the most honest language I hear today." In an interview with

Moyers, the poet Michael S. Harper (p. 185) defined the poet's task:"The job of the poet is to tell the truth no matter what. As James Baldwin said, 'Artists are here to disturb the peace' and by "the peace" he means our tendency to be vague and inactive and not attentive enough to the dynamism and the requirements of living."

2. Much of it is self-revealing, which takes, and demonstrates, courage that can be contagious. Gluck ((1994, p. 25,) called poetry a victory over shame. (I would call it a victory over the fear of shame). She also sees it as courageous to bear the silent, writers' block periods. The poet Victor Hernandez Cruz (in Moyers, 1995, p. 107) says, of his own work, " By explaining myself to myself, maybe other people can also see themselves."

A very vivid example is the poetry of Linda McCarriston (in Moyers, 1995, pp. 270–286) some of which describes her father's sexual, violent abuse of her as a child. Here (p. 273) is an example:

A Castle in Lynn

In the hometown tonight,
In the quiet before sleep,
a man strokes himself in the darkened
theater of memory, Best old

remembrance, he gets to play it
as slow as he needs, as his hand,
savvy tart of a million reruns,
plays the tune, plays the parts;

now hand is the hard bottom
of the girl. Now hand is full

of the full new breast. Now hand
—square hand, cruel as a spade—

splits the green girlwood of her body.
No one can take this from him now
ever, though she is for years a mother
and worn, and he is too old

to force any again. His cap hangs
on a peg by the door-plaid wool
of an elderly workingman's park-bench
decline. *I got there before*

the boys did, he knows, hearing
back to her pleading, back to her
sobbing, to his own voice-over
like his body over hers: laughter,

mocking, the elemental voice
of the cock, unhearted, in its own
quarter. *A man is king in his own
castle,* he can still say, having got

what he wanted: in a lifetime
of used ones, second-hand, one girl
he could spill like a shot of whiskey,
the whore only he could call daughter.

3. Poetry takes advantage of the way careful detailing can convey vividly.
For example, in her poem, "What the Living Do," Marie Howe (In Seiden,

2016, pp. 63–64) surrounds me with vivid, concrete details, that tell me about a mourner who is left unable make anything work right. I can easily join her there, with my own incapacities, and an aching remembrance of those who completed me while they were alive. Howe brilliantly brings me to the vicinity of this sorrow, but the sorrow is my own. Her poem reads like a letter to her brother, who, in reality, died of AIDS:

> Johnnie, the kitchen sink has been clogged for days,
>   some utensil probably fell down there.
> And the Drano won't work but smells dangerous, and
>   the crusty dishes have piled up.
> Waiting for the plumber I still haven't called. This is
>   the evening we spoke of.
> It's winter again: the sky's a deep headstrong blue
>   and the sunlight pours through
> the open living room windows because the heat's on
>   too high in here, and I can't turn it off.
> For weeks now, driving, or dropping a bag of groceries
>   in the street, the bag breaking,
> I've been thinking: This is what the living do. And,
>   yesterday, hurrying along those
> wobbly bricks in the Cambridge sidewalk, spilling my
>   coffee down my wrist and sleeve,
> I thought it again, and again later, when buying a
>   hairbrush: This is it.
> Parking. Slamming the car door shut in the cold. What
>   you called that yearning.
> What you finally gave up. We want the spring to come
>   and the winter to pass. We want

> whoever to call, or not call, a letter, a kiss—we want
> more, and more, and then more of it.
> But there are moments, walking, when I catch
> a glimpse of myself in the window glass,
> say, the window of the corner video store, and I'm
> gripped by a cherishing so deep
> for my own blowing hair, chapped face, and
> unbuttoned coat that I'm speechless:
> I am living, I remember you.

"What the Living Do" sings of sorrow, but it also sings of life. In fact, it juxtaposes longings. Alongside hopeless yearning for Johnnie, the poet feels the sharp, breath catching joy of being alive. She startles something in me, which wakes up along with her. She reminds me of what I already know, that life and death wait for me, side by side. Neither blocks my view of the other and neither can fully claim me, yet. But, eventually, one will.

The poet, like the analyst, makes a living from observations. Both usually turn toward the inner world, as well as the outer landscape. Both comb experience, searching for meaning. Both try to convey and, in that purpose, are interpersonal. Sometimes they convey through a telling detail.

Another poem, Sharon Olds' "The Race," (in Seiden, 2016, pp. 95–96) piles on details, moving from outer to inner reality and back again. I feel the urgency of the race as I read it. At least for me, the magic of this poem is that I come to care about the outcome so quickly, and so very much.

> When I got to the airport I rushed up to the desk,
> bought a ticket, ten minutes later
> they told me the flight was canceled, the doctors
> had said my father would not live through the night
> and the flight was canceled. A young man

with a dark brown moustache told me
another airline had a nonstop
leaving in seven minutes. See that
elevator over there, well go
down to the first floor, make a right, you'll
see a yellow bus, get off at the
second Pan Am terminal, I
ran, I who have no sense of direction
raced exactly where he told me, a fish
slipping upstream deftly against
the flow of the river. I jumped off that bus with those
bags I had thrown everything into
in five minutes, and ran, the bags
wagged me from side to side as if
to prove I was under the claims of the material,
I ran up to a man with a flower on his breast,
I who always go to the end of the line, I said
Help me. He looked at my ticket, he said
Make a left, and then a right, go up the moving stairs
and then
run. I lumbered up the moving stairs,
at the top I saw the corridor,
and then I took a deep breath, I said
goodbye to my body, goodbye to comfort,
I used my legs and heart as if I would
gladly use them up for this,
to touch him again in this life. I ran, and the
bags banged against me, wheeled and coursed
in skewed orbits, I have seen pictures of
women running, their belongings tied

in scarves grasped in their fists. I blessed my
long legs he gave me, my strong
heart I abandoned to its own purpose,
I ran to Gate 17, and they were
just lifting the thick white
lozenge of the door to fit into
the socket of the plane. Like the one who is not
too rich, I turned sideways and
slipped through the needle's eye, and then
I walked down the aisle toward my father. The jet
was full, and people's hair was shining, they were
smiling, the interior of the plane was filled with a
mist of golden endorphin light,
I wept as people weep when they enter heaven,
in massive relief. We lifted up
gently from one tip of the continent
and did not stop until we set down lightly on the
other edge, I walked into his room
and watched his chest rise slowly
and sink again, all night
I watched him breathe.

I think this poem epitomizes several of the qualities that enable poetry to convey emotion so forcefully. It has the ring of personal truth, and its details make the story so vivid that I feel as though I am running alongside her. The plain language and carefully scattered tiny details convey the humility of being at the mercy of impersonal external rules as well as the body's limitations. "Racing" describes my heart reading this poem. The poem's construction, its pace and shape, and the palpable rush of raw feeling all contribute to the effect. Olds so skillfully recruits us to fly along, outrunning one obstacle after another, both bureaucratic and physiological. At the lines "and then I took a deep breath, I said/ Goodbye to my body, goodbye to comfort..." I feel both fear she won't make it and awe at such concentrated purpose. That is what fear can do to us all. Seeing a tiger coming at us leaves no room for anything but fear and our particular way of reacting to fear.

Every detail contributes to the sense of desperation, and the sheer willpower with which she surpasses her usual limitations, both physical and psychological. She, who always goes to the end of the line, issues the urgent appeal, "help me." She, who has no sense of direction, gets every detail right. That full out dash leaves no time for periods. No rest, until she passes the Gate (17) of heaven. To me, this poem does what poems do best. With startling immediacy it recruits me into its emotional whirlwind. It gets me to care, instantly, profoundly. In less than two pages it makes me deeply identify with someone I will never meet. I get to know myself a bit better, too, as I recognize my own sense of trying with all my might to make something come out right, in some situations where I, too, am "under the claims of the material." In those moments I am trying so hard to be in control of something that has its own center of gravity. Everything in the poem conveys the single-mindedness with which the persona dashes, including the lines that can't pause at their ends, but jamb into each other. I certainly identify with the persona's willing herself forward, whether or not it looks like she has a chance of succeeding. She just keeps going, passes one hurdle, then the next. I would be cheering for her, rooting for her, even if I didn't so deeply identify with her. This is a poem that illustrates how poetry can be an experience, rather than just a description of an experience. Perhaps most importantly, it is an experience that suspends me in a different place and time, and shows me how we are all connected, all subject to the condition of vulnerable human beings. Sooner or later we know desperation. I have the feeling that each person in the plane has their own story; some need that pulled them onto this flight.

At the end of the poem, after feeling relief, I get lost in thoughts about heroism. Perhaps it is impossible to know what we are capable of, until we are called upon to fight for life, whether it is for ourselves, or others, or both. During and after 9-11, seeing pictures of terrified people fleeing, or jumping out of windows, we try to imagine what we would have/ could have done in their place. Stories of people going beyond themselves, during wars, in concentration camps, and other horrific situations, can elicit similar thoughts. In all these situations fear may well be central, but it isn't the only feeling. When augmented by fierce love, as it is in Olds' poem, it may give us surprising power. I think her poem communicates the exponentially augmented power of combined fear and love.

Like poets, analysts sometimes pierce with details. I think this is implicit in H. S. Sullivan's concept of the detailed inquiry. For example, in *Clinical Studies in Psychiatry* (1956, p. 373) he describes his motive for asking about the details of a schizoid woman's daily life, "I am simply hoping to crack the shell that surrounds all her feelings." I think sometimes a telling detail is what can crack the shell.

Here is a poem that makes this explicit. Its title is "Detail," by Eamon Grennan, and it is discussed by Henry Seiden (2016, pp. 40–43).

> I was watching a robin fly after a finch—the smaller
> chirping with excitement, the bigger, its breast blazing,
>   silent
> in light-winged earnest chase—when, out of nowhere
> over the chimneys and the shivering front gardens,
> flashes a sparrowhawk headlong, a light brown burn
> scorching the air from which it simply plucks
> like a ripe fruit the stopped robin, whose two or three
> cheeps of terminal surprise twinkle in the silence
> closing over the empty street when the birds have gone

about their business, and I began to understand
how a poem can happen: you have your eye on a small
elusive detail, pursuing its music, when a terrible truth
strikes and your heart cries out, being carried off.

The poem offers us the image of the predator robin, intent on demolishing the finch. The robin's full concentration is focused on his prey. The reader, too, is caught up in this picture. At that point we are unaware of our own unarticulated assumption that the robin and finch are the only players. There is a sudden shift. The sparrowhawk appears, and we, along with the robin, are jolted into awareness that our perspective has been too narrow. It takes only a second for unsuspecting predator to become terminally surprised prey. In psychoanalysis, a story is unfolding until, along with Edgar Levenson, (1991) for example, we ask what happened to the cat. And with attention to that detail our focus shifts, and the story attains a different meaning. I have found that poems often make me hyper-aware of my focus of attention as, itself, a significant action that expresses something personal. If I re-read a poem that is very familiar, and see something in it in a new light, I may learn about my present state of mind. Thus the "same" poem reads differently on Thursday than it did on Wednesday because I am not the same. This could be true of some prose, too, but poetry generally leaves more room for variation than literal, straightforward prose invites.

4. Because of their form, poems often make us stop and think about what is going on inside us. That can help us connect with our feelings. In the process of reading a poem, we often feel a need to think about the poet's words at the same time as we connect with our inner responses. Jane Hirshfield (2015, p. 159) pointed out that poetry "leaves in the tool chest a shining array of liftable, possible instruments for altering the angle of the seeing and feeling self." The poet and critic Edward Hirsch (1999) said (p. xiii):

"I'd like to believe that the ongoing initiation into art deepens our capacity for experiencing ourselves as well as others, thereby deepening our capacity for personhood, our achievement of humanity."

5. Poetry abounds in metaphors. Many years ago a teacher of mine defined the function of metaphor as making "the strange familiar and the familiar strange." In making the strange familiar, poet/reader (and analyst/analysand) discover connections that were previously unrecognized. In making the familiar strange, assumptions that have been taken for granted are questioned anew.

Another way to say this is that poetry fosters playful perspective taking. It makes the mind's angles and pathways into a playground. Some poets (e.g. T.S. Eliot) play hide and seek, luring us on with subtle, intellectually erudite clues. Chasing after them is good fun, and great exercise, for some readers. Others prefer more humble approaches. There is room in poetry for both. As Hirshfield (2015, p. 172) reminds us, reading poetry often requires an oscillating focus, looking inward laced with hearing the poet's voice.

Raffel (1984, p. 73) has an interesting take on metaphors in poetry: "And to a very considerable extent metaphor is exactly that: a frame of mind, a way of looking out from within an inner world of essentially personal thoughts and feelings. In the very act of expressing such inner worlds, the poet shares them with us." Hirsch (1999, p. 15) commenting on the work of the philosopher Ted Cohen, says that "...the maker and the appreciator of a metaphor are brought into deeper relationship with the other." Metaphors ask us to see connections between previously unconnected things, or ideas, or feelings. Poet and reader play roles in the meaning that emerges.

Gluck (1994, p. 39) tells us one way some poems communicate the connections they express: "This is the great advantage of formal verse: metrical variation provides a subtext. It does what we now rely on tone to do." The complexity of some poems allows them to communicate on several levels of consciousness at once. Poems often tap into the vast reservoir of unconscious thought, and juxtapose it with overtly disparate conscious perceptions. This distinguishes poetry from most prose, which thinks in more linear and sequential patterns. By connecting seemingly different things, poetry invites us to create something new. For me, reading poetry opens up avenues of thinking and feeling that are also available in reflecting on dream life. Feeling my way into a poem (or a dream) adds a dimension that makes inner life richer.

Still another angle on poetry's layering is its simultaneous expression of meaning and messages *about* that meaning. While reading a poem, in addition to comprehending the words, we are often asking how the words want us to read them. Poems require us to take up at least two thoughts at the same time. Jane Hirshfield (2015, p. 279) expressed this beautifully:

> From the first syllable then, we look for those forms and intentions: for words that sing as well as speak, for words that hear as well as speak, for thought and feeling unfrightened of depth and complication, for intensification, for implication, for playfulness, for all the surplus marks that increased attention leaves on language, which we call meaning, call pleasure, call beauty, call tenderness, call, sometimes, terror.

For me, personally, it has been interesting to think about the similarity between psychoanalytic listening and reading poems. Both ask me to pay attention to several layers of abstraction at once. Both require a rigorous, active listening process. Both insist on my looking inward, at my own process of hearing, at the same time as I hear a voice from another. This intensified awareness of how I take words in gives me an opportunity to try taking them in differently the next time they are presented to me. In other words, it gives me a chance to learn from an experience, and grow.

6. Built into the field of poetry is communication of the feelings of one generation to the next. Expressing profoundly felt experience in a poem is one way to leave a legacy, so that history will not be lost. This is powerfully expressed in a poem by Lucille Clifton. Its title is "fury" and it is dedicated "For Mama."

> remember this.
> she is standing by
> the furnace.
> the coals
> glisten like rubies.
> her hand is crying.
> her hand is clutching
> a sheaf of papers.
> poems.
> she gives them up.
> they burn
> jewels into jewels.
> her eyes are animals.
> each hank of her hair
> is a serpent's obedient
> wife.
> she will never recover.
> remember. there is nothing
> you will not bear
> for this woman's sake.
>   (In: Clifton, 2020, p. 151)

In interviews, Clifton has said that this is her mother's story. When her mother was invited to contribute her poems to a book, her father said she could not do it, so her mother burned them. Poetry keeps memories like this alive and passes them on.

Another poem, "Those Winter Sundays," by Robert Hayden (in Bialosky, 2017, p. 73) crosses the generational divide. I discuss this poem more fully in a subsequent chapter, but, for now, I mention it because to me it epitomizes the ache of the unsaid.

> Sundays too my father got up early
> and put his clothes on in the blueblack cold,
> then with cracked hands that ached
> from labor in the weekday weather made
> banked fires blaze. No one ever thanked him.
> I'd wake and hear the cold splintering, breaking.
> When the rooms were warm, he'd call,
> and slowly I would rise and dress,
> fearing the chronic angers of that house,
> Speaking indifferently to him,
> who had driven out the cold
> and polished my good shoes as well.
> What did I know, what did I know
> of love's austere and lonely offices.

This poem jumps many gaps: the chasm between the generations, the isolation of one family member from another, (especially in atmospheres of "chronic anger") and the silence that surrounds the unspoken. By mutual (often non-conscious) agreement, we avoid focusing on people we use. Few children pay homage to the person who made their oatmeal on Tuesday. But, twenty years later, making bowls of oatmeal for our own children, we remember, and send a love letter, in the form of a poem. Unlike usual love letters, the poem doesn't need an actual, alive, specific recipient. It is a message in a bottle, conveying its meaning to strangers.

7. Poetry can be simultaneously playful and disciplined. Generally, it taps into a long tradition and its construction follows rules set down over the centuries, and yet it may also pun and play with language. The combination of bound and unbound, measured and spontaneous, makes poetry an apt expression of all human experience. We live within the boundaries of space and time and our own bodies, and yet, in our sciences and so many other fields, we can act impulsively, unpredictably, adventurously breaking new ground. Edward Hirsch (1999, p. 2) declared, "I love the frame of mind, the playful work and working playfulness, the form of consciousness—the dreamy attentiveness—that comes with the reading of poetry."

A poem that is an example of the playful side, "My Maggie Machine," by Robert Pawlowski, was reprinted by Raffel (1984, pp. 60–61). In his witty poem, Pawlowski treats Maggie, his love, as though she were an assembly of mechanical parts that must be wound up and turned off when out of use.

This poem, carefully built around a metaphor, is obviously playful, witty, and meant to entertain. It creates its mood of teasing familiarity in very few words. It combines poetic economy with word play and sexual overtones. Perhaps ironically, the poet writes of his Maggie as a machine, but the *way* he writes it is anything but mechanical. This capacity to compress message and method typifies one of the strengths of poetry, as I understand it.

8. Poems are often intense in their language, and the experiences they reveal. This is due, in part, to poetry's general effort to use words economically, and, more specifically, to the rules of construction of various poetic forms. Raffel (1984, 23) gives this example of economy, and resulting intensity:

Pain penetrates
Me drop
by drop
    (Sappho, translated from Greek by Mary Barnard)

9. Poetry can be about the sound of the words, as much as it is about their meaning. This can express and relay to the reader unconscious thought, in the same way that music communicates. For the poet, focusing on the sound of a word may bring to mind another, similar in sound, and related in unconscious ways that only emerge after reflection. Emily Dickinson (in Vendler, 2010, Poem 23, p. 27) gave us a lovely example of alliteration expressing meaning through its music.

In the name of the Bee—
And of the Butterfly—
And of the Breeze—Amen!

This poem expresses Dickinson's version of the Trinity through its sound and sense. As Vendler (2010) succinctly describes it, the Bee represents Being, the Butterfly is the Psyche or Soul, and the Breeze is the Spirit. The poet has conveyed this in the meaning of the words chosen as well as their sound. "While the imagination is doing its work, a parallel investigation is being carried out by the ear, creating a link of sound—Bee, Butterfly, Breeze—to substitute for the "familial" links of the Trinity" (Vendler, 2010, p. 28).

How Poetry Fosters Emotional Modulation

What enables poetry to foster emotional modulation? The poet Sharon Olds said (in Moyers, 1995, p. 216) "Poets are like steam valves, where the ordinary feelings of ordinary people can escape and be shown." I think this release is part of what gives poetry its power to modulate affect, for both the poet and the reader. Poets such as Dante Gabriel Rossetti, Christina Rossetti, Jane Kenyon, and so many others, have let their poems speak about their depressive suffering. I think part of their power to help other sufferers is their ability to communicate that the reader is not alone in that state. In other words, their poems may decrease the loneliness in a depressed reader's overall emotional state, thus fostering greater balance.

1. Gluck, (1994. (p. 5) says, that poetry often deals in paradox, which I think can stimulate curiosity and invite refreshing perspectives. Personally, I am a student of the paradoxical-yet-true. I have always found it fascinating.

A poem by John N. Morris, "For Julia in the Deep Water" (In: A Holden and B. Holden, 2014, p. 213) captures one of life's essential paradoxes. I discuss it at length in chapter 3.

This poem gets to the heart of what is most difficult about being a parent or, for that matter, being a human being. Trying to help someone, we hurt them. Wanting to make something better, or easier, we make it worse, or harder. Sometimes when we mean to hug we strangle. It can be exquisitely painful to learn this (again). Finding it in a poem confirms that it is universal and unavoidable. There is some comfort in that.

2.   Poems frequently illuminate what is hidden and not a product of the will. Poetry dips (and dips us) into the interior world, expanding the context for thinking about our lives. Poetry's reach into unconscious territory allows it to consider issues under the surface of ordinary life, and sometimes, explore relationships between everyday experience and questions about our purpose and meaning that can't (yet) be within our conscious awareness.

A poem by W.S. Merwin (in Bialosky, 2017, p. 199) expresses poetry's effort to capture what can't be fully known on a conscious level.

Youth

Through all of youth I was looking for you
without knowing what I was looking for

or what to call you I think I did not
even know I was looking how would I

have known you when I saw you as I did
time after time when you appeared to me

as you did naked offering yourself
entirely at that moment and you let

me breathe you touch you taste you knowing
no more than I did and only when I

began to think of losing you did I
recognize you when you were already

part memory part distance remaining
mine in the ways that I learn to miss you

from what we cannot hold the stars are made

I find the last line, "from what we cannot hold the stars are made" mesmerizing. It eludes my grasp even as it speaks of what eludes grasp. I cannot hold what I cannot (yet) know. I have the sensation that something is there, waiting to take shape, but it needs to piggy back a dream, or a line of poetry. If I *could* hold it, my rational mind might take over and start explaining it, in the clearest *prose* I can muster. Poems invite me to a realm that can't be reached (consciously) and yet I yearn to try. Chasing after "what we cannot hold," striving for a clarity I cannot achieve, creates in me a sense of being fully alive.

3. Poems create intimacy with the reader, helping each of us feel less alone. This can help us bear sorrow and other painful feelings. In the language of emotion theory, (Izard, 1977; Buechler, 2008) poetry's capacity to modulate loneliness potentially changes the reader's balance of emotions, tilting it away from a stultifying mixture of unmodified sorrow and loneliness. Emotion theory suggests that our feelings exist in a system, so that a change in *any* emotion *affects the whole balance*. For example, feeling less lonely may take the edge off sorrow, and allow more positive emotions to emerge in time.

4. Gluck (1994, p. 29) praises the power of white space in poetry. The restraint of leaving some things out gives some poems "...the power to seem, simultaneously, whole and not final, the power to generate, not annul, energy." Like a good interpretation in psychoanalysis, some poems are alive, changing with each day's new understanding. This is possible because they are open-ended. They don't speak with finality, with absolute authority. They invite collaboration, by leaving space for it. In the poet, Michael S. Harper's words, (in Moyers, 1995, p. 173) "...*all* voids are not to be filled. You have to learn when to lay out because some space has to be left there to resonate. It is often the *absence* of sound, what is not going on, that people hear because so much has to do with measure, with what is said and with what is not said."

I am reminded of Keats' concept of "negative capability," the capacity to be "in uncertainties, mysteries, doubts, without any irritable reaching after fact and reason" (In Hirsch, 1999, p. 131). For example, here is a brief poem, by Julia Hartwig. (In Hirshfield (2015, p. 295):

Feeling the Way

The most beautiful is what is still unfinished
a sky filled with stars uncharted by astronomers
a sketch by Leonardo a song broken off by emotion
A pencil, a brush suspended in the air

I note the absence of punctuation at the "end" of the poem. Blank space can be beautiful if we are not afraid of it. For some, the blank sheet of paper is frightening, intimidating. In a state of curiosity it is challenging, invigorating, enlivening. I think we can guess what the poet, Emily Dickinson, would vote for.

I dwell in Possibility—
A fairer House than Prose—
More numerous of Windows—
Superior—for Doors—

Of Chambers as the Cedars—
Impregnable of eye—
And for an everlasting Roof
The Gambrels of the Sky—

Of Visitors—the fairest
For Occupation—This—
The spreading wide my narrow Hands
To gather Paradise—

(Poem 466, in Vendler, 2010, p. 222)

Commenting on the invitation this poem extends Vendler says, (2010, p. 224) "Through the poet's enumeration of its splendors, Possibility becomes (imaginatively speaking) real to us—so much so that we, now ashamed of our dreary Houses, might begin to construct in our minds a new House for ourselves, with sturdy doors, multiple windows, and an exalted 'Roof.' Visitors might come to such a House, fairer visitors than we have yet encountered."

In other words, not only does the unfinished leave room for collaboration, but it also stimulates curiosity. Elsewhere (2004) I have written of a continuum between alive curiosity and deadening paranoia. I think we are all, always, somewhere along this continuum. Tight, closed certainties are airless. An extreme of this would be the paranoid belief that everything that is happening to me can be explained by one fact: that I am Jesus Christ. In states of paranoia, anyone who doubts our passionately held "facts" is a traitor. At the other end is the curious state of the child, not bounded in by any assumptions, throwing a ball in the air just to see what happens.

I believe that much about poetry encourages curiosity. Not only the open ended poem, with wide unwritten spaces, but all the mysterious passages, can elicit in the reader a state of curious wondering.

In language I find particularly persuasive, Hirshfield recommends balancing encounters with the new (so as to stimulate surprise and curiosity) and encounters with the familiar. In her words (2015, p. 136):

Encounter with the unknown seems almost a nutrient in human life, as essential as certain amino acids—without it, the untested self falls into sleep, depression, boredom, and stupor. The trick then is discovering how much, and when, to admit the random, chaotic, unknowable, into our lives—if, that is, we are among those who have the privilege of choice at all. It is also a matter of balance. Personally, I find that both writing and reading some poems can give me a shot of this vital, and vitalizing nutrient.

5. We can turn to poetry to help us cope with our feelings because it is reliable. Clifton (in Moyers, 1995, p. 83) says: "...Poetry probably has saved my life. It has been *the* stable thing, something to love. Even in the midst of the most amazing and interesting things, there's a line that I could come to or that would come to me and help me through it. I think poetry has been the one faithful, good thing." Clifton has written many poems about her father's sexual abuse of her, which took place when she was a child. She calls some of these poems the "shapeshifter poems." (Clifton, 2020, p. 106) Here is the second one:

> who is there to protect her
> from the hands of the father
> not the windows which see and
> say nothing not the moon
> that awful eye not the woman
> she will become with her
> scarred tongue who who who the owl
> laments into the evening who
> will protect her this prettylittlegirl

6. Some poetry has the power to modulate the reader's emotional state by engendering its own live wire feelings. In an interview with Bill Moyers, the poet Joy Harjo (in Moyers, 1995, p. 165) is explicit about this.

Moyers: So what do you hope your poems do?

Harjo: I hope that on some level they can transform hatred into love. Maybe that's being too idealistic, but I know that language is alive and living, so I hope that in some small way my poems can transform hatred into love.

Moyers: Language has a healing capacity.

Later in the interview, Harjo (p. 168) explains that, for her, there is always love in the act of creation. No matter what the poem is about "Ultimately a poem has an electrical force field which is love. In one of my poems, 'Day of the Dead,' I have a line, 'Love changes molecular structure,' and that line describes something of what a poem does."

In a similar spirit, Edward Hirsch (1999, p. 3) says that "I don't think we should underestimate the capacity for tenderness that poetry opens up within us." In this connection he cites one of Walt Whitman's "Inscriptions," called "To You."

> Stranger, if you passing meet me and desire to speak to me,
>   why should you not speak to me?
> And why should I not speak to you?

The poet Gary Snyder talks about poetry's freedom.(Moyers, 1995, p. 368): "There's a freedom of mind, imagination, language, spirit that is granted you in poetry. It is the singing voice. It's the dancing body that is not in prose. It's ritual, it's ceremony, it's magic. The earliest hominid being we can touch comes out in poetry. It's the way natural systems work." I think that freedom is contagious, passing from poet to other poets, and other readers. Love (for aliveness itself, for others, for oneself, and so on) and joy are feelings that can be engendered by this exhilarating experience, and having such moments counters the pain life also brings.

7. It seems as though poetry is particularly apt at creating the sense of being part of the human community. In a way, poetry counters the "othering" of others. While pain can make us feel isolated, with some poetry (Hirschfield, 2015, p. 277) "...the ache of an elemental longing is slipped from hand to hand between writer and reader, a coin and token of recognition, and by that transaction is changed. What was carried alone is suddenly carried by two, by many."

I agree that pain can be extremely isolating, and the resulting loneliness adds to its weight. Alain de Botton and John Armstrong (*Art as Therapy*, 2013, p. 141) make the very obvious, but nevertheless interesting point that we perceive ourselves from the inside, but perceive others from the outside. "A central feature of human experience is that while we know ourselves from the inside, and have an immediate, intuitive grasp of what it is like to be ourselves, we meet others only externally. We may feel close, we may get to know them well, but a gap remains." Elsewhere (2008) I have written of the inevitability that the pain I feel today is shaped by my whole history of pain and, is, therefore, unlike anyone else's and, ultimately, unknowable by anyone else. People may say, "I feel your pain" but no one really does. They may feel something approximating it, but only I can feel my own pain, shaped by all the suffering that preceded it in my life. Suffering brings in its wake the memory of every pain I have ever felt. It pools, making it impossible for anyone else, who has not lived my life, to really grasp my pain.

This helps me understand *why* some suffering is accompanied by an extreme sense of isolation. I am reminded of Helene Deutch's (1973) autobiography, where she writes of loneliness as a product of knowing that you are the only one who sees things exactly as you do. Well-meaning people may mistakenly think that because they can recognize the *surface* of someone's pain, because it *looks like* a feeling familiar to them, they understand it. They don't understand how my pain is reverberating inside me, gathering echoes from past experiences. Much of the time I have no words for this accompaniment, so even I, myself, may not realize why I feel as I do.

In a lovely and characteristically self scrutinizing poem (Poem 550, in Vendler, 2010, pp. 250–254) Emily Dickinson tries to "measure" her pain against the sorrows she intuits others feel. In her mind's eye she "sees" a parade of mourners, and guesses about the sources of their suffering. She acknowledges that she may not label their sorrows correctly, though she would like to be able to presume that some are like her own. With her genius at introspection, Dickinson names the wish to erase the border between self and other, in order to feel a little less alone with life's inevitable burdens. Ironically her poetry is what has helped me feel less alone during many painful passages of my life.

In this light it is interesting to note how loneliness was described many years ago by the psychoanalyst Frieda Fromm-Reichmann. Exploring the differences between a comfortable state of aloneness and the painful state of loneliness, Fromm-Reichmann (1959) emphasized the lack of hope of human connectedness in the profoundly lonely person. This suggests to me that poetry can function as an antidote to extreme loneliness. While it is true that the suffering of the poet is never exactly the same as the suffering of the reader, it may be close enough to suggest the possibility of a connection.

8. Poetry is a meeting place between universal and individual experience. The poet and critic Edward Hirsch put it this way: (1999, pp. 4–5) "Reading poetry is a way of connecting—through the medium of language—more deeply with yourself even as you connect more deeply with another. The poem delivers on our spiritual lives precisely because it simultaneously gives us the gift of intimacy and interiority, privacy and participation." Personally, I feel that dwelling there can be healing in itself, apart from the particular experiences referenced. This reminds me of studies of the emotion of joy. Elsewhere (2008) I have summarized

that literature as suggesting two basic sources of joy: increased awareness of our membership in the human community and increased awareness of our own particularity. While these may sound contradictory they are both nevertheless true. (As stated above, I am a student of the paradoxical and contradictory-but-true). Some poems activate both of these sources of joy in the reader. As we read we become more aware of commonalities in the human condition. At the same time, we may become more focused on our own, particular, variation on the themes. There is potential for feeling joy in these moments of heightened awareness.

9. It is important to note that poetry's emotionally modulating effect is sometimes achieved by heading directly into a painful feeling, rather than avoiding it. The poet Rilke often commented on how meaningful that choice can be. He (in Baer, 2005, p. 98) advocated "...not to consider suffering from the outside...." When writing about our response to painful losses, Rilke (in Baer, 2005, p. 109) said "Our instinct should not be to desire consolation over a loss, but rather to develop a deep and painful curiosity to explore the loss completely, to experience the peculiarity, the singularity, and the effects of this loss in our life." In a similar spirit, Hirshfield (2015, p. 161) said that we go to certain poems, as a child might want to hear a particular story, in order to be "rightly frightened." I think the attitude, conveyed by some poets, of fully entering into pain fosters courage. It expresses the value of living everything to its fullest. Some poetry validates fuller experiencing, as well as freer expression of our emotional lives. For some readers this may be taken as permission, or, even, approval, of who they have always been (perhaps in secret). For others it may offer a glimpse of an entirely new way of living.

Linda McCarriston's poem, "Billy" is a particularly vivid example of heading directly into painful experiences. In an interview (Moyer, 1995, pp. 271–286) she explained that her childhood was filled with incidents of her violent father attacking her, her mother, and her brother. Many years later, as she revisited these incidents, trying to transform them by making them the basis of some of her poetry, McCarriston remembered (pp. 281–282) this terrifying scene:

Billy

As though a bare bulb hung
over your head as it does in
movie scenes of interrogation,
you are the single vivid thing
in the shades-of-gray memory,
the white center, out from which
the whole dank tenement
cellar—the dirt floor, the boulders
that formed the old foundation,
the three fat coal-burning
furnaces, one for each of the three
stories, the coal bins punky
across from each, the mud-thick
little windows above that were
coal chutes when the truck came,
the new table-saw, the new
table-saw overhead worklight,
and even our father,
who stood beating you with his fists
where he'd stuck you into
a barrel, as a mountaineer might plant
a banner into a peak, to keep your
skinny thirteen year old self erect

till he was finished-the whole
rest emanates and fades.
It was winter. You had driven
your homemade go-cart into a door
that he was saving for something,
I can see the little v's you made
in the paint. I see his upper body
plunging up and down like one
of those wind-driven lawn ornaments,
the one that is pumping.
The barrel reaches your bottom.
You must be holding onto it.
It must be braced against
his table saw. There are no words.
The barrel bangs and scrapes.
Your body sounds different than
a mattress. The noises he makes
are the noises of a man trying to
lift a Buick off the body of
a loved child, whose face he can
see, upturned, just above the wheel
that rests on her chest, her eyes right
on his eyes, as yours were on mine.

At first the poet's brother felt she was (p. 282) "too caught up in the past,"
and he didn't want to revisit these terrible memories with her. But when she
wrote this poem and asked his permission to read it at an award ceremony,
he came and (p. 283) "bravely and generously and lovingly" listened. The
poet's matter of fact tone and careful detailing bring us (readers/listeners)
into the scene. We can imagine we are standing where she stood in horrified

silence. Poetic structure accommodates a rich accumulation of contrasts, that intensify our feelings. In our mind's eye, this brutal father is pictured alongside an imagined loving parent straining to save his little girl trapped under a Buick. Her tortured brother's body is acutely vulnerable, unlike a mattress. Her sadistically whipped up father is not an innocent lawn ornament. Her brother is not a banner marking a victorious climb. The contrasts with the inanimate bring out the extreme vulnerability of a child's flesh. The last image moves me most. Two children, whose eyes meet, who know each other's wordless suffering. As she tells it, some forty years later, in the condensed, emotionally evocative format of poetry, Linda McCarriston found the words.

Of course there is a limit to how much exposure to pain we can endure. But denial, avoidance, and other defensive patterns take a toll. I think poetry has the capacity to *oscillate* between defensive and non-defensive postures. I believe that this is a very important point. Some of the world's most poignant works of tragedy, such as Shakespeare's *Hamlet* or *King Lear* have their comic, light-hearted moments. Similarly poems can sit astride the tragic and the comic, and/or the catastrophic and the everyday. For example, in poem 591, Emily Dickinson juxtaposes the mundane with the profound, and begins her poem by startling the reader:

> I heard a Fly buzz—when I died—
> The stillness in the Room
> Was like the Stillness in the Air—
> Between the Heaves of Storm—
>
> The Eyes around—had wrung them dry—
> And Breaths were gathering firm
> For that last Onset—when the King
> Be witnessed—in the Room—

I willed my Keepsakes—Signed away
What portion of me be
Assignable—and then it was
There interposed a Fly—

With Blue—uncertain—stumbling Buzz—
Between the light—and me—
And then the Windows failed—and then
I could not see to see—

(In: Vendler, 2010, p. 266)

This poem juxtaposes life's most solemn, final moments with the inconsequential buzzing of a fly. Vendler (p. 267) credits the poem with dry wit. My mind's eye wanders from the fly to the scene of mourning, and back again. Like a flying insect we circle the room, alighting here and there, wandering from the newly dead corpse, to the sobbing bereaved, to the stumbling fly. Vendler (p. 268) focuses on how the poem's truth defeats any and all illusions about our mortality. I think that, in addition, by engaging the reader in a kind of puzzle or mystery, Dickinson leavens the sorrow of the poem with surprise and curiosity. The reader is primed to wonder how the voice in the poem is speaking after her death and why the fly has such a prominent role. We think about the King, the non-assignable soul, and the religious meaning of the poem. These ideas, and the flitting fly, give us a needed break from the heaving breath and sobbing eyes of mourners, but the sadness is not denied. The magic of poetry allows the sorrowful and the inconsequential to hover, suspended side by side.

Raffel (1984, p. 70) claims for poetry a healing ability to create a space where parent-child love/ hate ambiguities can be probed. In his words: "Even to approach, to half articulate them, is itself threatening...Perhaps only in the half-world, the never-never world if you will, of a poem can we safely approach, safely articulate what otherwise might more than threaten us–might actually destroy us, or at least the balance of our sanity."

Dialoguing With Poems

The central premise of this book is that poetry, with its evocative capacity, has even more emotional impact in a dialogue with other poems and lines from plays. Poetry naturally falls into this dialogic role. As stated above, we can see poetry (and all the arts) as ways to conduct dialogues with our ancestors. We ask some of the same question that they did. From my (2004) point of view, as human beings we all face certain central issues, such as mustering the courage life requires, maintaining curiosity, bearing life's inevitable losses, and retaining a sufficient sense of integrity and emotional balance. Poems connect us with others who have faced these challenges.

More specifically, here are some reasons poetry is well suited to conversations spanning time and culture:

1. It deals with big subjects-time, loss, death, beauty, the good life, childhood, Nature, etc. For example, the poet Li Young Lee, who studied with Gerald Stern, hears ages old biblical stories of exile in his own and Stern's poems (Moyers, 1995, p. 259). In other words, poetry is a meeting place between the universal and the individual. As I said earlier, I think dwelling there can be healing.

2. Some poems connect us to our most fundamental feelings about life itself. The poet Stanley Kunitz said that "Poetry is the most difficult, the most solitary, and the most life-enhancing thing that one can do in the world." (In Moyers, 1995, p. 240). He sees poetry as full of secrets, just like dreams. Octavio Paz (Moyers, 1995, p. 442) said "I think the mission of poetry is to create among people the possibility of wonder, admiration,

enthusiasm, mystery, the sense that life is marvelous. When you say life is marvelous, you are saying a banality. But to make life a marvel—that is the role of poetry." Poets often keep open to confusion without any irritable grasping after reason (see concept of negative capability, above). To me this is similar to Rilke's injunction, in his "Letters to a Young Poet" (1934, p. 35) to "love the questions."

3. Reading poetry places us in a frame of mind that is conducive to associating the seemingly disparate. In this state we are less likely to experience in boundary bound binaries, such as the cognitive vs. the emotional, me vs. you, eighteenth century vs. now. As we read a poem and (especially, from my point of view) as we compare two or more poems, we are invited to let go of the usual demarcations. Some poems epitomize the interpenetration of mind, matter, and the spiritual. Raffel (1984, pp. 27–31) proposes Wallace Stevens as an example of a poet's expression of that interpenetration. Raffel offers two examples from Stevens' work. The first is a poem entitled "The House Was Quiet and the World Was Calm."

> The house was quiet and the world was calm.
> The reader became the book; and summer night
>
> Was like the conscious being of the book,
> The house was quiet and the world was calm.
>
> The words were spoken as if there was no book,
> Except that the reader leaned above the page,
>
> Wanted to lean, wanted much most to be
> The scholar to whom his book is true, to whom

The summer night is like a perfection of thought.
The house was quiet because it had to be.

The quiet was part of the meaning, part of the mind:
The access of perfection to the page.

And the world was calm. The truth in a calm world,
In which there is no other meaning, itself

Is calm, itself is summer and night, itself
Is the reader leaning late and reading there.

Raffel (1984, p. 28) points out how this poem crosses back and forth between mind and matter. I think this fusing contributes to the poem's mysterious power. When I read it I begin to feel myself going into a sort of trance state. The poem rocks me, like a lullaby, with its cadence and repetitions. With pleasure I lose track of all the boundaries of self, book, summer night, calm, scholar, house, words, thought, meaning, reading. This melange creates the feeling of intimacy and, simultaneously, a sense of the universality of the experience it is eliciting. Its appeal crosses cultures, individuals, ages, eras, professions. It speaks to anyone who has ever reverberated to anything rhythmic. I think it rises to Octavio Paz's challenge (see Chapter Two for discussion of this) to "make life a marvel."

The second Wallace Stevens poem cited by Raffel (1984, p. 29) is entitled "The Snow Man."

One must have a mind of winter
To regard the frost and the boughs
Of the pine-trees crusted with snow;

And have been cold a long time
To behold the junipers shagged with ice,
The spruces rough in the distant glitter

Of the January sun; and not to think
Of any misery in the sound of the wind,
In the sound of a few leaves,

Which is the sound of the land
Full of the same wind
That is blowing in the same bare place

For the listener, who listens in the snow,
And, nothing himself, beholds
Nothing that is not there and the nothing that is.

Raffel (1984, p. 30) focuses on the pleasure and excitement in this poem's evocation of the experience of the snow man. He points out the contrast between the perspective of a man of snow, who doesn't think of misery in the sound of the wind, versus the mind of a human being, for whom that misery would be inherent in the sound. In this poem I hear a song that celebrates empathic immersion and a peaceful surrender to experience. In order to understand the snow man we must approach him with a mind of winter. To feel what he feels, we must have been cold for a long time. Poetry can demonstrate this complete immersion, or what the poet, Rilke, called "inseeing" (Corbett, 2016, p. 99). I believe that the experience of entering another's center acquaints us with our own perspective more palpably than any other approach could. Becoming immersed in a mind of winter demonstrates how my mind is usually *not* a mind of winter. I am not a man of snow. I do hear misery in the wind and the paltry leaves. I am not made of cold water; I am not nothing. Perhaps that means I have trouble beholding nothingness. This poem's ability to seep into me *demonstrates* my permeability, even as it sings of it. We can imagine a theater critic, a biologist, a psychologist, a bird watcher, and anyone else, relating to its message.

Summary: What sets poetry apart from prose?

1. Its musicality (see Raffel, 1984, p. 92). Poetry often plays with musical rhythms and alliteration. We connect to it in a bodily sense, as we might connect with dance. Our own bodily rhythms reverberate with the poem's. It is often non-literal and non-linear (Raffel, 1984, p. 96). That is, it doesn't follow the rules of English syntax, grammar, and the purpose of conveying information, that are attributes of prose. Poetry conveys emotion, and stances, rather than information.

2. It often clarifies through contrasts. When I think about how contrast teaches, I recall one of my teachers (Edgar Levenson) saying that "the last one to know about water is the fish." That is, having been in water all its life, the fish doesn't see the water, since it has known nothing that contrasts with the water. Similarly, the child who goes to a friend's house for a "sleepover" may have the educative experience of seeing the functioning of a family other than theirs, thereby becoming clearer about their own family life. Poetry often teaches in a similar manner. It tells us what was so bred in our bones that we didn't know about it.

3. In poems, each word is very carefully chosen. In a good poem, changing any word feels like it mars the totality. In Raffel's (1984, p. 116) words, the poem *shows* us a state of mind, and does not merely talk about one.

4. Poetry celebrates the irrational and the nonlinear. Like prose, its aim is communication, but not the straightforward conveying of information that is often the aim of prose.

5. Poetry uses devices, like rhyme, which add pleasure to the poem. Rhyme creates a sensation that may please regardless of the poem's content. Alliteration (sequences of words beginning with the same consonant) can also give a kind of sensual pleasure, that may augment the poem's messages. Repetition can convey emphasis. These devices play supporting roles to the meaning of the poem. Similarly, refrains can add to the poem's musical quality. Allusion (alluding to a meaning that would be generally understood) often enhances a poem's richness. Finally, another device, onomatopoeia, employs sounds that communicate meaning. These are just some of the devices that add to a poem's ability to evoke ideas, images, and feelings to the reader.

I would like to end this chapter with a poem that illustrates how a state of emotion can be evoked on many levels at once, creating a reverberating experience in the reader. The poem is by Henry Timrod and titled "I Know Not Why, But All This Weary Day" (In Burt and Mikics, 2010, p. 182).

> I know not why, but all this weary day,
> Suggested by no definite grief or pain,
> Sad fancies have been flitting through my brain;
> Now it has been a vessel losing way,
> Rounding a stormy headland; now a gray
> Dull waste of clouds above a wintry main;
> And then, a banner, drooping in the rain,
> And meadows beaten into bloody clay.
> Strolling at random with this shadowy woe

At heart, I chanced to wander hither! Lo!
A league of desolate marsh-land, with its lush,
Hot grasses in a noisome, tide-left bed,
And faint, warm airs, that rustle in the hush,
Like whispers round the body of the dead!

Reading this poem, my first impression was of a meandering wanderer, directionless, unable, or unwilling, to exert effort, allowing himself to be blown around, like a leaf in the wind. A similar sense of fragility is conveyed by N.S. Nye (1995) in the poem, "The Art of Disappearing" (In: Bill Moyers, 1995, p. 323) in which our lives are likened to leaves which can tumble down at any point. The poet challenges us to hold onto the feeling of being a leaf as we decide what to do with our time. But, differing with Nye's thrust, Timrod doesn't sound like he could use the sensation to then "decide what to do with (your) time." Timrod remains in the indeterminate state.

Burt and Mikics (2010, pp. 182–185) let us in on the back story of this poem. Timrod, born in South Carolina in 1828, was a war correspondent during the Civil War. The battle of Shiloh, the bloodiest in American history, made an overwhelming impression. The poet, frail, tubercular, broken, sounds as though he never recovered from the traumatic experience of the war. He died at the age of 37. This poem was published that year.

As I hear it, the poem communicates a melancholic ennui with its images, word choices, and aspects of its structure. Form and content mirror each other. The persona seems not in control of his own movements, or of his emotions. Even the "control" of understanding the cause of his feelings is unavailable to him. He doesn't know why he feels as he does. Thus, in the opening line, we are told that he is not suffering from a defined sorrow over a specific loss. His experience (and ours) is de-centered. He roves, rather than walks. The images are hazy, with no destination, as he strolls "at random." His mind mirrors his meandering feet, floating from image to image. With him, we see a lost boat, gray clouds, a soaked, drooping banner, and muddy, marshy earth. The last line, "Like whispers round the body of the dead," brings in hushed sounds.

The poet creates an atmosphere, a dwelling place for readers, who fill it in with their own experience. Timrod's words string together hapless images and then, as the reader, I supply my own experience of haplessness.

But, since this is a poem, it evokes through its form, as well as its content. Burt and Mikics point out the reversal of the usual order. A couplet usually ends a poem, but Timrod puts it in the ninth and tenth lines (rhyming "woe" with "Lo!") and follows this with the last four lines of this 16 line sonnet. Here (pp. 184–185) is what the editors say about this reversal:

> The very striking reversal of the couplet and the third quatrain in Timrod's poem is a sign of this resistance to closure, the poet's refusal to pass on from melancholy to mourning. The couplet (here, lines 9 and 10) normally stands at the end of a Shakespearean sonnet: it summarizes, revises, and sometimes undermines the first twelve lines of the poem. But "I know not why" deprives itself of this encapsulating finish. The poem, like the poet, remains stranded.

Thus the reader is left without the sensation of closure. The poem's structure, like its content, leaves us with a vague, troubled, unfinished feeling. It has the timeless, endless quality of melancholy, or depression, as we would call it today. We hear the whispers around the dead, see the gray clouds, feel the unresolved ending, sense pointlessness. The poem is an experience, on conscious and unconscious levels, bringing together images, ideas, sensations, and emotions. It may well be that the poem I read, the experience I have, is somewhat different from yours, and no doubt different from Timrod's. A poem (as was discussed earlier) is a collaboration between poet and reader. But there also will be commonalities between your "I Know Not Why,

THE POWER OF POETRY TO EVOKE EMOTIONS

But All This Weary Day" and mine. Both of us will probably *not* feel a quickening pulse of joy, or sense an expanding horizon of hope. For us both, the mood conveyed will be somber. But, I think, for all of us, reading this poem offers us a chance to feel there have been others who, like ourselves, have felt lost in a "desolate marsh-land."

2.

How Poetry Restores Emotional Balance

If I had to name one writer who has made our common humanity a palpable, living experience, it would be Shakespeare. Reading him we can't help but recognize the pain of jealousy, (*Othello, A Winter's Tale*) the agony of loss (the death of Cordelia in *King Lear)* the joy of first love, (Romeo and Juliet) the infinite ruthlessness of vengeance, (*Richard III)* the shame and sorrow of falling from grace (Richard I") the self-torture of indecision, (*Hamlet)* the nightmare of guilt (*Macbeth)* and so much else. Sometimes what we recognize on the age is a feeling that is, in itself, painful. But the experience always includes an awareness that the author must have known these emotions, as we have, to depict them with such accuracy and stunning compassion. Implicitly, we are taken into the human fold, by reading an incredibly beautiful expression of what we, ourselves, have felt. We participate in the creative process, in that we bring our life experience to the page, which colors how we hear Shakespeare. We live an experience that affirms that great art can be made out of the emotions human beings have in common. I believe that art's presence in our lives can contribute to healing. This chapter reflects on the power of the poet to modulate the reader's emotional balance.

First, a word about the phrase "emotional balance." Earlier in my career, with Cal Izard, I studied the first expressions of each of the "discrete" emotions in the first two years of life. We looked at the first times infants' faces showed joy, sadness, curiosity, anger, fear, and other feelings. Based on Izard's earlier studies of adult emotions (1972) we explored the idea that the emotions always exist in a balance, with the intensity of each affecting the level of all the others. That is, if I am feeling extremely angry that will impact my level of curiosity and, likewise, intense curiosity can affect the level of anger. Emotions operate as a system, with each affecting the experience of all the others. Elsewhere (2004, 2008, 2012, 2015, 2017, 2019) I have written at length about many possibilities for clinical applications of these ideas. Here I am pursuing another angle: the power of poetry to evoke modulating experiences in the reader that can restore or enhance emotional balance.

Many have written about the alive and transformative power of poetry; its ability to "...bridge the gulf-the chasm-between people otherwise unknown to each other." (Hirsch, 1999, p. 6) Hirsch goes on, quoting Robert Graves, to write of poetry as a "living entity" that can affect readers with its "stored magic." He also cites (p. 7) Emily Dickinson's oft quoted high bar. "If I read a book (and) it makes my whole body so cold no fire can ever warm me I know that is poetry. If I feel physically as if the top of my head were taken off, I know that is poetry..." For these people, and many more, poetry can do what countless clinical practitioners aim for—to use words to create an actual, living experience that changes another person's life. In my own language, a poem can shift the balance of our feelings. For example, if a poem helps the reader feel less lonely, other emotions, such as curiosity, hope, and even joy, might take hold. Octavio Paz put it this way, "I think the mission of poetry is to create among people the possibility of wonder, admiration, enthusiasm, mystery, the sense that life is marvelous. When you say life is marvelous you are saying a banality. But to make life a marvel-that is the role of poetry." (In Bill Moyers' "The Language of Life," 1995, p. 442) In a gorgeous poem titled "Dedications," Adrienne Rich addresses the hunger for poetry, which can be more intense in times of adversity. It is a long poem, so I am quoting just a few lines.

I know you are reading this poem
In a room where too much has happened for you to bear
where the bedclothes lie in stagnant coils on the bed
and the open valise speaks of flight
but you cannot leave yet....
I know you are reading this poem listening for something, torn
    between bitterness and hope...

(In Moyers, 1995, pp. 343–344)

Loneliness

A particularly moving and inspiring story I heard in a taped interview ("Poetry in America, Season One, by Elisa New, PBS, DVD, 2019) confirmed poetry's potential to diminish isolation. When the late senator John McCain was a political prisoner in Vietnam, he, like many others, was held in solitary confinement and, for the latter period of his incarceration, brutally tortured. The terror and extreme loneliness inherent in this situation are hard to imagine. When asked how he survived, he described the routine he and the prisoner in the next cell devised, for tapping lines of poetry on the wall between them. He would memorize each line and add it to his store of poems. This story epitomizes many aspects of human beings. We can unleash sadistic cruelty on others, and we can sustain each other in the most horrendous circumstances. I think it also illustrates the power of poetry to connect us to each other and to enhance the will to survive.

For me, personally, poems sometimes provide a welcome spiritual home. I am not sure where that is, but I know it isn't New York in 2020. If I forget that I am in alien territory, the assault of well disguised advertisements, unremitting noise, screen absorbed pedestrians, and many other reminders disabuse me of any illusions. And the absence of little book and record stores

45

and quiet cafes confirms the message. But for moments at a time some poems carry me into a different time and place. I sit by a fire and listen to Emily Dickinson's description of a mourning so like my own, in her poem, "After Great Pain, A Formal Feeling Comes."

> After great pain, a formal feeling comes—
> The Nerves sit ceremonious, like Tombs
> The stiff Heart questions 'was it He, that bore,'
> And 'Yesterday, or Centuries before'?
> The Feet, mechanical, go round—
> A Wooden way
> Of Ground, or Air, or Aught—
> Regardless grown,
> A Quartz contentment, like a stone—
> This is the Hour of Lead—
> Remembered, if outlived,
> As Freezing persons, recollect the Snow—
> First-Chill-then Stupor-then the letting go—
>   (In Vendler, 2010, Poem 372, p. 168)

I imagine that Dickinson must have known many an hour of lead, with its chill, then stupor, and then the letting go. Of course, even if I lived in her century she would not have invited me to share her fireplace. But I think I would have felt more spiritually at home than I do now, at least able to imagine that a kindred spirit lives nearby. The values in a poem often include some of those that are so familiar to me from years of psychoanalytic practice: directness, restraint, economy, truthfulness, courage, and willingness to look at ourselves and at life, no matter what we see. When I hear a poem that embodies these qualities, I feel I belong.

For me, the feeling of not belonging can easily morph into loneliness. The difference between tolerable, or even pleasurable aloneness and painful loneliness has long been of great importance to me. Generally, loneliness has been thought by many to involve some type of painful loss. Thus, for example, Rollo May (1953, pp. 23–30) writes of loneliness as a response to a threatened sense of self. Because we need human relations in order to orient and know ourselves, unending isolation poses a threat to the feeling of the self's cohesion. The loss that loneliness entails is given a different slant by Fromm Reichmann (1959). Her writings emphasize the lack of hope of human connectedness in the profoundly lonely person. She focuses on the significance of hope of future interactions and the subjective meaning of the loneliness in explaining its effect. She explores possible antidotes to loneliness, such as a feeling that the loneliness has a purpose, that it is, for example, in the service of a cause. She also suggests that mental stimulation may somewhat relieve the feeling. Thus for Fromm-Reichmann, the most profound loneliness would entail the loss of hope, purpose, and stimulation. This is the loneliness I know best. It is a painful feeling that brings with it a sense of its permanence.

I suggest that poetry can be an antidote to many aspects of loneliness. Poetry can evoke a feeling of being whole; an interconnectedness between thought, feeling, and the spiritual self, since it often appeals to us on all of these levels at once. And poetry is a superb medium for transmitting the feeling that even someone we have never met might empathize with us. Hearing the poet express experiences similar to our own is conducive to hoping we *can* be understood by another human being. This is not unlike the feeling some patients express in treatment, that in order to accurately mirror them, the analyst must have felt similarly, at some time. In addition, poets (e.g. Rilke, 1934) have explicitly touted the value of solitude, thus supplying a sense of its validity and potential purpose. In other words, instead of judging ourselves as socially inadequate when we are alone, poetry might help us appreciate what aloneness offers us. Finally, it is unquestionable that poetry can supply intense stimulation, if one is open to its imaginative leaps. When I look at all poetry potentially offers (sense of wholeness, hope of being understood with empathy, feeling of being respected in our solitude, and experience of being engaged imaginatively) for me this description closely resembles the ideal analytic relationship. As I read a marvelous book by the poet Jane Hirshfield (2015) I kept thinking of analogies between what we would hope treatment would confer and what she sees as the powers of the poem to transform experience. Writing of a poem by Pound, Hirshfield (2015, pp. 276–277) says, "...the poem dissolves loneliness, by bringing the confirmation of shared experience. This happens, I think, in reading almost any good poem, though it is only noticed, or needed, when the poem has to do with pain. Pain, at its bluntest, separates and culls, isolates self from others. It lives inside the skin and pulls our available awareness with it. Yet in reading this poem, the ache of an elemental longing is slipped from hand to hand between writer and reader, a coin and token of recognition, and by that transaction is changed. What was carried alone is suddenly carried by two, by many."

While poems can leaven loneliness, to some degree, it is still there. Some poems confirm my belief that, as Rilke put it, "... for at bottom, and just in the deepest and most important things, we are unutterably alone...." (1934, p. 23). My way of understanding this is that no one else has lived my history of emotional experiences, so no one can fully "know" my pain or my joy, or other feelings. If someone says they feel your pain, I believe they are feeling *their version* of something triggered by your pain, which can't be exactly the same. The aloneness, of each of us, encased in our own unbridgeable experience of life, *is* permanent, and forms the basis of loneliness, at least for me.

What if outer reality mirrors this inner state? That is, what if feeling marooned with internal experiences that can never be fully communicated is also duplicated by *being* (in some sense) marooned in an unfamiliar external world? I am thinking of the experience of a child suddenly finding themselves transported to an unfamiliar culture. Sometimes all the child can express is a fear or reluctance to go to school with children who speak a foreign language, play unfamiliar games, and live according to different customs and values. Some of the difficulties for a child in this situation are apparent. But, I would suggest, the outer situation sometimes powerfully reinforces a deeper isolation. A poem by Aracelis Girmay captures the loneliness and anxiety of suddenly finding oneself cut off from anyone who truly understands and cares.

> Second Estrangement
> Please raise your hand,
> whomever else of you
> has been a child,
> lost, in a market
> or a mall, without
> knowing it at first, following
> a stranger, accidentally
> thinking he is yours,
> your family or parent, even
> grabbing for his hands,
> even calling the word
> you said then for "Father,"
> only to see the face
> look strangely down, utterly
> foreign, utterly not the one
> who loves you, you
> who are a bird suddenly
> stunned by the glass partitions

of rooms.

How far
the world you knew, & tall,
& filled, finally, with strangers.

(In Sieghart, 2019, p. 87)

No wonder science fiction touches a chord when it paints a picture of being a stranger in a strange land. Stories (like Shirley Jackson's (Farrar, Straus, and Giroux, New York: 1982, pp. 291–305) popular short story, "The Lottery") connect with our dread of finding ourselves alone, endangered, at the mercy of an uncaring horde. Poetry, too, can sometimes make vivid the powerful combination of uncanny dread and profound loneliness. What is it like to be a child separated from their parents at a border, or anyone, dying in a nursing home in the Covid era, where visitors are not permitted, attended only by heavily masked strangers? Or to be surrounded by people who hate your skin, who deny your humanity, crying that you can't breathe? I imagine a profoundly agitated loneliness, frantically searching for a familiar face, in a world "...filled, finally, with strangers."

Another poem, "Musee Des Beaux Arts," by W. H. Auden (in Bialosky, 2017, pp. 158–159) captures the essence of our isolation when we suffer in a cold, unregistering sea.

About suffering they were never wrong,
The Old Masters: how well they understood
Its human position; how it takes place
While someone else is eating or opening a window or just walking
dully along;
How, when the aged are reverently, passionately waiting
For the miraculous birth, there always must be

50

Children who did not specially want it to happen, skating
On a pond at the edge of the wood:
They never forgot
That even dreadful martyrdom must run its course
Anyhow in a corner, some untidy spot
Where the dogs go on with their doggy life and the torturer's
    horse
Scratches its innocent behind on a tree.

In Breugher's Icarus, for instance: how everything turns away
Quite leisurely from the disaster; the ploughman may
Have heard the splash, the forsaken cry,
But for him it was not an important failure; the sun shone
As it had to on the white legs disappearing into the green
Water; and the expensive delicate ship that must have seen
Something amazing, a boy falling out of the sky,
Had somewhere to get to and sailed calmly on.

This poem has a powerful effect on me. The words of the poem exist in my mind side by side with my memory of Brueghel's painting. Bialosky (2017, p. 160) tells how Auden came across the painting in a visit to the Brussels museum. It depicts the moment, in the myth of Icarus, when he flouted his father's advice not to fly too close to the sun, and plummeted into the sea. We see two frantic legs plunging into the cold water as everyone else calmly carries on with their ordinary tasks. Auden's poem declares that, like other masters, Brueghel was never wrong about the place suffering occupies. One of us is falling into an abyss as the rest of us go on with our lives. The figures in the painting are not spectators, in that they don't seem to notice the fall. It is a non-event for them, as Auden suggests. For Icarus it is the end of his chance at life; for others it is an unimportant little splash. In fact, looking at the painting, I am struck by its unnatural stillness. The plowman, the animals, the boat form a kind of tableau, frozen in time. The moment is preserved, like a snowy scene in a Christmas paperweight. As I read the word "leisurely," and the phrase "not an important failure" I feel how alone each of us is when disaster strikes. It is as though we were encased in a bubble or stranded in outer space. And, then, I have the feeling that by staring at the scene in a way I participate. I am at the border, encapsulated in my own stillness, looking on.

I think it is Breughel's genius that invites me to feel like desperate Icarus at the same time as I identify with the nonchalant plowman. I know what it feels like to sink, helpless, watching life recede out of reach. But it is just as clear to me that I know what it is like to be indifferent to the tragedies on the next block, out of sight, out of mind. Because it is happening over there, it is easy to let it remain unreal. By painting it as a tableau, Brueghel has invited me to inhabit a separate capsule, like the plowman and the horse, to know myself as them, just as I also know myself as Icarus. I can stand apart, as the plowman does, and as Sandra does, watching the scene unfold in her mind. I am in a different zone, where there are no legs hopelessly beating the cold, unyielding water one last time. In a moment a gradual fall will become a permanent absence, all useless effort ceasing as the legs sink into death. The poem brings back to me times when I was most alone with a grief no one else could really share. For me, Auden's poem has an even greater impact than the painting. When I look at the painting I feel most for Icarus, that dying boy who paid for his vaulting daring with his life. But when I read the poem I see that I am Icarus and the plowman, and all the other figures. I wall myself off from the tragedies around me, more often than I can possibly know. For me, the greatness of the poem, and its tremendous impact, comes from how it conveys the complexity of being a human being. We cling to the very defenses that keep us from greater compassion with sufferers. In our oblivion, we don't even know when we "had somewhere to get to and sailed calmly on."

As I think about this poem, I am also reminded of the first line of a poem by Jack Gilbert ("Falling and Flying," in Sieghart, 2019, p. 163). It begins, "Everyone forgets that Icarus also flew," and goes on to remark that when marriage ends in divorce we tend to focus on the "failure" of the relationship and not on the earlier fulfillments. But when I read Gilbert's line I am jolted into realizing that I never thought about the Icarus story that way. He got to fly. The jolt tells me about the limitations of my focus. I had heard the story only from the vantage point of how it ended, until Gilbert showed me another perspective. This confirms my feeling that poems can converse with each other and bring out new meanings. It also makes me less lonely, as Gilbert adds his point of view to mine.

I will illustrate how a poem can sometimes leaven my own loneliness by discussing two of Robert Frost's poems. Frequently, Frost elicits emotions in me that he then mirrors back. Reading his work, I often feel the same melancholy, wistful yearning that regularly haunts me while listening to Samuel Barber's "Adagio for Strings." As a first example, here is his poem, "Stopping By Woods on a Snowy Evening."

> Whose woods these are I think I know.
> His house is in the village though;
> He will not see me stopping here
> To watch his woods fill up with snow.
>
> My little horse must think it queer
> To stop without a farmhouse near
> Between the woods and frozen lake
> The darkest evening of the year.

He gives his harness bells a shake
To ask if there is some mistake.
The only other sound's the sweep
Of easy wind and downy flake.

The woods are lovely, dark and deep.
But I have promises to keep,
And miles to go before I sleep,
And miles to go before I sleep.
(In: "The Art of Robert Frost," T. Kendall, 2012, p. 319)

As I read the poem, I enter into it, in my imagination. Then, at first, I feel like a stranger to myself. This is not like me. I am deliberately lingering where I am not supposed to be! But, thankfully, the owner will not catch me loitering in his woods, since his house is far away, and though my horse understands my trespass, he has no recourse. So I can wallow in this spell, pulled toward the peaceful death that beckons me from those lovely woods. No one will witness the spell the woods cast over me. But, of course, spells don't last forever, and I am bound to remember the promises I am obliged to keep and the miles I must go before I sleep. At the end of the poem I feel I have been returned to my more usual, dutiful self, after having had a brief but rejuvenating escape. Then comes that whiff of haunting, familiar melancholy. For me, what is most delicious is that I don't have to ask whether my experience is "in" the poem, or entirely my projection. As Winnicott (1971) suggested so long ago, culture (unlike most of the rest of life) can give us a break from the tedium of having to answer that question.

Raffel (1984, p. 127) explores the structural qualities that give this poem its hold. "Quietly yet vividly musical, Frost's poem also involves a fine asymmetrical balance, with three stanzas devoted to the woods and only one to the 'promises ('I have) to keep,' and as delicate a contrast as a poet can muster, in the final stanza." Personally, I find it almost hypnotic.

But what if I am unable to go on vacation from myself when I read a poem? What if it doesn't give me a break from lonely self-enclosure? Remembering a poem by W.H. Auden ("Loneliness," In Mendelson, 1991, p. 866) makes it clear to me how much worse that could be.

> Gate-crashing ghost, aggressive
> invisible visitor,
> tactless gooseberry, spoiling
> my tete-a-tete with myself,
> blackmailing brute, behaving
> as if the house were your own,
> so viciously pursuing
> your victim from room to room,
> monotonously nagging,
> ungenerous jabber,
> dirty devil, befouling
> fair fancies, making the mind
> a quagmire of disquiet,
> weakening my will to work,
> shadow without shape or sex,
> excluding consolation,
> blotting out Nature's beauties,
> grey mist between me and God,
> pestilent problem that won't
> be put on the back-burner,
> hard it is to endure you.
>
> Routine is the one technique

I know of that enables
your host to ignore you now:
while typing business letters,
laying the table for one,
gobbling a thoughtless luncheon,
I briefly forget you're there,
but am safe from your haunting
only when sound asleep.

History counsels patience:
tyrants come, like plagues, but none
can rule the roost for ever.
Indeed, your totter is near,
your days numbered: to-morrow
Chester, my chum, will return.
Then you'll be through: in no time
he'll throw you out neck-and-crop.
We'll merry-make your cadence
with music, feasting, and fun.

Auden writes of the haunting presence of loneliness. During the day, Auden's only weapon is routine, until his real life chum returns. I am reminded of the analyst, Winnicott, (1971) who studied how our internal life determines whether or not we can derive needed comfort from culture's gifts. He looked to our internal life to understand what allows some to assuage loneliness with what he called "transitional space." This poem paints a less rosy picture. The way Auden describes his foe makes loneliness sound like an obsessive state of mind, allowing for few distractions, making the mind, in his words, a "quagmire of disquiet." Routines give only momentary relief. Sleep stills the enemy, temporarily.

Only the presence of a real other (not one encountered in a poem, in imagination) effectively breaks loneliness's spell. I am fascinated by his images of a tyrannical loneliness, "that won't be put on the back-burner." To my way of thinking, that is exactly what we most need to do, in states of loneliness. We can't make it disappear, (at least, not by an act of conscious will) but, unless it takes the shape of a stubborn obsession, we may be able to move it to the background, or, in Auden's words, briefly forget it is there. Auden's incredibly acute conjuring of loneliness's pursuit makes me feel less alone than I did before I read it. He is so very vivid, so alive to me, as he sets his table for one and gobbles his thoughtless luncheon.

My own self-reflections have led me to distinguish a benign (even pleasurable) aloneness from painful loneliness by thinking about who I am alone with, when I am alone. This is just another way to refer to Winnicott's "internal objects." Are they kind, loving, comforting, or degrading, disrespectful? Elsewhere (2008) I wrote about how shame about being alone can foster the slide from pleasant, or at least tolerable aloneness to devastating loneliness. In my mind it is not just the presence of a negative emotion (such as shame, guilt, regret, anxiety, and anger) that turns aloneness into a kind of torture. It is also the *absence* of self-love. This message is vividly conveyed by a generative and beautiful poem by Derek Walcott.

Walcott's poem, entitled "Love After Love" (In Seighart, 2019, p. 37) celebrates the caring we can extend to ourselves when we are alone after suffering loss. We can recognize and take pleasure in the person we see when we look in the mirror. That ongoing familiar being, that self, deserves a hearty welcome. To me, this poem speaks of a cherishing of oneself that can be of comfort and leaven the pain of a loss.

To know and love ourselves is such a rich concept, and, surely, one honored in my (psychoanalytic) profession. Self-knowledge and self-acceptance that is thorough, and automatic, and guided by a loving heart, is a worthy goal for anyone. I think of it as an especially important aspect of the equipment of a clinician, since, inevitably, there will be many painful moments, many losses, uncertainties, and challenges to personal and professional self-esteem. I think it takes an especially loving superego (Schecter, 1979) to engage, with due humility, in any of the "helping professions." Without adequate self-love the position of the clinician can be too lonely to bear.

Another poet, Robert Hass, reminds me of the special quality of loneliness when we are in the company of someone with whom we feel out of joint. From his long poem, "Heroic Simile," I quote the striking final lines: (In Seiden, 2016, p. 50):

> A man and a woman walk from the movies
> to the house in the silence of separate fidelities.
> There are limits to imagination.

Once in a while, absorbed in a poem, I get a little shock to discover my secret feelings in someone else's words. How did they know? When Robert Frost (in Mendelson, 1991, p. 179) wrote "The Road Not Taken," could he have had any familiarity with my regrets? Here is the poem.

> Two roads diverged in a yellow wood,
> And sorry I could not travel both
> And be one traveler, long I stood
> And looked down one as far as I could
> To where it bent in the undergrowth
>
> Then took the other, as just as fair,
> And having perhaps the better claim,
> Because it was grassy and wanted wear;

Though as for that the passing there
Had worn them really about the same,

And both that morning equally lay
In leaves no step had trodden black.
Oh, I kept the first for another day!
Yet knowing how way leads on to way,
I doubted if I should ever come back.

I shall be telling this with a sigh
Somewhere ages and ages hence:
Two roads diverged in a wood, and I—
I took the one less traveled by,
And that has made all the difference.

In the poem Frost seems to me to be looking for a way to choose one road over the other. He decides to choose the one that has not been worn down as much, even though "...both that morning equally lay/In leaves no step had trodden black..." He convinces himself that one road has "the better claim." His mind game is delightful to me, and so like my own! I would like to think my reasons for my choices came first, but, really, the choices precede the reasons most of the time. The reasons provided a story line, much like Frost's (arbitrary?) assertion that the least worn road is most worthy of his steps.

I hear in this Kierkegaard's idea that we have to live life forwards but can only understand it backwards. In other words we have to make choices not really knowing why we make them or where they will lead. This is part of the human condition. I think the poem adds a note of humor and a kind of peace, a tranquility, to the musings. What would my own life have been like if I had made different choices? Did I even see the crossroads as crossroads? Does it make sense to me to choose on Frost's basis? Maybe I would rather choose well-worn paths. But what does *that* say about me, if it is true? In any case, reading this poem has led me to confront the pattern of some of my choices in life. Similarly, in a treatment, we often see the "thread in the carpet," (a phrase used often by my teachers in psychoanalytic training) that is, the way our choices fit together. As a result of both treatment and reading (and writing) poetry ,when they are at their best, we can feel more whole. Personally, looking at Frost's poem, I feel a greater peace about how little any of us can really know about the outcome of our choices when we make them. The threads in the carpet are so much easier to see in retrospect! Any poem (or any other form of expression) that confronts us with life's basic terms can take the edge off the inevitable loneliness of living within them.

But so much that offsets loneliness can be shared by the tight community of poet and reader. Both take pleasure in words; their sounds, rhythms, music, beauty. Edward Hirsch (1999, p. 260) put this mutual collaboration so well. In the first chapter I quoted his expression (1990, p. 260) of how poets and readers make meaning together, as readers wrestle with poems, talk back to them, and become more fully themselves in the process.

I love a description (Raffel, 1984, p. 63) of the rewards for the reader of poems. He comments that poetry gets at some truths that ordinary, straightforward, non-metaphorical language can't express. He goes on to say that "each poem, if it is a good poem, creates a kind of small world of its own. We as readers of the poem are allowed to penetrate, to experience that small, different world." Being allowed into this world has often assuaged loneliness, for me. Reading a poem lets me share the links someone else experiences. For example, in Dickinson's poem (372) that begins "After great pain, a formal feeling comes..." (Vendler, 2010, p. 168) her linkage of the aftermath of pain with the idea of formality is something I would not have thought of, on my own. She has given me that (precious) connection. I will never forget it. In sharing this thought with me, she has let me into her mind (a little). This opening into the poet's mind acquires some of its emotional effect from poetry's evocative language. With great economy, Dickinson's phrase "formal feeling" conveys more than any prose description could. It *evokes* its layered meanings, rather than just describing them. Image after image weighs us down, as we read. I think of the many meanings of the word "gravity." I imagine how I might illustrate this poem as I read it, because images capture some of what Dickinson's words evoke. But they always fall short.

Another way to think of poetry as an antidote for loneliness is that it connects us with ourselves at the same time as it connects us with others. As I think about this, I remember the words of the psychoanalyst and author Erich Fromm, who understood alienation from oneself and others as a central problem of modern life. Fromm saw isolation as at the heart of suffering. He advocated what he called the "direct encounter," with oneself and others. Another way to put this is that we need to be in touch with the "stranger" in ourselves, as well as the "stranger" in others. Here are Fromm's own words ("Beyond the Chains of Illusion," 1962, p. 171).

> This attitude toward the stranger is inseparable from the attitude toward oneself. As long as any fellow being is experienced as fundamentally different from myself, as long as he remains a stranger, I remain a stranger to myself, too.

Some poems take us by the hand and introduce us to the stranger, in ourselves and in other human beings. They widen who we are to ourselves. In her unusual autobiography, which focuses on how particular poems affected her life, Jill Biolosky (2017, p. xiv) says, "Like a map to an unknown city, a poem might lead you toward an otherwise unreachable experience; but once you've reached it, you recognize it immediately." I think of Langston Hughes poem, "I, Too," (Bialosky, 2017, pp. 29–30).

> I, too, sing America.
>
> I am the darker brother.
> They send me to eat in the kitchen
> When company comes,
> But I laugh,
> And eat well,
> And grow strong.
>
> Tomorrow,
> I'll be at the table
> When company comes.
> Nobody'll dare
> Say to me,
> "Eat in the kitchen,"
> Then.
> Besides,
> They'll see how beautiful I am
> And be ashamed—
>
> I, too, am America.

Otherness is confronted by the proud assertion of membership in the human family. We hear the rage of the excluded. We face the results of injustice, prejudice. We step closer to an empathic understanding of stored up determination to overcome soul-crushing barriers. I feel this poem invites me to connect with ways I have excluded the external *and* internal other. Who is storing up strength to demand a place at my table? Who is my (*internal/external*) "darker brother," waiting to be recognized? Of course finally acknowledging how I have relegated him to an unseen corner will bring shame. Whether we consider a literally darker skinned human being or an internal "not me" that has been rejected from conscious awareness, these "others" don't accept their exclusion forever. Eventually they demand respectful attention. But while I cut myself off from them, I isolate part of my own humanity from the rest. I alienate, in the sense of dissociating a part from the whole, and in the sense of creating disaffection.

Many years ago I took a course on the metaphor. We were taught to use words to "make the strange familiar and the familiar strange." I have always loved that phrase. Making the strange familiar means, to me, finding commonalities, for example, between myself and the stranger. Making the familiar strange asks me to see from new angles. Both of these tasks, so central to the creation of a poem, are also central to countering prejudice.

Although it is in the form of a play and not a poem, nothing speaks to me of prejudice's distortions more than Shakespeare's "The Merchant of Venice." In this play we are forced to face how the prejudiced lose part of their humanity, and how their victim, Shylock, becomes dehumanized by his thirst for revenge. Here is his fervent plea for inclusion. (Act III, Sc. 1, lines 54–62).

...Hath not a Jew eyes? Hath not a Jew hands, organs, dimensions, senses, affections, passions?—fed with the same food, hurt with the same weapons, subject to the same diseases, healed by the same means, warmed and cooled by the same winter and summer as a Christian is? If you prick us, do we not bleed? If you tickle us, do we not laugh? If you poison us, do we not die? And if you wrong us, shall we not revenge? If we are like you in the rest, we will resemble you in that.

By the gut wrenching end of the play, Shylock has lost his daughter and his fortune, and has been forced to convert from his religion. But, more profoundly, he has lost his capacity for compassion. He is a lonely, empty shell. With this play Shakespeare has held up a mirror, in which we can see, in ourselves, the face of the excluding and the excluded. In the way that I think great art (and psychoanalysis) works, seeing our own alienation brings both pain and an *easing* of that alienation. We are no longer wasting energy by walling off part of ourselves from awareness, or walling off part of humanity from the rest of it. What we see in these mirrors may not please us, but in the act of looking we affirm a desire to do better. I am not suggesting that this performs miracles. But I do think it can contribute to a movement toward a less lonely, alienated state.

Sorrow and Grief

Assuaging loneliness is only one of poetry's restorative powers. As suggested in the discussion of Dickinson's poem (above) it can also help us bear life's inevitable sorrows. Hirsch (1999, p. 80) had this to say about how poetry can fill a gap society leaves vacant. Though written more than 20 years ago, his statement strikes me as still apt:

We live in a superficial, media-driven culture that often seems uncomfortable with true depths of feeling. Indeed, it seems as if our culture has become increasingly intolerant of that acute sorrow, that intense mental anguish and deep remorse which may be defined as grief. We want to medicate such sorrow away. We want to divide it into recognizable stages so that grief can be labeled, tamed, and put behind us. But poets have always celebrated grief as one of the deepest human emotions. To grieve is to lament, to let sorrow inhabit one's very being.

Hirsch goes on (p. 81) to describe the poet's task, as understood by Robert Frost. Frost saw grief as potentially enlarging us, not diminishing us. The poet's role is to be stubbornly unwilling to be reconciled, and determined to forge words that transform our deepest feelings into art. By furnishing us with this attitude, poetry implicitly grants us permission to grieve in our own way. In a very similar spirit, (as I discussed in chapter one) Rilke wrote that we should not aim to be consoled when suffering loss, but, rather, we should aim to develop the curiosity to explore the loss completely (in Ulrich Baer, "The Poet's Guide to the Wisdom of Rilke, Modern Library, 2005, p. 109). I notice how Rilke implicitly assumes that curiosity (an emotion, according to emotion theory, as defined by Izard, 1977) can help us bear sorrow, another intense feeling. Elsewhere (Buechler, 2008) I have written about how Rilke's wisdom anticipated many of the research findings of emotion theory.

A luminous story ("Since my house burned down") by Mary Yukari Waters (2003, pp. 17–33) illustrates poetry's potential for helping us bear grief. The protagonist is a seventy-six year old Japanese woman, who lives through the death of her husband in World War Two, the death of her only daughter, (a victim of pneumonia). periods of severe privation, the gradual diminishment of her physical being with aging, and the loss of much of her culture as her world becomes more and more westernized. Despair looms, as she is forced out of her kitchen, her only occupation, by her aggressive daughter in law. At one point she says to herself (p. 30) "My whole life has been a process of losing security. Or identity. Perhaps they are the same thing." But then a poem from her childhood floats into her mind.

Since my house burned down
I now own a better view
Of the rising moon.

The memory is accompanied by an unclenching of something in her chest, and she is comforted by the sounds of a nearby river. To me, it is as though the poem has the power to contextualize her life in a new way. Even loss has more than one side. It puts what we have left in higher relief. It reminds us of our membership in the human community, where one of the prices of survival is living through losses. We know that everything life gives us will be taken from us, in one way or another. We have to value sand castles that will be washed away by inevitable tides. None of us is unique in bearing this burden. There is something so sad, and yet, peaceful, in embracing this. Poetry can facilitate embracing, and not just surviving these truths. I wonder whether part of its power comes from poetry's readiness to live by (varying degrees of) stringent rules. Some poems, like this one, speak their truth within the strict limitations of their structures, which are the products of handed down poetic traditions. This poem, in its severe economy, obeys stringent laws, and yet tells its story with undiminished creativity. It is fully alive, within its strictures. I think it challenges us to do something similar; to maintain the spark of life within, and, in some senses, because of the limiting laws that govern us all.

Another way to look at the emotional power of this and other poems is that its impact derives from what it leaves out. It suggests a philosophy of life, a worldview, and we are left to fill in its meaning to us. Despite its strong conviction, it doesn't force us to any conclusions. But it has an unequivocal voice, the deep rooted voice of wisdom.

Interestingly, another Japanese poet, Izumi Shikibu (translated by Jane Hirshfield with Mariko Aratani) wrote a deeply resonant poem, about a thousand years ago (In Seighart, 2019, p. 9). This spare poem acknowledges that although their ruined house admits the terrible wind, it allows the moonlight to leak between the planks of its roof.

Like the poem in Waters' story, this poem promotes the idea that an opportunity can accompany a hardship. The house's state of ruin invites the invasion of harsh winds, but it also permits moonlight to leak between its planks. The gap in covering creates both vulnerability to the wind and exposure to the light. I think the challenge is to *expect* an opportunity to exist in the midst of ruin. I love the word "although" in this poem. It guides us to hold onto both sides at once; what is missing in the ruin and what is present in that very same state. If we focus only on the roof's inadequacy in keeping out the wind we might miss what is also true about it.

Rilke provided a demonstration of absence's power in his poem "The Archaic Torso of Apollo" (in Rachel Corbett, "You Must Change Your Life," 2016, pp. 210–211).

We cannot know his legendary head
with eyes like ripening fruit,
And yet his torso

is still suffused with brilliance from inside,
like a lamp, in which his gaze, now turned to low,
gleams in all its power.

Otherwise
the curved breast could not dazzle you so, nor could
a smile run through the placid hips and thighs
to a dark center where procreation flared.

Otherwise this stone would seem defaced
beneath the translucent cascade of the shoulders

and would not glisten like a wild beast's fur:

would not, from all the borders of itself,
burst like a star: for here there is no place
that does not see you. You must change your life.

Corbett, who studied Rilke's relationship with the sculptor, Rodin, describes the poem as starting out with a tour of parts of the torso. How to explain the statue's power? Rilke turns to the absence of the head for an explanation. Were it not for this absence "...the curved breast could not dazzle you so, nor could/a smile run through the placid hips and thighs...." At the end of the poem, in one of the sharpest turns I have ever read, Rilke says "...for here there is no place/ that does not see you. You must change your life." Corbett understands this as the moment when the searching becomes mutual, and the boundary between the torso and the poet dissolves, as does the boundary between poet and reader. As I hear it, if the statue had eyes, its sight would be limited to a certain field of vision. But the headless torso "sees" with its whole being. When we dissolve boundaries, including the line between white space and torso, "thing" and surround, background and foreground, we are on the way toward changing our lives. We are no longer holding on to the illusion of a separate self. That illusion gave us a misleading clarity, that kept us from any truly meaningful transformation.

In trying to explain poetry's power to move us, Edward Hirsch (1999, p. xi) quotes Paul Valery, who said, "The power of verse is derived from an indefinable harmony between what it *says* and what it *is*. Indefinable is essential to the definition." (italics in original). Two aspects of this explanation are particularly striking to me, partially because they remind me of the power of a transformative interpretation in psychoanalysis. In calling the harmony "indefinable" Valery is pointing to the irreducible mystery of what makes a poem, an interpretation, or any creative product profoundly affect us. I think of the "harmony" he credits as an organic relationship between content and process. Regardless of the medium, this gives an expression power. If I talk about kindness kindly, what I say may more easily touch you. To me, this is not just about the words I choose. It is also about the pace, tone, shape of how I speak. I can talk about kindness in a clipped, staccato, sharp manner that belies my words. In that case, I don't think they will have much impact, or the impact might be different from what I (consciously) intend. For example, in Hirsch's own poem, "Fast Break" (in "The Living Fire," 2011, p. 51, and discussed more fully below) Hirsch writes an elegy for a friend who died very young, and was the poet's basketball buddy. The poem is written as one long sentence that races, weaves, darts. Its form conveys the feel of players moving forward in tandem on that basketball court, as though connected by invisible strings. And then one, off balance, "inexplicably" falls. Which brings us back to the dedication of the poem, "In memory of Dennis Turner, 1946–1984."

Like this poem, some poetry brings home to us, in vivid terms, what we do and don't inevitably forfeit when we bear significant losses. Hirsch lost Dennis Turner, but not his memories of their brotherhood on the basketball court.

Poetry's ability to conjure up images, along with its rhythmic qualities and frequent direct appeals to the heart, make it an ideal medium for integrating mind, body, and emotion. Many poems have helped me put myself together during times of sorrow. An example is Heaney's "Clearances." Here are just a few lines.

> So we'd stretch and fold and end up hand to hand
> For a split second as if nothing had happened
> Beforehand, day by day, just touch and go,
> Coming close again by holding back
> In moves where I was X and she was O

Inscribed in sheets she'd sown from ripped—
out flour sacks.

(In Ogden, 2001)

My mind's eye sees a mother and son dancing a stately do-si-do. My body feels the rhythm of the poem's slow, steady movement. My thoughts are engaged in trying to understand the mystery of "coming close again by holding back." At the same time I remember that Heaney's mother died close to when this poem was written. I feel for a son who so profoundly misses his reliable partner. The sheets speak of his mother's frugality and steadfast industry. I am moved by this son's careful observations. It is as though he is putting her together again, matching up her way of folding sheets with her way of mothering him. I wonder what he feels about their rituals now that she is gone. Did they "come close" enough? Did they both need to feel "as if nothing had happened/beforehand...."?

By engaging me on so many levels at once, this poem centers me. Responding to it, my mind, heart, and body are gathered into one place. And, of course, that place is not new to me. It is full of memories of my own losses; of my own dance partners.

Another poem, by Marie Howe, illustrates loss and remembrance with heart stopping clarity. I discussed this poem in the first chapter, but I want to bring out different aspects of it here. The poem is entitled "What the Living Do."

Johnnie, the kitchen sink has been clogged for days,
    some utensil probably fell down there.
And the Drano won't work but smells dangerous, and
    the crusty dishes have piled up.
Waiting for the plumber I still haven't called. This is
    the evening we spoke of.

It's winter again: the sky's a deep headstrong blue
    and the sunlight pours through
the open living room windows because the heat's on
    too high in here, and I can't turn it off.
For weeks now, driving, or dropping a bag of groceries
    in the street, the bag breaking,
I've been thinking: This is what the living do. And,
    yesterday, hurrying along those
wobbly bricks in the Cambridge sidewalk, spilling my
    coffee down my wrist and sleeve,
I thought it again, and again later, when buying a
    hairbrush: This is it.
Parking. Slamming the car door shut in the cold. What
    you called that yearning.
What you finally gave up. We want the spring to come
    and the winter to pass. We want
whoever to call, or not call, a letter, a kiss-we want
    more, and more, and then more of it.
But there are moments, walking, when I catch
    a glimpse of myself in the window glass,
say, the window of the corner video store, and I'm
    gripped by a cherishing so deep
for my own blowing hair, chapped face, and
    unbuttoned coat that I'm speechless:
I am living, I remember you.

                                        (In Seiden, 2016, pp. 63–64)

Sometimes poetry names what can't yet be borne so, at least, it can be
spoken. This poem helps me to feel seen in my own grief. Poetry often helps
me feel seen, for what I am, not what others want me to be, or assume I am,

or project. So often it is a small detail that blasts me with the enormity of the loss of those I loved. This mourning can be deeper than what is called up by a photo or even the remembrance of a memorable occasion. The ordinariness of relying on Johnnie to unclog the sink makes manifest that, while he was alive, his sister was not aware of the assumption that he would always be there. Just as sinks would always be there, Johnnie would always be there. So, when the sink is clogged, and there is no one to holler at to fix it, the hollering reverberates inside the poet. Howe leads me by the hand to see my own reflection, haunted by losses, yet still cherishing life. She must see me seeing myself, since she writes just the right words to describe what I feel. My sorrow is the neighbor of my cherishing. They live in houses that adjoin. The walls keep each one in its rightful place. They don't try to mix or visit or move in with the other. The know their place. They know that if they keep to this arrangement they can stay forever. In other words, if guilt over still loving life prods me to give mourning exclusive sway, my state is ultimately untenable. Similarly, if the joy of being alive prompts me to deny my sorrow it bursts in when least expected. The poet sees all this and, in her spare lines, tells me she feels all this too. "I am living, I remember you." I note the comma. "I am living" needs "I remember you" fully as much as "I remember you" needs "I am living."

In his essay on Howe's poem (2016, pp. 62–65) Seiden writes about Howe's ability to find something numinous, a spark of life, in the mundane. I agree with his assessment that Howe found words that actualize this quality for the reader. Seiden also points to the resilience and life force that shine through. He lauds (p. 64) the poet's ability to "think big and write small." With this thought, Seiden has named one of poetry's greatest strengths, in my opinion. Poetry has the ability to create pictures of everyday details *at the same time* as it evokes our deepest reflections on the meaning of life itself. Of course poetry doesn't have a monopoly on this capacity. But I find it more frequently in verse, and Howe's poem is a great example. Since this poem is stated as about the slow death of the poet's brother, from AIDS, I will write about the poet, rather than the poet's persona. She conjures up our focus on her spilled coffee, and, just a few lines later, the stubborn recalcitrance of the life force. Our mind's eye still sees the coffee running down her sleeve as we muse, with her, about our own unyielding desires. Tiny, truthfully etched, perfectly ordinary moments beside profound questions about whether "to be or not to be," as Hamlet put it. What effect does this have? I think it can actually change our vision. The everyday takes on weighty meaning. The spilled coffee says that, despite (or because of?) a brother's unspeakable suffering, coffee tastes good enough to want to buy it and carry it home. It's not just inconveniently messy brown liquid.

But, at least for me, there is something more. My mind is forced to do two things at once. I am focusing on small details as though examining a photograph. And I am also musing, in a dreamy, associative state. I am thinking with feeling and feeling thoughtfully. I am focused and unfocused, attentive to Howe's images and inwardly absorbed. In other words, I am having an experience, not just reading words. And that experience seems to me to be not unlike what the poet describes herself undergoing.

This poem affects me profoundly, like a gut punch, no doubt in part because I strongly identify with the poet/speaker. But not all poetry is this direct a communication from poet to reader. Raffel (1984) reminds us that in some poems the speaker is someone other than the poet. He refers (p. 10) to this as a kind of mask, or persona. For me, this extra layer between me and the poet can sometimes distance me from a direct experience of grief, and function as an end run around my defenses, allowing the poem to penetrate me when I might otherwise resist. I am sometimes most in need of the "gut punch" and, at other times, the "end run," so I am very glad to find both in the poetry I love.

In a way Howe celebrates everyday life persisting amidst tragedy. W.H.
Auden has a very different view but, for me, his poem "Funeral Blues" packs
just as much of a gut punch.

> Stop all the clocks, cut off the telephone,
> Prevent the dog from barking with a juicy bone,
> Silence the pianos and with muffled drum
> Bring out the coffin, let the mourners come.
>
> Let aeroplanes circle moaning overhead
> Scribbling on the sky the message He Is Dead,
> Put crepe bows round the white necks of the public doves,
> Let the traffic policemen wear black cotton gloves.
>
> He was my North, my South, my East and West,
> My working week and my Sunday rest,
> My noon, my midnight, my talk, my song;
> I thought that love would last forever: I was wrong.
>
> The stars are not wanted now: put out every one;
> Pack up the moon and dismantle the sun;
> Pour away the ocean and sweep up the wood;
> For nothing now can ever come to any good.
>
> (In Mendelson, 1991, p. 141)

This poem comes the nearest of any I know to portraying some moments of
my own grief. Ongoing life can seem incongruous, even obscene. Sometimes,
in a state of unbearable sorrow there just isn't any room for the tension
between the everyday and the profound. Auden's poem conveys to me the
feeling that the everyday and the profound have been lost with the death of

the beloved. Since *he was* "my working week and my Sunday rest," *all* is lost, from the tiniest ordinary detail through the deepest meaning. This strikes me as quite different from Howe's celebration of ongoing mundane joys.

When my own grief is accurately described in a poem it comforts me, partly because it takes place when I am alone. It is entirely free. No strings attached. I don't have to applaud, appreciate, give feedback, or anything else. Like a mirror it is there solely to help me know myself. I don't have to keep furtive track of a debt.

Another poem, (mentioned briefly above) Edward Hirsch's " Fast Break," (in Hirsch, 2011, pp. 51–52) also balances grief and cherishing. He sneaks up on his sorrow which I think makes it more powerful. "Fast break" is several stories skillfully braided into one poem. But, aside from this, to read it is a physical, imaginative, and emotional experience. "Fast break" makes it clear that a poem can incarnate bodily experiences, which is less common in prose. This means it moves us on many levels at once. *We feel it in our bodies as we are thinking it in our minds, and reeling from it in our hearts.* "Fast break" catapults us into the rush of basketball's pace, as, at the same time, it sweeps us into the sorrow of a dear friend's tragically premature death.

A hook shot kisses the rim and
hangs there, helplessly, but doesn't drop,

and for once our gangly starting center
boxes out his man and times his jump

perfectly, gathering the orange leather
from the air like a cherished possession

and spinning around to throw a strike
to the outlet who is already shoveling

an underhand pass toward the other guard
scissoring past a flat-footed defender

who looks stunned and nailed to the floor
in the wrong direction, trying to catch sight

of a high, gliding dribble and a man
letting the play develop in front of him

in slow motion, almost exactly
like a coach's drawing on the blackboard,

both forwards racing down the court
the way that forwards should, fanning out

and filling the lanes in tandem, moving
together as brothers passing the ball

between them without a dribble, without
a single bounce hitting the hardwood

until the guard finally lunges out
and commits to the wrong man

while the power-forward explodes past them
in a fury, taking the ball into the air

by himself now and laying it gently
against the glass for a lay-up,

but losing his balance in the process,
inexplicably falling, hitting the floor

with a wild, headlong motion
for the game he loved like a country

and swiveling back to see an orange blur
floating perfectly through the net.

This poem is dedicated in memory of Dennis Turner (1946–1984). Turner was Hirsch's fellow faculty member, with whom he enjoyed playing basketball, until cancer claimed Turner's life at the age of 38. I have yet to get to the end of this poem with dry eyes.

This poem *embodies* its content in its fluidity and forward motion. It operates as an experience, and not just a description of an experience. It is also an elegy, which can mean that it comments on the afterlife of those we have lost, as they live on in our minds and hearts. Some poems vividly and palpably illustrate what I have elsewhere (2008) suggested about mourning being an ongoing relationship, rather than a process of letting go. In "Fast Break," Hirsch shows how the relationship continues partly through an activity he and his friend Dennis both loved, the exhilarating dance of basketball. Now the activity is a medium that helps the poet carry on the relationship by doing something in the outer world that brings them together in Hirsch's inner experience. Furthermore, there is humor in the midst of sorrow in this poem. Hirsch's ironic jab ("for once the player got it right") is a joke the poet and the deceased would have enjoyed together, so it honors their relationship. I think this grief tugs at the heart harder because it is understated.

Elegies often embody grief in another sense. They take us *toward* and *into* sorrow. They don't leave us room enough to defensively skirt it. They aim for the bull's eye, pain's epicenter. In a sense, they obey Rilke's advice to go toward, and not avoid, our heart's most profound losses (as discussed more fully above).

What I hear in this is that our losses are *constituents* of our selves. We shouldn't aim to "get over" them, any more than we should aim to "get over" being who we are. When we look in the mirror we should recognize how they have shaped us. It is not for us to judge their markings as good or bad, but just to recognize them.

But do we think of our sorrows as integral parts of ourselves, or as burdens we carry? These differences can be subtle, but, I think that holding each can have meaningful consequences. I discuss some of these differences in a later section, but, for now, I quote a poem by Jane Hirshfield that takes a definite stand.

Burlap Sack

A person is full of sorrow
the way a burlap sack is full of stones or sand.
We say, "Hand me the sack,"
but we get the weight.
Heavier if left out in the rain.
To think that the sand or stones are the self is an error.
To think that grief is the self is an error.
Self carries grief as a pack mule carries the side bags,
being careful between the trees to leave extra room.
The mule is not the load of ropes and nails and axes.
The self is not the miner nor builder nor driver.
What would it be to take the bride
and leave behind the heavy dowry?
To let the thin-ribbed mule browse the tall grasses,

its long ears waggling like the tails of two happy dogs?

(In Sieghart, 2019, p. 29)

In a kind of intermediate position, a poem by Lucille Clifton sees our sorrows as beautiful assailants clinging to us, yet separate enough to have their own wings. They scar, scab, attach themselves to us, and overwhelm our protestations.

Sorrows

who would believe them winged
who would believe they could be

beautiful who would believe
they could fall so in love with mortals

that they would attach themselves
as scars attach and ride the skin

sometimes we hear them in our dreams
rattling their skulls clicking their bony fingers

envying our crackling hair
our spice filled flesh

they have heard me beseeching
as I whispered into my own

cupped hands enough not me again
enough but who can distinguish

one human voice
amid such choruses of desire

(In: Clifton, 2010, p. 216)

Prose can't capture the luminosity of this poem. As it drifts on the page it also drifts through my mind and heart. I, too have been the cupped hands that resist sorrows assaults, and I, too, have understood how useless it is to resist. That they scar and leave their mark is familiar. But, for me, these creatures are novel as conveyances of grief. While I immediately understand how their numbers overpower, and I intuitively sense their envy, I have never before seen them as beautiful.

I think all these poets would agree that there is no shame in crying. In many poems pain is told to come out into the open, rather than hide its tears. Poetry reverses the usual conventions. We are supposed to *dwell* on pain, not move away as quickly as we can. Other conventions are also up-ended. We don't have to follow the rules of logic. Like children, we are free to cry in public, to wail, or to let the poem hold the heartache in a safe place, waiting for us to be ready for it. We do our best to keep hold of the inner tie to those we have lost. We may try to live in the ordinary world until momentum gathers, or disaster shatters, and we break into sorrow.

"Permission" to grieve openly has an interesting history. The story behind a poem by Henry Wadsworth Longfellow gives us a window through which to view it (In: Burt and Mikics, 2010, pp. 202–205). The poem is entitled "The Cross of Snow."

In the long, sleepless watches of the night,
A gentle face—the face of one long dead—
Looks at me from the wall, where round its head
Here in this room she died; and soul more white
Never through martyrdom of fire was led

80

To its repose; nor can in books be read
The legend of a life more benedight.
There is a mountain in the distant West
That, sun-defying, in its deep ravines
Displays a cross of snow upon its side.
Such is the cross I wear upon my breast
These eighteen years, through all the changing scenes
And seasons, changeless since the day she died.

Eighteen years before Longfellow wrote this poem his wife, Fanny, died in a fire at their home (Burt and Mikics, 2010, p. 202). He was badly burnt in the fire too, trying to save her, but failed to do so. He wrote the poem in 1879, but it wasn't published until 1886, after his death. Writing a biography of the poet, his brother chose to include the poem. Burt and Mikics suggest (p. 202) that the poet didn't publish the poem because it was too personal or too painful. But then they add:

The sonnet (one of dozens he composed in the last decade of his life) describes his continuing grief over Fanny, and, in doing so, violates standards of Victorian and postbellum American taste, by which (as Matthew Arnold put it) suffering should find "some vent in action," grief (especially grown men's grief) some end.

In this poem Longfellow admits the truth, that his grief is endless and "changeless since the day she died." Fanny is long dead, but her husband's grief lives on, unmitigated by any comforts provided by either Nature or religion. He has chosen to put her portrait on the wall opposite his bed even though, presumably, it elicits memories and feelings that contribute to his "sleepless watches." As Rilke advised (above) he heads *toward*, not away, from his pain. In the language I used to discuss Marie Howe's poem (above) Longfellow's sonnet is a gut punch, rather than an end run around his sorrow. But he judged that society was not ready to hear it, or, at least, he wasn't ready to share it in the world at that time.

Both Howe and Longfellow express intense grief that endures, but Howe describes a cherishing of her own aliveness that exists at the same time, for her. In my own mind I am separating the philosophical assumptions that dictate heading *toward* pain from the assumptions and values that would have us strive toward a *balance* of intense pain with the intensity of positive feelings. I don't think that expressing loss in direct and vivid language has to limit us to just grief, and nothing else. I am not suggesting that Longfellow did or didn't achieve that balance, but, only, that he didn't write about it in this poem. Burt and Mikics imply that, in that era, to be respected, grief had to be limited in time and result in some purposeful action. Women were allowed more latitude for limitless, purposeless grief. But men were expected to master their grief, as expressed by limiting its duration and transforming it into action.

Interestingly, two psychiatrists (A. V. Horwitz and J.C. Wakefield, 2007, *The Loss of Sadness.* New York: Oxford University Press) traced the history of their profession's treatment of sadness as an illness, failing to differentiate it from depression. Their work suggests a broader application of this attitude. Their evidence reflects the stigmatizing of lengthy sorrow for women as well as men, and well into the twentieth century.

Howe (above) achieved the insight that grief balanced by cherishing life is not, necessarily, less intense than grief felt without it. I think Waters, in just three lines, captured the spirit of the compensations that can offer balance. But regardless of whether or not they put forth the idea of balancing grief with other feelings, all of these poets give voice to an ongoing relationship with the departed.

Elsewhere (2008, p. 150) I have argued that internal efforts to maintain ongoing relationships with the deceased are inherently limited. Theories that highlight them describe one important aspect of mourning, but may not give adequate emphasis to needs that can't be met internally, but require an actual, *external* interaction. I quote this at some length because I feel I still have no better way to express it.

> ....I believe that a true grasp of our interpersonal natures forces us to conclude that the loss of actual, specific, intimately known others is irreplaceable. We need to feel their breath, to hold their hand, to watch them laugh, to experience them in the living moment, through every sense, and not just in memory. This need is given poignant voice by survivors like Didion and Bayley who will settle for nothing less than the continuing presence of their beloved. Anything else denies the importance of the body, of surprise, of the unpredictable moment. No matter how mature and well developed our inner life, there is no object relational substitute for an alive partner when you want to go dancing.

Over the years I have grown more comfortable with realizing that contradictory ideas may be true. I still feel that there is no substitute for an alive partner when you want to go dancing. The loss of the body of the other can be immeasurable. And yet it seems true that those who have fully entered into me are never lost to me. They are the air I breathe. A beautiful poem by Mary Elizabeth Frye makes this point.

Do Not Stand At My Grave and Weep

Do not stand at my grave and weep,
I am not there; I do not sleep.
I am a thousand winds that blow,
I am the diamond glints on the snow,

I am the sun on ripened grain,

I am the gentle autumn rain.

When you awaken in the morning's hush

I am the swift uplifting rush

Of quiet birds in circling flight.

I am the soft starlight at night.

Do not stand at my grave and cry,

I am not there; I did not die.

(In Sieghart, 2019, p. 165)

Some sorrows challenge us to accept both the limits and the extent to which we can learn to bear the pain of living. It shouldn't surprise us that Emily Dickinson (Poem 419, in Hirshfield, 2017, pp. 157–158) wrote a subtle poem on the subject.

We grow accustomed to the Dark—

When light is put away—

As when the Neighbor holds the Lamp

To witness her Goodbye—

A moment-We uncertain step

For newness of the night—

Then-fit our vision to the Dark—

And meet the Road-erect—

And so of larger—Darkness—

Those Evenings of the Brain—

When not a Moon disclose a sign—

Or star-come out-within—

The Bravest-grope a little—

And sometimes hit a Tree

Directly in the Forehead—

But as they learn to see—
Either the darkness alters—
Or something in the sight
Adjusts itself to Midnight—
And life steps almost straight.

What happens to us in our darkest and most uncertain times? Do we falter and then right ourselves, until we can, once again, "meet the Road-erect-"? And then, despite our most courageous efforts, what if we inadvertently steer ourselves directly in harm's way? At that point something has to give, and (hopefully) either the situation improves or we learn to take it in differently. As Hirshfield (2017, p. 163) points out, the last line carries the knowledge that there are events in our lives from which no recovery is possible. Hirshfield sees the poem as declaring that, while we may be capable of dogged persistence, life has the last word.

While I get the sense that Hirshfield reads this qualifier as devastating, I have a different feeling about it. That I see it so differently is, in itself, meaningful to me, since it illustrates how each reader may find a somewhat different poem in the poet's lines. For me, the word "almost" *rescues* the poem from an unrealistic optimism about our ability to bear adversity. In my experience there are times when no amount of dogged persistence can get life to step straight. Elsewhere (2019) I have discussed the limitations of therapeutic ventures that aim for a full "adjustment" to reality. In some situations adjusting is a necessary component of coping, but it doesn't eradicate pain.

One of poetry's comforts is so embedded in its fabric that it may be hard to isolate. Some poems focus on the everyday in a way that lends it greater significance. I think this can actually affect our perspective on life, in sorrowful times and throughout our lives. We read these poems, look around us, and see the timeless in the time bound details. Visual arts can serve a similar function. Here is one poem, Poem 591 (In: Vendler, 2010, p. 266) by Emily Dickinson, that suavely performs this feat. (I discussed this poem in Chapter One, but want to revisit it here to look at other aspects of it). Dickinson juxtaposes the mundane with the profound, and begins her poem by startling the reader:

> I heard a Fly buzz-when I died—
> The stillness in the Room
> Was like the Stillness in the Air—
> Between the Heaves of Storm—
>
> The Eyes around—had wrung them dry—
> And Breaths were gathering firm
> For that last Onset—when the King
> Be witnessed—in the Room—
> I willed my Keepsakes—Signed away
> What portion of me be
> Assignable—and then it was
> There interposed a Fly—
>
> With Blue—uncertain—stumbling Buzz—
> Between the light—and me—
> And then the Windows failed—and then
> I could not see to see—

Everything I see or hear or touch or smell, even the smallest fly, can signal my aliveness. When I die, some of me will be passed on; "assignable" to others. But my window on the world, my particular way of seeing it, will die with me. However, life itself will go on. There will still be buzzing flies.

Some poems seem to stop life's dogged forward motion, which is a magic many of us appreciate. In doing so, I think they render the reality of time's passage just a bit more bearable. In general, art makes time stand still for a few moments. In our absorption, we literally lose track of time. Also, as Keats's Grecian urn (In: *Immortal Poems of the English Language*, ed. Oscar Williams, 1952, Simon and Schuster, p. 315) illustrates, art's beauty endures. Taking this a step further, Frost's poem "Nothing gold can stay," fosters our ability to distinguish and accept what outlives time and what won't. (In: *A Book of Modern American Poetry*, ed. Jane McDermott and Thomas Lowry, 1970, Harcourt Brace Jovanovich, Inc. NY, p. 55).

> Nature's first green is gold,
> Her hardest hue to hold.
> Her early leaf's a flower;
> But only so an hour.
> Then leaf subsides to leaf.
> So Eden sank to grief,
> So dawn goes down to day,
> Nothing gold can stay.

This poem adds a softer, mellow note to the drumbeat of time and the approach of death. By stopping time, even if it is just for a moment, and by creating something beautiful that *will* last forever, the poet has balanced what is finite with what is infinite. The poet gives us "the second that goes on living for hundreds of years." (as expressed in the poem "Vermeer" by Tomas Transtromer, *in Art and Artists*, Ed. Emily Fragos, 2012, pp. 23–24). Thus time is transformed into something we may be able to accept because:

1. We have had a vacation, escaped it for a while.
2. We see that beauty will last after we are gone.

3. We may shift our emotional investments, prioritizing that which endures.

I think of this transformation as akin to the clinician's art of reframing. Much of the world's culture partakes of the benefits of this transformation of meaning. In Tolstoy's (1886/1982) "Death of Ivan Ilyich," a father's suffering and approaching death become sacrifices he can make to free his family of their stilted attention to him. In Shakespeare's (1972, Arden edition) *King Lear,* the old man's death becomes a poignantly desirable relief, for himself and all who love him. Life can become unbearable enough for death to seem more like a release than a sorrow. Much poetry reframes our losses into marks of the natural passage of a season. With great simplicity, Edna St. Vincent Millay (in Bialosky, 2017, p. 133) tells us "summer sang in me/a little while, that in me sings no more." To me, this evokes sweet, soft, sad nostalgia, a mood more than any specific memory or thought. In this mood I am more easily reconciled to the passing seasons of my own life.

To sum up, in this mood, with Howe (above) I can still value my life, alongside mourning my losses. I am unashamed of my tears (Rilke) and determined to move toward my deepest feelings, rather than try to avoid them. With Dickinson, I recognize that healing will be limited. But, with Hirsch, I also know that what I have shared with others can help me continue our relationship after they die. The timeless wisdom of Frost and Edna St. Vincent Millay may help me accept life's seasons with greater equanimity. These poets tell me my grief is not avoidable or pathological, but simply human, and I am not alone in it. Some say I can fully enter it with my body, my heart, and my mind, and still cherish life. Some of them celebrate ongoing life, even in the midst of deep grief, while others insist on our recognition that loss changes everything. There are poets that see sorrow as a (potentially separable) burden we bear, while others position it as integral to who we become forevermore. Some see sorrows and joys as different sides of the same life experiences, with each side highlighting the presence of the other side. In other words, our absences *define* what is present. Other poems focus on sorrow and joy as distinct feeling states that, at best, can balance each other. While various poets emphasize different nuances, all acknowledge the inevitability of loss itself. Eventually I will lose everyone, and everything I hold dear. As I hear them, each of these poets has a meaningful perspective on living with this knowledge.

Fear

The challenges of absorbing life's blows can be magnified by fear. That is, the concept of a system of emotions means that painful feelings can exacerbate each other, just as well as modulating moods and emotions can soften each other. For example, fear (and its more complicated cousin, anxiety) can greatly add to the difficulty of bearing the sorrow of the inevitable losses that accompany aging. Anxiety can be seen (Izard, 1972, 1977; Buechler, 1995) as a more complex array, with fear at its center, but other feelings in its makeup. Regardless of the fine points of this distinction, it is clear that some form of fear of aging and dying can intensify our sorrow about the passage of time. How can poetry help us with this potent brew?

Fear bids us shrink away, but poetry heads us toward the threat, leaving no room for avoidance. By presenting it in close-ups, every aspect vividly detailed, poetry tells us (implicitly) that our fears *can* be faced. Just as Rembrandt looked squarely into his aging face, never leaving out the sagging flesh, the tired eyes, the mottled skin, the creeping advance of sorrow, so some poems refuse to squint. By articulating every particle, they perform an autopsy even before dread dies. I am reminded of my own work on the nature of courage (2004) and its *equidistance* from rashness and timidity. Some poems exemplify this courage, this hard glance right into life's greatest challenges. As Jane Hirshfield says (2015, p. 161) "We go to certain good poems as children go to certain stories, to be rightly frightened."

Fear can be a response to slight alterations in the way situations normally read, causing us to question our sense of reality. A poem can articulate this in a way that is conducive to facing it. It can also awaken our curiosity, which may modulate the fear. Take, for example, the marvelous poem "Lion," by Michael Hettich (In: Raffel, 1984, pp. 44–45).

> Behind that door
> in a white room we keep
> a man who thinks
> he is a lion.
> You can see he's kept safe.
> He thinks he's a lion!
> Once he escaped
> and ran through the city
> Disappeared.
> Changed his name.
> Actually this isn't him,
> This is a lion
> And this is a picture
> Of the African plains.
> We'll slip it beneath
> his door now; he'll look at it
> smiling, draw
> an animal on it
> and himself running
> to catch it, slip
> the picture back under
> the door.

thus we study
the workings of his mind.
Today he's drawn
a bowl, that's a bowl
of soup, being carried
by a stick figure, a woman.
That's him smiling.
Notice the hair
is wild, that he wears
no shirt.
Each day the picture
is different, but he always
smiles. Tonight his dinner
is soup, of course,
and a woman, but what
do you think of his smile,
his naked chest, skinny
after months in the white room
but still wild—
What do you think
he looks like, who do you
think he is, who do you
think he thinks
he is, we are? These are some
of the questions we ask ourselves.
A wild man! A lion!

The poem interferes with our comfortably settling on one viewpoint. Is it the story of a wild man, lion-like, who paces in solitary confinement? Of a patient in a mental hospital? Of a subject in a bizarre observational experiment? Of a childish boy/man who draws stick figures? Of a mythological lion-man? Of a totemic figure in a clan that has been conquered and caged? Of a symbol of the power of the instincts (for food, a woman, and self-expression in the drawing)? Or a symbol of how the "wilder" aspects of us are "tamed" by a coldly observant society? Or, perhaps, a situation where those in the role of "taming" can project their own "wildness" onto their victims? Or is it an actual lion, with onlookers wondering about what he thinks and feels?

After trying out one or another of these readings (or other possibilities). only to have each disconfirmed, we are forced to "give up the fist." Categorization, that neat obsessive way to delimit felt fear and anxiety, has failed us. "Either or" has to give way to "And also," or "I don't know." Rigid thinking must be abandoned or, at least, its limitations are made obvious. For me, this leads to a moment of humorous self-recognition. The contrast tells me that my thinking is usually obsessively neat. The effort I have to make, to try a hypothesis, (e.g. that this is a delusional man) and then discard it when it is disconfirmed ("Actually this isn't him,/ This is a lion") beckons me to hold my hypotheses lightly. Or, at least, it could, if I am open to hearing this lesson. The poem also challenges the reader to accept a lack of "resolution" at the end, which, to me, is another valuable lesson with applications to much of life, as I experience it. Perhaps it also reminds me of my situation as a child, not always understanding what is being said and what is going on; not yet possessing the categories that would allow me to put moments in boxes and store them for safe keeping.

How might reading Hettich's poem, "Lion," help me live my life? If I am ready for it, I think it could contribute to shaking up fixed assumptions about the value, and the limitation, of making sense of things. For those with a tight, rational approach to life, it might nudge us toward alternative approaches. But most importantly, at least for me, it startles me, and this gives me a chance to know something about the fear and anxiety I usually avoid. Of course, reading this poem would not be enough to change life—

long ways of coping. I am not at all suggesting that. It is a poem, not a substitute for years of treatment. But it points toward how frightening it can be to be uncertain about reality. It offers the reader a chance to embrace, rather than avoid, uncertainty. Going further, the poem is an opportunity to become curious rather than afraid. What is the poet trying to say, and trying to evoke? Why do I react to it as I do? If I truly wonder, I am less likely to feel pressure to "know" the "right" answers. I might even be a bit less afraid of the mystery. As Jane Hirshfield says (2015, p. 149) "...to be human is to be unsure, and if the purpose of poetry is to deepen the humanness in us, poetry will be unsure as well." Just (same page) a bit later, she says "...good poetry helps us be more richly uncertain in more profound ways."

Perhaps another way to say this is that poetry is unafraid of obliterating all the lines between self and non-self, inner life and outer life, and reality and non-reality. These divisions, which some have considered so vital to mental health, are violated in poetry, as we will encounter many times. I find this enormously bracing. I hear it as validating so many of my own experiences of floating entirely unmoored. Raffel (1984, p. 28) quotes T.S. Eliot, who referred to music "heard so deeply that it is not heard at all, but you are the music while the music lasts." Of course poetry is not the only art form that blurs or entirely erases these lines, but I think it is especially well suited for this task. Like a good story, poetry can open up new vistas. But stories usually have certain restrictions that poems can more easily escape. Take, for example, "The Wizard of Oz," ("Annotated Wizard of Oz," 2000. Frank L. Baum 1900, ed. M.P. Hearn, WW Norton NY) a story in which we are led, along with its protagonist, Dorothy, to visit a strange world. This new world may have some parallels to ours, but there are differences, most especially in what is possible in it. In the story, Dorothy starts out in the quintessential *obsessive* conflict. She is caught between what she wants to do (keep her dog, Toto) vs. what she has to do (obey parental authorities and give him up). It seems utterly insoluble, not unlike most such dilemmas. But Dorothy is rescued by magic. She has a fantastic adventure, which exposes her to the clash between good and evil, and teaches her to look beneath surfaces. For example, a fierce looking lion may be quaking in fear. Eventually, Dorothy is freed to want what authorities would want her to want-that is, to go back home. She listens to her heart and finds the power within herself to get there. That she chooses home may help the reader bear our own return to reality when the story ends. In a sense, home has been re-framed, from a harsh place that endangers little dogs, to a welcome haven. In the audience we participate in the magic of re-framing, sighing with relief when Dorothy makes it back to Kansas. The structure of this tale is clear: we start in a difficult reality, are lifted to a fantasy land, and return, glad to be back in reality. It is as though we couldn't appreciate the rational, sensible, rule-bound world until we experienced a place where all reasonable limits didn't apply. We had a real vacation from order, we had wonderment, and now it is time to go home.

As we have seen, both prose and poetry can lift us from reality. But, compared with prose, I think poetry can more easily embody a *fluidity*, back and forth, between fantasy and reality. For example, while the content of the characters and situations Dorothy encounters is pure fantasy, the structure segregates reality from the fantasy realm. Of course poetry is not the only art form that can portray simultaneous reality and fantasy, or swift alternations between them. But I think poetry is the ideal medium for creating a *flickering* between the real and the imagined. In Hettich's poem, at one point, we are getting comfortable that we are dealing with the reality of a human being ("Once he escaped/and ran through the city/Disappeared./Changed his name..."). But then the poet throws us a curve ball ("Actually this isn't him,? This is a lion...."). The poem dances, dizzyingly light on its feet. As I chase after it, I feel how different this is from my usual mode. I am accustomed to segregating non-reality to night time dreams. But in this poem reality and fantasy play dodge ball, weaving around each other. I feel unsettled. Do I try to force the poem to tell me a story within my comfort zone? Or do I let it filter through me, spreading its uncertainties? When I feel unhinged who do I become? Can I remain curious when I am thrown into an unmoored state? Hettich's poem invites me to do just that, in a relatively low stakes situation for, after all, I can just turn away from it any time I want. In that sense, a poem like "Lion" gives us practice in bearing uncertainty in a relatively safe situation. Like training a muscle, we can start with a manageable exercise, taking a step toward developing the capacity to maintain curiosity amidst greater, or more consequential chaos. Or, as the poet Rilke advised (1934, p. 35) "learn to love the questions....."

But sometimes the loss of bearings feels too extreme. Sullivan (1953, p. 10) used the word "uncanny" to mean emotions that "...have a sort of shuddery, not of this earth component," including feelings of dread, horror, and loathing. For Sullivan, experiencing the uncanny can be greatly disorienting, and, even, damaging. Some poems present uncanny moments in ways that inch toward our feeling (just) able to survive them. In a poem I have always found astonishing Elizabeth Bishop (In Seiden, 2016, pp. 22–27) describes an uncanny experience, presumably from her own childhood. This poem has the fascinating ability to paint an extremely clear picture but remain, at least for me, full of mysteries. Little Elizabeth, just shy of her seventh birthday, sits in the waiting room while her aunt gets treated by the dentist. Hearing her aunt's sudden cry of pain, Elizabeth is not surprised, because she already assessed her aunt as foolish and timid. But something else was a shock. Here are some lines from the beginning and middle of the poem:

In Worcester, Massachusetts,
I went with Aunt Consuelo
to keep her dentist's appointment
and sat and waited for her
in the dentist's waiting room...

Suddenly, from inside,
came an oh! of pain
—Aunt Consuelo's voice—
not very loud or long....
... What took me
completely by surprise
was that it was me:
my voice, in my mouth.
Without thinking at all
I was my foolish aunt,
I-we-were falling, falling....
I knew that nothing stranger
had ever happened, that nothing
stranger could ever happen...

Elizabeth has been jolted out of ordinary life and into a slippery territory, where she feels she is falling and falling and, maybe, never landing on solid ground again. But, by the end of this long poem, she finds herself back in Worcester Mass., in February, 1918. Seiden (2016, p. 22) calls the poem a "spookily beautiful evocation." He uses the clinical terms, dissociation and depersonalization, to describe Elizabeth's traumatic awakening. "Other" and "self," "familiar" and "stranger" refuse to keep to their usual places. In the remainder of the poem, Bishop creates a vivid image of how this shakes the child's foundations:

The waiting room was bright
and too hot. It was sliding
beneath a big black wave,
another, and another.

Then I was back in it.
The War was on. Outside,
in Worcester, Massachusetts,
were night and slush and cold
and it was still the fifth
of February, 1918.

Hirsch (1999, pp. 236–243) also discusses this poem, and its expression of the terror of a sudden loss of identity. Hirsch notes what he calls the "epiphanic moment" or crisis, in the line: "Suddenly, from inside,/came an oh! of pain…" This moment is a very sharp turning point, after which experience is never the same. Of these moments, he says (p. 243) "They move from the ordinary to some other extraordinary realm of experience in order to negate time itself. The experience is shockingly painful since it involves being separated from daily life and losing one's former self. The compensation is a new knowledge and consciousness. The everlasting splendor of dramatizing epiphanies may well be the mystery of communicating moments when the self is both lost and found."

By finding words for the uncanny, it seems to me that Bishop has moved it one step away from the entirely taboo, or, in Sullivan's language, the "not-me." For Sullivan, the "not me" means the motivations we can't know are our own without serious negative consequences (Sullivan, 1953). Later in the poem, I hear the child asking what can help ground her, when her foundation seems to be dissolving. She glues her eyes to a magazine cover and its specific date, and remembers her own age, attempting to locate herself in the dimension of time. She glances over at other bodies (knees, trousers, skirts, boots, hands) trying to use her observations to discover the relationship between physical characteristics and identity. Finally, she turns to logic, asking why she should inhabit her particular self and not another. I think she is attempting to contain the uncanny by using her mind to find an explanation for it. The poem seems to me to ask whether we are best off defending ourselves by reasoning with the uncanny, or is it best to move as quickly as possible back to reality, to Worcester, Massachusetts, the fifth of February 1918? Clearly, interrogating the disruptive experience ("Why should I be my aunt,/ or me, or anyone?") doesn't argue it away. And yet, she *has* opened up a dialogue with herself. I would assume she, and all of us, spend our whole lives in that waiting room, hoping that soon our niche will make sense. Perhaps the best we can do is use our strengths to hold terror at bay enough to continue the dialogue, rather than shutting it down, which may give us a chance to get used to life in the waiting room. In her biography of Bishop *(Elizabeth Bishop: A Miracle for Breakfast* ,Houghton Mifflin Harcourt, NYC, 2017, p. 210) Megan Marshall writes:

This fall into self-consciousness was almost more than the child could bear. The 'bright/and too hot' waiting room carried her 'sliding/ beneath a big black wave,/ another and another.' Yet it was not too much. Thinking saved her; poetry—'a way of thinking with one's feelings'—saved her. She could think then and, decades later, define and contain the unsettling moment in verse...

Not surprisingly, different poems point us in somewhat different directions, as we cope with fear and anxiety. Some suggest we head straight for what we are afraid of. Others seem to recommend a more cautious approach. Some poems (not unlike the theories of emotionality I discuss elsewhere, 2004, 2008) recommend putting another evocative experience alongside our apprehensive imaginings. This is clearly spelled out in the poem, "The Peace of Wild Things" by Wendell Berry (in Sieghart, 2019, p. 3). The poet, despairing, wakes and lies down to rest where wood drakes and herons make their home. These creatures are not troubled by anticipating future grief. In the presence of the still water and shining stars he feels free, resting in the world's grace.

It seems to me that if we "come into the peace of wild things," and "rest in the grace of the world" we live moments that contrast with our fearful imaginings. Perhaps this provides a temporary vacation from them. Or, maybe, it gives us that and something more. I think it soaks us in the experience of what will survive. That transforms what we fear we will lose from foreground to background. Ongoing life takes center stage. This life is without fear, because fear predicts and mourns future losses while (presumably) the wood drake and heron do not. Wild things have not been tamed by fear. In their presence, perhaps we are less tamed by it, too. Afterwards, we may go back to fearing, but something has changed, in that we have had an experience of being unafraid, so, forevermore, it will exist withinthe realm of possibility.

Shame and Guilt

Bouts of unsettling anxiety are not the only painful feelings poetry helps us bear. Sometimes poems confront us with our least acceptable attributes, challenging us to deal with potential shame and guilt. Differences between shame and guilt (and, sometimes, between each of these and anxiety) have always been of interest to me. When I have had to explain their meaning I have often resorted to a story. If I got a failing grade on an exam, and I didn't study, I might feel guilt, for not living up to my own standard. But if I failed even though I did study, I might feel shame, or a sense of insufficiency. And if I worried about how I could be punished for failing, I would feel fear or anxiety.

One of my favorite poems, Dickinson's Poem 1263 (in Vendler, 2010, p. 451) seems to me to be the perfect antidote to a certain form of shame.

Tell all the truth but tell it slant—
Success in Circuit lies
Too bright for our infirm Delight
The Truth's superb surprise
As Lightening to the Children eased
With explanation kind
The Truth must dazzle gradually
Or every man be blind—

This is quite an extraordinary statement, especially from someone for whom the truth was so central, and its surprises were so cherished. And yet she advises us (and, I presume, herself) to tell it circuitously. Vendler puts it beautifully when she says (p. 433) "We all begin as children knowing practically none of the truths of body or selfhood. Little by little, 'the facts of life' (emotional and intellectual, as well as physical) are conveyed to us; but even so, we only half-formulate many of them...It takes a poem to make our eyes gradually accept the brilliant light of the Truth hitherto shaded."

Two concepts from the literature in psychology and psychoanalysis come to mind. The first, from Freud, (1926/1959, Standard Edition, 20, 87–175) is the idea that trauma is the ego overwhelmed. That is, regardless of the content of what we have to cope with, if it is more than our strengths can bear, it is traumatic. The second is the definition of shame as a sense of insufficiency (Izard, 1977). In each of these we see a self, aware it *can't* cope with what it *must*. Elsewhere (2008, p. 57) I have called this shame/anxiety, to point to what I think is its hybrid nature. Compassion bids us feed children (and adults) difficult truths gradually enough to avoid this experience, whenever possible.

Early in my career I didn't understand this. Like many other neophytes, (starting, in fact, with Freud,) I thought if I could just tell my patient The Truth it would be mutative. First of all, this presumed that there was a Truth,

100

and I knew what it was. I now feel these were the illusions of someone young, inexperienced, idealistic, and insufficiently humble.

I won't take all the blame for why this illusion held sway over me for as long as it did. I think psychoanalytic training fosters it, in its goal of diminishing the power of the defenses. (I discussed this issue at length in Buechler, 2012). I think this facilitated my clinging to the idea that if I could just get around, or under, or through the patient's defenses, or disable them, or help the patient need them less, The Truth would set them free, as the saying goes. Sometimes it actually does work that way. The energy employed to defend against knowing something is freed for other uses. I believe that if the treatment partners discover something just at the point where it was almost already clear, it may be useful. Then it may "dazzle gradually" enough not to "blind." But if the clinician conveys the attitude that cowardice is preventing the patient from grasping the truth, this is likely to cause shame (if the patient takes it to heart) or, perhaps, rage.

A superb example of traumatic, overwhelming truth was portrayed in Elizabeth Bishop's poem, "In the Waiting Room" (discussed above). Seven year old Elizabeth was forced to confront more truth than she could bear, and felt "...the sensation of falling off/ the round, turning world/ into cold, blue-black space." (In Seiden, 2016, p. 24). To go back to Dickinson's idea of gradual vs. sudden realizations, it is as though Elizabeth simply hadn't the resources to cope with her own questions, such as: in what way are we all related? What does it mean to have a specific identity? What separates each of us from others? Elizabeth was as unprepared to deal with these questions as Dickinson's imagined children given a premature treatise on the causes and dangers of lightning.

So Dickinson advises us to take it easy. When in the business of dispensing Truth, take your time. Approach it in a roundabout way, gradually sidling up to it, perhaps using indirect forms of communicating it. In my own language, spoon feed rather than force feed.

But, as Vendler (p. 431) reminds us, the poet does say to tell it all. She doesn't compromise her allegiance to the truth. She is merely commenting on the manner in which it is conveyed. In my view, her attitude retains dignity and integrity without sacrificing empathic concern. We can be both brave and kind. We don't have to choose.

Another poem of Dickinson's (Number 326, in *The Complete Poems of Emily Dickinson,* Ed. Thomas H. Johnson, 1960, pp. 154–155) deals with her limitations with a somewhat different attitude. It declares, "I cannot dance upon my Toes…" and then goes on to portray what she *can* do, at least, in imagination:

> I cannot dance upon my Toes—
> No Man instructed me—
> But oftentimes, among my mind,
> A Glee possesseth me,
>
> That had I Ballet knowledge—
> Would put itself abroad
> In Pirouette to blanch a Troupe—
> Or lay a Prima mad,
>
> And though I had no Gown of Gauze—
> No Ringlet, to my Hair,
> Nor hopped to Audiences—like Birds,
> One Claw upon the Air,
>
> Nor tossed my shape in Eider Balls,
> Nor rolled on wheels of snow
> Till I was out of sight, in sound,
> The House encore me so—

Nor any know I know the Art
I mention—easy—Here—
Nor any Placard boast me—
It's full as Opera—

According to Vendler (2010, p. 1) Dickinson published few poems within her lifetime, out of the nearly 1,800 She wrote. Yet she continuously sought publication, sending her work to Thomas Wentworth Higginson, (among others) bearing rejection after rejection. I will not try to imagine myself into her feelings about this. But I do find it striking that, in this poem, she juxtaposes what she can't do in the real world (because no man has instructed her) vs. her glorious performances in fantasy. The inner world can so often compensate us for what is unreachable in the outer world! And what profound acclaim she imagines she could have "among" her mind! Since no word is random in her poetry, I assume she is of several minds, only one of which dreams of amazing successes. In that mind, she shocks troupes and stuns audiences, who reward her with multiple encores. She is a star, the brightest star. She doesn't have to stoop to stunts ("Nor tossed my shape in Eider Balls/ Nor rolled on wheels of snow...") to get the audience's attention. Her talent is enough.

Where does a sense of being sufficient come from? Theories abound (Kohut, 1971; Lansky M.,& Morrison, A. 1997). Do certain people need external validation, so as not to suffer from the shame/anxiety I mentioned in relation to the previous Dickinson poem (above)? Can some of us retain the feeling of being "enough" on the basis of the fantasies we spin in one of our minds?

There are poems that help us face our whole selves by making us aware that the underside of our strengths may include our least noble aspects: that is, those that could elicit our shame and/or guilt. I find this concept enormously helpful and, somehow, peaceful. It reminds me of Sullivan's often repeated dictum that we are all more human than otherwise (1953). I find it conducive to greater self-acceptance to understand how everything about us, our greatest assets and most profound limitations, is connected in ways we may only partially comprehend. Poetry often presents to us the truth that all motives are mixed, to varying degrees, and that human beings are ambivalent creatures. I think there is potential for helping us bear our shame and guilt in this message. While many creative forms might convey it, I think poetry is a particularly felicitous medium for this task. In some poems, our hybrid natures are expressed so subtly that we might not always consciously notice this point, perhaps allowing it to pervade our being without our resistance. Take, for example, the gorgeous declaration of love in W. H. Auden's poem, "Lullaby." (in Seiden, 2016, pp. 18–19)

Lay your sleeping head, my love,
Human on my faithless arm;
Time and fevers burn away
Individual beauty from
Thoughtful children, and the grave
Proves the child ephemeral:
But in my arms till break of day
Let the living creature lie,
Mortal, guilty, but to me
The entirely beautiful.

Soul and body have no bounds:
To lovers as they lie upon
Her tolerant enchanted slope
In their ordinary swoon,
Grave the vision Venus sends
Of supernatural sympathy,

Universal love and hope;
While an abstract insight wakes
Among the glaciers and the rocks
The hermit's carnal ecstasy.

Certainty, fidelity
On the stroke of midnight pass
Like vibrations of a bell
And fashionable madmen raise
Their pedantic boring cry:
Every farthing of the cost,
All the dreaded cards foretell,
Shall be paid, but from this night
Not a whisper, not a thought,
Not a kiss, nor look be lost.

Beauty, midnight, vision dies:
Let the winds of dawn that blow
Softly round your dreaming head
Such a day of welcome show
Eye and knocking heart may bless,
Find our mortal world enough:
Noons of dryness find you fed
By the involuntary powers,
Nights of insult let you pass
Watched by every human love.

Is there a more tender expression of love in the English language? If there is, I don't know it. And yet, he declares his lover "...mortal, guilty, but to me/ The entirely beautiful." This part of Auden's message is spelled out especially emphatically. It is possible to be flawed and yet entirely beautiful in the eyes of someone who loves us. A comforting, and, perhaps, even, an enlightening thought. Toward its end I think this poem spells out our greatest challenge, "Find our mortal world enough..." How can we, ephemeral, guilty creatures, accomplish this? And, given clear vision of each other, how can we still love? I hear Auden as saying we can suspend our focus on these truths and, for a night, let love happen. Even while we are "suspending disbelief" (somewhat as we do watching a performance in the theater) we still really know reality. In the theater we know we are not looking at the forest of Arden. We know our lover will disappoint us, perhaps be unfaithful, perhaps leave us, maybe die before we do. But we can (temporarily) background this and foreground their sweet beauty and our love for them. I believe that being able to do this can be life saving, in many senses. It shifts the emotional balance, in my terms. It adds joy and love to the equation.

The message is more complicated but, I think, profoundly similar in W.B. Yeats' evocative poem (in Seiden,2016, p. 140) "Crazy Jane Talks With the Bishop."

I met the bishop on the road
And much said he and I.
"Those breasts are flat and fallen now,
Those veins must soon be dry;
Live in a heavenly mansion,
Not in some foul sty."

"Fair and foul are near of kin,
And fair needs foul," I cried.

My friends are gone, but that's a truth
Nor grave nor bed denied,

Learned in bodily lowliness
And in the heart's pride."
"A woman can be proud and stiff
When on love intent;
But Love has pitched his mansion in
The place of excrement;
For nothing can be sole or whole
That has not been rent."

Seiden (2016, p. 141) suggests that this poem "gives us a concise assertion of the argument against even the possibility of purity..." I agree, and read in the poem the question of how we can continue to love life, and ourselves, given the impurities of both. Or, as I have asked elsewhere (2019) can we love life, ourselves, and others, anyway? Jane and the bishop take opposite sides, as I hear them. He emphasizes the ugliness of Jane's life now, and raises the question of whether she should go on with a dirty, hardscrabble life or give it up. Jane argues for the value of it. She sees foul and fair as needing each other, for there can't be one without the other. Perhaps ironically (since he is a bishop and she is supposedly crazy) Jane presents a more spiritual, holistic perspective. Beneath our pretensions we are all, always imperfect creatures, having to acknowledge our impure bodies, thoughts, and hearts, and the painful losses of those we love.

I think this poem demonstrates the idea (discussed in the previous chapter) that it is essential for us to be able to embrace contradiction. Nothing is whole that has not also been rent. We are torn from our mothers' bodies, born amidst blood and other matter; angels and devils, pure and impure hybrids. Embracing who, and what we are, and life's many-sidedness could help us remain in life, even when our breasts are fallen and our friends are gone. Love itself has unsavory aspects. I hear Jane as "crazy" in the same way that Shakespeare's "fools" are fools. Both tell truths that society might prefer to tuck out of sight. But, once faced, perhaps they make it just a bit easier to look in our own mirrors and see whatever we see.

But given society's influence, looking in the mirror can become more daunting, and shame producing, as we age. One poem in particular takes this on, with a spirit I find bracing, entertaining, and, somehow, contagious.

Warning

When I am an old woman I shall wear purple
With a red hat which doesn't go, and doesn't suit me.
And I shall spend my pension on brandy and summer gloves
And satin sandals, and say we've no money for butter.
I shall sit down on the pavement when I am tired
And gobble up samples in shops and press alarm bells
And run my stick along the public railings
And make up for the sobriety of my youth.
I shall go out in my slippers in the rain
And pick the flowers in other people's gardens
And learn to spit.
You can wear terrible shirts and grow more fat
And eat three pounds of sausages at a go
Or only eat bread and pickle for a week
And hoard pens and pencils and beer mats and things in boxes.
But now we must have clothes that keep us dry
And pay our rent and not swear in the street
And set a good example for the children.
We must have friends to dinner and read the papers.
But maybe I ought to practice a little now?
So people who know me are not too shocked and surprised
When suddenly I am old, and start to wear purple.

Jenny Joseph, in: *Poems to Learn By Heart*
(Ed. Ana Sampson, 2013, pp. 124–125).

From my point of view, this poem demonstrates how a pinch of assertion/ aggression can alter shame. It is easy to take in society's message that getting older is something to try to hide, using "products" pitched to us for that purpose. To me this poem says, flaunt it! There is nothing to be ashamed of.

For another humorous, gently chiding poetic expression, I turn to the poem "A Reckoning." This poem makes a subtle distinction between shame and guilt. It is by Richard Wilbur (2009). The poet has decided that it is time to chalk up his sins. What comes to mind are embarrassing memories. In retrospect his foolish words cause him shame.

After differentiating embarrassing faux pas from genuinely guilt provoking behavior, Wilbur makes what I think is an unusually insightful point. Holding oneself to a very high standard, and, as a result, feeling shamefully insufficient, is itself prideful. I am sure we have all encountered (or been) people who exclaim at how inadequate they are while expecting super human achievements from themselves. They often see their flaw as the failure to live up to those high standards, while Wilbur sees the standards themselves as problematic.

These poems invite us to question our negative self-evaluations. I am not suggesting that all shame and guilt is unwarranted. But, as I read these poems I feel less likely to be ashamed of my humanness. I am a limited, sometimes ambivalent, sometimes prideful, always flawed, constantly aging person. I may *earn* shame or guilt *from how I behave* but that is different. These and other poems evoke my re-appraisal of what should, and what shouldn't elicit shame or guilt in me. I have always believed that people deserve some credit for looking in the mirror, no matter what they see when they look. When I read these poems I see myself reflected, along with countless others, as part of the human fold. I can describe the poems' effect on me, using the concept of the emotions as a system. As I read and contemplate how hard it is to be a person, and live a decent life, my own shame, guilt, and loneliness tend to decrease, and my curiosity and empathy are enhanced.

Anger

Among our other profound human challenges is adequate integration of anger and its related emotions (rage, hate) into our overall makeup. In emotion theory terms, anger is considered a fundamental emotion, basic to human experience. It might sound odd to consider how poetry can help us bear (and, even, use) our anger, but I believe it can. "A Poison Tree," by William Blake (in Raffel, 1984, pp. 64–65) gives us some ideas.

I was angry with my friend:
I told my wrath, my wrath did end.
I was angry with my foe:
I told it not, my wrath did grow.

And I watered it in fears,
Night and morning with my tears;
And I sunned it with smiles,
And with soft deceitful wiles.

And it grew both day and night,
Till it bore an apple bright.
And my foe beheld it shine,
And he knew that it was mine,

And into my garden stole,
When the night had veiled the pole;
In the morning glad I see
My foe outstretched beneath the tree.

What a complex and insightful theory of human emotionality is contained in this poem, and years before Freud! I hear it declare, in simple but evocative language, that sharing anger can ameliorate it, that one emotion (fear) can exacerbate another (anger). and that the "fruit" of such a union can be deadly. Raffel cites this poem as an example of an extended, controlling metaphor. For me, the poem creates an indelible image that pictures a truth it would be hard to express in any other way. Once anger is "planted," and especially when its growth is facilitated by fear, it develops a life of its own. So much that goes on between human beings can be understood in these terms. Anger (for example, at a group in society) can be made more potent by the addition of fear. In this poem the fear is experienced as a misery, expressed in tears. I think of the fundamentally incendiary situation created when one group fears that its survival is threatened by another.

I believe that this poem's power comes, partially, from its simplicity and economy. It creates its imagery in a language that could be understood by a child. In fact, it reminds me of children's fables. It is, in a sense, a morality tale. I can imagine a storybook illustration in my mind's eye. Personally, I feel lulled by the first 14 lines, and a bit stunned by the last two. At first, I am expecting the speaker to become contrite. He failed to express his anger to his foe, resulting in it bearing bitter fruit. But then, at the end, the speaker is gleeful about his foe's demise. This turn engages me emotionally, more than I would be without it. I become an active participant, going along with the speaker, until I am caught up short. I think this renders the poet's message much more powerful than it would be otherwise. It prepares me to wonder how I have "watered" my own angers, and what dangerous "fruits" they might bear.

A poem by Charles Lamb, titled "Anger," makes related points, differentiating constructive from destructive forms of the emotion.

> Anger in its time and place
> May assume a kind of grace.
> It must have some reason in it,
> And not last beyond a minute.
> If to further lengths it go,
> It does into malice grow.
> 'Tis the difference that we see
> 'Twixt the serpent and the bee.
> If the latter you provoke,
> It inflicts a hasty stroke,
> Puts you to some little pain,
> But it never stings again.
> Close in tufted bush or brake
> Lurks the poison-swelled snake
> Nursing up his cherished wrath;
> In the purlieux of his path,
> In the cold, or in the warm,
> Mean him good, or mean him harm,
> Whensoever fate may bring you,
> The vile snake will always sting you.
>
> (In: *Poems to Learn by Heart, Ed.* Ana Sampson, 2013, p. 71)

Lamb's "good" anger seems inherently tame (or has it been tamed?). It stays in its place, and doesn't overstay its welcome.

It is interesting to look at Blake's and Lamb's poems together. In Blake's poem, anger becomes problematic when it is *unexpressed* and *nurtured*, as is more likely with a foe than with a friend. Lamb 's dangerous anger is also nurtured ("Nursing up his cherished wrath;...") but the question of whether or not it is expressed is not mentioned.

What constitutes "nurture" of anger? I think there is a truth in the idea that indulging in angry fantasies, luxuriating in them, immersing oneself, bathing in angry monologues can preclude feeling anything else. It may then preclude feelings that might otherwise modulate the anger, such as lingering positive feelings or, even, fear about the consequences of expressing the anger.

Who does the "vile snake" always sting, the angry one or the object of their anger? From the poem it sounds more like the latter, but it isn't clear to me. I read the last three lines as saying that when we are the object of someone's nurtured wrath, whatever else fate has in store for us, and whatever our own motives might be, we will eventually suffer. Anger's poison has a kind of inevitability. Interestingly, the concept of anger as a poison is implicit in Blake's poem and explicit in Lamb's. It inescapably infects.

As a psychoanalyst, I am especially drawn to two points: Blake's argument that unexpressed feelings eventually erupt and cause problems, and the concept of the harmful effects of "nurturing" anger (which I hear as akin to an obsessive preoccupation with it). The need for emotional expression is a basic premise in all the psychoanalytic theorizing, which developed well after Blake's and Lamb's poems were written. Abraham, Freud, and their psychoanalytic followers explored the dangers of getting lost in obsessive thinking. I think these poems contain the kernels of some of their ideas.

Another approach to the place of anger in a balanced emotional life suggests that, sometimes, we need anger to rescue us from limitless sorrow, or incapacitating helplessness. Here, again, poetry can be our teacher. For example, in Dylan Thomas's moving poem, "Do Not Go Gentle Into That Good Night," (in K. Young, 2010, p. 19) the persona begs his father to fight the incursions of aging. He desperately wants to remember a fierce father.

> Do not go gentle into that good night
> Old age should burn and rave at close of day;
> Rage, rage against the dying of the light.
>
> Though wise men at their end know dark is right,
> Because their words had forked no lightning they
> Do not go gentle into that good night.
>
> Good men, the last wave by, crying how bright
> Their frail deeds might have danced in a green bay,
> Rage, rage against the dying of the light.
>
> Wild men who caught and sang the sun in flight,
> And learn, too late, they grieved it on its way,
> Do not go gentle into that good night.
>
> Grave men, near death, who see with blinding sight
> Blind eyes could blaze like meteors and be gay,
> Rage, rage against the dying of the light.
> And you, my father, there on the sad height,
> Curse, bless me now with your fierce tears, I pray.
> Do not go gentle into that good night.
> Rage, rage against the dying of the light.

The persona in this poem begs his father for a memorable legacy. Curse or blessing matters less than that it is fierce, passionate until the end. As I hear it, he is not in favor of his father's gradually letting go of investments in life, in order to more easily give life up. He doesn't want his father weak and tenuous at the end. He wants to remember him in all his intensity. It matters less whether it is a loving father, so long as it is a father full of life. The poem counsels that the way to maintain full blooded aliveness is to embrace and embody rage. Don't meekly, sorrowfully accept the loss of everything you hold dear. Go down fighting.

Whether or not we agree with this philosophy, it does reflect a belief in the value of using an anger related emotion to cope with adversity. Faced with the ultimate challenge, anger can serve to mobilize our strengths. A similar belief was poignantly expressed by King Lear, at a key moment of his own emotional descent. (*Arden Shakespeare*, 1997, Act II, Sc. 2, lines 465–468, p. 256)

> ...touch me with noble anger,
> And let not women's weapons, water-drops,
> Stain my man's cheeks...

Lear counts on anger to prevent him from dissolving in helpless grief. As I read it, this play asks the question of whether Lear's towering rage can be a resource, to hold him together, or must it pave the way to madness. It seems as though the balance tilts toward the latter, and Lear's terrible, hurt rage undoes him. But he (and so many others) hoped anger would lend him coherence. Personally, I think it sometimes does. For example, if we fight against the destruction of the environment we might save ourselves from dissolving in grief about its desecration. Or, as another example, I imagine that organizations, like "Mothers Against Drunk Driving," or politically active groups of parents of children who perished in bombing attacks have known tremendous sorrow, but, alongside it, mobilize anger that allows them to pour themselves into fighting against further losses of life. I think that anger sometimes centers us, giving pain a shape and a purpose.

But anger can't always be managed. This is forcefully expressed in Lucille Clifton's poem "fury" (In: Clifton, 2020, p. 151). Please see the text of this poem above, in Chapter One. It contains a powerful description of a searing rage that can defeat us *or* coalesce us in a determined resistance. Briefly, Clifton, with a quiet ferocity, portrays her mother destroying precious pages of writing because Clifton's father forbade the mother from publishing them. Clifton's "fury" is a cry of rage and pain, that makes itself felt in many ways at once. For me, it is very hard to read past the line "her hand is crying." I find it devastating. The simple, straightforward statement, "she will never recover" has a finality that doubles the devastation. The poem makes its impact in few words, with no capital letters, seething. I picture it spoken between clenched teeth. No exclamation points, although so many phrases might seem like they deserve one. But this is a poem that doesn't shout its anger, which, I think, adds to its power. It portrays, and conveys, stifled life. One of its lines declares that this mother *must* be remembered.

"Remember this" brings to mind the ghost's pleas to Hamlet. Remember me. Avenge me. Justice must be served. In Clifton's poem mama's potential was crushed, ostensibly for the sake of her husband's pride, on the altar of obedience.

Clifton's poem conveys a series of amazingly vivid images. They are unforgettable, partly, I think, because they join nouns that are not usually connected. Eyes are not generally seen as animals and hanks of hair are not often described as "a serpent's obedient/wife." Yet each word is so right!

Here rage is called upon to steel the poet's determination "...there is nothing/ you will not bear/ for this woman's sake." But I am left wondering if, ultimately, rage that hot can be channeled. Of course, I will never know.

Love

Extending the concept of balance, it is important to focus on the positive feelings poems can foster, as well as the painful ones they can help us modulate. Love is, of course, a central positive feeling, but there is also joy, hope, curiosity, and inspiration. My general premise is that poetry is an art uniquely suited for evoking a whole spectrum of feelings, due to its subject matter (as well as its musicality and other aspects of its construction). As Raffel (1984, p. 16) suggests, poems can be about emotions, with or without reference to the people feeling those emotions. Some poetry celebrates the saving graces of these elevating feelings and easily evokes them.

It is not surprising that Shakespeare beautifully expressed how a positive emotion, such as love, can balance and modulate negative feelings. Three of his sonnets teach this, in ways I find profoundly uplifting. In my reading each conveys the point in its own, delicate voice. In each, we see how love can save us from being overwhelmed by a painful emotion.

Sonnet 73

That time of year thou mayst in me behold
When yellow leaves, or none, or few, do hang
Upon those boughs which shake against the cold,
Bare ruined choirs, where late the sweet birds sang.
In me thou seest the twilight of such day
As after sunset fadeth in the west,
Which by and by black night doth take away,
Death's second self that seals up all the rest.
In me thou seest the glowing of such fire
That on the ashes of his youth doth lie,
As the death-bed whereon it must expire,

117

Consumed with that which it was nourished by.
This thou perceiv'st, which makes thy love more strong,
To love that well which thou must leave ere long.
(In: H. Vendler, *The Art of Shakespeare's Sonnets*, 1997, p. 333)

Here, once more, we come upon the opposition between love and the potentially crushing sorrow of death and loss. Which will tip the emotional balance in its favor? Shakespeare gives us the heartening message that when someone loves us, *despite* knowing they will soon lose us, their love has proven its strength. To me this is one of the most profound human challenges. In my language, can we "love anyway," alongside the feelings evoked by the knowledge that one of us will die first?

Mary Oliver, in "In Blackwater Woods," issues a similar challenge. Loving another person, and being loved, both seem to me to declare that something is stronger than sorrow, worth risking being sunk by grief, worth bearing whatever comes (I discuss her stunning poem at length in chapter 3).

For Shakespeare love could triumph over aging, as well as impending sorrow.

Sonnet 116

Let me not to the marriage of true minds
Admit impediments; love is not love
Which alters when it alteration finds,
Or bends with the remover to remove.
O no, it is an ever-fixed mark
That looks on tempests and is never shaken;
It is the star to every wand'ring bark,
Whose worth's unknown, although his heighth be taken.

Love's not Time's fool, though rosy lips and cheeks
Within his bending sickle's compass come;
Love alters not with his brief hours and weeks,
But bears it out even to the edge of doom.
If this be error and upon me proved,
I never writ, nor no man ever loved.

(In: H. Vendler, 1997, p. 487)

Once again, Shakespeare declares that love can win in the balance, "even to the edge of doom." No decline or infirmity overcomes true love. Shakespeare calls love "...the star to every wandering bark..." but I can see his poem itself as providing shining guidance. Its beauty inspires.

Lest we think Shakespeare's paeans to love overly serious, he also offered us this, more humorous sonnet.

Sonnet 130

My mistress' eyes are nothing like the sun;
Coral is far more red than her lips' red;
If snow be white, why then her breasts are dun;
If hairs be wires, black wires grow on her head.
I have seen roses damasked, red and white,
But no such roses see I in her cheeks,
And in some perfumes is there more delight
Than in the breath that from my mistress reeks.
I love to hear her speak, yet well I know
That music hath a far more pleasing sound;
I grant I never saw a goddess go—
My mistress when she walks treads on the ground.
And yet by heaven I think my love as rare

As any she belied with false compare.

(In: H. Vendler, 1997, p. 555)

Here we see the poet still making comparisons, but in a lighter tone. I hear in this a teasing, but still loving affirmation. Like Auden, (see above) whose lover is "mortal, guilty, but to me/The entirely beautiful," so, too, is Shakespeare's beloved imperfect. Could he feel critical, even disdainful? Might he sometimes wish for a more perfect creature? Of course, but these are not the feelings that prevail. Love weighs heavier in the balance.

In another sonnet (138) Shakespeare compares the idealized version of ourselves we would like a lover to see versus the reality. He seems to say that when we love we treat the idealization as though it were the reality. Or, at least, we don't insist that those we love verbally acknowledge the difference.

When my love swears that she is made of truth,
I do believe her though I know she lies,
That she might think me some untutored youth,
Unlearned in the world's false subtleties.
Thus vainly thinking that she thinks me young,
Although she knows my days are past the best,
Simply I credit her false-speaking tongue:
On both sides thus is simple truth suppressed.
But wherefore says she not she is unjust?
And wherefore say not I that I am old?
O love's best habit is in seeming trust,
And age in love loves not to have years told.
Therefore I lie with her, and she with me,
And in our faults by lies we flattered be.

(In Vendler, 1997, p. 584)

Vendler (p. 586) tells us that there are two schools of thought about this sonnet. The first sees it as a portrait of a pair of cynically untruthful partners, while the second, lighter interpretation imagines it as an expression of the universal tendency to flatter those we love. I hear in it an expression of how we balance the need for truth with the need for tact. In a sense, I think we are always somewhere on a continuum between these two values. I wrote about this aspect of relationships in a chapter on kindness (2004). Neither truth nor tact is fully responsible, without some observance of the importance of the other. In a sense, this issue forms an important fulcrum in Shakespeare's " *King Lear,* in which Cordelia at first tells her truth without a consideration of tact but gains greater wisdom over the course of the tragedy. I will consider this issue more fully in a chapter on the play.

In his paper, "The Dyer's Infected Hand: The Sonnets and the Text of Hamlet" (in Kinney, 2002, pp. 101–111) Philip Edwards likens Shakespeare's dilemma in writing the sonnets to a similar difficulty in writing the plays. The plays necessitated a compromise between what he would want to write, from a literary standpoint, and what he had to write so that the play could be performed, and so that the audience would enjoy it. Similarly the sonnets had to please a patron. Interestingly, this issue is woven into the *content* of Hamlet, when Rosencrantz and Guildenstern tell Hamlet the Players have come (Act II, Sc. 2). Hamlet asks why they have left London, and Rosencrantz and Guildenstern refer to the fashion for children's companies. Hamlet compares the fickleness of theater audiences to the adulation of the new king, when he did not command any interest before he was crowned. In a sly way, I think Shakespeare is commenting on fashion as an arbiter of critical acclaim. Whether he likes it or not, when he strives to fulfill his artistic ambitions he also has to please critics, patrons, and the audience members who ultimately foot the bill. More on how this problem wove its way into the text of *Hamlet* in the chapter on this play.

Satisfying the other (lover and/or patron) necessitates some image building prevarication. In Sonnet 138 Shakespeare seems to be saying that the wiser course is for both to wink. Play along to get along. Present the persona the other person needs to see, and pretend the other has been equally convincing. Of course we can't know how much Shakespeare's tongue is planted in his cheek, and how much he is cheekily deriding the "business end" of courtship, as well as patronage. Or should we take at face value that he is telling us that tact sometimes *should* triumph over truth?

For a rather bitter assessment of the cost of idealizing, I turn to a much more recent poem, by Wendy Cope (in Sieghart, 2019, p. 151). Briefly, in her poem "Defining the Problem," Cope declares that she loves the person she thought her lover to be, but not the person he is.

In a spare four lines, Cope has described a seemingly impossibly tangled web. Once the flattering portrait is drawn (collaboratively) its effect can't be undone. The persona in the poem has fallen hopelessly in love with someone who doesn't exist. Giving up the real "other" entails giving up the illusory, idealized other. This cannot be done. It betrays the compact. The persona has, implicitly, promised to overlook imperfections. It would be a betrayal to go back on that promise. And it would cause the persona the unbearable grief of the loss of a perfect love.

Perhaps Shakespeare was right, and the wisest course is to pretend one of us is really young, and the other is really "true," despite all evidence to the contrary. What is more important, being right or being loved? Similarly, what is more important, writing a "perfect" play, or writing one that can be staged and speak to an audience? In an ideal world we wouldn't have to choose. But neither Shakespeare nor we live in an ideal world. "Pure" truth can lack sufficient evidence of love to make it palatable. "Pure" tact can lack sufficient truthfulness to give it meaningful resonance. Each, without the other, is inimical to love.

Joy

Clinicians can sometimes help patients remember and revive life's joys to modulate its sorrows. I think poets are some of the world's experts at this. Jane Hirshfield (2015, p. 208) suggests that what good poems restore to us is something close to what is meant by animal joy. As if by magic, they transform grief, or, at least, leaven its pain. Some poems are alive, changing with every reading, and seem to convey a kind of joy or life force to the reader. There are poems whose music haunts us all our lives, and others whose words we recite in our most anguished moments. Poems provide the grace notes in some lives, while for others they are central to survival. Cultures have found different languages for explaining the sources of their power but, perhaps, poetry's capacity to literally and figuratively move us will always remain somewhat mysterious.

Elsewhere (2008) I have contemplated as to why joy is so poorly understood, compared with other emotions. And yet, it is a fundamental emotion (Izard, 1972) and, certainly, a highly significant aspect of life. Humorously, Heisencamp (Buechler, 2008) remarked that there was very little freud (joy, in German) in Freud. In a section of one of his poems the Israeli poet, Yehuda Amichai (in Seiden, 2016, pp. 4–5) gives one explanation.

The Precision of Pain and the Blurriness of Joy

The precision of pain and the blurriness of joy. I'm thinking
how precise people are when they describe their pain in a doctor's
    office.
Even those who haven't learned to read and write are precise:
"This one's a throbbing pain, that one's a wrenching pain,
this one gnaws, that one burns, this is a sharp pain

and that—a dull one. Right here. Precisely here,
yes, yes." Joy blurs everything. I've heard people say
after nights of love and feasting, "It was great,
I was in seventh heaven." Even the spaceman who floated
in outer space, tethered to a spaceship, could say only, "Great,
wonderful, I have no words."
The blurriness of joy and the precision of pain—
I want to describe, with a sharp pain's precision, happiness
and blurry joy. I learned to speak among the pains.

We discern throbbing pain from wrenching, burning, sharp, dull, and other varieties, but, in contrast, joy is just one undifferentiated blur. Adding to the mystery Seiden, a psychoanalyst and poet, reminds us (p. 5) that "For one, everything we've been taught about repression and, more recently, about dissociation would have us think that we should be better able to talk about joy than about pain." And yet, Amichai clearly has a point. Is it, as he suggests, that we are more familiar with pain? As children did we need to express our pain more than we needed to express our joy? This seems plausible. But I would add a slightly different slant. I wonder if words and joy are, in a sense, inherently further apart than words and pain. Joy seems to me to have no specificity. Where is it felt? Can we pinpoint when it is over? In contrast I think we can often say that a pain (physical or emotional) is gone. Words may seem too precise to capture our joy. But this is just a conjecture.

But there have been some writers who have identified some fundamental sources of joy. I am able to name three, and I feel that poetry is especially suited to evoking each of them. I have written about the wellsprings of joy elsewhere (2008) so I will make only brief mention of them and concentrate on some poems that I think have the power to evoke joy in the reader. Briefly, the three sources I consider are: the joy of self-expansion, the joy of connecting more fully to the rest of humanity, and the joy of increased recognition of one's own particularity. I discuss each more fully below. In most instances joy is evoked by both the content of the poem and something else about the experience of reading it. In certain of these poems the reader is given insight into how painful feelings can be transcended, with joy as a result. Sometimes poems capture the expansive power of the life force that the poet feels in their creation. Self-expansion is the overt content of many poems, as well as the result of the reader's encounter with them. Take, for instance, the poem "The Writer," by Richard Wilbur (1989, pp. 23–24). In this beautiful and inspiring poem, Wilbur gives us a window into the feelings of a father whose daughter is suffering from writer's block. The father's love ignites a passionate desire for her to triumph over whatever holds her back. Wilbur focuses on the moment when it is unclear whether or not the daughter will find the strength to go on writing. He gives us a poignant expression of the daughter's purposeful determination, and her father's anxious love. In the poem, the father listens at the door, to hear whether or not his daughter has become able to overcome her block. He hopes to hear the clack of her typewriter. As he waits, he remembers a time another creature, a helpless trapped bird, also needed great resolve.

Wilbur vividly describes the bird's determined escape. Time after time, the creature battered against a closed window, fell, and waited for the strength to try again. Finally, it cleared the window sill and flew to freedom.

Reading this poem, I feel the thrill of leaping over obstacles; of sensing I have widened my perspective or deepened my comprehension. It also brings to mind so many moments (as a clinician, as a person) when I have witnessed others take that leap. Regardless of whether it is me or someone else who clears the sill of the world, it always brings me joy, and I believe I am not alone in this. When a child takes their first steps, when an athlete beats the odds and crosses the finish line, when my eight year old patient says her first words to me after two years of angry silence, when health is restored after a long battle with illness, when a long term patient recognizes the part they often play in marital disharmonies, it *is* always a matter of life or death. For that moment, life won, expansion won, and the resultant joy can balance our inevitable sorrows. Some poetry serves to remind us that, once in a while, we have beaten a smooth course for the right window, and, maybe, we can do so again.

Many poems suggest connections we might not have made on our own which, in a sense, expands our consciousness. When Wilbur links breaking through writer's block to matters of life or death I feel a shock of recognition. I wouldn't have put them together myself, but, once I read it, it felt so right. This line of poetry added to my understanding of my experiences of not being able to write. As has been true for me in countless moments as a patient and as an analyst, there is a joy in this deepened self—awareness.

The second source of joy I will consider, in poetry, therapy, and the rest of life, is the feeling of being connected with the whole of humanity. Of course, this is not entirely different from the self-expansion noted above. But this source puts the accent on connection rather than triumph or transcendence of an obstacle.

In considering the joy of connecting with our common humanity, poets and analysts truly have been on the same page. The early Interpersonal theoretician, Schachtel (1959). defined joy as "a feeling of being related to all things living" (p. 42). He went on to describe joy as a continuous turning toward the world. It is, in his words, "the felt experience of the ongoing acts of relatedness." Similarly, the poet Wordsworth (1805/1988) captured the joy of connecting to life in his "Ode: Intimations of immortality from recollections of early childhood." For Wordsworth, sensing that we are part of the vast fabric of life can bring profound joy. When life presents itself to him, in any form, his heart bears witness. As he expresses it, "to me the meanest flower that blows can give/ thoughts that do often lie too deep for tears." In a similar spirit, Pablo Neruda (Quoted in Hirsch, 1999, p. 262) wrote of the life changing moment when he suddenly felt a kind of love between himself and strangers, a feeling that "widens out the boundaries of our being and unites all living things. That exchange brought home to me for the first time a precious idea: that all of humanity is somehow together..."

In college and beyond my intellectual "heroes" were Erich Fromm, Frieda Fromm-Reichmann, and Harry Stack Sullivan, among others, all of whom wrote about the emotional satisfaction of recognizing our membership in the human fold. In fact for Fromm, the healthy, evolving, biophilic person's love of self grows along with love for others, and love for all forms of life. As I understand it, according to Fromm we care about ourselves *and* the other because we reverence life. Basically, Fromm's belief is that if the other is a stranger to me, I am a stranger to myself. To know myself completely is to know that the humanity I share with others is the most significant thing about me, and can lead me toward compassion. This seems to me similar to Harry Stack Sullivan's famous maxim (1953) that we are all more simply human than otherwise. Sullivan was emphasizing that the schizophrenic patient is a human being, with significant similarities to any other, and, therefore, potentially knowable. But the humanistic orientation in his thinking is similar to Fromm's in spirit.

Fromm believed that finding a place in the human family brings the kind of satisfaction we feel in exercising a muscle, or using our minds to capacity. In his (1968, p. 72) words, "Because I have eyes, I have the need to see, because I have ears, I have the need to hear, because I have a mind, I have a need to think; and because I have a heart, I have a need to feel. In short, because I am a man, I am in need of man and of the world. "

In other words, there is joy to be had from fulfilling our potential to connect with humanity. Some poets help us remember that potential. For me, no other is as able to facilitate that as Shakespeare. Every time I see *King Lear*, I marvel at the transformation of this initially insensitive, self-centered man into one with a real capacity to love (as I see him). As *he* becomes able to connect with the human condition, I feel my own connection strengthen. Shakespeare makes palpable what the character gains from his hard won appreciation of his own humanity. But we, in the audience, have a chance to mingle our own tears with his, and to know how sharing sorrow can elicit sublime joy. The joy and the sorrow don't cancel each other out. They are byproducts of the exercise of being human together.

There are countless descriptions of the benefits of catharsis, the empathic process in appreciating art. More generally, there are many ways to describe what happens when we encounter products of the creative process. Perhaps there is no single "right" description. But I would suggest that the joy it can bring comes, at least in part, from art's vivid reminder that we are all more human than otherwise.

Some poems express, and can evoke, both of these first two sources of joy. They offer instances of self-expansion as well as connection to the rest of humanity. While (as described above) blurring, or even erasing, the line between self and non-self can elicit anxiety, it is also a potential wellspring of joy. This is another of life's mysteries. What makes one boundary-less experience terrifying and another transporting? The stuff of nightmares and horror movies can sometimes resemble the fabric of awe inspiring, transcendent moments. Just as a roller coaster can be more fun than frightening or more frightening than fun, leaving our well defined borders can be a joy ride or a horrifying dislocation.

The joyful side is highlighted in Wallace Stevens' poem, "The House Was Quiet and the World Was Calm." (I discussed this poem previously, but here I want to focus on other emotions it stirs).

> The house was quiet and the world was calm.
> The reader became the book; and summer night
> Was like the conscious being of the book.

The house was quiet and the world was calm.
The words were spoken as if there was no book,
Except that the reader leaned above the page,

Wanted to lean, wanted much most to be
The scholar to whom his book is true, to whom

The summer night is like a perfection of thought.
The house was quiet because it had to be.

The quiet was part of the meaning, part of the mind:
The access of perfection to the page.

And the world was calm. The truth in a calm world,
In which there is no other meaning, itself

Is calm, itself is summer and night, itself
Is the reader leaning late and reading there.

(In Raffel, 1984, pp. 27–28)

In writing about this poem, Hirsch (1999, pp. 250–253) emphasizes its power to transport us to a spiritual realm. For him, this is a deeply fulfilling poem that reports, and evokes, the experience of reading, late at night, "...in the dark hour when the secular world recedes and consciousness is loosened for poetic reverie" (p. 250).

For me this poem has the quality of a lullaby. It evokes a quiet joy that I find very hard to put into words, perhaps because it taps into experiences that are both before and beyond words. Differentiations are elsewhere. For the moment I am at one with the house, the world, the book, the night, and summer. I think of magic spells and enchantment. I am pleasantly drifting where there is no need for a separate self. I am not trying to find my bearings (and, therefore, not terrified that I can't). Perhaps this state is akin to what Freud *(Standard Edition*, "Civilization and Its Discontents," Vol. 21, p. 64) called the "oceanic" feeling. It encompasses two potential wellsprings of joy—the expansion of the self, and the interconnection of all of life.

The third source of joy may sound, at first, like a direct contradiction of the others, but I think it just as reliably elicits joy. Perhaps here is yet another of life's many mysteries. This third root is the positive feeling that can come from a recognition of our unique particularity. When I find myself reacting in a characteristically "Sandra" way, the pleasure I may feel could be understood as a feeling of being whole, or well-integrated. I am suggesting that joy can result from experiences where we let go of the separation of self from non-self, as well as moments where we are most clearly evincing that specific self.

Elsewhere (2004) I have developed a viewpoint on the importance of a sense of wholeness, or integrity, in clinicians and their patients in treatment. My generation of analysts, schooled in the Interpersonal tradition, were taught to look for the "red thread," that is, the unifying, recurring patterns in the patient's ways of experiencing and behaving in the world. I developed my style of doing treatment based on the idea that it is inherently beneficial to know oneself as a particular individual, with a unique history of experience with each of the fundamental emotions (Buechler, 2004, 2008). For example, I have a lifetime of specific instances of living with Sandra-when-she-is-sad. I bring that history to every sad moment in the present. No one else can know "my" pain exactly as I do, because no one else has lived that history exactly as I have. For me, this is a crucial insight, that helps me understand the limits of empathy and, more generally, the limits of perception.

In my experience the process of becoming whole, and recognizing my particularity, can bring moments of joy. Erich Fromm (1976, p. 106) once said that, "Joy, then, is what we experience in the process of growing nearer to the goal of becoming ourselves."

Poetry can be seen as a celebration of the unique, individual voice. I think that makes it inherently joyous. Here is a description by Raffel (1984, p. 103) "...the "magic" of a poem does not come from some extraordinary, some suprahuman power, but from all men's indefinable and undeniable uniqueness, the force of an individual personality. To the extent that a poet truthfully and uniquely expresses who and what he happens to be, his poems too will express that unique self, in music as in their other component parts." I would add the magic and the joy come, at least partially, from this source. And, of course, "men" should be replaced by a gender neutral noun.

One of the joys of poetry is its capacity to convey both the uniquely personal and the universal in the same breath (literally). As we read some poems, we hear their words on all these levels at once. Consider the moving poem, "Those Winter Sundays," by Robert Hayden (in Bialosky, 2017, p. 73). I think it is a model of both powerful particularity *and* universality.

> Sundays too my father got up early
> and put his clothes on in the blueblack cold,
> then with cracked hands that ached
> from labor in the weekday weather made
> banked fires blaze. No one ever thanked him.
> I'd wake and hear the cold splintering, breaking.
> When the rooms were warm, he'd call,
> and slowly I would rise and dress,
> fearing the chronic angers of that house,
> Speaking indifferently to him,
> who had driven out the cold
> and polished my good shoes as well.
> What did I know, what did I know

of love's austere and lonely offices.

The boy in this poem is a specific child, growing up in a particular house, (with its chronic angers) with a unique father, with a recognizable pair of weathered hands. Writing this poem, as well as reading it, brings us nearer to this father and son, though we can never fully understand their experience. Hearing its narrative is likely to evoke thoughts of our own childhoods, however similar or different they may be. There can be a joy in this moment of self-recognition, even if what we see is painful. But, at the same time, in the same space, the poem speaks to us of universal human experience. Generations so often fail to understand and appreciate each other. Each of us lives with regrets born of such misunderstandings. We have failed in the fundamental human challenge, to see a situation from another's perspective as it is unfolding, rather than only in hindsight. We were loved in ways we didn't recognize at the time, because they didn't read as love, but, perhaps, as duty, if they registered at all. Or, more likely, they were absorbed into routines that never made it to the foreground of our attention, so were not given any meaning. One aspect of the situation (maybe the chronic angers) shaped our experience so completely that the house felt "cold" even when the father worked to warm it. Thoughtlessly, we take lit fires for granted, never bothering to see the human being who lit them. He is, for us, his "office;" his function as a fire-lighter and shoe shiner, and no more. It never occurred to us to wonder what it was like for the father to get up each morning and tend fires. Did he ever ask himself if he wanted to do it? Did he ever expect to do what he wanted, rather than what needed to be done? Was choice always a luxury he knew he couldn't afford? Did he wish, for once, someone else would take up the task? Did he notice that no one was thanking him? Did it hurt? In our own lives, who do we treat as a function, rather than a whole human being? Reading the poem is rich in its capacity to speak to us, in the same breath, as a specific story and as a universal truth. It can induce in us a like-minded search for our own particular stories and their simultaneous universality. Finding these unique/universal stories can bring joy. Perhaps the poem also touches on what we take for granted about ourselves, or ways others take us for granted, and can help us empathize with our own experience. Have we absorbed the feeling that what went unappreciated about us was not worthwhile?

In my previous work (2008) I called joy the universal antidote, in that when it is present it can mitigate all our negative feelings. I still believe that it can. A poem that exemplifies this is Maya Angelou's "Still I Rise." This poem belongs here, but also fits in a subsequent section about what inspires us. I will quote it in both. "Still I Rise" thrills me, every time I read it. Miraculously, it draws from all three of the wellsprings of joy I described above. With a soupcon of anger threaded through it, and a glitter of pride, "Still I Rise" is an anthem to the power of the unquenchable human spirit. Its title, and its stirring words epitomize the capacity to rise above every obstacle.

Still I Rise

You may write me down in history
With your bitter, twisted lies,
You may trod me in the very dirt
But still, like dust, I'll rise.

Does my sassiness upset you?
Why are you beset with gloom?
'Cause I walk like I've got oil wells
Pumping in my living room.

Just like moons and like suns,

With the certainty of tides,
Just like hopes springing high,
Still I'll rise.

Did you want to see me broken?
Bowed head and lowered eyes?
Shoulders falling down like teardrops,
Weakened by my soulful cries?

Does my haughtiness offend you?
Don't you take it awful hard
'Cause I laugh like I've got gold mines
Diggin' in my own backyard
You may shoot me with your words,
You may cut me with your eyes,
You may kill me with your hatefulness,
But still, like air, I'll rise.

Does my sexiness upset you?
Does it come as a surprise
That I dance like I've got diamonds
At the meeting of my thighs?

Out of the huts of history's shame
I rise
Up from a past that's rooted in pain
I rise
I'm a black ocean, leaping and wide,
Welling and swelling I bear in the tide.

Leaving behind nights of terror and fear
I rise
Into a daybreak that's wondrously clear
I rise
Bringing the gifts that my ancestors gave,
I am the dream and hope of the slave.
I rise
I rise
I rise. (In Sieghart, 2019, pp. 107–108)

Like this poem, joy rises. It leaps over gravities that would pull us down. It embodies the expansive power of the life force. It soars over narrowing prejudice, gallops past constricting rigidities. With Angelou we expand into more inclusive, richer selves. We grow beyond delimiting categorizations. The poem trumpets a triumph over whatever, and whoever, would drag down this beautiful fighting spirit. But it also forges connections to the whole of humanity. She is me, she is you, and everyone who has ever lived. And yet, she is also a very particular woman, whose eyes blaze with passion. She is strong in her determination, absolute in her conviction, rooted in a fierce insistence on respect, on freedom, on her right to be recognized.

Hope

Hope is also capable of making the painful aspects of life more bearable, and strengthening the resolve to live as fully as possible. Emily Dickinson subtly conveys many of hope's most significant aspects. (in Vendler, 2010, p. 118).

'Hope' is the thing with feathers—

That perches in the soul—
And sings the tune without the words—
And never stops—at all—

And sweetest—in the Gale—is heard—
And sore must be the storm—
That could abash the little Bird
That kept so many warm—

I've heard it in the chillest land—
And on the strangest Sea—
Yet-never-in Extremity,
It asked a crumb-of me.

Vendler points out (2010, pp. 118–120) a few very interesting aspects of Dickinson's conception of hope. It has an aspiring nature, (wings) is expressed in a melody without words, is unstoppable, (although this is questioned by the end of the poem) is sweetest in the most extreme circumstances, and does not ask for recompense. I find this poem extremely evocative. It bids me question my own experiences of hope, and challenges me to understand them better. My own spirits lift in the process.

I sometimes gather hope from a poem's ability to magically transport me to another era, where I see that today's troubles are not very different from those that have been endured in the past. For example, in Wordsworth's poem, "The World Is Too Much with Us" (in Raffel, 1984, p. 81) the poet's sorrowful reflections sound eerily contemporary.

The world is too much with us; late and soon,
Getting and spending, we lay waste our powers;
Little we see in Nature that is ours;

We have given our hearts away, a sordid boon!
This sea that bares her bosom to the moon,
The winds that will be howling at all hours,
And are up-gathered now like sleeping flowers,
For this, for everything, we are out of tune;
It moves us not.—Great God! I'd rather be
A Pagah suckled in a creed outworn;
So might I, standing on this pleasant lea,
Have glimpses that would make me less forlorn;
Have sight of Proteus rising from the sea;
Or hear old Triton blow his wreathed horn.

In these lines, Wordsworth has shown me that the crass, materialistic world I see today is nothing new. We have lived according to non-humanistic values for a long time. Somehow, we lost touch with spirit, bartered it for "getting and spending," and rendered ourselves "out of tune" with Nature. Of course the poem does nothing to lessen the sorrow and sheer danger of being out of tune with it now. But hearing Wordsworth voice my despair makes me feel less alienated. I feel as though I received a message from a kindred spirit, which, perhaps, assuages loneliness enough to dare to hope for a better future.

In my 2004 book, *Clinical Values,* I devoted the second chapter to hope's part in treatment. Hope has certainly sustained me in many moments of my personal life, and in many moments doing clinical work. I would agree that it has an aspiring nature, but I think its sweet song *can* be silenced, at times. Like Dickinson, I see hope in a kind of tug of war, opposed to the storms that come crashing down on us. Personally, I don't think one side or the other always prevails. Some storms are too "sore" to be survived. But I do agree that there are times when hope lends us enough warmth to keep battling life's cold indifference.

In that previous work, I distinguished cognitive expectations from emotionally motivating hopes, cited Schachtel's (1959) distinction between active and passive hopes, suggested that in clinical work sometimes the patient's hopefulness is a gift to the clinician, or, a belief in the clinician's integrity, and differentiated between realistic hope and "hope for the wrong thing," (a hope based on a rigid effort to control life). This last idea was my take on a clinical vignette contributed by Stephen Mitchell (1993). Mitchell quoted T.S. Eliot's (1943) poem, "East Coker," which warns us about hope for the wrong thing.

I think hope is not always free. In some situations I would quarrel with Emily Dickinson's idea that it has no price (never "asked a crumb-of me."). In fact many depictions of hope in therapeutic settings (Buechler, 2004, 2012) emphasize its costs. Hopes can be irrational, magical, passive, wishful expectations that can actually interfere with more constructive strivings.

In my own clinical experience, I was sometimes treated as a danger to patients who felt I might engender their unrealistic hope. Hope can be seen as exacerbating the pain of dreams that won't come true. Perhaps it is not fair to blame hope for that, but people often do.

In a similar spirit, Langston Hughes asks what happens to a dream deferred. "Harlem," his moving poem, brings us to the broken dreams of individuals and groups. Written in 1951, it was part of a larger work, entitled "Montage of a Dream Deferred" (In: Rampersod, A., 1995, p. 387).

What happens to a dream deferred?

Does it dry up
like a raisin in the sun?
Or fester like a sore—
And then run?
Does it stink like rotten meat?

Or crust and sugar over,
like a syrupy sweet?

Maybe it just sags
like a heavy load.

Or does it explode?

Does this mean we should abandon hope? Is there a way to distinguish healthful from misdirecting hope? What role can poetry have, in recognizing these differences and deepening our capacity for beneficial hope?

Personally, I think hope's positive or negative impact depends on its emotional context. In my previous writing (as already mentioned) I described some forms of "hope for the wrong thing" (2004, pp. 35–36). Fundamentally, these problematic hopes narrow how life is lived. They would include the (schizoid) hope to achieve safety by muting emotionality and limiting relationships, and the (obsessive) hope for an unrealistic degree of control of other people. But, on the other hand, some expansive hopes can be life enhancing. Take, for instance, the Richard Wilbur (1989) poem, "The writer," (cited above). There, a father's hope, growing out of profound love for his daughter, resulted in an experience of great joy, as he heard the clatter of her typewriter announce her triumph over writer's block. In T.S. Eliot's terms, this was a hope for the right, and not the wrong thing. It was steeped in love, and founded in faith in his daughter's capacity to cope. Hope was not "flying solo," to go back to Dickinson's feathery thing. It was in a context of love and faith.

For me, the question of what makes some hope life enhancing requires us to look at what else is present in the hopeful moment. Here I think poetry's components make it an optimal resource.

I want to look at the properties of poetry that render it ideal to enhance hope and, more generally, to have an impact on the reader's emotional balance. Here I am not primarily concerned with the poem's words, or, even their meaning (by itself) but, rather, with poetry's form. How does reading a poem affect us emotionally, and how might this differ from the emotional effect of prose?

Of course, nothing I can pinpoint will be true of all poetry (or all prose). But, for example, poems are usually relatively compact. This sets up a particular relationship to time. I think of it as a highly respectful relationship, where, implicitly, time is treated as precious. Every word in (at least some) poems does a great deal of work. Again, I am generalizing, and nothing I say will apply to all poems. But I think it is often true that poems try to say a great deal in a short time. For example, in Robert Hayden's great poem "Those Winter Sundays," (cited above, in Bialosky, 2017) the last two lines read:

> What did I know, what did I know
> Of love's austere and lonely offices.

I first notice how much meaning is contained in these two short lines. I can't know whether my reading conforms to what the poet meant to say (more about that later). But the lines elicit a whole array of distilled thoughts. To me, this is a poem laced with regret, for missed opportunities to recognize his father's expressions of love. In the repeated phrase "what did I know," these four short words suggest a lifetime of neglected chances to feel loved, to express appreciation, to recognize each other. These four words speak to me of the difference between the perspective of the young, and our outlook as it shifts with age and experience. And then, in the next six words, the poet creates an even more emotionally complex array. I could think about these six words for days. What are love's austere and lonely offices? I think

Hayden expresses his profound understanding of human beings in these lines. He asks us to look at the disparity between the outward appearance of someone simply taking care of business and the intense, loyal love that expresses itself in this prosaic form. This is a love that does not ask for recognition, a love devoid of drama. This love is quiet, and has to be inferred from cracked hands, from duties fulfilled for decades without complaint. And all this, in a few lines!

My point here is not simply to extol the virtues of this poem (although I greatly admire it). Rather, I am pointing to what can be its effect on the reader's emotional balance. Of course the meaning of the words is vital to its impact. But I am also considering the effect of the poet's economical use of words. This form doesn't allow my attention to wander off. When I read the words "love's austere and lonely offices," my mind immediately asks what are love's offices, and what could be austere and lonely about them?

My attention is riveted and I am locked into an encounter. I feel curious, alive. Hope is kindled, in that I believe something important is about to be revealed to me; something that could change my way of thinking about myself, and others, and life. I feel new perspectives are possible. I might see someone who I took for granted as expressing silent love. I might see my own routine dutiful behavior differently. I might see love differently. By giving me only the few words that are necessary the poet has moved me, not just in the sense that I am emotionally touched, but in a literal sense I am *moved* from one position to another. Hayden has shown me how much can be communicated between people, how much finding just the right words can matter. I have a little greater hope for words, for understanding, for human beings touching.

I am not the same after I read this poem. Its economy is only one aspect of how its form affects me. When I read it I think of Winnicott's (1971) concepts of transitional space and the transitional object. "Transitional," in these concepts, means neither entirely created by the "maker" nor entirely created by the "consumer," but a product of the contributions of both. For example, a teddy bear has a shape that has been determined by its manufacturer, but the child who receives it has an impact on how it feels to them. Similarly, Hayden had meanings in mind when he wrote the words "love's austere and lonely offices." These words shape readers' possible interpretations, to some degree. But different readers would understand them differently. I might say that I have the Hayden I most need to create from his words.

I have already quoted Edward Hirsch's (1999, p. 260) lovely description of the collaborative meaning making process between poet and reader, but I would like to return to it here.

We make meaning together, we wrestle with what we read and talk back to it, we become more fully ourselves in the process. We activate the poem inside us by engaging it as deeply as possible, by bringing our lives to it, our associational memories, our past histories, our vocabularies, by letting its verbal music infiltrate our bodies, its ideas seep into our minds, by discovering its pattern emerging, by entering the echo chamber which is the history of poetry, and, most of all, by listening and paying attention. *Attentiveness is the natural prayer of the soul.* (italics in original).

How does this collaboration in transitional territory affect the reader emotionally? Personally I believe it resonates with interchanges with caregivers from our earliest days of life. What makes "peek-a-boo" so delicious? Two faces have an impact on each other. I smile at a baby smiling at me, who smiles back, and a miraculous, life affirming dance has begun. Hopefully it sustains us throughout our lives, and only ends with our death. I read lines that Hayden and I have worked on. They are "his," in a literal sense. He (presumably) has the copyright. But I know they are also mine, because their meaning isn't straightforward. For example, when I read a sentence like "The temperature in New York is 52 degrees," it has an objective meaning.

It is one degree warmer than 51 degrees. I feel no personal ownership of that sentence. Anyone could have written it. It doesn't express who I am as a human being. But my Hayden poem does. No one else brings to the poem the same life experiences that I bring. I have my memories of "austere" love, and "lonely" love. No one else has exactly the same collection. No one could. Similarly, when someone says "I feel your pain," I say, "No." You may feel your version of my pain, or pain triggered by seeing mine, but only I can feel my pain.

So when I read the words Hayden wrote, and they take on the meaning I give them, I feel hope, joy, and melancholy. I think the hope comes from a shared creative process. Once again I learn that I can have these moments, that it is possible for strangers to complete each other's thoughts. I think the joy comes both from the expansive experience of shared humanity, and the self-recognition of a "Sandra" way of interpreting. The sadness comes, for me, from the sense that my understanding of Hayden's meaning will always be limited by who I am, by what I can and can't empathically perceive.

But that is not all. Body, mind, and heart are moved by this poem. My body responds to the rhythm, to the music of "love's austere and lonely offices." My mind appreciates the quirky individuality of this description of love. I am surprised by the word "offices." I didn't expect it. I love that jolt. It tells me not to assume I know what word is coming around the next corner. The surprise enhances my emotional (that is, motivating) curiosity. What will I hear if I read the poem again?

My emotional balance is affected by several boundaries, other than those already mentioned, that some poetry challenges. Aside from the creative mix-up of poet and reader, and poetry's frequent flickering between reality and non-reality, there is what Raffel (1984, p. 29) calls the "interpenetration of mind and matter" that we find in some poems. In this context Raffel cites (pp. 27–29) the poem by Wallace Stevens, "The House Was Quiet and the World Was Calm." I mentioned this poem in another context, but will expand my understanding of its "interpenetrations" here. Please see the text of the poem, quoted earlier in this chapter.

As Raffel (1984, p. 28) understands it, "Stevens moves back and forth between mind and matter, interlacing the mental and the physical." The house, the reader, the book, the summer night interpenetrate. When I read this I think of staring directly into the sun long enough to lose a sense of my own separateness from the light. It is not just the content of the poem that intertwines what we usually think of as separate. It is also how the poem moves, that communicates an experience of blurred boundaries. Elements keep floating up, like buoyant objects in water. We see the quiet house, imagine the summer night, reader, book, and then the quiet house floats up again, to be displaced by the intent reader, only to come back to our awareness as "part of the meaning." All are components of the truth, even though we usually separate them from each other.

Reading this I feel the same sense of joyous freedom I have so often experienced standing in front of Monet's "Water Lilies." The poem loosens my grip on how I usually perceive. I don't know if this is true for others, but I can say for myself that there is great hope joined with joy in this freedom. The content of the poem with its declaration of interpenetrations, and the poem's movement, all contribute to its powerful emotional effect.

Many people avoid poetry, believing they can't "understand" it. In one sense, I think they are right. Much poetry refuses to be grasped immediately. It is shy about being known, requiring us to work for it. Writing that can be quickly taken in may be reassuring. It is certainly convenient, a quality which is prized in our fast paced world. Like dreams, like anything that springs from the unconscious, poetry often takes time to unpeel. It yields wisdom only to those patient enough to persist.

The experience of digging around in a poem can elicit hope partially because of what it forces us to relinquish. In a sense we have to "give up the fist." Our usual reliance on logic, on rational, straight line thought, can leave us baffled as we confront a poem. We can't will ourselves to understand it. Questions multiply, rather than subtract, and we find ways to live with uncertainty. I can never be sure I "get" what Hayden meant by love's austere and lonely offices. This tells me that I may (or may not) grow as I continue to chase after the line. But I can hope. I am always reminded of certain paintings of J.M Turner, where a scene is almost emerging from the mist.

Gluck (1994, p. 29) said that poetry has "the power to seem, simultaneously, whole and not final, the power to generate, not annul, energy." Like the best psychoanalytic interpretations, it is alive and excites thought. Interpretation (of almost anything) can be deadening, pro forma, closing down active exploration. But interpretation, like poetry, can bring us to the growing edge of our conscious minds. I think it is an inherently hopeful place to be. In that space I can feel that I may comprehend more tomorrow, even if I don't see how. Gluck suggests (1994, p. 16) that poetry can help us "endure the desert," until greater clarity is possible. I think the experience of enduring one desert can help us believe we can endure others. I believe this can bring both hope and joy. As I have suggested earlier, one source of joy is the experience of self-expansion. Tomorrow this poem may teach me something that makes me wiser. Another source of hopeful joy could be a sense that I will know myself better. Delving into the ambiguous phrase "love's austere and lonely offices" may acquaint me with my less than conscious attitudes about love.

I think poetry's impact does not stem from its ambiguity so much as its comfort with contradictory truths, with magic, and with shifting perspectives. The poem "Lion," which I discussed earlier (by M. Hettich, In Raffel, 1984, pp. 44–45) exemplifies all of these qualities. Its protagonist is, and is not a lion. It seems to shape shift magically as the poem progresses. Our perspective alters with each stanza. Are we trying to penetrate the hallucinations of a disordered mind? Or is the confusion a product of our own flights of fancy? This poem takes us on a mental roller coaster ride. Its sharp, hairpin turns can leave us breathless. It calls perception itself into question. I am reminded of an inpatient I met decades ago when I worked in a state mental hospital. He frequently exhorted other patients and staff to listen to him preach, claiming to be Jesus Christ. In his earlier life he had been a lawyer, and some of his previous oratory skills still survived. When I tried to "reality test" his thinking he looked at me and asked, "How do *you* know I am not Jesus Christ?" I never forgot his challenge to me. There can be something exhilarating about questioning fundamental beliefs. How *do* I know which of my perceptions are "objective"?

To take this one step further, I would say that much poetry brings us to the edge of our current understanding of some of life's most urgent and profound questions, like the meaning of our lives, time, death, reality, loss, and so much else. I think this can mean that poetry can evoke any and all of the fundamental emotions. It touches us nearly, sometimes eliciting hope, or joy, or sorrow, or fear, or any other feeling or combination of feelings. When it reaches us, it activates our minds, our emotions, our spirits, and our body's rhythmic resonances.

Curiosity

This brings me to another of poetry's strengths: the power to activate curiosity and wonder. In emotion theory terms (Izard, 1977) curiosity is a "fundamental" or "discrete" emotion. It is present from birth. In my own clinical work (2004) I have found it to be one of the greatest sources of movement in treatment, particularly when it is joined by love and other positive feelings. Curiosity can so often motivate us to keep looking at ourselves and our world, despite obstacles. As a clinician, I tried to extend credit (to myself, as well as others) for looking in the mirror, no matter what we see. Curiosity can help us overcome the shame, or fear of shame, the

146

guilt, fear, anger, and other negative feelings that might otherwise paralyze us. If we watch young children pick up toys, and throw them down just to see what happens, we can grasp how fundamental, and ubiquitous curiosity is in human behavior. I see poetry as particularly well suited to function as an inducement to curious wondering.

From my perspective, one of poetry's greatest gifts is that it nurtures attitudes that foster curiosity. For one thing, as has already been mentioned, poetry promotes the proclivity/ability to see from more than one perspective. Poetry exercises the mind, just as any muscle building activity exercises the body. One of these "muscles" grows from repeated experiences of persisting, in writing poems or reading them, when we don't understand them (yet). This is mentioned (above) in relation to hope, but it applies to the deepening of the ability to be curious, too. Mystery takes on the connotation of a fascinating challenge, rather than a foreboding obstacle. As I proceed with a poem I don't "get," I am making a "bet" that this can change. In Robert Frost's language (in the poem "The Road Not Taken" in Mendelson, 2012, p. 179 and discussed above in section on "loneliness") I am expressing faith that "way leads on to way." In the context of reading poetry what that says to me is that finding a meaning for the first line may lead to a tentative understanding of the second line. In other words, I am voting that the *process* of trying is, in itself, worthwhile, whether or not I ever feel I "got it." And, of course, we can never know how much we "got" what the poet meant to say. This may come to matter less than what we reach internally, via the process of exploring the poem. I think of this attitude as a necessary building block for curious exploration of paintings, flowers, other people; in short, anything and everything in the internal and external worlds. Much like the concept of play, as an activity done for itself, reading and writing poems trains us (or, rather, retrains us) to pursue for the sake of pursuit. As children, we are likely to have acted in accordance with this value. Most of us lose it, in the bustle of an adult's everyday activities, done for the sake of a practical outcome. Poetry can help us regain the inclination to wander, with Wordsworth, among daffodils, (or words) with only the goal of enjoying their beauty. (W. Wordsworth, "Daffodils" in: *Immortal Poems of the English Language,* Ed. Oscar Williams, Simon and Schuster, Inc. 1952, p. 250).

Poetry requires us to relate differently to time, a "muscle" that I think facilitates curious exploration. Reading a poem hundreds of times accustoms me to a pace that allows me to wonder about much else. I might first read the poem, listening to its music, its rhythms, its flow. Some words may jump off the page, for their sheer beauty. I notice how right they are, how they fit, and how wrong any other word would be in their place. Images may take over in my mind, and then, perhaps, meanings, personal associations, memories, connections with other poems, and so on. "Way leads on to way."

According to this way of thinking, the destination of a journey evolves. We could say that the "road" develops a life of its own. A poem by Sheenagh Pugh gives voice to this idea.

What If This Road

What if this road, that has held no surprises
these many years, decided not to go
home at all; what if it could turn
left or right with no more ado
than a kite-tail? What if its tarry skin
were like a long, supple bolt of cloth,
that is shaken and rolled out, and takes
a new shape from the contours beneath?
And if it chose to lay itself down
In a new way; around a blind corner,
Across hills you must climb without knowing

what's on the other side; who would not hanker
to be going, at all risks? Who wants to know
a story's end, or where a road will go?

(In Sieghart, 2019, p. 103)

I love the image of the snake-like tar skinned road shape shifting its own way. But I wonder if the poet thinks us more adventuresome than we are. Not all of us "...hanker to be going, at all risks..." and some of us do want "... to know/ a story's end, or where a road will go..." Or, at least, we want this predictability some of the time. That freedom to follow the road, wherever it may lead, is a precious gift. Who, or what, bestows this gift? That is, what allows any of us the freedom to follow a course without knowing its outcome? How do we come to trust the "tarry road" this much? Or is it ourselves we trust to find a viable path, no matter where a particular road takes us?

I can only speculate that, since I see curiosity as inborn, the freedom to follow an unknown road is not so much a gift bestowed as it is a capacity that, in the fortunate, has been allowed to thrive. That is, while no one enjoys only positive experience on open "roads," for the lucky exploration has been (even if just slightly) more exciting than frightening. I think relishing the unfamiliar has profound intrapersonal and societal significance. Interestingly, I would say, I asked in 2004 (pp. 12–13) "Are we intrigued by the stranger, or do we become defensively closed off? Our ability to remain open to the strange and unfamiliar (nonfamily) has great political and psychological significance in our post-September 11, 2001, world. Our society as a whole needs to learn how to find enough that is familiar in the strange(r) to evoke more curiosity than fearful defensiveness. But we also need to find enough that is unfamiliar so as to elicit sufficient active curiosity." If anything, this seems even more true now (2020).

Being truly curious is an openness to new experience. (Buechler, 2004). I have written about it as the opposite of a paranoid frame of mind (Buechler, 2004, Chapter 1). Reading/writing poetry can be an exercise in prying ourselves loose from previous assumptions. Some poems (like Hettich's "The Lion" discussed above) require us to hold any hypotheses lightly. "Understanding" becomes an evolving, fluid, infinite process of adjusting and readjusting our last "take." Perhaps T.S. Eliot (1943) said it most succinctly in part of his poem, "East Coker."

> There is, it seems to us,
> At best, only a limited value
> In the knowledge derived from experience.
> The knowledge imposes a pattern, and falsifies.
> For the pattern is new in every moment
> And every moment is a new...and shocking
> Valuation of all we have been (p. 26).

Rilke's concept of "inseeing" (in Corbett, 2016) is relevant here. As Corbett describes it (p. 99) inseeing, for Rilke, is "...the wondrous voyage from the surface of a thing to its heart, wherein perception leads to an emotional connection." To fully enter a poem we leave our usual boundaries behind.

Some poems explicitly, or more implicitly invite us to "insee." Take, for example, Wallace Stevens' poem, "The Snow Man." (In Bialosky, pp. 48–49). I have already explored this poem, but here I want to apply the concept of "inseeing" to it.

> One must have a mind of winter
> To regard the frost and the boughs
> Of the pine-trees dusted with snow;

And have been cold a long time
To behold the junipers shagged with ice,
The spruces rough in the distant glitter

Of the January sun; and not to think
Of any misery in the sound of the wind,
In the sound of a few leaves,

Which is the sound of the land
Full of the same wind
That is blowing in the same bare place

For the listener, who listens in the snow,
And, nothing himself, beholds
Nothing that is not there and the nothing that is.

What, exactly, does it take "...not to think/ Of any misery in the sound of the wind,"? We have to "white out" all our previous experience and open to the snow man's point of view. In a "mind of winter" the world looks and sounds different from the environment we have known. "Inseeing" the snow man means to me wiping my mind clear of everything I have been and seen previously, and then, "nothing" myself, I can behold "nothing that is not there and the nothing that is." That step, of *not* beholding what I think should be there, or what has been there in the past, is crucial to "inseeing" and to profound curiosity. From a psychoanalytic point of view, it can be thought of as similar to the effort we make in treatment to help people distinguish the past from the present. It is hoped that this effort stimulates the patient's curiosity about how current interpersonal situations compare to those that occurred in their earlier life. I am reminded of H.S. Sullivan's understanding of health: the ability to benefit from new experience (Sullivan, 1953, 1954).

Fundamentally, it is only when we perceive how new experience differs from old expectations that we can learn new ways of relating.

Emily Dickinson can serve as a model of curiosity. Nothing could stop her unquenchable thirst for understanding her inner and interpersonal world. Few have been as brave in their exploration of themselves. On paper, at least, she doesn't seem to flinch, regardless of what her delving uncovers. Her search for truth is indomitable. Personally, I find her attitude contagious. It is expressed in so much of the content of her poems, but, also, in their style. Her economy can literally pack a (gut) punch. To me it says we can look straight into our inner lives and squarely face the truth, whatever it is.

For example, Dickenson's poem 550 (in Vendler, 2010, pp. 250–251) probes her own pain and compares it with the suffering of others.

I measure every Grief I meet
With narrow, probing eyes—
I wonder if it weighs like Mine—
Or has an Easier size—

I wonder if They bore it long—
Or did it just begin—
I could not tell the Date of Mine—
It feels so old a pain—

I wonder if it hurts to live—
And if They have to try—
And whether—could They choose between—
It would not be—to die—

I note that Some—gone patient long—

At length, renew their smile—
An imitation of a Light
That has so little Oil—

I wonder if when Years have piled—
Some Thousands—on the Harm—
That hurt them Early—such a lapse
Could give then any Balm—

Or would They go on aching still
Through Centuries of Nerve—
Enlightened to a larger Pain—
In Contrast with the Love—

The Grieved—are many—I am told—
There is the various Cause—
Death—is but one—and comes but once—
And only nails the Eyes—

There's Grief of Want—and Grief of Cold—
A sort they call "Despair"—
There's Banishment from native Eyes—
In sight of Native Air—

And though I may not guess the kind—
Correctly—yet to me
A piercing Comfort it affords
In passing Calvary—

To note the fashions—of the Cross—

And how they're mostly worn—
Still fascinated to presume
That Some—are like my own—

Discussing this poem, Helen Vendler (2010, p. 251) stated that "Dickinson's 'narrow, probing eyes' could, with a psychological penetration trained by her own scrupulous and unforgiving introspection, indeed scrutinize and 'measure every Grief' she met." Just a bit later (p. 252) Vendler remarks on Dickinson's effort to understand time's effect on the experience of pain. As Vendler describes, Dickinson's "…practice is now to note and wonder, rather than to 'measure,' but with some of the same precision. Her scrutiny has shown her that some sufferers can smile again, but their smile is a pale shadow of their former one; the lamp of their inner light is burning very low." Dickinson delves inside herself and outside at others, and takes pain apart, as though she were taking apart a clock, to discover just what makes it tick. For me, her poem has a quiet dignity in the face of suffering. She stares at it, with an open minded curiosity that makes me want to look at my own experiences and compare them with hers.

In poem 288, (In Bialosky, 2017, p. 79) Dickinson brings humor to her self—examinations.

I'm Nobody! Who are you?
Are you-Nobody-Too?
Then there's a pair of us!
Don't tell! they'd advertise—you know!

How dreary—to be—Somebody!
How public—like a Frog—
To tell one's name—the Livelong June—
To an admiring Bog!

Bialosky (2017, p. 80) quotes from a letter Dickinson wrote to friends "Perhaps you laugh at me! Perhaps the whole United States are laughing at me too!...I can't stop for that!" Pride was no match for her relentless pursuit of every truth she could unearth.

Rainer Marie Rilke was another poet with a great appetite for curious (intra and interpersonal) exploration (Ulrich Baer, 2005, Modern Library Edition, Random House, NY, *The Poet's Guide to the Wisdom of Rilke*). Rilke was particularly expressive about the need to be open to our experiences of loss, rather than to close off inquiry into their meaning, even when it causes us extreme suffering to do so. For example (In: Baer, 2005, p. vii) in the Duino Elegies, Number 9, he says

All that we
can achieve here, is to recognize ourselves completely
in what can be seen on earth.

Of course these words speak to the heart of the psychoanalyst in me! I think poets and analysts are alike in our privileging of self-recognition as a goal in life. In his study of Rilke's letters, Ulrich Baer (2005) (p. xxvi) characterizes Rilke's investigative attitude. "We must look *everywhere*, including in sites that strike us as unpleasant: in his life, similarly, he could not pretend to ignore the parts that did not make sense, hurt him or others badly, or that he would have rather denied, repressed, and forgotten-hence the large number of letters to his wife, and his efforts to understand himself as both an artist and a father." (italics in original).

In one of his letters, Rilke (in Baer, p. 10) wrote, "Life has been created quite truthfully in order to surprise us (where it does not terrify us altogether)." Perhaps tongue in cheek, nevertheless this is a very interesting way of framing the unexpected. Curious exploration of life can pave the way for surprises which are tolerable, or even enjoyable, if they are not too threatening.

For Rilke, paying attention to what our senses tell us can be very informative. It is largely a matter of focusing on their input. "All that is necessary is for our eye to be a trace more seeing, for our ear to be more receptive, for the flavor of a fruit to enter us more completely, for us to be able to tolerate more scent, and, in touching and being touched, to be more present-minded and less oblivious-in order to receive from our most immediate experiences consolations that would be more convincing, more significant and truer than any suffering that can ever unsettle us" (Baer, 2005, p. 60).

I find this statement extremely evocative. In his call for us to sharpen our senses, by being more "present-minded and less oblivious," I hear him highlighting the role of focus. This statement contains a way of thinking about emotional balance. Openness to full sensory experiences has the potential to "consol" us for life's pain.

One of Rilke's poems, "Archaic Torso of Apollo," makes his point by focusing us on the restorative, inspirational power of works of art: (In Burt and Mikics, 2010, p. 230). I have already written about this poem (above) but here I look at its powerful call for us to fully perceive the beauty around us. Please refer to the text of this poem, that appears earlier in this chapter.

Rilke published this poem in 1908, in his volume, *New Poems*. Burt and Mikics tell us (2010, p. 231) that at the time Rilke wrote this poem he was concentrating deeply on objects in the physical world around him. This poem celebrates the sculpture of the Torso of Miletus in the Louvre's collection. The poem was translated from the German by Edward Snow who, according to Burt and Mikics, found the poet's "insistence on the objective" "disconcerting" and "almost ruthless." Burt and Mikics go on to interpret the poem as telling us (p. 231) that "Transcendent beauty shocks us: we are forced out of our usual defensive, possessive stance. We suddenly have a task: the world waits for us to realize it, and wants that realization." This poem suggests many questions and, as Rilke told us in his *Letters to a Young Poet* (1934, p. 35) we must learn to "...love the *questions themselves* like locked rooms and like books that are written in a very foreign tongue." How does the sight of beauty interrupt our usual functioning? Can that be enough to inspire profound curiosity and change? How can we understand the task that is waiting for us?

Both this poem and Rilke's letters celebrate the unfinished. The line that comes to my mind, from Keats' "Ode on a Grecian Urn" is "Heard melodies are sweet, but those unheard/ Are sweeter..." (In: *Immortal Poems of the English Language*, ed. Oscar Williams, 1952, p. 325). In an earlier chapter I commented on this poem's celebration of poetry's ability to communicate in its white spaces. What is left out conveys messages that may be as important as what is written. In a sense, Keats's sweet unheard melodies are like the absence of the torso's head and eyes in Rilke's poem. This absence focuses us on the body's gleam. Would we be able to focus on that gleam in the presence of the head and eyes? My mind then asks whether we could appreciate life if it weren't for its looming absence. Death, hovering over us, presses us to change our lives by making optimal use of them. Without death's shadow, every glisten wouldn't "burst forth from all its contours/ like a star..."

The last two lines of Rilke's poem deliver two jolts. "...for there is no place/ that does not see you. You must change your life." Who does the seeing, the statue or the art lover, the observer or the observed? I think that for Rilke there is no boundary between observer and observed. This, again, makes reference to his concept of "inseeing," which I mentioned above. When we are fully absorbed there is no line between us and things (and other people) in the world. We see into the other, which sees into us. As Rachel Corbett, author of a biography of Rilke and Rodin, commented (2016, p. 211) "When Apollo speaks to him, Rilke consummates the empathic union of object and beholder, author and reader. This new being could now communicate; it was whole." Corbett's biography, which traces the relationship between Rilke and the sculptor Rodin, was titled *You Must Change Your Life*.

Fully grasping this *would* change our lives. Beauty can be the antidote to time, in that it transfixes us. A thing of beauty would be like a shooting star, bursting "all its contours." A curving breast, a semi-circle of thighs would bring enchantment. We would savor every enchantment, like a light that momentarily interrupts the darkness.

When our focus changes, from one aspect of the world to another, a surprise may be in store. Seeing this can have the power to enhance our curiosity, as well as our appreciation of what we see. "Details," a poem by Eamon Grennan (in Seiden, 2016, pp. 40–43) vividly conveys this. I discussed this poem in the first chapter, but re-visit it here in relation to the emotion of curiosity.

> I was watching a robin fly after a finch—the smaller
> chirping with excitement, the bigger, its breast blazing,
> silent
> in light-winged earnest chase—when, out of nowhere
> over the chimneys and the shivering front gardens,
> flashes a sparrowhawk headlong, a light brown burn
> scorching the air from which it simply plucks
> like a ripe fruit the stopped robin, whose two or three
> cheeps of terminal surprise twinkle in the silence
> closing over the empty street when the birds have gone
> about their business, and I began to understand
> how a poem can happen: you have your eye on a
> small
> elusive detail, pursuing its music, when a terrible
> truth
> strikes and your heart cries out, being carried off.

As I discussed in chapter one, this poem portrays the predator robin, intent on his prey, the finch. The robin is entirely focused on the finch, and the reader's mind's eye is entirely focused on the robin. Thus, we are unaware of our unformulated assumption—that the robin and finch are the only players. Then, suddenly, the scene changes with the appearance of the sparrowhawk, and we, along with the robin, are forced to notice that our perspective has been too narrow. The unsuspecting predator has become the terminally surprised prey. What is relevant here is that the reader has had the experience of being caught unaware of how an unconscious assumption can limit our focus, thus skewing how we see reality. The poem has given us an important lesson in why it pays to keep our eyes wide open. Hopefully, this jolt awakens our curiosity about what else we may miss. More generally, it demonstrates the importance of maintaining a lively curiosity about what we may be unaware we are overlooking.

As metaphor is such a staple ingredient in poetry, the properties of metaphor characterize many poems. Elsewhere (2008) I have written about my own lessons in how metaphors can alter perception. In brief, they can often make the strange familiar, and the familiar strange. In making the strange familiar, poet/reader and analyst/analysand discover connections that were previously unrecognized. In making the familiar strange, assumptions that have been taken for granted are questioned anew. In a sense, metaphors foster our (metaphoric) peripheral vision.

In our everyday lives, when our focus centers on practical matters, we may miss opportunities for open minded, open hearted wonder. This is so stunningly expressed in a poem by Denise Levertov.

Primary Wonder

Days pass when I forget the mystery
Problems insoluble and problems offering

their own ignored solutions
Jostle for my attention, they crowd the antechamber
along with a host of diversions, my courtiers, wearing
their colored clothes; cap and bells.
    And then
once more the quiet mystery
is present to me, the throng's clamor
recedes: the mystery
that there is anything, anything at all,
let alone cosmos, joy, memory, everything,
rather than void: and that, O Lord,
Creator, Hallowed One, you still,
Hour by hour sustain it.

                                 (In: Sieghart, 2019, p. 11)

Our antechambers get more and more crowded, as we juggle imperative tasks and a steady stream of distracting "input." In the midst of proliferating sources of information (and misinformation) we lose focus on what Shakespeare (*King Lear*, Act V, Sc.3, line 16) called the "mystery of things," and what Levertov calls "the mystery/ that there is anything, anything at all..." But Levertov challenges us to *focus on our focus on the mundane.* When we are conscious of what we pay attention to, we can also become aware of what escapes our attention. We can realize that, mesmerized, we have lost the forest, buried in the myriad branches of a single tree. Levertov restores perspective, which invites us to a wider (or, in her words, a more primary) wonder.

Inspiration

Although hope is not one of the fundamental emotions (Izard, 1972) sometimes it can be a significant source of the strength to survive and thrive, as is its close cousin, inspiration. Inspiration is hard to define but, in my experience, unquestionably important. Sometimes seen as a gift from a muse, inspiration has been devoutly desired by artists, musicians, writers, and others throughout the ages. Aside from its role in fostering creativity, it plays a highly significant part in helping human beings maintain the will to survive difficult circumstances. I connect it with the "sense of purpose" I have written about elsewhere (2004). I would put Gwendolyn Brooks' poem, "To prisoners," on the top of my list of poetry that makes a direct, unabashed, deliberate appeal for inspiration.

I call for you cultivation of strength in the dark.
Dark gardening
in the vertigo cold.
in the hot paralysis.
Under the wolves and coyotes of particular
silences.
Where it is dry.
Where it is dry.
I call for you
cultivation of victory Over
long blows that you want to give and blows you are
going to get.

Over
what wants to crumble you down, to sicken
you. I call for you

cultivation of strength to heal and enhance
in the non-cheering dark,
in the many mornings-after;
in the chalk and the choke.

(Disembark, Third World Press, 1981)

Poet as conjurer, summoning healing spirits to counter the prisoner's internal and external adversaries. I think this poem beautifully illustrates how poetry can glide from the universal to the particular, from the particular to the universal, and, even, address both at once. Those who are (literally) prisoners are subjected to extremes, of temperature, of rage, of violence, of dark. Brooks calls for the cultivation of the inner strength to bear these conditions. Part of the prisoner's challenge is finding life—giving spirit from within. Brooks says these capacities must be nurtured, deliberately cultivated. Prisoners must find the will to overcome all that could destroy them so as to heal and, perhaps, eventually, use their passage through pain to enhance their connection to life. It is hard to imagine what this must take. As I hear it, this is some of the poem's specific application to the literally physically imprisoned. But I read the poem as meaningful on a universal plane as well. Aren't we all prisoners, in some senses? Don't we suffer within vulnerable bodies, sometimes subject to conditions beyond our control? Don't we have to bear blows and, at times, long to deliver them? Don't we all sometimes wake in the non-cheering dark? I believe that this poem speaks to the all-important balance of the feelings that threaten to destroy us versus those that strengthen our attachment to life.

Affirmation of the life force is also celebrated in the justly famous poem "Still I Rise," by Maya Angelou. I quoted this poem in the section of this chapter on "joy," but I want to discuss it further here, since I think it is inspiring, as well as joyful. Please revisit the text of the poem.

162

Like Brooks, Angelou sings of the power of the will to overcome adversity. But Angelou is not so much calling for that power, as she is insisting we recognize that she already brims with it. Adversity has crystallized her determination to be seen, to be heard. Her eyes flash, and she knows that she dazzles. If we fail to see her for what she is, that will reflect on us, not on her. She shines with inspiration and challenges us to be willing to see the light. If we disrespect her, she turns our disdain back onto us, forcing us to look for its sources in ourselves. I think she inspires through her absolute belief in herself. She is all in, which (through contrast) points out our equivocations. Recognizing how her rootedness in her values, and her value, solidly center her, we feel called upon to find our own roots. What passionate determination can inspire us to a similar pitch?

As mentioned above, I believe that inspiration feeds, and is fed by, a sense of purpose. As I suggested (2004) the sense of purpose is not simply a specific goal, or meaning, but, rather, a more general attitude, that purposes drive us, even when we are not consciously aware of them. The overall sense of purpose, and more specific goals, are sources of inspiration that make our lives meaningful to us. Purpose is a "thread" that coalesces the story of our lives. The idea of a thread creating a sense of wholeness is beautifully expressed in a poem by William Stafford.

The Way It Is
There's a thread you follow. It goes among
things that change. But it doesn't change.
People wonder about what you are pursuing.
You have to explain about the thread.
But it is hard for others to see.
While you hold it you can't get lost.
Tragedies happen; people get hurt
or die; and you suffer and get old.

Nothing you do can stop time's unfolding.
You don't ever let go of the thread. (In: Sieghart, 2019, p. 17)

I think of Ariadne. The thread saves us from being lost. In my experience as a clinician, and in my own personal experience, threads are often understood in retrospect, rather than on an ongoing basis. But I believe they guide us unconsciously, and, perhaps, even more firmly when we become consciously aware of them. One of the greatest gifts a treatment (or any other process) can give is the clarification of a thread that runs through a person's life, and gives that life its structure, meaning, and cohesion. Recognizing the arc of our narrative, finding the through-line, enables many to make peace. Even the sorrows have been part of the story, and have had a role in making us who we are. What is uplifting is the feeling of making sense to oneself, and the empowerment of the message that, while we can't prevent tragedies or "time's unfolding," we can hold tight to the thread. At times, pattern creates beauty. This relates to the section on joy, (above) where I suggested that one source of joy is recognizing our particular signature style of living. I know myself partly by knowing the way I anger, sorrow, regret, and so on. I am Sandra in my laughter and my tears. When I see her (me) being quintessentially Sandra, and responding to life in Sandra style, I feel centered. However I may judge that style, whether or not I approve of it, at least I feel known to myself. And understanding what holds my life story together may help guide me at choice points in the future. Perhaps, when I see threads, I learn something about what I want to repeat, or I learn something about what I don't want to repeat, or some of both, or neither. But I learn something that could inspire my future direction.

Another poem, "The New Colossus," by Emma Lazarus, (David Lehman, Ed. "The Oxford Book of American Poetry", 2006, Oxford University Press, p. 184) has inspired many generations. It is a sonnet, etched inside the pedestal of the Statue of Liberty, in New York's harbor.

Not like the brazen giant of Greek fame,
With conquering limbs astride from land to land;
Here at our sea-washed, sunset gates shall stand
A mighty woman with a torch, whose flame
Is the imprisoned lightening, and her name
Mother of Exiles. From her beacon-hand
Glows world-wide welcome; her mild eyes command
The air-bridged harbor that twin cities frame.

"Keep, ancient lands, your storied pomp!" cries she
With silent lips. "Give me your tired, your poor,
Your huddled masses yearning to break free,
The wretched refuse of your teeming shore.
Send these, the homeless, tempest-tost to me,
I lift my lamp beside the golden door!

What gives this poem its power to inspire? As may always be true, it is a combination of the words and the music. It is addressed to the entire human family, not any specific group. I am fascinated by just what it calls out and calls for, from each of us, and how it attains its ever-lasting ability to inspire.

What I notice first is its unequivocal quality, manifested in the content and the style of the poem. This lady doesn't mince her words. She is sharp tongued about who she is *definitely not*. From the first line, she makes it known that we should never confuse her with her European, masculine, conquering counterparts. She leaves no room for doubt about the position she will assume: "Here at our sea-washed, sunset gates shall stand/ A mighty woman with a torch..." The words are fierce, shaped in one assertion after another. The rhyming adds to the musical quality, and helps lock the poem in place in our minds. Like the statue itself, the lines stand firm, and the rhyme and rhythm make each of the two stanza's feel as though it can bear its weight on its own. Nature is represented by mention of land, sea, sun(set). and air(-bridged). This frames the human pilgrimage and adds a note of universality to the picture. The contrast between the muddle of human beings, and the grandeur of their natural setting could not be more extreme. The grace of the images of "sea-washed, sunset gates" is matched by the sheer beauty of the soft sibilant sounds of the line.

The power and majesty of the statue forms a sharp contrast with the powerlessness of the poor "tempest-tost" supplicants.

What do the images of the "huddled masses" inspire? There is no individual face to give their plight particularity. They are simply human, to paraphrase H.S. Sullivan's oft quoted (1953) phrase. They are tired, they suffer, they yearn to breathe free. Perhaps we feel for them out of natural human compassion, or maybe we want to align with the mild-eyed Mother of Exiles (and/or against the pomp that reigns on other shores). Or, from another angle, we may want to think of ourselves as compassionate, out of religious beliefs or other motives. Religion teaches us to love our neighbor as ourselves or, as a sixteenth century rabbi, Moshe Cordovero put it, "do good to whomever needs your goodness." (In Estelle Frankel, 2003, p. 184). Much of the world's philosophy and literature deals with our obligations to the "other." (for example, D. Orange, 2010).

Whether for the good of our own souls, or out of duty, or fear of being judged, or from empathic identification with the sufferer, we are called upon to open our gates to those in need of our care. Among many philosophers who have explored our ethical obligations to other human beings, Eric R. Severson (2011) writes that responsibility for each other is required of us, despite knowing that "The other person needs more than I can give, hurts more than I can see, has been through more than I can understand, and hopes more than I can imagine" (p. 20). The impossibility of the task doesn't let us off the hook. Further on he states (p. 24) that "...responsibility is the fundamental property of human existence. Ethics thus precedes all philosophy." Severson quotes and builds on the work of the philosopher Emmanuel Levinas, who is often cited for his convincing accounts of what we owe to other human beings. Levinas forged his thinking from reading, and from his own experiences, including five years of imprisonment in concentration camps during World War II.

Lazarus's poem's power seems to me to come from its (sometimes subtle) comparisons, contrasts, surprises, and poetic logic. Unlike Europe's aggressive conquering heroes, Liberty's hand holds a guiding light, not a weapon. This lady is a giant, but not brazen.. She is *both* powerful and mild-eyed. She commands in order to welcome, not in order to subdue. The beautiful, poetic phrase, "imprisoned lightening," captures the poem's subtleties. Much has been written speculating as to what these words mean. Lazarus was an activist and advocate for Jewish refugees fleeing persecution in Czarist Russia. (D. Lehman, ed, 2006, *The Oxford Book of American Poetry*, Oxford University Press p. 184). On one level, her words relate to this experience. But there may be other meanings as well. It may refer to electricity, and connote the industrial revolution in progress when the poem was written (1883) and cast (1903). I am more interested in its emotional effect. "Imprisoned" is not what I expect lightening to be. The phrase tells us that Lady Liberty has captured this force, not to exert authority, but to use it as a torch, to light the way toward her welcoming shore.

She includes in her welcome those who have not (yet) proven their worth. Here lies some of the poem's inspirational quality, at least in my reading of it. In a sense, it alludes to a great leap of faith, taken by both the immigrant and the country allowing entry. By coming here, the homeless masses, "wretched refuse" in their own lands, assert that they do not deem themselves forever unworthy of a better life. They are making a crucial bet on themselves. This must be an act of faith, since faith, by

definition, needs no proof. By welcoming them, Lady Liberty is also acting on faith. I think Lazarus's poem evokes passion about our basic obligations to the stranger, partly by creating such a stark image of nameless, homeless, tired, wretched human beings. Their yearning to breathe, contrasting so sharply with our air-bridged harbor, is poised to inspire an invitation to share what we have. Sadly, we know that we have not always done so, and sentiments opposed to such generosity have great sway as I write this today (March, 2020). But, on the other side, protesting voices, speaking on behalf of those seeking a better life, have not been silenced.

The poem comes to rest with a softly alliterative, lilting line, "I lift my lamp beside the golden door!" For this poem, at least, the harsher alliterations, the "tempest-tost" times, are over.

Summary: Poetry As An "Emotional Apothecary"

Erich Fromm was an analyst but, in some of his writing, he expressed ideas that are more frequently encountered in works of philosophy. He was a fierce advocate for our being fully present in the moment. In this regard, he saw our principal obstacle as alienation from our own inner life and from other people. In his language, what we must aim for is the "direct encounter" with ourselves and with others (Funk, 2019). For Fromm, to quote the title of a recent book about his thinking, (Funk, 2019) "Life Itself Is an Art." Funk, who was Fromm's last assistant and has translated many of his books, experienced being with Fromm as "exhilarating" (p. 7).

This chapter is my effort to suggest ways poetry can acquaint us with our most basic emotional experiences. At the same time, it connects us with the feelings of those around us, including strangers, as well as those who are intimately known. A case can be made that all the arts perform a similar function, but I feel poetry has a special claim. Here is a very brief list of some of its frequent components.

1. Poetry celebrates what is beyond the power of will and/or irrational. In both its form and content it is conducive to a dreamy state of mind.
2. It specializes in expanding our horizons, sometimes shifting our perspective, and admitting the presence of complex, or even emotionally contradictory truths.
3. Poetry is not afraid of magic. It is not put off by the bizarre. In poems we are allowed to hope for, and imagine, anything.
4. Poetry helps us (Gluck, 1994, p. 16) "endure the desert," until greater clarity is possible. Over time, reading poems, we can develop some faith that it is likely that a meaning will emerge to us, even when we can find no evidence of it, as yet.
5. It has (Gluck, 1994, p. 29) "the power to seem, simultaneously, whole and not final, the power to generate, not annul, energy." Rather than closing down our thinking, poetry often opens it to new directions. We have the chance to experience a dialogue (with the poet and with ourselves) that is alive, rather than pro forma.
6. Poetry can sometimes generate a sense of connection to the rest of humanity because it deals with the big subjects-life, death, time, reality, loss—in ways that suggest our commonalities.

My own belief is that the products of culture, in general, and poetry, in particular, can have a significant part in helping each of us maintain some measure of emotional resilience and equilibrium. I come back to the story of John McCain, quoted in the beginning of this chapter. By his own account, during solitary confinement, tapping out poems with the prisoner in the next cell helped him maintain emotional strength.

After commenting (p. 50) on how hard it can be to achieve, and retain emotional balance, an essay entitled "What is culture for?" (published by an organization entitled "The School of Life," London, 2018) suggests this remedy. "...it is an issue that culture is particularly placed to help us with, for works can put us powerfully in touch with concentrated doses of our missing dispositions, and thereby restore a measure of equilibrium to our listing inner selves." The essay goes on (same page) to say that "It is an emotional skill to be ready to sense an inner imbalance and then to take the steps necessary to rectify it with the help of culture. We might register that we are suffering from a mood of longing and disenchantment with what strike us as our rather humdrum and ordinary lives. The realization isn't complex in itself; what counts is the confidence to see that culture might have a solution to our mood—as well as the imagination to seek it out." The essay ends (p. 109) by lamenting our difficulty retaining equilibrium and maturity, and declaring that "Culture is our emotional apothecary, a storehouse of humanity's finest bottled wisdom and compassion, with whose help we have the best chance of riding out our many inevitable moments of fragility and folly." I say "amen," and express my personal belief that, even within the vast storehouse of culture, poetry is unusually well suited to play the role of emotional apothecary.

3.

Poems Conversing

———∿∿∿———

Bearing Loss

"One Art" (Elizabeth Bishop) and "Blackwater Woods" (Mary Oliver) each suggest a way we might learn to bear our losses gracefully. Bishop believes practice makes perfect, or as nearly so as we mortals can get. Oliver turns to Nature, as though we could learn by imitating her. I hear their songs as harmonizing. In my mind, though they are not the same approach, they don't contradict each other. What happens when we put them side by side?

One Art (Elizabeth Bishop) In: K. Young, 2010, p. 215

The art of losing isn't hard to master;
so many things seem filled with the intent
to be lost that their loss is no disaster.

Lose something every day. Accept the fluster
of lost door keys, the hour badly spent.
The art of losing isn't hard to master.

Then practice losing farther, losing faster:
places, and names, and where it was you meant

to travel. None of these will bring disaster.

I lost my mother's watch. And look! my last, or
next-to-last of three loved houses went,
The art of losing isn't hard to master.

I lost two cities, lovely ones. And vaster,
some realms I owned, two rivers, a continent.
I miss them, but it wasn't a disaster.

—Even losing you (the joking voice, a gesture
I love) I shan't have lied. It's evident
the art of losing's not too hard to master
though it may look like (Write it!) like disaster.

Leaving aside, for the moment, how much Bishop's tongue is planted in her cheek, this poem reminds me of the Skinnerian approach to learning (B.F. Skinner, 1968). which has been adapted in some forms of psychotherapy (B.F. Skinner, 1976). Basically, if you are trying to cure a snake phobia, you confront the person with more and more lifelike representations, helping them gradually approach what they fear. Of course I am not suggesting that Bishop was a Skinnerian. But the poem builds, from a very temporary and minor loss (lost door keys) to the greatest loss, ("losing you"). The art of losing raises the stakes in step wise fashion. First we learn the skill with the easiest examples, and then we generalize what we have learned, applying it to the greater and greater challenges.

Bishop brings Nature into the learning process, not for guidance, (as Oliver does) but to get us up to speed. With Bishop we are not looking to Nature to learn *her* grace in bearing losses. She tells us that losing Nature's vast treasures (two rivers, a continent) affords us valuable *practice* because it stands closest to the greatest loss of all, the loss of a beloved and irreplaceable human being.

But just what is Bishop asking us to "learn"? Again, taking the poem literally, by *willing* loss (practicing it) we change it. We also learn that we can withstand it ("None of these will bring disaster"). Loss can be tamed. In my (Buechler, 2004) language, if we are not afraid that we can't stand loss, we can (just) bear the sorrow. By implication, it is only when we don't believe we can survive it that we lack the strength we need, to bear the irreducible sadness. Elsewhere, (2019) in my own explorations of grief, I have suggested that any feeling, added to sorrow, that saps our strength, can compromise our ability to bear loss. This is contrary to Freud (in "Mourning and Melancholia," 1917) who wrote that ambivalence is the emotional state that most often turns sorrow into something more complex. I think the complicating emotion is just as likely to be fear, or shame, or guilt, or regret, among other possibilities.

Bishop's last lines have always fascinated me (along with so many other readers). It seems to me she is saying that she is not being defensive or evasive when she says that she can bear her loss, even if appearances are to the contrary. But then she has a remarkably transparent conflict. She informs us that she has to tell herself to write it. What are the two sides of the conflict? Is she of two minds about calling her loss a disaster? Is that because it would too clearly admit (even to herself) how much the loved one means to her? Or is she telling us that *writing* about this takes an act of will? Or both, or something else?

I hear this poem as a paean to self—discipline, and strength of will. And, maybe, to pride as a motivator. It suggests that, in lieu of the control of our diminishing possessions (perhaps as we age, or just as life unfolds) we can substitute self—control and self -exploration. As T.S. Eliot suggests (1943) old men ought to be explorers. When we lose the capacity to tour outer territories, we can turn toward the inner world.

With a different prescription, Mary Oliver focuses on the outer world for examples of how to bear loss. For her, Nature provides *guidance*, not practice. In her poem, "Blackwater Woods," (In: A. Holden and B. Holden, 2014, pp. 231–232, also discussed in the present volume in chapter 5. Please see the wording of the poem there) Oliver counsels us to look to the natural world for models of acquiescence to life's unopposable forces. Like trees, cattails, and ponds, we must bend to inner necessity and embrace our mortal condition. The inevitability of loss cannot keep us from passionately loving, just as profound love cannot inhibit us from letting go when it is time.

I find this poem extraordinarily moving. I have never read the last lines without crying, and I doubt I ever will. ("…you must be able/to do three things:/ to love what is mortal;/to hold it/ against your bones knowing/your own life depends on it;/and when time comes to let it go, to let it go.") It speaks the kind of truth Bialosky (2017, p. 200) referred to, when she said that some poems tell us what we already know.

I notice that, like Bishop, Oliver brings in the issue of will. In Oliver's poem Nature bends toward its losses, providing us with many examples of grace. The trees turn their own bodies into pillars. We might imagine they are obeying their Maker's orders, but, nevertheless, outwardly they act without prompting. Having turned as they were designed to do, they give off the fragrance of fulfillment. The ponds don't seem to protest the loss of their identities (names). The long tapers float away, accepting their diminishment. Salvation is in yielding.

For me, the delicacy of this poem's construction adds to its impact immeasurably. The wispy lines are feather light. Most are incomplete without each other. Each seems to me to be inexorably falling into the next, like souls coming to rest.

Oliver follows the inevitable turns of Nature's seasons and, gathering up what she has learned, offers it to us. She advises us to embrace (and not just accede to) life's terms. Ultimately, we must yield. The only choice is whether to open ourselves to loving enough for loss to be excruciating. But here Oliver doesn't suggest, but, rather, exhorts. We *have* to take the path that leads into the pain, not away from it. I have thought a great deal about those moments, when life requires us to counter the instinct to protect ourselves. I hear Oliver as calling for the courage it takes to walk into the line of fire; "the fires/ and the black river of loss."

These two poems focus on somewhat different sources of the capacity to bear sorrow, but, perhaps, the differences are not as great as they seem. When I first read them, I saw Bishop as relying on will, and Oliver as emphasizing submission to life's terms. But, with each reading, I felt less clear about this comparison. Are they really so different? Isn't what Oliver expects from us, in accepting life's terms, actually the product of an enormous act of will?

Losses Inherent in Aging

What does it take to love, knowing that, inevitably, one person will be left by the other? Subtly contrasting views sit side by side in Shakespeare's Sonnet 73. I discussed this poem in Chapter Two, but want to look at it again.

That time of year thou mayst in me behold
When yellow leaves, or none, or few, do hang
Upon those boughs which shake against the cold,
Bare ruined choirs, where late the sweet birds sang.
In me thou seest the twilight of such day
As after sunset fadeth in the west,
Which by and by black night doth take away,
Death's second self that seals up all in rest.
In me thou seest the glowing of such fire
That on the ashes of his youth doth lie,

As the death-bed whereon it must expire,
Consumed with that which it was nourished by.
This thou perceiv'st, which makes thy love more strong,
To love that well which thou must leave ere long.

(In: Vendler, 1997, p. 333)

Does this sonnet say that only a very strong love can survive knowing that one lover will inevitably leave the other bereft? Thinking of it in the context of the Bishop and Oliver poems, I might imagine all three are saying that it takes personal strength ("practice," to quote Bishop, or, perhaps, wisdom acquired through life experience, in Oliver's poem) to love mortal beings. But, as I hear it, Shakespeare's sonnet's last couplet adds another possibility: that love may *strengthen as the end approaches*. Its fire, built upon the ashes of youth, glows bright. With that Idea in mind, can we see Bishop's well practiced loser ever more fiercely loving the familiar jokester at the end? Having reaped wisdom from Nature and life experience, does Oliver see us holding onto mortal others with *increasing* passion? Is Shakespeare telling us that knowing we must leave can make our love grow stronger, as the end approaches? Vendler (pp. 334–336) compares the three models of aging in this sonnet, suggesting that the third differs most from the others. It offers an image of " ...an elan vital within the ruin, of a steady heat in the twilight." Vendler attributes the more positive third model to "the speaker's gradual withdrawal from the idealization of his own youth."

Vendler concludes (p. 335) that Shakespeare is telling us that the "... only locus of true life is the present..." I think this reading of the sonnet beautifully accords with Oliver's conclusion. How else, but firmly ensconced in the present, could we hold what is mortal against our bones, and, when the time comes, let it go?

A rich array of other poems and plays portray the losses that often accompany our last years. For example, the famous "seven ages" speech in

Shakespeare's play, "As You Like It," presents a rather gloomy picture. I will briefly comment on this and other expressions of what it can be like to grow old. I see each of these works as meaningfully dialoguing with the others, opening up questions that might not occur if each piece is viewed on its own. I believe that in poetry (as in psychoanalysis) we are best off if our questions lead to more interesting questions, rather than to answers that might close down inquiry.

In "As You Like It," Jacques, an aging cynic, can be counted on to present life in fatalistic and pessimistic terms. (In: *Complete Works of Shakespeare*, 2015, Act II, Sc. 7, lines 141–169). His words create an unforgettable portrait of our losses as we age, and a formidable challenge to us to find a way to bear them.

All the world's a stage,

And all the men and women merely players:
They have their exits and their entrances;
And one man in his time plays many parts,
His acts being seven ages. As, first the infant,
Mewling and puking in the nurse's arms.
And then the whining schoolboy, with his satchel
And shining morning face, creeping like snail
Unwilling to school. And then the lover,
Sighing like furnace, with a woeful ballad
Made to his mistress' eyebrow. Then the soldier,
Full of strange oaths, and bearded like the pard,
Jealous in honor, sudden and quick in quarrel,
Seeking the bubble reputation
Even in the cannon's mouth. And then the justice,
In fair round belly with good capon lined,

With eyes severe and beard of formal cut,
Full of wise saws and modern instances;
And so he plays his part. The sixth age shifts
Into the lean and slipper'd pantaloon,
With spectacles on nose and pouch on side;
His youthful hose, well saved, a world too wide
For his shrunk shank; and his big manly voice,
Turning again toward childish treble, pipes
And whistles in his sound. Last scene of all,
That ends this strange eventful history,
is second childishness and mere oblivion,
Sans teeth, sans eyes, sans taste, sans everything.

Back to the "bare ruined choirs" in Shakespeare's Sonnet 73 (discussed above)! With acerbic wit, Jacques skewers every phase of life, but none of the earlier periods compare in devastation to the last. Those hose that are too wide may be inconvenient, or even embarrassing, but they don't stack up to much next to oblivion. In this vision aging inevitably brings total loss of every human faculty. Every prop to pride is foreclosed. Each phase of life brings us one step closer to doom. Jacques leaves no room for any other conclusions, in two senses of that word. There is no room for us to come to any other conclusions, or beliefs. And there is no other way our lives can conclude. What awaits us all is the loss of everything we have ever been.

Garber (2004, p. 452) points out an interesting contradiction to the thrust of Jacques's speech, presented by another character, the old, faithful servant, Adam. As Garber says, "...in his dignity and self-awareness he gives the lie to everything Jacques has just said about the depredations and mortifications of old age." Earlier in the play, when Adam is trying to convince Orlando to let him accompany him on his journey into Arden, the old man says,

Let me be your servant:
Though I look old, yet I am strong and lusty:
For in my youth I never did apply
Hot and rebellious liquors in my blood,
Nor did not with unbashful forehead woo
The means of weakness and debility;
Therefore my age is as a lusty winter,
Frosty, but kindly; let me go with you;
I'll do the service of a younger man
In all your business and necessities.

(Act II, Sc. 3, 40–49)

Quite a different picture from Jacques' inevitable and total decline! Here behavior when young (I presume, the behavior that avoids syphilis, among other afflictions) plays a role in shaping the course of old age. Overall, I think the playwright keeps us guessing as to his own view of aging. According to the chronology I have (text prepared by Arthur Henry Bullen, Stratford Town Edition, Sterling Publishing Co. NY: 2015) Shakespeare wrote this play after he had completed about 20 others. His capacity to play with disparate, competing views was well honed. Garber (2004, p. 438) sees this play as a send-up of pastoral comedies, with many contrapuntal notes. It easily accommodates differing takes on the inevitability and severity of losses as we age.

I am juxtaposing the views of aging in "As You Like It" with those in Sonnet 73, to bring out their similarities and differences. Both the play and the sonnet can be read as summarizing some negative and positive attitudes about aging. With Adam (as a positive model) and Jacques (as the negative) in mind, we can ask again in just what ways the quality of later life depends on behavior while young. As already suggested, the wording of the sonnet leaves room for this question. The aged's "glowing fire" rests on youth's ashes. It is "...Consumed with that which it was nourished by." Vendler interprets this as meaning (1997, p. 335) that we die simply from having lived. I wonder if it can be taken to mean that the fierceness of the fire in our youthful bellies affects the "glow" of our fire when we age. Adam from "As You Like it" teaches us that a zestful young man can become a zestful old man. In the language of Sonnet 73, the ashes of his youth prepared a "glowing fire" to warm his aging. Not so for everyone.

The inevitability of decline and the relationship between youthful behavior and aging are two of the questions in my mind. Jacques's speech draws me toward another issue. He portrays the aged as ridiculous, not just depleted. The picture of the old man, baggy pants, sagging hose, and childish, high pitched voice, is a clownish portrait. I have long wondered about this aspect of some popular views. The aged can be seen as more than just diminished, but also unsightly; inherently, shamefully, uncontrollably humiliated. Lines from T.S. Eliot's "Prufrock" come to mind. He, too, suffers from baggy pants!

> I grow old...I grow old
> I shall wear the bottoms of my trousers rolled.
>
> Shall I part my hair behind? Do I dare to eat a peach
> I shall wear white flannel trousers, and walk upon the beach.
> I have heard the mermaids singing, each to each.
>
> I do not think that they will sing to me...
>
> (In: T.S. Eliot, 1998, p. 15).

Elsewhere (2019) I have written that for me this poem epitomizes the view that the aged are inevitably shamed for being found wanting, in more than one sense of the word. We are found wanting what is unavailable to us, and we are also found to be inadequate, compared with younger people. Is there something *inherently* shameful about having attained the seventh stage, in Jacques's "seven ages"? How much is culture (in Shakespeare's era and our own) the source of the shame? Natural human yearnings evoke almost unbearable shame in T.S. Eliot's unforgettable poem. A man whose desires are likely to be met with derision had better not eat any peaches in public, and he is best off assuming that the mermaids will never sing to him. Perhaps our greatest shame comes from reaching for the unavailable peach, or listening for a mermaid who will never again deign to sing to us. We feel devastated by showing we were not even aware of our position. I wonder whether the Shakespeare of the first two quatrains of Sonnet 73 could have reached for the lover in the third quatrain. Garber suggests (2004, p. 335) that in the first two quatrains the self-image is as a victim, but the speaker is released from that perception by the third. To me it seems that the speaker in the first two parts is a victim of shame. His boughs are bereft; his day has lost its sun. He is defined by what he has lost (perhaps like the "kingless" Richard II, by the end of the play, or old *King Lear*, when he has given up the crown). But in the third, while death is still inevitable, he burns brightly based (literally and figuratively) on his youthful fires.

What can we conclude about bearing our losses, including those that accompany growing old? Bishop and Oliver have given us our marching orders. Practice losing! Embrace (your own and others') mortality and head into its pain, not away from it! Eliot and Shakespeare face us with the clownish caricatures that can make this humiliating, as well as sorrowful. But there is another potential attitude, that sees youth's flaming passions as preparing a brightly lit place to come, eventually, to rest.

Careful Love

When I think about parenting teenagers, certain sacrifices come to mind. Of course each parent-child pair is its own country, but there are patterns that frequently repeat. For example, how does a parent bear caring enormously about how well their child fares, while knowing they are powerless to affect the outcome? Several poets address this, in very touching, heartfelt poems. Morris's poem, "For Julia, in the Deep Water," portrays a parent's internal struggle. I have mentioned this poem before, but here cite it for comparison with others that deal with similar conflicts.

I think anyone who has ever loved a teenager can connect with Morris's poem (In: A. Anthony and B. Anthony, 2014, p. 213). In it, a father reflects that he hired an instructor to teach his daughter, Julia, to swim because he knew that this task required a stranger's capacity to bear the child's panicky progress. Both father and mother express devotion by refraining from intervening when Julia screams. Nothing could be harder. They believe Julia will always remember feeling in over her head, with her cries for rescue unanswered, and ultimately finding the skill to survive. Personally, I would find it hard to know whether what Julia learns strengthens her self-confidence, or just acquaints her with terror. But I am very clear that there are times when the hardest, and most necessary parental task is to let the child we deeply love flounder.

When I read this poem, I keep thinking of Seamus Heaney's 2001 description of a mother and son coming close to each other by holding back. For the mother in Morris's poem doing nothing was the hardest thing she ever did. For me, the two acts of love are similar.

Because she doesn't love Julia the instructor can be both merciless and encouraging, in the face of Julia's desperation. I think some of our best "instructors" teach us that the degree to which we need something to happen doesn't necessarily dictate its likelihood. We can utterly need respite, or saving, but that doesn't mean we will get to rest or be saved.

The instructor shows faith that Julia has what it takes to surmount her terror. The mother and father can hire her, and, through sheer willpower, force themselves to do nothing in response to Julia's screams. But they know they wouldn't be able to do what the instructor does. Doing nothing is their sacrifice, their great gift, and an achievement, all done for love.

Aside from love, I think this poem evinces faith, in Julia as a particular person, and in human growth. The father imagines that the memory of this moment will give Julia a fundamental strength. She will remember being in "over her head" (both literally and figuratively) and surviving.

What allows any of us to survive mortal dangers? More generally, how does any person (parent or otherwise) convey the grit to stare at mortality and keep going? I don't really know, but my fantasy is that Julia understood that her parents' courage came from their love for her. Speaking to Julia in his imagination, the father says she will learn her way toward her parents. I understand this to mean that she will become like her parents in their loving and courageous stance toward life.

In "The Writer" (Richard Wilbur, 1989, pp. 23–24) another father holds his breath, listening at his daughter's door, and hoping to hear the clack of her typewriter, which would signal that she has overcome her writers' block. I discussed this poem's joy in the section on that emotion in chapter two. Here I refer to Wilbur's poem again, to compare it with the Morris poem.

Morris and Wilbur portray fathers who silently cheerlead their daughters forward. Interestingly, each has an element of the natural world as a backdrop: for Morris, water, and for Wilbur, air. Each has a fervent hope that their child will be able to confront the world, conquer fear, and stride toward more life. Both poems are suffused with an anxious, powerless, but also hopeful love. They are powerless because, paradoxically, to intrude, even to save their daughters, would be to rob them of their chance to succeed.

To extend a helping hand is to destroy. Each father needs to dwell, alone, struggling to believe in his daughter's capacity. As happens so often for me, I think about where faith comes from, and that, by definition, it needs no proof. Did someone, perhaps years earlier, demonstrate that faith in Morris and Wilbur?

Wilbur's poem stirs me in a somewhat different way from Morris's. At first, with Wilbur, I drift, lulled by associations and images of a beautiful creature finding its way to freedom. But then I am caught up short, as I begin to realize that the stakes are always so high for those fighting to overcome fearsome obstacles. For the iridescent bird, for the struggling writer, for the bold who face adversity, it is always a matter of life or death, as Wilbur reminds us.

But with Morris there is no lull. We are in deep (in several senses) by the third line ("Leads you into the deep water,/ The deep end"). With him a loving parent's insoluble conflict is more palpable. The father can't help yearning to save his daughter from her terror, if not from real danger, but knows that in this situation the "instructor" is the better equipped authority figure, "because she does not love you." Morris's war with his own natural impulses is (if you will pardon me) apparent. Compared with the instructor, Morris's far greater emotional investment in his daughter's welfare renders him *less* capable of helping her through this situation. The best he can do is restrain himself and refrain from any action. Perhaps Wilbur feels a similar conflict, but it isn't spelled out that way. His burden is the uncertainty; the hopeful but worried waiting to see if she makes it.

Morris also points to how this moment will be remembered by his daughter. Even though this is not explicitly addressed by Wilbur, I think there is a point of convergence in their both seeing their daughters' struggles as matters of life and death. Each roots for life and, to the extent that their daughters intuit their feelings, each has an opportunity to grasp something about love and the sacrifices of peace of mind that it can inspire.

Adding a third poem to this mix illuminates other aspects. Here is Rita Dove's "Party Dress for a First Born" (In: *The Art of the Sonnet,* S. Burt and D. Mikics, 2010, p. 377).

Headless girl, so ill at ease on the bed,
I know, if you could, what you're thinking of:
nothing. I used to think that, too,
whenever I sat down to a full plate
or unwittingly stepped on an ant.
When I ran to my mother, waiting radiant
as a cornstalk at the edge of the field,
nothing else mattered: the world stood still.

Tonight men stride like elegant scissors across the lawn
to the women arrayed there, petals waiting to loosen.
When I step out, disguised in your blushing skin,
they will nudge each other to get a peek
and I will smile, all the while wishing them dead.
Mother's calling. Stand up: it will be our secret.

The poet has written that this poem (same page) is a response to the Greek myth of Demeter and her daughter Persephone, who is kidnapped by the god Hades, and kept as his wife. Demeter gets the god Zeus to ask Hades to give her back, but Persephone, having eaten the food of the dead, is only permitted to come back for half each year. Hence our seasons, in which, with Persephone, crops thrive (in Spring and Summer) but, in Fall and Winter, along with Persephone, crops are below ground, and Demeter grieves.

The voice of the adolescent talking to her dress, her headless companion, is Dove's persona in this poem. I am imagining her in the company of Wilbur's writer-daughter and Morris's Julia. From their point of view, the courage of their parents, nudging them into the future, might be a mixed blessing, at best. Dove's teenage persona remembers a simpler time in her life, a time before the complexities of ambivalent love. That time of innocence shimmers, seemingly endless. Even a rupture could be mended by her faultless mother, forever standing by, waiting to heal every tear. Back then, she saw her mother from inside their cocoon. Now her mother is a woman, seen from outside, calling on her daughter to step forward. Wilber's and Morris's parental personas imagine that when they encourage their daughters forward, they are promoting them to the next stage of life. Like Prospero in Shakespeare's *The Tempest* they are sacrificing what has given them exquisite joy: exclusive love from a non-ambivalent child. Out of love, they are beckoning their daughters to advance toward the future. But what do the daughters feel? In Dove's poem, it is now time to put on a disguise and a fake smile, become ready to be judged, and harbor secret hate. Mother's call has to be obeyed. There is no choice, since it is no longer possible to think "nothing." Those days are gone. Prospero could have been speaking for all these parents when he says "I have done nothing but in care of thee,/ Of thee, my dear one, thee my daughter…" (Act I, Sc. 2, p. 172). But Rita Dove adds a disquieting note to my imaginary conversation between the young daughters. How does the parent's "promoting" call feel to the child? In a sense, all these parents are voting in favor of their children's growth, whatever sacrifices this might entail on the parents' part. The parents may all assume they are being generous, by welcoming their children into the rest of their adult lives. But, to the children, how does this invitation feel?

From my point of view, one of life's ironies is that the invitation that can cost the parent heartache to extend may also disillusion the child, with varying consequences. I wonder whether we all need a time when we can count on our "…mother, waiting/ radiant as a cornstalk at the edge of the field…" How long might we need to believe in the illusion of a powerful, protective parent? What happens if this period is curtailed too soon, by life circumstances, or the parent's eagerness to promote the child's independence, or, more simply, the parent's other preoccupations? On the other hand, what happens if this period is so prolonged that the child never comes to trust their own ability to protect themselves? Perhaps it is fortunate that the illusion can't last long, since so much is beyond the parents' control, as is vividly portrayed by Vernon Scannell's poem, "Nettles."

> My son aged three fell in the nettle bed.
> "Bed" seemed a curious name for those green spears,
> That regiment of spite behind the shed:
> It was no place for rest. With sobs and tears
> The boy came seeking comfort and I saw
> White blisters beaded on his tender skin.
> We soothed him till his pain was not so raw.
> At last he offered us a watery grin,
> And then I took my billhook, honed the blade
> And went outside and slashed in fury with it
> Till not a nettle in that fierce parade
> Stood upright any more. And then I lit
> A funeral pyre to burn the fallen dead.
> But in two weeks the busy sun and rain
> Had called up tall recruits behind the shed:
> My son would often feel sharp wounds again.
>
> (In: Seighart, 2019, p. 123)

Is this father hacking away for his son's welfare, or to pretend he can protect him from harm to comfort himself, or for both? Is it fortunate or unfortunate that the son will "feel sharp wounds again," and, perhaps, have the experience that they heal in time? Or, is three too young to learn that no one, not even a loving father, can keep nettles from stinging? Are the father's protective instincts somehow communicated and, in themselves, protective?

Regardless of the answers to these questions, all of these parents struggle to give their children a good start. I believe that their conflicts come from the inherent gap between meaning well and doing well; to my mind a disparity that is laced into every phase of life. Unfortunately, not all parents wrangle with their own self—interest at all. Some simply indulge themselves, at their children's great expense. I have written about Lucille Clifton's shattering "shapeshifter" poems in Chapter One, where I quoted the second in the series. In these works, Clifton finds words for the indelible impact of her father's sexual abuse when she was a young girl. Here is the fourth of the poems.

> the poem at the end of the world
> is the poem the little girl breathes
> into her pillow the one
> she cannot tell the one
> there is no one to hear this poem
> is a political poem is a war poem is a
> universal poem but is not about
> these things this poem
> is about one human heart this poem
> is the poem at the end of the world

These poems are heart-breaking. With every reading, I struggle to endure what they evoke in me. But I think we owe it to Clifton (or, rather, to her memory since she is dead) not to shy away when she asks us to bear witness.

Presumably, since the poet called these poems "shape-shifter," her father assumed different shapes, and some of them were more benign than others. Indeed, in her interview with Moyers, Clifton (1995) asserts that she wants to think of her father "wholly," and not, just, as an abuser (p. 93). In her own words: (same page) "...surely I am one of the people I want to see wholly, and my father is another person I want to see wholly since I inherited from him so many strong and good qualities, including stubbornness, strength, intelligence, and curiosity. He was a remarkable man."

We can never know her inner experience, or the experiences of the others who were the subjects of the other poems in this section. In most respects, the situations depicted couldn't be more different. Morris and Wilbur sound extremely empathic, acting out of genuine concern and love *and holding back* from acting on their own impulsive desires. I don't think Clifton would make that claim for her father's sexual behavior, but she is adamant that in other contexts he took on much more positive "shapes." Clifton insists that her father's legacy is more complex than could be described by any single word or dimension. He was abusive, but he was not just abusive. Yet in an especially poignant line, she writes of having only her pillow to confide in, for "there is no one to tell." The isolation and helplessness of a child in that position is hard to bear imagining.

Putting the poems side by side brings out, even more starkly than each poem on its own, the contrast between a child (Morris's daughter) who cries to her mother to protect her, and a child who can only confide in her pillow. There is only one commonality, as I hear it. *Both* children may learn from these experiences that desperate need does not, necessarily, result in rescue. This is a highly significant lesson and, often, a very painful one to bear, even under good circumstances.

I think in some situations in life, and very often when we are still relatively helpless children, we have to learn that the intensity of one's need doesn't always determine whether or not one gets help. Life and death can be (or feel as though they are) at stake, and yet the other person may still remain unmovable. It is important to consider how abandoned and alone a child may feel while learning the skills necessary for survival. The girl in Rita Dove's poem is alone with her false bravado, and Wilbur's daughter has to face her demons by herself. Even when parents are not abusive, are trying their best, are well-intentioned and refrain from impulsive self-gratification, at some point I think we each face the shocking truth that we need to develop those survival skills for ourselves. Going back to Morris's poem about Julia in the deep water, I wonder whether our best teachers, in these times, are the "instructors" who aren't *overly* attuned. Perhaps with them we have less of an expectation of being saved, and they have less of a need to rescue us. Julia's instructor can trust her to the water, and to her own, developing skills in living in what kills us all. But, I can't imagine how someone who has been sexually abused by their father can learn this lesson. Can it feel to her that *anyone* who doesn't rescue her is *really* acting on her behalf? Will it ever feel like it is for the abused child's sake? I am thinking that perhaps that is part of the collateral damage of abuse. Even when parents are not abusive, are trying their best, are well-intentioned and refrain from impulsive self-gratification, at some point I think we each face the shocking truth that we need to develop those survival skills for ourselves.

Parents don't have a monopoly on finding ways to entice children to conquer their fears. In a succinct poem, "Come to the Edge," Christopher Logue (In: Sieghart, 2019, p. 41) aptly portrays one person coaxing another to be trusting and brave. Other family members, teachers, clinicians, friends, and colleagues can sometimes provide encouragement. But what does it take to give the push, and what does it take to respond by leaping forward? We can see both actions as expressions of faith/trust. On the part of the one who pushes, I think it takes faith/trust in one's own motives as primarily benign. Most of us can only inhabit the urge to push if we trust that we mean well. The impulse comes upon us. Without really thinking it through we shout COME TO THE EDGE. And we trust our instincts enough to follow that with a push. We must also have faith in the recipient's strength and willingness to fly, once over the initial hump. I think the recipient needs a similar faith, in us, and in themselves. In psychoanalytic treatment, the recipient needs to feel that the pushing clinician has basically good intentions. Both have to believe that the recipient is willing to let it work out well. That is, the recipient must not be overly determined to make the clinician fail. Please note that I qualified each intention. For example, the one who gives the push has to have *primarily* benign motives. I don't think anyone's motives are completely benign. But, hopefully, they are benign enough, so that when we feel the urge to push, we are relatively comfortable with it. It helps if, in the past, others (like the parent in Morris's poem) prioritized our welfare over their own needs.

What allows this gift to be well received? Once again, it is hard for me to imagine the child in Clifton's poems as growing up trusting pushes to be well intentioned but, fortunately, it happens sometimes. I can imagine a certain form of anger as the internal partner that might still make leaps possible. The inner dialogue would go something like, "Damn it! I won't be cowed by fear! I won't be limited to crawling through life. I want to fly!" Ultimately, though, for me there is still a mystery about the wellsprings of the courage to live. Morris said "it is with our skill/ we live in what kills us." Wilbur's dazed starling waits, "humped and bloody,/ For the wits to try it again." In Dove's poem, when the mother calls, the girl orders her party dress (and herself) to stand up. Clifton ended the interview (Moyers, 1995, p. 95) by saying "Every day there is something that would make you afraid, and you have to try not to let it stop you. That's where the honor is. Honor is *not* acting because you are afraid. Nor is there honor in acting when you are not afraid. But acting when you *are* afraid, that's where the honor is" (italics in original).

Turning Away From Suffering

Musee Des Beaux Arts
(In: W.H. Auden, *Collected Poems,* Ed, E. Mendelson, 1991, p. 179. Please refer to the text of this poem in Chapter Two)
I explored this poem in Chapter Two, in the section on loneliness, where I looked at its expression of how suffering isolates us from each other. Here I look at it again, in concert with a fascinating poem that was explicitly written in response to Auden's. It is called "Musee des Beaux Arts Revisited," by Billy Collins (In: *Art and Artists: Poems,* Ed. Emily Fragos, 2012, pp, 65–66).

As far as mental anguish goes,
the old painters were no fools.
They understood how the mind,
the freakiest dungeon in the castle,
can effortlessly imagine a crab with the face of a priest
or an end table with genitals.

And they knew that the truly monstrous
lies not so much in the wildly shocking,
a skeleton spinning a wheel of fire, say,
but in the small prosaic touch
added to a tableau of the hellish,
the details at the heart of the horrid.

In Bosch's *The Temptation of St. Anthony,*
for instance, how it is not so much
the boar-faced man in the pea-green dress
that frightens, but the white mandolin he carries,

not the hooded corpse in a basket,
but the way the basket is rigged to hang from a bare branch;

how, what must have driven St. Anthony
to the mossy brink of despair
was not the big, angry-looking fish
in the central panel,
the one with the two mouse-like creatures
conferring on its tail,
but rather what the fish is wearing:

a kind of pale orange officer's cape
and, over that,
a metal body-helmet secured by silvery wires,
a sensible buckled chin-strap,
and, yes, the ultimate test of faith—
the tiny sword that hangs from the thing,
that nightmare carp,
secure in its brown leather scabbard.

I hear Auden's poem, written on the brink of a calamitous world war, as a horrified, perhaps embittered, but certainly saddened, examination of our mortal dangers and empathic limitations. Falling into the unforgiving water, we are invisible and impenetrable to each other.

Collins focuses on the bizarre, uncanny sources of unease or, perhaps, disease. He eyes a different painting, Bosch's *The Temptation of St. Anthony*. Collins makes a fascinating point about what inspires our greatest terror. It is the less obvious tampering with reality, rather than the floridly strange. It makes sense to me that these smaller departures would trigger a greater confusion about reality. I discussed this idea at some length, in regard to the poem "Lion" (section on fear in chapter two).

Reading Collins engages my mind, but doesn't trouble my conscience the way Auden's poem does. With Auden I identify with the uncomprehending bystander, as much as with the boy fatally plunging to his death. Auden makes me look at myself. His challenge is as much ethical as it is emotional and intellectual. As I read the poem I feel the cold cruelty of the boy's loss of life being "not an important failure" to myself and others. With Auden I become one of those uncaring bystanders, when I am not identifying with Icarus and plunging into the sea. Words like "leisurely" ("how everything turns away/ Quite leisurely from the disaster;") confront me with the casual callousness in my own disregard for fellow human beings who are suffering. Auden evokes many crosscutting feelings, including sorrow, guilt, and rage. Like the painting, the poem has many layers, as does my response. I remember being in Brussels, standing in front of Bruegel's "The Fall of Icarus," in its position beside two other great paintings by the same artist, and admiring how he conveyed the differing perspectives of the figures, each on his own plane, each in his own world. Auden captured suffering's "human position," which we each may relegate to someone else's plane, whenever we can.

With Collins I feel intellectually curious about the parallels to the Auden poem, sometimes amused by his dry wit, and tremendously admiring of his vivid language and his insight about fear. I enjoy this poem. I am captivated by lines like "They understood how the mind,/ the freakiest dungeon in the castle,/ can effortlessly imagine a crab with the face of a priest/ or an end table complete with genitals." But, unlike with Auden's poem, with Collins' I don't imagine I will discover deeper layers of the poem and/or of myself when I come back to it in a year.

I can imagine a conversation between Auden's poem and one by Adrienne Rich, "Eastern War Time," #10 (in "Poems that Make Grown Men Cry" Ed

Anthony and Ben Holden, 2014, pp250–251). Auden refers to those who can turn away, "Quite leisurely from the disaster;" for whom it is "not an important failure." Rich relentlessly explores what some of those disasters are like for those caught up in them, who don't have the choice to turn away.

Eastern War Time 10

Memory says: Want to do right? Don't count on me.
I'm a canal in Europe where bodies are floating
I'm a mass grave I'm the life that returns
I'm a table set with room for the Stranger
I'm a field with corners left for the landless
I'm accused of child-death of drinking blood
I'm a man-child praising God he's a man
I'm a woman bargaining for a chicken
I'm a woman who sells for a boat ticket
I'm a family dispersed between night and fog
I'm an immigrant tailor who says *A coat
is not a piece of cloth only* I sway
in the learnings of the master-mystics
I have dreamed of Zion. I've dreamed of world revolution
I have dreamed my children could live at last like others
I have walked the children of others through ranks of hatred
I'm a corpse dredged from a canal in Berlin
a river in Mississippi. I'm a woman standing
with other women dressed in black
on the streets of Haifa, Tel Aviv, Jerusalem
there is spit on my sleeve there are phonecalls in the night
I am a woman standing in line for gasmasks
I stand on a road in Ramallah with naked face listening

I am standing here in your poem unsatisfied
lifting my smoky mirror

Commenting on this poem, the sculptor Anish Kapoor (In: Holden and Holden, 2014, p. 249) says "Reading this poem jogs a sense of indirect guilt we feel when we are faced with the plight of humanity and our own inability or unwillingness to act." This poem pulls at my heart, too. Although Rich cautions me about the fallibility of memory, I am flooded with memories, of the Jewish cemeteries, synagogues, memorials, shtetls I have visited over the years. Memories of the man who showed me around the prison in Berlin, where, as an adolescent, he had been incarcerated for the crime of trying to swim from East to West Berlin. Perhaps, as a Jew myself, I have found it a little harder to accept some "failures" as "unimportant."

Rich's poem triggers images of shtetls crammed with ragged people eking out just enough money for food for their families to survive. Of parents terrified that the next pogrom will claim their children's lives. Of what mothers will sell for a chicken, or a boat ticket. Can I allow myself to imagine the agonizing choices parents are making, right this moment, about whether to risk a dangerous journey in the hope that they and their children will be allowed to try to make a better life in this country? In my mind, in my heart, can I "look" at the children in cages, separated from their parents, their only "crime" being their parents' decision to embark on a desperate journey? Without even making a conscious decision, am I failing to register the splash of water as today's Icarus pays with his life for his high hopes?

Reading Rich's poem, I am haunted by the idea of walking children "through ranks of hatred." I picture terrified boys and girls of color summoning their courage on the way to school. With Rich's lines about what she has dreamed, I think of Martin Luther King's dreams, and all the parents who fervently prayed, and still pray for a time when their children "could live at last like others."

By piling high the indignities, Rich makes it hard to turn away, leisurely, to use Auden's word. The tailor demanding respect for his trade, the Jew accused of killing the Christ child, the spat upon, bear witness to the human capacity for murderous contempt. The mass graves and corpse filled canals tell of the literal murders that have resulted from prejudice gone wild. Prejudice renews itself in each generation. Today's newspaper (*New York Times Magazine*, Sunday, Nov. 3, 2019, "The Haunted," pp. 32–43, by Jennifer Perry) describes children tortured for years by ISIS, and men and women raped, sold, murdered. A twelve year old boy, captive for five years, starved, his body covered with scars. A girl who had been captured by ISIS at 4 and was now 9, bleeding from everywhere, her forehead marked from being beaten every day with a metal bar. A woman tells that an ISIS member put her two-year old in a tin box and left her in the sun, and then, in front of the mother, broke the baby's back by slamming her on the floor. He told the mother that this is how all disbelievers have to die. Another ISIS fighter explains that Yazidis have to die because they are not human. Rich's poem and today's newspaper tell similar stories.

The form, the rhythm, and tone of Rich's poem disallow oblivion. Saying "I'm a mass grave" makes the statement more powerfully than any other wording I can imagine. The repetition of what I am keeps coming at me and beats me. Can I still lift a smoky mirror after reading it? Probably. But (I hope) it will be harder to do.

Another poem, by Ilya Kaminsky, issues a similar challenge (in: *Deaf Republic*, 2019, p. 3)

We Lived Happily during the War

And when they bombed other people's houses, we

protested

but not enough, we opposed them but not

enough. I was
in my bed around my bed America

was falling: invisible house by invisible house by invisible house—

I took a chair outside and watched the sun.

In the sixth month
of a disastrous reign in the house of money

in the streets of money in the city of money in the country of
    money,
our great country of money, we (forgive us)

lived happily during the war.

As I read this poem, its jolts remind me of Jane Hirshfield's concept of windows, those sudden transitions that multiply a poem's layers. Here is one of her descriptions of her concept: " A 'window' offers a different kind of plunging, the swerve into some new possibility of mind" (2015, p. 153).

The dislocations in Kaminsky's poem are part of the subject matter. We are watching from a "chair outside." This poem gives us a way to describe America's moral decay. Our patriotism has always had a dose of elitism, but, more and more, we see ourselves as the exception to the rest of the world's sorrows. I think some of us secretly believe that we can buy our way out of them. They happen elsewhere, in the "less developed" countries.

In its jagged lines, enjambed, Kaminsky doesn't let us settle down. What would it take to protest enough? What would it take (eventually) to forgive ourselves and to be forgiven?

Pursuing Life with Animated Intensity:

Mary Oliver's "When Death Comes" and Gerald Stern's "I Remember Galileo"

One way poetry inspires is by celebrating the life force. Here are two poems that forcefully convey it, in very different ways.

When Death Comes
When death comes
like the hungry bear in autumn;
when death comes and takes all the bright coins from his purse

to buy me, and snaps the purse shut;
when death comes
like the measle-pox;

when death comes
like an iceberg between the shoulder blades,

I want to step through the door full of curiosity, wondering:
what is it going to be like, that cottage of darkness?

And therefore I look upon everything
as a brotherhood and sisterhood,

and I look upon time as no more than an idea,
and I consider eternity as another possibility,

and I think of each life as a flower, as common
as a field daisy, and as singular,

and each name a comfortable music in the mouth,
tending, as all music does, toward silence,

and each body a lion of courage, and something
precious to the earth.

When it's over, I want to say: all my life
I was a bride married to amazement.
I was the bridegroom, taking the world into my arms.

When it's over, I don't want to wonder
if I have made of my life something particular, and real.
I don't want to find myself sighing and frightened,
Or full of argument.

I don't want to end up simply having visited this world.

(In: K. Young, 2010, pp. 269–270)

I Remember Galileo

I remember Galileo describing the mind
as a piece of paper blown around by the wind,
and I loved the sight of it sticking to a tree,
or jumping into the back seat of a car,

and for years I watched paper leap through my cities;
but yesterday I saw the mind was a squirrel caught crossing
Route 80 between the wheels of a giant truck,
dancing back and forth like a thin leaf,
or a frightened string, for only two seconds living
on the white concrete before he got away,
his life shortened by all that terror, his head
jerking, his yellow teeth ground down to dust.

It was the speed of the squirrel and his lowness to the ground,
his great purpose and the alertness of his dancing,
that showed me the difference between him and paper.
Paper will do in theory, when there is time
to sit back in a metal chair and study shadows;
but for this life I need a squirrel,
his clawed feet spread, his whole soul quivering,
the loud noise shaking him from head to tail.
O philosophical mind, O mind of paper, I need a squirrel
finishing his wild dash across the highway,
rushing up his green ungoverned hillside.

(In: Seiden, 2016, p. 115)

Oliver counts on fierce curiosity. Not just casual, thoughtful considering, but passionate observation of all that is alive. Stern also believes in something beyond abstract considerations. His is a full throated love for life, driving a determined, animal pursuit of it. They agree in rejecting anemic approaches to living. Neither wants to roll back in an armchair and watch life go by, or nestle into theories about it.

But I think Stern goes further, counting on the life force to propel us. His is a more urgent drive. Interestingly, both look to the animal kingdom to find models. I imagine Oliver's bodies, those lions of courage, have much in common with Stern's squirrel. They both exemplify a hearty determination.

Oliver focuses more on wanting to be a full participant in her life. I hear her warning herself not to stand on the sidelines, as though that were a temptation. To me it is as though her better angels are arguing with her more passive inclinations. She seems to be telling herself to step up, while there is still time. Don't allow (yourself) to live an armchair life. Get in the game, become something, fully embrace the whole world, and you will delimit your regrets when your life is over. Inhabit your curiosity, let it lead you everywhere that something is alive. Oliver seems to me to be saying that if we nurture our curiosity about life, we will be able to approach death similarly. Perhaps she means that a lifetime of being " a bride married to amazement" can prepare us best for the time "when death comes," for then it will be just another season that cannot be denied, as natural as a hungry bear in autumn.

For the emotion theorist in me, this is a very compelling poem. It celebrates the power of curiosity and believes in its power to avert regret. I also think of Erich Fromm when I read the line "And therefore I look upon everything/ as a brotherhood and a sisterhood,...." For him caring about anyone's life, including one's own, is impossible without caring about all that is alive (Fromm, 1956). Oliver's poem first introduces a definitive, imperious death dealer, then tours life forms with a lighter touch, and finishes with declarative determination. Its form is satisfying, like a rounded piece of music. In form and content it speaks to me of a fully realized, fulfilled life.

From my point of view this poem epitomizes one of poetry's greatest strengths. It flickers. In this case it flickers between an idea (everything that happens is part of Nature) and an emotion (intense, unquenchable curiosity). The idea without the emotion wouldn't be as riveting. The emotion without the idea would be an empty platitude. Oliver tells us to be curious at the same time as she tells us what to be curious about. She puts in a plug for life-long childish wonderment. Reading it feels to me like "an iceberg between the shoulder blades." Its first lines distinguish it from weary bromides about life and death. When that purse snaps shut, a shock passes through me. It is the recognition of death's unfathomable finality. But a different feeling quickly follows: the peaceful calm of accepting inevitabilities; of surrendering to life's rhythms. I can get comfort from seeing myself as an instance of life. I am reminded of one of Hamlet's last soliloquies. It is the one I love best. For me, it has a gentle wisdom beyond any other.

> ...we defy augury: there 's a special providence in the fall of a
>   sparrow. If it be now, 'tis not to
> come; if it be not to come, it will be now; if it be not now, yet it
>   will come: the readiness is all:
> since no man knows what aught of what he leaves, what is't to
>   leave betimes? Let be.
>   Act V, Sc.2, lines 218–224

Let be. But how can we embrace *both* calm surrender and unrelenting curiosity? Or, (answering Hamlet's early question "to be or not to be") how can we "be" (passionately) at the same time as we "let be"? I think it is poetry's magic that it can subtly insinuate questions such as these, without "irritably" reaching for an answer (following Keats's recommendation in his concept of negative capability, discussed in chapter one).

When I read Stern's poem, I think of Rilke's cry "You must change your life!" (in his poem, "The Archaic Torso of Apollo," in Corbett, 2016, pp. 210–211). Stern relies on narrative. His squirrel, an unlikely protagonist, becomes a hero by the end of the story. How does Stern get us to care about him and root for him? How did he make me feel anxious, until the squirrel successfully completed "his wild dash across the highway"? Stern gives us fine details ("...his head/ jerking, his yellow teeth ground down to dust") that bring the squirrel off the page. With consummate skill the poet forges the association between the urgent squirrel and a human life lived with urgency. Contrast clearly plays a role in this. Leaping paper, light in substance, is compared with that desperate squirrel, with his "lowness to the ground." Running parallel we have airy theories of the mind versus grounded, passionate theories of the mind as an organ dedicated to preserving life. Living according to this second theory means making headlong dashes up the next steeply ascending inclines, no matter how ungoverned they may be.

Let us put Stern's squirrel in Oliver's animal (and human) kingdom. The juxtaposition is meaningful to me. The squirrel's purposeful mad dash is pure animal instinct. If we were to see it as a prescription for the good life, we might be inclined to privilege impulse (or sensation) over other motives, and live, energetically, in the present moment. I see no room for ambivalence in his headlong dash; no space for contemplation or even curiosity. Every fiber is dedicated to forward motion.

I think there can be a kind of joyous exhilaration in full-out commitment, whether to physical exertion or a more intellectual or spiritual pursuit. Pedal to the metal. No brakes. It is akin to fairy tales of good and bad spirits. Somewhat like some stories of combat, the heroes are clear from the beginning. These tales can be deeply satisfying to us as children, and well beyond that phase of life. In psychoanalytic terms, they can be products of the "splitting" or total separation of positive from negative forces.

Obviously, the absence of nuance can pose a danger, among its other limitations. Giving ourselves (or others) an absolute green light, seeing ourselves as fighting the good fight, or fighting to survive crossing Route 80, can be used to justify all sorts of actions. From one angle it is passionately, stunningly single minded. From another it is ruthless and amoral. How many lives have been taken in its name? How many villainous actions condoned?

Personally, I sometimes need to access Stern's squirrel. Its caption can be what I call life's "necessary ruthlessness." But (in myself and others) I am also afraid of what his instincts can justify.

"I Am Living, I Remember You":

Marie Howe's "What the Living Do" (In: Seiden, 2016, p. 62) and Jason Shinder "Coda" (In: K. Young, 2010, p. 278)

Sometimes a poem seems almost like a direct answer to someone else's work. It really is an answer in the case of Jason Shinder's "Coda," which tells Howe how *he* sees what the living do. I discussed Howe's poem in Chapters One and Two. (Please see the text there). I return to it here, to comment on the convergence between that poem and Shinder's "Coda."

Previously (Chapter Two, section on grief) I wrote about how the mundane details in this poem mesh with the poignant wish she could still take her brother's everyday presence in her kitchen for granted. Joy at being alive lives side by side grief in this poem, as it does in our lives. I noted that, in the last line, there is a comma between "I am living" and "I remember you," as though the two phrases need each other in equal measure.

Here is Shinder's reply in his poem, "Coda"

And now I know what most deeply connects us

after that summer so many years ago,
and it isn't poetry, although it is poetry,

and it isn't illness, although we have that in common,

and it isn't gratitude for every moment,
even the terrifying ones, even the physical pain,

though we are grateful, and it isn't even death,

though we are halfway through
it, or even the way you describe the magnificence

of being alive, catching a glimpse,

in the store window, of your blowing hair and chapped lips,
though it is beautiful, it is; but it is

that you're my friend out here on the far reaches

of what humans can find out about each other.

I hear Shinder as finding meaning from truthful dialogue, and not (solely) from aliveness itself. I don't think there is disagreement here, but just a difference in emphasis. Howe celebrates the catch in the throat from the sheer joy of being alive. Like Gerald Stern's squirrel, (above) who literally lunges for life, Howe cherishes her own reflection. Feeling the spark of life (and seeing it reflected) is enough to bring her joy.

Shinder most joyously celebrates something perhaps less visceral—a friendship based on no-holds-barred honesty. In a sense, to paraphrase the saying that the truth sets us free, for Shinder the truth sets his joy free. That search for an extreme encounter, for the dropping of every self-protective defense, is what he counts on. It sounds to me as though everything else, every other aspect of the shared human condition, is not as crucial for him.

206

Shinder poses the central question (what most deeply connects us) and then gives us several wrong answers, until, at the end, he reveals the right one. In response to this, I found myself guessing. What could it be? As with so many poems, when the answer comes it seems like I knew it all the time. Yet, it is very satisfying to have it articulated.

But Howe's remembering and Shinder's no holds barred friendship are not to everyone's taste. Through several sets of poems I next explore their potential pitfalls.

"No Holds Barred" Vs "Tell It Slant"

What are the dangers of Shinder's "no holds barred honesty"? Even for someone who cherishes and stoutly pursues Truth, like Emily Dickinson, there are times it is wisest to "tell it slant." For most of us, there are very many times when the truth may be too much to bear. I have already discussed Dickinson's remarkable recommendations for moderating truth (see Chapter Two). I reprise her poem to juxtapose it with one by Sherman Alexie, and some others. First, I look at the need to "slant" truths that are just too painful to bear when confronted head on. In a subsequent section, I explore the need to moderate truths that might threaten to overwhelm relationships with friction.

> Tell all the truth but tell it slant—
> Success in Circuit lies
> Too bright for our infirm Delight
> The Truth's superb surprise
> As Lightning to the Children eased
> With explanation kind
> The Truth must dazzle gradually

Or every man be blind—

(Poem 1263, In: Vendler, 2010, p. 431)

In a marvelous poem by Sherman Alexie, "Grief Calls Us To The Things of This World" (In Seiden, 2016, pp. 1–2) the poet (or his persona) wakes in a hotel room and notices a blue telephone in the bathroom. He decides to share this juicy bit of modern absurdity with his father, calls home, and asks to speak to him. His mother answers the phone and gasps at his request, which triggers his remembering that his father has been dead for a year. The poet apologizes, but his mother quickly chimes in that she has made similar mistakes, such as forgetting her husband is dead and preparing coffee for him. When his mother laughs, the poet references angels who meet our praise for forgetfulness with harsh replies. Their wings slap our souls, they burden us and unbalance us, ride us piggyback, and, finally, haul us into the dust. We are their prey, as we pray for the sweet oblivion of moments of relief from sorrow.

Alexie is probably all of us, at one time or another. We resist our version of the "angels" pulling us down into gravity's realm. But, in addition to telling us about a slip, when, for one precious moment, a wish triumphed over reality, he also portrays *how* this can happen. I notice that it is only when the mother gasps that the poet remembers that his father is dead. Of course he "knew" about the death of his father, nearly a year earlier. It is as though when he thought of telling his father about the bathroom telephone, and imagined their shared chuckle about the absurd things of this world, anticipation filled his mind. The "file," of knowledge of his father's death, was unopened for that moment, perhaps in the back of the "cabinet," out of sight. Then the mother gasps, shocked. *Then* (I imagine) the poet registers that something is out of joint. The "file cabinet" is quickly scanned, and the poet remembers. And apologizes. As though he has been inconsiderate?

Insensitive? As though "forgetting" was an act of indifference? Or, as though it could sound this way to his mother?

But she reassures the poet that she has made similar mistakes. I imagine this is to tell him that she understands his slip did not come from an uncaring heart. She knows how she loved the father, and she has made similar faux pas. So loving and "forgetting" are not incompatible.

Then comes what for me is the most fascinating part of the poem. Alexie paints a picture of angels alert to catch us enjoying forgetfulness. They take this as an opportunity to drag us down. Alexie has created a battleground. Just when we most appreciate our (defensive) oblivion, we are punished, slapped, hauled into dust.

The light, playful tone is entirely gone. This is war. On one side the poet, the poor prey, praying for peace of mind. On the other, those furious, hell bent, avenging angels, insisting that he fully face the harsh reality of his loss. I have always questioned (psychoanalytic and other) portrayals of noble battles against defenses. Does it have to be war? Are the angels always right? Why should we be punished for longing for sweet oblivion? I notice that Alexie's angels haul the miscreant *down*, as though (like Icarus?) he was guilty of trying to escape gravity, in many senses of the word. Just who do we imagine these fallen angels really serve?

But I think Alexie has been fair to both sides. The angels win, of course, in the end, but the "forgetful," defensive poet has been portrayed sympathetically. In my language Alexie balances the value of facing the truth with the equally worthy value of tact. As a clinician I believed that the defenses are there for a reason, and must be respected. The impulse to barrel through them, and "haul" the poor "prey" to face reality can "unbalance" a patient, or anyone else someone tries too hard to confront with The Truth. In my experience it is a mistake made most often by young clinicians, who get excited and eager about sharing an "insight" they think they see, not unlike the young Freud, who tried to circumvent the defenses through hypnosis

POETIC DIALOGUES

to deliver Oedipal truths directly into the patient's mind. As evidenced, for example, by Dora's abrupt termination of her treatment with Freud (Freud, 1905) it didn't always work. Sometimes, it was smarter than it was wise.

Even supposing we know a truth, often it is kinder and more effective to let it dazzle gradually. I am reminded of the wisdom in Winnicott's (1949) advice that clinicians who feel hate toward their patients should hold it in storage, since telling the patient about it in the moment might be too difficult for the patient to hear. But Winnicott went on to say that this truth must be told before the treatment ends, or it has not been completed.

In my opinion, the sage poet Jane Hirshfield (2015, p. 114) has best expressed the importance of tactful timing.

> Perhaps one message to be taken from the many myths that speak of a broken concealment is the need for tact. In life, as in literature and myth, the desire to strip reality down to some bare and blunt truth reflects delusion, hubris, or reductionism's inedible dust. As there is a connection between modesty, the generative, and a clear-seeing compassion, there is one also between hubris and an ensuing blindness. *What is bared without sufficient respect may not be bearable, or bearable only at enormous cost.* (Italics mine).

My thought is that intensity of grief, or anger/hate, or any fierce painful feeling can get us to long for forgetfulness, that is, try to defend ourselves. The question is not whether the truth of these feelings must *eventually* be faced but, rather, how. The attitude that our souls must be "slapped" with "cold wings" comes, I believe, from a belief system not unlike Freud's (and many other analysts, of every generation). In this way of thinking it is assumed that war must be waged to defeat defenses that originally were adopted for protection, but have become obstacles to a healthier life. I think there is some validity in these assumptions. I do believe that the truth sets us free. But I don't agree that waging war is the way to get to it. The problem with this approach is not only that it pits clinician and patient in opposition. It also pits one aspect of the patient against another. The underlying message is that the patient's (cowardly) efforts to avoid pain must be confronted and defeated, for the patient's own good. Medicine has to be distasteful to be effective.

In this context Hirshfield mentions (2015, pp. 113–14) the myth of Psyche, which I think can be considered the clinician's origin myth. As you may remember, Psyche is the beautiful girl married to Venus's son, Eros, and the object of Venus's jealousy. Eros, worried about his bride's safety, conceals himself from Psyche, visiting her only at night, and warning her not to try to see him. Spurred on by her sisters, Psyche brings a lamp to look at him as he sleeps. Oil from the lamp awakens Eros, he flees, and Psyche's difficulties begin. Thus we have a story where security and curiosity pull in opposite directions. Both can't be served at the same time. As Hirshfield makes clear, (p. 114) this poses a dilemma. "Until she engages the world with oil lamp and open eyes, Psyche cannot become what her name has come to mean: a soul, a being fully engaged in the living through of her own deep existence."

My feeling is that Psyche's problem isn't her curiosity, it is Venus. The context is what pits one of Psyche's needs (to truly see) against another (to remain secure and in her new role). I believe that compassion can render seeing compatible with security. Letting my own fantasies play, I would like to ask Eros to look at his new wife with compassion for her position, summon all his tact, and talk to his mother! While I am not serious about re-writing the myth, I do really believe the message we take from it matters. Like Psyche, clinicians and their patients need to be able to shed light on their realities, but only compassion can render the process safe, freeing, and enlightening at the same time.

These issues take on special meaning in times of grief. In my own times of searing loss, my strongest, most palpable need has been for compassion.

Both as a patient and as a clinician, I know that any effective treatment process inevitably evokes pain. But I think it must always feel like the pain was unavoidable. When it comes as a result of a tactless attack on the defenses it is at best ineffective, and at worst harmful. Loss can be a tremendously isolating experience. It is then that we most need Eros, the god of love, at our side.

In her poem, "Myth," Natasha Tretheway brings a heart-breaking expression of love into the discussion (In: K. Young, 2010, p. 127). Tretheway writes of a beloved person whose death occurred while the poet was sleeping. As I read it, this allowed the poet to maintain the loss in an ambiguous space, somewhere between real and not real. In dreams, the beloved lives on, but dies again each morning.

Tretheway uses the language of being forsaken, as though her beloved comes to her at night but then chooses to abandon her each morning. She imagines the dead slipping through a rift. Rifts, of course, are of many kinds, including angry interchanges. This poem softly switches, back and forth, between the persona (the poet) having and not having agency. At one point it seems as though the poet is able to hold onto the beloved, but, then, she is once again helplessly forsaken. The words carousel, round and round, night turning into day, day into night, dream into reality, and so on, until, at the very end, we are back to the poem's first words.

The dizzying circularity of the language in this poem puts me in a dreamy state. I find it almost hypnotic. By the end sense is less important to me than music. The poem creates its content in its way of engaging with the reader (or, at least, this reader). Some words start dancing with new partners. Round they go. Order no longer matters, nor do literal meanings.

The title of the poem fascinates me. Does it refer to a nightly resurrection? Rollo May *(The Cry for Myth,* 1991, p. 26) says that myth "...unites the antimonies of life: conscious and unconscious, historical and present, individual and social." Later on (attributing the idea to Thomas Mann p.

212

27) he says that myth represents eternal truth in contrast to empirical truth. Perhaps Tretheway's title refers to the empirical truth (the death of someone she cared about, realized in the cold light of day) and the eternal truth (Tretheway's night time experience of the ongoing internal existence of the loved person).

Many myths come to mind, that portray aliveness and deadness reigning at alternating times (e.g. the Greek myth of Demeter and Persephone). Regardless of what Trethewey had in mind with her title, her poem is entrancing. Unlike Alexie, Trethewey doesn't have to fight with herself about remaining aware of her loss. No "fucking angels" need to ride her piggyback. Rather, she attributes her daily abandonment to her beloved's retreat. As she wakes he (or she) slips "through some rift." In Alexie's poem, it is he that "slips," but his is a Freudian slip, as he "forgets" his father died. But, in their own ways, I think each of these poems pays tribute to the human need to intermingle awareness of loss with awareness of ongoing (if only internalized) life.

Another voice chimes in, as I think about how much our brief vacations from awareness are worth, or are not worth the subsequent, inevitable shock. It is Joseph Brodsky's in his lovely, tuneful poem "A Song" (in K. Young, 2010, pp. 130–131).

I wish you were here, dear,
I wish you were here.
I wish you sat on the sofa
and I sat near.
The handkerchief could be yours,
the tear could be mine, chin-bound.
Though it could be, of course,
the other way around.

213

I wish you were here, dear,
I wish you were here.
I wish we were in my car,
and you'd shift the gear.
We'd find ourselves elsewhere,
on an unknown shore.
Or else we'd repair
to where we've been before.

I wish you were here, dear,
I wish you were here.
I wish I knew no astronomy
when stars appear,
when the moon skims the water
that sighs and shifts in its slumber.
I wish it were still a quarter
to dial your number.

I wish you were here, dear,
in this hemisphere,
as I sit on the porch
sipping a beer.
It's evening, the sun is setting:
boys shout and gulls are crying.
What's the point of forgetting
if it's followed by dying?

It is hard not to sing this melodic poem. But I stop singing at the end. I have answered his parting question differently at different times in my own life (and, even now, my answers are not consistent). Sometimes

I feel "the point of forgetting" is simply to have a few minutes off. Whether or not they are worth it depends on how badly I need them. At other times I feel differently. Given how painful the aftermath is (Trethewey's "constant forsaking") maybe it is just not worth it. But, it isn't a (conscious) choice.

Still, this lilting poem evokes old fashioned porches and songs to sweethearts. As with so many other poems I love, its form fits its content perfectly. As I come to the last lines, the song chokes in my throat. The very momentary forgetting is followed by a painful jolt. Once again, Alexie's angels have hauled me down.

Avoiding disclosing our feelings, or avoiding facing them ourselves, can have a wide array of meanings. Sometimes we wish to spare ourselves from sinking into grief, and at other times we are trying to preserve our own self-image or a fraying relationship. Of course, these wishes can overlap, and very often they do. This thought brings me back to Henry Wadsworth Longfellow's "The Cross of Snow" which I would like to re-read alongside Christina Rossetti's "Later in Life 17."

The Cross of Snow (In: Burt and Mikics, 2010, p. 202)

In this poem, Longfellow expresses his grief about the death of his wife, Fanny, who died eighteen years earlier in a house fire. I discussed this poem in chapter two, but reprint it here to compare it with Rossetti's.

> In the long, sleepless watches of the night,
> A gentle face—the face of one long dead—
> Looks at me from the wall, where round its head
> Here in this room she died; and soul more white
> Never through martyrdom of fire was led

To its repose; nor can in books be read
The legend of a life more benedight.
There is a mountain in the distant West
That, sun-defying, in its deep ravines
Displays a cross of snow upon its side.
Such is the cross I wear upon my breast
These eighteen years, through all the changing scenes
And seasons, changeless since the day she died.

Briefly, in the previous discussion of this work, I commented on how Longfellow expressed his unabated sorrow, his ongoing relationship with the image of his wife, and that nothing in the poem suggests that his grief is balanced by other feelings. The history of the publication of this poem is interesting in itself. Written eighteen years after his wife's tragic death, it was not published in the poet's lifetime. Presumably he didn't want to expose his grief because he thought it would be too personal and/or too painful to do so. After Longfellow's death, the poet's brother published a biography of him, and included this sonnet. The editors (Burt and Mikics) suggest that Longfellow's reluctance to publish the poem was probably partially based on his society's attitudes about grief. Particularly in men, it was thought that grief should be time limited, and should be transformed into action at some point. The editors' explanation sounds plausible to me, though, of course, we will never know why Longfellow didn't publish the poem. Whether or not their theory has truth, it usefully brings up the question of how we preserve, or are unable to preserve, our self-esteem in times of grief. In my own work (2015, 2019) I have highlighted the role of self-esteem in mourning. Briefly, whereas Freud (1917) saw ambivalence toward the departed as the central complication that can turn grief into melancholia, (depression) I believe that (while ambivalence certainly can complicate grief) mourners need to be able to *empathize fully with themselves*, which may not be possible in states of shame, guilt, or profound regret. I posed (2019, p. 46) the question as to whether the mourner has a self-nurturing attitude, as they go through a difficult time. Bearing loss can take every strength we can muster, and it is made harder if society pathologizes us, or we ourselves feel our ongoing sorrow is something we have to hide. It is vital to me that we separate grief, in our minds, from the condition of depression, which may well need treatment. Here is how I put it in 2015 (p. 113):

Depression is both like and unlike grief, as Freud (1917) and countless others have suggested. As with grief something has been lost. But, I suggest, in depression the loss is more fully interior. One has lost one's own light. While an exterior loss may have contributed, the depressed person mourns him or herself. This death in the midst of life transfixes us, like specimens caught in amber.

Just a bit further (p. 114) I conclude that "...while grief can last as long as depression, in grief the sense of self-worth is less likely to be profoundly diminished. I believe that while the grieving person and the depressed person have both suffered some form of loss, the lowered self-esteem often present in depression complicates self-care."

With this distinction in mind, I turn to the poem, "Later Life 17," by Christina Rossetti.

Something this foggy day, a something which
Is neither of this fog nor of to-day,
Has set me dreaming of the winds that play
Past certain cliffs, along one certain beach,
And turn the topmost edge of waves to spray:
Ah pleasant pebbly strand so far away,
So out of reach while quite within my reach,

As out of reach as India or Cathay!
I am sick of where I am and where I am not,
I am sick of foresight and of memory,
I am sick of all I have and all I see,
I am sick of self, and there is nothing new;
Oh weary impatient patience of my lot!—
Thus with myself: how fares it, Friends, with you?

(In: Burt and Mikics, 2010, p. 206)

Burt and Mikics (p. 207) tell us that this sonnet is part of a sequence of poems, titled "Later Life" because the poet was fifty years old. They then suggest that this poem "...is atypical of her verse: however deep its melancholy, it substitutes, for any more pious conclusion, an unexpected, almost cheerful humor." I agree with the word "melancholy," which was a term used for depression in the past. But I am not sure whether I hear the "cheerful humor." The poet is turning away from her self-reflections, but I don't feel I know her emotional state. I could imagine that last line expresses a pressing need to escape an increasingly irritated "impatient patience" with herself.

In any case, I am *not* attempting to diagnose or analyze the poet, but just to point out that I think her poem beautifully illustrates a difference between sorrow and depression. Many lines in the poem point to familiar aspects of depressive states: fog, pleasure seeming out of reach, sorrowful feelings about where she is in her life, disgust with her own thinking process, pervasive disenchantment with herself, the sense that there is nothing new for her to experience, that her life is an endless repetition, and contemplating it stirs a weary impatience (although she is trying to have patience). After what seems to me like thirteen lines of description of a melancholic state, Rossetti turns away from looking at herself, to shift the spotlight to her friends.

I hear the poet as feeling unable to access anything that has given her pleasure in the past. I imagine some of these feelings have to do with aging, since the poem is part of a sequence titled "Later Life." In any case, the sense that "…there is nothing new" is certainly familiar to me, from working with patients who feel their experience of life has been narrowed by depression. The world lacks color; life is unexciting, and the self is impoverished. Rossetti so clearly describes the monotony of depression when she says "I am sick of all I have and all I see,/ I am sick of self, and there is nothing new;…"

Burt and Mikics understand (p. 209) the last line as hopeful. "Rossetti suddenly notices that she might have an audience, an awareness that must console her no matter what answer her question gets. If we feel unlike her (sunnier, less foggy). perhaps tomorrow she will feel more like us; if we feel like her—if we share her restlessness—at least she can know that her pain is shared."

Maybe. *I don't think we can know, from the poem itself.* In my experience, while the presence of someone else who feels better might console the sufferer, it could also elicit envy, jealousy, shame, and, even, an exacerbation of the depression. The other's sunnier state of mind could seem like another unreachable "pleasant pebbly strand so far away/ So out of reach while quite within my reach…" Sometimes a reminder that others are enjoying their lives only reinforces the isolation and sense of inadequacy that often accompany the pain of a pervasive depressive state.

Still another slant on defensive avoidance of the truth is contributed by a fascinating poem (In Burt and Mikics, 2010, p. 246) by Edwin Arlington Robinson, called "Firelight." Here what is at stake in confronting the truth is risking a breach in the maintenance of a smoothly operating relationship. Does that change our assessment of the best balance of the needs for tact and truth?

Firelight

Ten years together without yet a cloud,
They seek each other's eyes at intervals
Of gratefulness to firelight and four walls
For love's obliteration of the crowd.
Serenely and perennially endowed
And bowered as few may be, their joy recalls
No snake, no sword; and over them there falls
The blessing of what neither says aloud.

Wiser for silence, they were not so glad
Were she to read the graven tale of lines
On the wan face of one somewhere alone;
Nor were they more content could he have had
Her thoughts a moment since of one who shines
Apart, and would be hers if he had known.

A couple has chosen serenity with each other over other possibilities. Each lets their thoughts wander to these other potential lovers, but neither speaks their thoughts out loud. Do we agree they are "wiser for silence"?

I am reminded of a wonderful scene in Shakespeare's *The Merchant of Venice* (2000, Ed: A.R. Braunmuller). Portia, disguised as a lawyer, witnesses Bassanio giving away the ring she had entrusted to him. Earlier, as Portia and Bassanio declared their love and intention to marry, she had bestowed the ring on him, telling him that if he parted from the ring, lost it, or gave it away, it would "presage the ruin" of their love (Act III, Sc. 2, lines 171–173). In the later scene, Portia, in disguise, hears Bassanio declare to his friend Antonio:

Antonio, I am married to a wife
Which is as dear to me as life itself;

But life itself, my wife, and all the world
Are not with me esteemed above thy life.
I would lose all, ay, sacrifice them all
Here to this devil, to deliver you.

Portia sees Bassanio choose to part with the ring, for the sake of his friend. Later, when Portia and Bassanio reunite, and Bassanio tells her what he did she responds angrily, and Bassanio begs: (Act V, Sc. 1, lines 248–249):

Pardon this fault, and by my soul I swear
I never more will break an oath with thee.

At this point all is revealed, and all is forgiven. Portia knows the meaningful choice Bassanio made, in giving away her ring, but she prioritizes harmony, as do all the other characters by the play's end. I can imagine Portia and Bassanio, ten years later, as in the poem "Firelight," seeking "each other's eyes at intervals/ Of gratefulness to firelight and four walls/ For love's obliteration of the crowd."

Of Robinson's poem, Burt and Mikics (p. 247) write that "...what looks like a sad outcome might be the best any of us could do." They have left behind other potential lovers ("the wan face of one somewhere alone;" and "one who shines/ Apart, and would be hers if he had known"). The word "compromise" comes to my mind, with all its positive and negative connotations. To be able to compromise is a virtue, but to be compromised can mean "to give up one's interests, principles, or integrity" according to my dictionary. I think Robinson's poem implies that both are inevitable in a relationship. Shakespeare's Portia (who earlier in the play delivered the exquisite monologue about the "quality of mercy") has learned the limits of Bassanio's love for her. We might see her "compromise" as, partly, mature wisdom, but, just as much, bleak resignation. Similarly, Robinson's couple buys their serenity at the cost of buried secrets and unexplored "roads not taken" (to quote Robert Frost's well known line). Firelight gives off a soft glow, but leaves some of the room in shadows.

While these couples' pacts are, in many respects, different from Alexie's "forgetting," what they have in common is the challenge we all face, sooner or later. When is it wisest to prioritize truth over tact, within ourselves, and with each other? I would suggest that clinicians face this challenge every hour. When should sleeping dogs be left to lie (pun intended)? When should defensive avoidance be respected, and not tampered with? How "slant" should we tell our truths (to go back to Dickinson's phrase) if we tell it at all?

While I will discuss Shakespeare's *King Lear* separately, in this context I want to mention one "slant" on this great play. When I was much younger, I fully identified with Cordelia's attitude when she insists (in Act I, Scene 1, lines 95–103) on expressing only the "truth" of her feelings toward her father, the king. But, as I have aged, I see it somewhat differently. Was her stance ungenerous, as well as honest? Couldn't she have told her truth a bit more "slant" to salve her aging father's ego? When Lear says, a few lines later (line 128) "Let pride, which she calls plainness, marry her" doesn't he have a point? Isn't Cordelia's being prideful, as well as truthful? Of course, if she is, the apple hasn't fallen far from the tree, but that is not really the issue. Kent, another truth teller in this scene, has a different motive. He is desperately trying to save Lear from making a horrendous mistake, even at the risk of his own life. And the Fool is doing his job by telling the truth in his convoluted way. The profession of Fool has always reminded me of myself and my colleagues, as psychoanalysts, since we so often couch our truths in parables, aphorisms, analogies, and abstractions, to soften them for the other person (and, sometimes, to seem intelligent and witty to ourselves).

From this vantage point I have sometimes seen *King Lear* as (in part) about Cordelia becoming able to leaven her truth with an empathic recognition of the needs of the other person. So, toward the end of the play (Act IV, Scene 7, lines 73–77) when Lear, awakened in more than one sense, asks her forgiveness, she utters two of my favorite words in the play "No cause." With these two words I think she expresses a wholly different outlook from the one she had at the beginning. After all, strictly speaking, she *does* have cause to be angry. He publicly denounced her, disowned her, and banished her. But I think Cordelia has learned that truth, by itself, unmitigated by empathy, is not sufficient. In that, I think she has something in common with many of Shakespeare's strongest characters, including Isabella in *Measure for Measure*, and, of course, Portia in *The Merchant of Venice*. An empathic capacity to forgive is among Prospero's achievements in *The Tempest* too. "No cause" is one of Shakespeare's profound lines that, in just two words, expresses a world of hard won wisdom.

Much of the world's literature explores the dangers of unexpressed intense feelings, including love. For example, in *Twelfth Night*, Shakespeare's characters, the Duke and Viola, say (Act 2, Sc. 4, lines 105–114):

> Viola: My father had a daughter loved a man
> As it might be, perhaps, were I a woman
> I should your lordship.
> Duke: And what's her history?
> Viola: A blank, my lord. She never told her love,
> But let concealment, like a worm i'th'bud,
> Feed on her damask cheek. She pined in thought,
> And with a green and yellow melancholy
> She sat like patience on a monument,
> Smiling at grief. Was not this love indeed?

For me, this is a fascinating passage. Here what is concealed is love, not anger. But it takes the form of a poisonous worm (not unlike the snake in the poems about anger by Blake and Lamb in chapter two). The concealment feeds on the woman, and she grows melancholic (which is an earlier version of the word "depressed"). Like the cultivated anger in Blake's and Lamb's poems, Shakespeare's poisoning lovesickness is nurtured by its host. In a sense, if we feed our concealed emotions, we don't get past them, and they invariably end up stinging us.

Another expression of this idea can be found in Dickinson's complex Poem 165 (in Vendler, 2010, p. 50).

> I have never seen "Volcanoes"—
> But when Travellers tell
> How those old—phlegmatic mountains
> Usually so still—
>
> Bear within—appalling Ordnance—
> Fire, and smoke, and gun—
> Taking Villages for breakfast,
> And appalling Men—
>
> If the stillness is Volcanic
> In the human face
> When upon a pain Titanic
> Features keep their place—
>
> If, at length, the smouldering anguish
> Will not overcome,
> And the palpitating Vineyard
> In the dust, be thrown?

If some loving Antiquary,
On Resumption Morn,
Will not cry with joy, "Pompeii"!
To the Hills return!

Vendler (p. 51) connects this poem with part of another that Dickinson wrote (but never sent) to her friend Catherine Anthon:

Divulging it would rest my Heart
But it would ravage theirs—
Why, Katie, Treason has a Voice—
But mine—dispels—in Tears.

Both of these poems speak of intense, suppressed, anguished feelings. In Poem 165 they are volcanic but not expressed on the persona's unmoving face. In the second poem, (1429) expression of the emotions would be relieving to the persona but devastating to others.

Here is how Vendler (p. 52) paraphrased part of Poem 165, "If it is not serenity one sees on this human face, but rather repression of pain, will not, at length, the smouldering anguish overcome the stoicism, and destroy the palpitating heart behind that face?" However, Vendler sees (p. 51–52) the last part of the poem as presaging a happy ending for the persona, who is reunited with her beloved ("loving Antiquary") on "Resumption" Day (which Vendler understands as Dickinson's version of Resurrection Day).

I think Vendler means "suppression" rather than "repression," at least in the technical sense, because surely the anguish is conscious to the persona, as she struggles to maintain an unmoving face. (Vendler seems to me to use the two terms interchangeably). The effort to conceal the anguish is futile. If we discuss the two poems together, as Vendler did, it seems as though some intense feelings are a danger to the self, if not expressed, and to others, if vented. Is it the very intensity of the feelings, or the tremendous effort to suppress them, that creates the disaster? This is not clear to me, from my reading of the poem. But the destructive potential of smoldering emotions, kept under an impassive expression, is quite clear.

Shakespeare and Dickinson portray a recessed layer of dangerously roiling feelings that can "bubble up" to the surface and wreak havoc. I think they presage the conflict theories that prevailed in Freud's era, where a teeming Id is met with the leavening powers of Ego and Superego. Aggression and passion are to be modulated enough to prevent disaster. The psychoanalytic model trusts internal workings (aided by the analyst) and not a future "loving Antiquary" to save the day.

Letting Go Of Life

I refer to Dylan Thomas's great poem "Do Not Go Gently..." in several other chapters, so I will not reprise it here, but I want to juxtapose its position about fighting death with work that suggests the value of being able to let go of life. Briefly, in his poem Thomas begs his father not to "go gently," since that would leave the poet with the painful memory of a father who submitted to death. An example of a very different philosophy is expressed in Joseph Campbell's (2004) book, *Pathways to Bliss*. According to him, an important psychological function of myth is to carry the individual through the stages of life. At life's end, the myth functions to help the aged become *disengaged* (p. 10) and gently, peacefully, adapt to the aging process. In his words (p. 14) as we age we begin to lose our grip, in many senses, and long for sleep. Faced with a vigorous younger generation, the wise elderly think "Well, let them have it."

There are many champions of this viewpoint among the poets. Yeats' poem, "When you are old" (In: *A Treasury of Poems*, 1996, Ed.: Sarah Anne Stuart,

p. 7) recommends the company of memories, to help us *adapt* and let go of life gracefully. Most especially, hopefully, we can turn to memories of being young and being cherished.

> When You Are Old
> William Butler Yeats
>
> When you are old and gray and full of sleep,
> And nodding by the fire, take down this book,
> And slowly read, and dream of the soft look
> Your eyes had once, and of their shadows deep;
>
> How many loved your moments of glad grace,
> And loved your beauty with love false or true;
> But one man loved the pilgrim soul in you,
> And loved the sorrows of your changing face.
>
> And bending down beside the glowing bars,
> Murmur, a little sadly, how love fled
> And paced upon the mountains overhead
> And hid his face amid a crowd of stars.

In his poem, "Terminus," Ralph Waldo Emerson (In: Stuart, 1996, pp. 7–8) expresses an even more extreme level of adaptation. We should go beyond *merely accepting* aging and death. We should *embrace* them gladly. In his own words:

> Terminus
> Ralph Waldo Emerson

It is time to be old,
To take in sail...
Fancy departs: no more invent,
Contract thy firmament
To compass of a tent.
There's not enough for this and that,
Make thy option which of two;
Economize the failing river,
Nor the less revere the Giver,
Leave the many and hold the few.
Timely wise accept the terms....
As the bird trims her to the gale,
I trim myself to the storm of time,
I man the rudder, reef the sail,
Obey the voice at eve obeyed at prime:
'Lowly faithful, banish fear,
Right onward drive unharmed;
The port well worth the cruise, is near,
And every wave is charmed.

So it is up to us to "trim" ourselves "to the storm of time." It is our duty to march to death unafraid and unresisting. Anything less is sacrilegious. To fear or regret death is to fail to have faith in heaven and, ultimately, in God.

A very different (but, for me, personally resonant) reason to submit willingly to death was suggested by W.A. Auden's poem, "Old Peoples' Home" (In: Mendelson, 1991, p. 860). This poem is more fully discussed in chapter 5.

This quietly devastating poem imagines death as a release from (at least one of) the rings of hell. It brings several ideas into a discussion of why some might not want to "rage against the dying of the light," as prescribed by Dylan Thomas. First, Auden considers the times (1970's) and mores regarding aging. Unlike in previous generations, where family provided functions for grandparents, this was a time when older people were often stowed out of sight, like "unpopular luggage." Auden also mentions the handicap that the more intact might suffer more often. Having intellectual awareness of their situation might make them even more miserable than the "terminally incompetent." Auden's characterization of the classes, from "elite" to "unspeakable," is acutely accurate and acutely painful. Looking at his poem beside the last three (Thomas, Yeats, Emerson) makes for an interesting exchange. While their lenses are certainly focused on very different realities, what fascinates me is the differences in what they imagine would be helpful. Thomas tells us to protest our losses. Yeats recommends a slide back into loving, warm, youthful memories. Emerson counsels a religious forbearance. Auden, wondering about his own response, prays for a speedy end to the suffering old person's life. It is interesting to me that he is concerned about whether he is being "cold," given that he knows she has the same prayer. Auden is not counting on an emotion or memory or belief system to comfort the old woman. The only mercy would be deliverance. Regardless of who (or what) is responsible for making this person into merely an obligation, the only humane answer would be for her misery to end. Unlike Dylan Thomas, Auden is not hoping for a memory of her going down fighting, or, even, retaining her identity as she dies. The only thing that matters is an end to her suffering.

Another perspective sees death as simply part of life; not necessarily to be valued as a relief from suffering, but, in more fortunate, peaceful circumstances, to be embraced when its time comes. Paul Durcan's poem, "Maureen Durcan," (in: Sieghart, 2019, p. 171) expresses this with a feather light touch. In the poem Paul sees a large butterfly and imagines it is his ninety -four -year-old aunt, Maureen, smiling down on him, and telling him that she died while he was sleeping. She then exclaims that it is a glorious morning. My mind played with this line, responding that it is also a glorious mourning.

Prose can't really match this poem's delicacy. It floats from line to line. Death provides its first full stop. The poem can't be spoken without also being enacted. It is a wisp, just like Auntie Maureen. It offers us a different way of looking at death, as altering Auntie Maureen's shape, but not her spirit. She still hovers over everything, beautiful as ever.

But, sadly, many end our lives more like Auden's "unspeakable" than Durcan's Auntie Maureen. A pair of poems ("Grief" by C.K. Williams and "The Spots" by Joel Brouer) together bring out the bizarre horror of death at the hands of modern medicine, one ghastly procedure after another. Surreal, heartless, methodical, every moment is an amalgam of faint hope and certain dread. These poems also vividly portray the pain that can be felt by those who love someone ending their lives this way. "Grief" is a very long poem, so I am only quoting its first section.

> Gone now, after the days of desperate, unconscious gasping, the
> reflexive staying alive,
> tumorous lungs, tumorous blood, ruined, tumorous liver
>   demanding
> to live, to go on,
> even the innocent bladder, its tenuous, dull golden coin in the
>   slack
> translucent bag;
> gone now, after months of scanning, medication, nausea, hair loss
> and weight loss;
> remission, partial remission, gratitude, hope, lost hope, anxiety,
>   anger,
> confusion,
> the hours and days of everyday life, something like life but only as

dying is like life;
gone the quiet at the end of dying, the mouth caught agape on its
 last
bite at a breath,
bare skull with its babylike growth of new hair thrown back to
 open
the terrified larynx;... (In: K. Young, 2010, pp. 123–126)

"Grief" captures the way the dying become collections of body parts and test results. Even to say "the dying" robs human beings of their identities. Someone who liked poached eggs and coached baseball becomes the "tumorous lungs" in Room 34A. The dehumanization feels unintended, which creates more abject sorrow where it might be better to have rage. Submission to the machines (out of fear? out of hope? out of passivity? habit?) and moments of residual assertion play out in Joel Brouwer's poem:

The Spots (In: K. Young, 2010, pp. 54–55)

Appeared to her in Massachusetts. Purple and green.
And immediately

vertigo rushed up like an angry dog
to a fence. She went white, fell down a well

of herself and wept.
Late at night, in the motels, when she'd fallen

asleep, I cried too. I whispered curses to the awkward stacks
of white towels. Hating anything out of balance. Hating

her, her new failure. In the mornings
my checkbook voice returned, low and soft. For an angry dog

whose yard you wish to cross.
We both hated my balance, hated her imbalance, needed each.

Sudafed acupuncture ear candle.
Yoga chewing gum Zoloft Chinese tea.

She was afraid of going blind. She constantly described
colors and shapes, as if I had gone blind.

They turned orange. They floated. They darted.
We went arm in arm without passion, like elderly French.

Internist neurologist ophthalmologist.
Otolaryngologist neurologist psychiatrist.

She would not allow the warm towel over her face in the MRI.
The nurses seethed. She set her jaw and vanished

into the gleaming white tube. The machine banged like hammers
on a sunken ship's hull. She listened to Beethoven through
    headphones.

The magnetism passed through her mind in waves,
like wind through chestnut trees, touching

everything and changing nothing. Her courage! If courage
is what stones have. My God, how I loved her. Badly.

The spots were like metaphors. They told us something
by showing us something else. And so I believed they were
    metaphors.
They were not.

How entirely life can change! This reminds me of Tolstoy's (1886/1982) story, "The Death of Ivan Ilych." One day Ivan has what seems like a very slight accident, and never recovers, to the amazement of Ivan and everyone else. Mind so often fails to fully register the body's incremental failure. How much more manageable metaphoric spots would be, compared with the reality of these actual spots. The mind can't play mind games with the meaning of these spots. The dying woman is fed to the MRI, like a letter going into an envelope. By listening to Beethoven, by refusing the towel, she tries to hold onto some semblance of herself. But the spots, the endless parade of doctors, and death itself, are all relentless.

Together these poems tell how hard it is to isolate the enemy, when in the process of dying (or witnessing it). In "Grief," it can seem as though the enemy is the liver's will to live. If only it would give in! But no, the enemy is the tumor, and, in Brouwer's poem, the spots. Or, in both, is it the "procedures" that prolong the agony, whether or not there is anything real to hope for? The tumor has already won and so have the spots. But, in "Spots," two people did get to show each other who they were: she with her stone-like courage, and he with his secret tears. In "Grief," as in "Spots," love is expressed in exquisitely detailed observation. Every aspect of the body's defeat is preserved on the page. Words form an effigy. But each poem makes it clear how much a specific, beloved human being, who got lost in dying, will be missed.

Pangs of Regret

Sometimes the person we lost changes his or her meaning to us after they die, and, from that point on, we will mourn the loss of that newly constituted loved one. Some deaths alter the balance of our feelings, freeing us to feel differently about the deceased. Often, what allows us a new appreciation of the dead is simply that we grow up and gain new perspective. But with this enhanced insight can come painful regret that we didn't appreciate what we had at the time. Regret is an extremely important aspect of most lives, as is the fear of future regrets. I explored its role in a chapter of my 2008 book. A poem I love, Hayden's "Those Winter Sundays," ends with plaintive regret for not having thanked his caretaking father. I quoted the poem, in full, in Chapter Two.

Occasionally it seems to me as though two poets are singing to each other, which, of course, could be literally true. But more often I think they harmonize because of the universality of some aspects of human experience. When Hayden repeats, "What did I know..." I hear the haunting refrain of a poem by W.S. Merwin, (1973, p. 25). The poem's title is "Something I've Not Done."

Something I've not done
is following me
I have not done it again and again
so it has many footsteps
like a drumstick that's grown old and never been used
In late afternoon I hear it come closer
at times it climbs out of a sea
onto my shoulders
and I shrug it off
losing one more chance

Every morning
it's drunk up part of my breath for the day
and knows which way
I'm going
and already it's not done there
But once more I say I'll lay hands on it
tomorrow
and add its footsteps to my heart
and its story to my regrets
and its silence to my compass.

Hayden's unsaid "thanks" to his father and Merwin's elusive lost chances both speak of "sins" of omission. They add an everlasting silence to all our compasses. Some aspects of the pain of being human haunt us. Regret can greatly exacerbate loss. Regrets can trail us throughout our lives, and some sorrows strip us of parts of ourselves. For example, if my dear friend Ben dies, an aspect of myself may also perish. Let's say Ben was the only person on earth who cherished a particular brand of my humor. Just a wink would be all we would need to burst into gales of laughter that left everyone else baffled. Maybe someday I will share this mirth with someone else. Maybe not. But, at least, for now, that part of me is gone, along with my loss of his grin. Similarly, in a devastating sense, when a parent loses a child he or she will never be exactly that parent to any other child. It can be impossible to look back at what happened without profound regret. Some regrets never die, and some losses never end.

Opening Our Hearts And Homes

In a previous chapter I commented on the inspiring poem, "The New Colossus," that is etched beneath the Statue of Liberty in New York harbor. I find that this poem, composed by Emma Lazarus, gains new meanings for me when I juxtapose it with a much more recent poem by Rita Dove, a former poet laureate of the United States (1993–1995). I reprint Lazarus's poem, to create a dialogue with Dove's.

"The New Colossus," by Emma Lazarus, (In: *The Oxford Book of American Poetry*, 2006, D. Lehman, Ed., p. 184)

> Not like the brazen giant of Greek fame,
> With conquering limbs astride from land to land;
> Here at our sea-washed, sunset gates shall stand
> A mighty woman with a torch, whose flame
> Is the imprisoned lightning, and her name
> Mother of Exiles. From her beacon-hand
> Glows world-wide welcome; her mild eyes command
> The air-bridged harbor that twin cities frame.
>
> "Keep ancient lands, your storied pomp!" cries she
> With silent lips. "Give me your tired, your poor,
> Your huddled masses yearning to break free,
> The wretched refuse of your teeming shore.
> Send these, the homeless, tempest-tost to me,
> I lift my lamp beside the golden door!

Previously I explored this poem's capacity to inspire. Putting it alongside Dove's poem, I discover aspects of each that I didn't see before.

"Lady Freedom Among Us" by Rita Dove (In: Moyers,1995, p. 111)

don't lower your eyes
or stare straight ahead to where
you think you ought to be going

don't mutter oh no
not another one
get a job fly a kite
go bury a bone

with her oldfashioned sandals
with her leaden skirts
with her stained cheeks and whiskers and heaped up trinkets
she has risen among us in blunt reproach

she has fitted her hair under a hand-me-down cap
and spruced it up with feathers and stars
slung over one shoulder she bears
the rainbowed layers of charity and murmurs
all of you even the least of you

don't cross to the other side of the square
don't think another item to fit on a tourist's agenda

consider her drenched gaze her shining brow
She who has brought mercy back into the streets
and will not retire politely to the potter's field

having assumed the thick skin of this town

its gritted exhaust its sunscorch and blear
she rests in her weathered plumage
bigboned resolute

don't think you can ever forget her
don't even try
she's not going to budge

no choice but to grant her space
crown her with sky
for she is one of the many
and she is each of us

In an interview (Moyers, 1995, pp. 109–128) with Bill Moyers, Dove explained that this poem was written when the statue was brought back, after being cleaned, and returned to its place atop the Capitol Building in Washington, DC. Dove is writing as though the statue were a homeless human being, demanding our attention.

Each poem conjures up a strong woman who represents freedom. Lazarus's poem is a tough minded invitation, to "huddled masses," to come to this country, to "breathe free." It draws a contrast with an Old World, Greek, conquering Colossus. This Lady is firm in her message, which invites and promises.

When I turn to Dove's poem I hear an equally strong female voice, but this one rings with anger as well as power. Instead of Lazarus's use of the negative to form a contrast, ("Not like the brazen giant...") Dove's message is more like "don't you dare!" ("don't think you can ever forget her..."). By telling us what *not* to do, Dove suggests what we *would* do, if left to our own devices. We would look away, ignore, avoid, label, condemn the suffering poor. Like children who, around the age of four, think if they close their eyes others actually disappear, we would close our eyes.

These two poems form a sequence in my mind. In an earlier era, in the USA, there existed an ideal of extending an open hearted invitation to share our home. But, somehow, it seems to me that even the ideal has been lost. At one time we believed we were a country that opened our arms and hearts wide. At least we held this *ideal*, even though the reality always left much to be desired. But, as Dove suggests, we have added contempt for the poor to our avoidance of them. Even if the contempt was really always there, at least we *also* nurtured a belief in generosity of spirit. Dove's Lady of Freedom won't, and shouldn't be ignored. What happened to Lazarus's "worldwide welcome"?

Seeking Attention: Strength or Sin?

Other "old fashioned" ideals are increasingly challenged, or even forgotten. What place does privacy have in the Facebook era? Is modesty, humility, still valued? For many, angling for a spotlight can still feel unseemly, but refusing to "post" can mean lonely obscurity. These issues are hardly new, but they take a somewhat different shape when being "liked" on social media can bring instant celebrity, and one ill considered comment can ruin a career, or, even, a life.

Still, even in earlier times, it was unclear whether or not it was shameful to seek attention. As a psychologist, I remember when it was frowned upon to have a professional listing in the "Yellow Pages." It was unseemly to advertise. Poets, too, had trepidations about the seeking the limelight. But, on the other hand, strict isolation could be considered eccentric, or even abnormal. Emily Dickinson's reclusiveness elicited endless speculation. At some point did she profoundly want the world's attention and then withdraw when it wasn't forthcoming? Or was she increasingly protective of a seclusion that she felt was necessary for the fullest cultivation of her talent? Or should we look elsewhere in her biography for a better understanding? I am not going to speculate about this, but I do want to raise the fascinating question of how each of us feels about attention seeking and self-promotion in creative and professional spheres. Is the wish for our voices to be heard and our paintings to be seen itself unseemly? How far can we go toward self-advertising without becoming vulgar and being (and being seen as) selling out? In a way, even those who only consume creative products, rather than create them, should examine their views on this issue. I think these attitudes can have a subtle impact on how much we appreciate what we read, see, and hear. When an artist (or anyone else) seems to beg for our attention and approval, does this impact our judgment of their worth?

A poem written to Emily Dickinson, and several poems of her own, can form an interesting dialogue on this subject. In his poem, "To Emily Dickinson," (In: Burt and Mikics, 2010, p. 269) Hart Crane makes his empathy for her conflicts clear.

To Emily Dickinson
You who desired so much—in vain to ask—
Yet fed your hunger like an endless task,
Dared dignify the labor, bless the quest—
Achieved that stillness ultimately best,

Being of all, least sought for: Emily, hear!
O sweet, dead Silencer, most suddenly clear
When singing that Eternity possessed
And plundered momently in every breast;

—Truly no flower yet withers in your hand,

The harvest you descried and understand
Needs more than wit to gather, love to bind.
Some reconcilement of remotest mind—

Leaves Ormus rubyless, and Ophir chill.
Else tears heap all within one clay-cold hill.

Commenting on this poem, Burt and Mikics (p. 270) write that Crane saw Dickinson as "...a poet who turned not toward imagined crowds, but toward her own solitary contemplation, who saw for herself not a public future but a private endurance, in art that could live on after her body died." Dickinson's work certainly has lived on. Burt and Mikics suggest that Crane's subtext was the question of whether the true poet must turn away from the world and the pursuit of fame. They also supply a quote from the Book of Job that explains the reference to Ophir: "..in the Book of Job, 28: 16–21, wisdom cannot be valued with the gold of Ophir...for the price of wisdom is above rubies..". Ophir was a wealthy Near Eastern city.

Of course, we will never know just what Emily Dickinson did desire, though we can speculate that some "hunger" drove her to her prodigious output. Did she yearn for fame, despite her deliberately secluded life? Or, did she simply want her voice heard? Did she hope for responses to her work, that might help her improve it? Did she yearn for interactions with fellow poets respectfully regarding each others' ideas? We do know (Vendler 2010) that, even though she was repeatedly told her poems were not fit for publication, she kept sending them to the noted critic Thomas Wentworth Higginson, asking for his opinion. He repeatedly advised her not to try to publish her poems, and responded critically to their unorthodox punctuation and other aspects. Dickinson wrote about 1,800 poems in her lifetime. About 8 were published, all anonymously.

One of Dickinson's poems (519, in Vendler, p. 237) has as its first line "This is my letter to the world."

> This is my letter to the World
> That never wrote to Me—
> The simple News that Nature told—
> With tender Majesty
>
> Her Message is committed
> To Hands I cannot see—
> For love of Her-Sweet-countrymen—
> Judge tenderly-of Me.

Of this poem, Vendler (p. 238) comments that its boldness has not been adequately recognized. In the poem Dickinson appoints herself the messenger of Nature, and draws a parallel between that office and the disciples of God's messages. I am struck by the second line, "That never wrote to Me-." I can't help hearing a melancholy note. Vendler (p. 2) tells us that Higginson responded to the "eccentricity" of her poems with editorial suggestions that Dickinson gracefully acknowledged but did not adopt. Vendler writes that Dickinson's poems and letters reveal a longing for an audience, yet when Higginson suggests that she was seeking publication, Dickinson replied that publication was foreign to her mind. Significantly, when her poems were first published, her editors "corrected" their punctuation and diction and censored her most innovative ideas.

So one way to understand Dickinson's ambivalent relationship to publication might be that she was simply afraid that the cost of it would be that her work would lose its originality in the hands of an editor. But what might have been her other fears?

In her poem, (poem 326, pp. 154–155 in *The Complete Poems of Emily Dickinson,* ed. Thomas H. Johnson, 1960) Dickinson paints a picture at the other end of the spectrum from her actual solitude and the world's disregard: a portrait of a fabulous star, garnering enthusiastic attention from multitudes.

I cannot dance upon my Toes—
No Man instructed me—
But oftentimes, among my mind,
A Glee possesseth me,

That had I Ballet knowledge—
Would put itself abroad
In Pirouette to blanch a Troupe—
Or lay a Prima mad,

And though I had no Gown of Gauze—
No Ringlet, to my Hair,
Nor hopped to Audiences—like Birds,
One Claw upon the Air—

Nor tossed my shape in Eider Balls,
Nor rolled on wheels of snow
Till I was out of sight, in sound,
The House encore me so—

Nor any know I know the Art
I mention-easy-Here—
Nor any Placard boast me—
It's full as Opera—

In a fascinating taped discussion of this poem, Elisa New and several guests examine what it might mean about the poet ("Poetry in America," WGBH, PBS, 2019, Season One, DVD Disc One). The second line ("No Man instructed me") could be heard as ironic or sarcastic; a bitter recrimination against a patriarchal system, in which only men judge the worth of a woman's creative products, and decide whether or not they should be published and made known.

To me the line also contrasts a complicated skill (dancing on one's toes) with magical inspiration (Glee that can take possession of one of one's minds). A skill can be taught by a Man. But no one, man or woman, can teach us to have glee. I am especially appreciative of her phrase "among my mind." I don't know if this is what she means, but I certainly feel that the spirit that sometimes carries me away when I am writing is only one of my minds. My more discerning, judging, whittling mind is another. I try to keep the second quiet while the first reigns.

Dickinson celebrates that gorgeous glee, which doesn't need instruction. It doesn't have to be dressed to the hilt, in eider balls or gauzy gowns. It is beautiful on its own, without any ringlets in its hair. It doesn't need to beg by hopping around a stage like an entreating bird.

I think the richness of Dickinson's imagination and the glory of her glee can be appreciated with or without the recrimination, but it seems likely that the contrast was a deliberate expression of what *was* available, whether or not it was recognized. No one could take away her glee, and the fullness of an internal experience that was as complete as opera. Perhaps we can say that Dickinson was denied some potential joys (satisfaction of the human needs for response and affirmation) but fulfilled in the exercise of her creativity.

Burt and Mikics (2010, p. 270) see Crane's poetic bow to Dickinson as, in part, about "...aesthetic and commercial failures he feared for himself..." I am not sure about the word "failure" here. Did Crane (or Dickinson, or her readers) see her as having failed? We come back to the (unanswerable) question of what she really desired. Personally, I have a more sanguine view of Crane's last lines, where he writes of Dickinson's "harvest." What does he say it needs? More than wit, or even love. It needs "Some reconcilement of remotest mind-." I think of Wallace Stevens' poem, "The Snowman," in which he says that to penetrate the experience of the snowman we must have a mind of winter. To enter into a Dickinsonian line, we must have a mind of Dickinson. Once again I am reminded of the inherent limitations of prose explanations of poetic insights. I can't put into words what a "mind of Dickinson" is. It is an experience, not an idea. But, at least for me, that mind holds a rich potential for glee.

One last note. If Emily Dickinson did yearn for fame, or, at least, acknowledgment of her talent and the worth of her poems, and didn't get much of it (during her lifetime) is this shameful? Is it more shameful the more she yearned and the less she received? I think this attitude is one way our culture has not changed, despite the many years that have transpired. With T.S. Eliot ("Prufrock," 1930) we mock the old who wish the mermaids still sung to them. To save her pride, the child who wanted a toy she can't have may engage in the "sour grapes" excuse that she didn't really want it, after all. But I can see this another way. Isn't it even *more* of a testament to Emily Dickinson's perseverance if she continued to perfect her art, despite getting so little recognition, if she sorely *wanted* to be recognized? Might we see as heroic those who will not be silenced by the world's silence? In his poem, Crane calls Dickinson a dead Silencer, and the editors ponder the meaning of this line. Is it about how she can be intimidating to poets who would follow her example? Or, is it about her enclosure into her own silent internal world? My own variant of these interpretations might be that Dickinson's economical lines contain a wisdom that can't be captured by our explanations. In that sense, they leave us silent.

Prejudice

I have already addressed some poems born from the grief and rage of those who have been targets of prejudice (see section of this chapter on "opening our hearts and homes"). Now I want to explore some sources of the strength to confront it.

"America"-Claude McKay (In: Burt and Mikics, 2010, p. 250)

Although she feeds me bread of bitterness,
And sinks into my throat her tiger's tooth,
Stealing my breath of life, I will confess
I love this cultured hell that tests my youth!
Her vigor flows like tides into my blood,
Giving me strength erect against her hate.
Her bigness sweeps my being like a flood.
Yet as a rebel fronts a king in state,
I stand within her walls with not a shred
Of terror, malice, not a word of jeer.
Darkly I gaze into the days ahead,
And see her might and granite wonders there,
Beneath the touch of time's unerring hand,
Like priceless treasures sinking in the sand.

How does a human being survive a "cultured hell," "...with not a shred/ Of terror, malice, nor a word of jeer."?

Claude McKay's America was the Harlem Renaissance of the 1920's, although he was born in Jamaica. He found work as a waiter in a railroad dining car. Danger lurked everywhere for him as a man of color. Burt and Mikics (2010, p. 250) quote McKay as saying that "We stuck together, some of us armed, going from the railroad station to our quarters. We stayed in our quarters all through the dreary ominous nights, for we never knew what was going to happen."

What, exactly, does McKay love about his America? Does he love *it because* he triumphed over its stringent test? In spite of those tests? Or is it the culture in the "cultured hell" that inspires his love? Surely it is *McKay* that transformed his country's "hate" and "bigness" into his own fierce strength. Does he love America for being the occasion of this transformation? Or simply for her beauty; for the sweep of her vast grandeur? Or is his love born of melancholy foreknowledge that, inevitably, America's wonders had to sink under the weight of its legacy of injustice (which, arguably, explains some of our present moment in 2020)?

The work of Langston Hughes comes to mind.

You and Your Whole Race

You and your whole race.
Look down upon the town in which you live
And be ashamed.
Look down upon white folks
And upon yourselves
And be ashamed
That such supine poverty exists there,
That such stupid ignorance breeds children there,
Behind such humble shelters of despair—
That you yourselves have not the sense to care
Nor the manhood to stand up and say
I dare you to come one step nearer, evil world,
With your hands of greed seeking to touch my
throat, I dare you to come one step nearer me:

When you can say that
you will be free! (In: Bialosky, 2017, p. 29)

Other poets have testified about tensile strength as a product of surviving racism. At the Dodge Poetry Festival in Waterloo, New Jersey (transcripts published by Bill Moyers, 1995) the poet Lucille Clifton (mentioned in several chapters) spoke of her experiences of racism, sexual abuse, profound loss, and other severe trials, and memorably declared that every day something has tried, and failed, to kill her.

Burt and Mikics mention (2010, p. 252) the very different America celebrated in the poem "The New Colossus" by Emma Lazarus, which is etched into the Statue of Liberty in New York harbor (discussed in a previous chapter and a section of this one). What a contrast! "The New Colossus" pictures a country with open arms, inviting the tired and the poor, well aware that its diversity will contribute to its strength. Very different from the bigoted America that feeds McKay "the bread of bitterness/ And sinks into my throat her tiger's tooth,/ Stealing my breath of life..."

Perhaps the clearest picture emerges from flickering from one poem to the others. I think each contributes something about pluck in survivors. Toward that end, I want to refer again to Rita Dove's poem, "Lady Freedom Among Us," (discussed in the previous section along with "The New Collossus." Please see the text of the poem above) because it so vigorously points out our tendency to look away, rather than frontally face, our disparate Americas.

As I indicated in the previous section, Dove, a woman of color, explained that this poem was written when a statue of the Lady Freedom was brought back, after being cleaned, and returned to its place atop the Capitol Building in Washington, DC., in 1993. Dove speaks for the statue, as though she were a homeless human being. In the interview with Moyers (p. 112) Dove expressed her hope that readers of the poem would think more deeply about freedom.

Though these poems were written in different eras, some things about racism and "otherness" in the United States remain unchanged. Personally, I cope best if I let my attention flicker, from the United States of Emma Lazarus to the country loved by Claude McKay, survived by Lucille Clifton, and challenged by Langston Hughes and Rita Dove. For me, the resulting kaleidoscope is the truth, to the extent that there is one at all. Perhaps the greatest challenge is to garner McKay's "strength erect" without succumbing to the poisonous hate Clifton warns us to avoid.

This brings me to think again about some of McKay's lines, in his poem "America," quoted above.

> Yet as a rebel fronts a king in state,
> I stand within her walls with not a shred
> Of terror, malice, not a word of jeer.
> Darkly, I gaze into the days ahead,
> And see her might and granite wonders there,
> Beneath the touch of time's unerring hand,
> Like priceless treasures sinking in the sand.
>
> (In: Burt and Mikics, 2010, p. 250)

Perhaps for McKay there is no need to take up arms, since the "cultured hell" will collapse on its own. Hughes believes shame will teach the greedy, and he will be recognized if he grows strong, and Clifton certainly embodies a life force prevailing over those who would abuse. In these voices I hear some differences in what each poet relies on, with some gathering sustenance from rage and others looking elsewhere. Can our country's "vigor" (McKay) nourish our capacity to have faith in a more fair future? Will "shame" (Hughes) at our inaction become a potent motivator to work toward change? What can protect our souls as we confront abuse, as Clifton reminds us to do? I think the greatest danger to our future was named by Dove. It is the pull to avoid witnessing suffering and "lower our eyes." Elsewhere (2019 p. 166) I referred to a New York Times opinion piece (by Ross Douthat, October 29, 2017, New York Times Sunday Review, p. 9, "The Misery Filter") that described our culture's inclination to focus away from sufferers. We tend to avert our eyes from the hungry child on the subway platform. It can sometimes seem more polite, and, often perhaps, feel as though it will make for a less painful ride *for us*. To me this is our biggest danger, because, like all denial, it allows the unacceptable to be overlooked, and, therefore, tolerated. This is one of the reasons I believe in flickering; keeping one eye on Emma Lazarus's "New Colossus," with its humane ideals, and the other eye on McKay's "tiger tooth/ Stealing my breath of life..," as well as Hughes' "hands of greed seeking to touch my/throat." Holding on to the ideals of the new colossus might help keep me aware of the freedom of my own breathing, and the *contrast* with my brothers and sisters whose free breathing is still inhibited.

When a Child Loses Track

In my mind, juxtaposing Elizabeth Bishop's poem "In the Waiting Room" with George Eliot's "Brother and Sister 7 and 8" yields a fascinating conversation about children baffled by the world as it is constructed by adults. The children in both poems come upon something that doesn't make sense, from their perspective. Each poem asks a question that the other tries to answer.

I looked at Bishop's "In the Waiting Room" in the previous chapter, so I will just quote a few lines to juxtapose them with George Eliot's work. Bishop's poem, which was discussed by the psychoanalyst and poet Henry Seiden, (2016, pp. 22–27) is, in itself, a fascinating study of a child's astonishment, as well as her horror, as she tries to situate herself in the wider world. Here are a few of its lines.

> Without thinking at all
> I was my foolish aunt
> I-we-were falling, falling...
> I knew that nothing stranger
> had ever happened, that nothing
> stranger could ever happen.
> Why should I be my aunt
> Or me, or anyone?

Why am I Person A, and not Person B? What creates an identification, with a gender, or a family, or a place or period of time? What if, in a dissociative moment, I fall away from being Sandra, with my usual descriptors? Why do adults make assumptions that assign labels to people, putting them in separate categories and sticking a name on each file? What if, at a particular moment, my attention wanders and my focus blurs, and sounds get separated from their sources?

Such a blur occurs in the poem by George Eliot (Mary Ann Evans) in her poem "Brother and Sister 7 and 8," reprinted in Burt and Mikics, 2010, pp. 190–191. "Brother and Sister" is a series of sonnets Evans wrote about her childhood with her beloved older brother, Isaac. Later, in their adult lives, Isaac rejected Eliot, refusing all contact with her. According to Burt and Mikics this was in response to learning that Eliot was living with a married man who could not obtain a divorce from his first wife.

But the poem remembers a time when brother and sister went fishing. The little girl, left in charge of the fishing line, momentarily loses focus, dissolved in a dreamy state of mind. As a barge approached her brother shouted for her to rescue the line from the water, but she was off in her own fantasies.

Sudden recognition of the barge snapped her back to a terrified attention. As luck would have it, her lapse was rewarded with a fish, and she received compliments on her skillfulness later at home. Eliot ends the poem with the lesson learned, that "luck was with glory wed." Children assume that glory is supposed to crown good behavior, not irresponsible lapses. While the practical gardener got the story straight, others gave her praise she felt was undeserved, which led her to question some of her basic assumptions about how the world works. As she put it "In secret, though my fortune tasted sweet,/ I wondered why this happiness befell."

Both children lost track. In Bishop's poem the child has "...the sensation of falling off/ the round, turning world/ into cold, blue-black space..." For the child in Eliot's poem "...sky and earth took on a strange new light/ And seemed a dream-world floating on some tide—/ A fair pavilioned boat for me alone/ Bearing me onward through the vast unknown." When the children in both poems let go of the mooring of focused attention, they get swept into an uncanny void. Each child questions something that usually goes unquestioned, in the safety of ordinary daily life. Bishop's child asks something like: How was it determined that I would be Elizabeth, a girl of seven, in a town called Worcester, in a country called the United States of America, in a year called 1918? Eliot's child asks something like: How is it determined that people characterize me as having a certain talent? If the fish hadn't happened to bite the bait, would I still have that talent? Both might ask, if life is really as arbitrary as it seems to me, right now, what can I be sure of?

Presumably, in some sense, both children represent the poets when they were young. So, we can assume they were both greatly talented, precocious, and immersed in imagination, not by accident, but by nature. But in the poems they have yet to find their footing. Each learned that life can snap us to attention with a shock when we dare to dream. Lines of time, place, person, melt. Haze envelops the world, and, then, it may feel arbitrary that

Elizabeth still belongs in 1918, and Mary Ann Evans was not hit by the barge, and came home to be lauded for her dexterity in fishing. Is it safe to dream, or day dream? What else won't make any sense, as time and grown up life unfold?

In Praise of Tolerance

Taken together, Margaret Bruner's poem, "A Plea for Tolerance" and Lucille Clifton's poem, "Sam" make what I think is a convincing argument.

Plea for Tolerance
Margaret E. Bruner (In: S.A. Stuart, Ed., 1996, p. 32)

If we but knew what forces helped to mould
the lives of others from their earliest years—
Knew something of their background, joys and tears,
And whether or not their youth was drear and cold,
Or if some dark belief had taken hold
And kept them shackled, torn with doubts and fears
So long it crushed the force that perseveres
And made their hearts grow prematurely old,—
Then we might judge with wiser, kindlier sight,
And learn to put aside our pride and scorn...
Perhaps no one can ever quite undo
His faults or wholly banish some past blight—
The tolerant mind is purified, reborn,
And lifted upward to a saner view.

I think Bruner's "tolerant mind" is exemplified by the poet, Lucille Clifton, whose work I have discussed in several chapters. Many of her poems deal with her father's sexual abuse of her when she was a child. In an interview with Bill Moyers (1995) she said that, although she very much wants to name what happened, in part to help others name their own experiences, she does not want the abuse to define her, or her father. She wants to be seen as a whole, and to see him as a whole, including the history that helped make him who he was. In Clifton's words, (Moyers, 1995, p. 93)"...I don't want to make the whole judgment because, ultimately, if you fill yourself with venom you will be poisoned, and I don't want to be. I'm a survivor from my heart. I figured that out a long time ago." It sounds to me as though a philosophy not unlike Bruner's plea for tolerance has helped Clifton become a survivor from her heart. Here is Clifton's poem about her father.

Sam (In: Clifton, 2020, p. 135)

if he could have kept
the sky in his dark hand
he would have pulled it down
and held it.
it would have called him lord
as did the skinny women
in Virginia. if he
could have gone to school
he would have learned to write
his story and not lived it.
if he could have done better
he would have. oh stars
and stripes forever,
what did you do to my father?

Along with Clifton, and, in the spirit of Bruner, should we say about anyone, whatever their actions, that if they could have done better they would have?

Inevitable Loss and Inevitable Renewal

In the previous chapter I quoted Frost's poem, "Nothing Gold Can Stay," and discussed how it helps us distinguish between what outlives time and what doesn't. I suggested that becoming reconciled to this difference may help us bear the losses that accompany aging. Here I would like to contrast this poem with one by Tolkien, that emphasizes renewal. Interestingly, the two poems resonate, even using some similar images, but, I think, their underlying insights part company.

Here is Frost's poem, again.

Nothing gold Can Stay

Nature's first green is gold,
Her hardest hue to hold.
Her early leaf's a flower;
But only so an hour.
Then leaf subsides to leaf.
So Eden sank to grief,
So dawn goes down to day,
Nothing gold can stay.

(In: *A Book of Modern American Poetry*, ed. Jane McDermott and Thomas Lowry, 1970, p. 55).

In J.R. R. Tolkien's poem the color gold is also central, but its message is very different. The title of his poem is "All That Is Gold Does Not Glitter" (in Sieghart, 2019, p. 13). Tolkien's optimistic poem heralds the promise of renewal that tomorrow can bring. I hear its message as the opposite of Frost's warnings about the inevitable effects of time. Frost's gold shines in his first line, but it is doomed to yield to green. Tolkien tells us that gold sometimes hides its glitter, passing up chances to shine, but readying for its renaissance. We might be fooled into thinking that losses are permanent when, in reality, they are ephemeral. For Frost, it is the golden glory that is ephemeral. Where Frost sees inevitable decay, Tolkien insists on inevitable renewal. But for both appearances can be deceptive. Frost seems to imagine a reader who wants to believe the early promise of gold will ripen, enriching over time. To that reader, Frost breaks the news that nothing gold can stay. On the other hand, Tolkien's imagined reader is unduly pessimistic. His news is of a joyful resurrection. Tolkien has taken the saying, "All that glitters is not gold," and turned it completely around. More generally, I think he is asking us to question our stock assumptions, but, of course, to do that we first must become aware of them.

In sum, with Frost we lose Eden; with Tolkien we gain heaven. Perhaps each reader gravitates

toward the poem that confirms their outlook on life, but I think that together the two poems make the contrast sharp. Reading both could lead us toward awareness of what we tend to assume or, in the phrase that has always meant a great deal to me personally, contrast teaches.

I see the difference between these two poems as echoed in another pair, Clifton's "Sorrows" and Hirshfield's "Burlap Sack." With life experience do our sorrows gather around us, surrounding us, attaching themselves to us, unalterably changing our lives, so that we are never the same? Or are they a burden we can put down, and reclaim our inherent, ongoing selves? I discussed these two poems in a previous chapter, but will quote them here to briefly connect their differences with the Frost/ Tolkien dialogue.

Sorrows

who would believe them winged
who would believe they could be

beautiful who would believe
they could fall so in love with mortals

that they would attach themselves
as scars attach and ride the skin

sometimes we hear them in our dreams
rattling their skulls clicking their bony fingers

envying our crackling hair
our spice filled flesh

they have heard me beseeching
as I whispered into my own

cupped hands enough not me again
enough but who can distinguish

one human voice
amid such choruses of desire

(In: Clifton, 2020, p. 216)

In this poem by Lucille Clifton, we helplessly host our sorrows. They love
us too much to let go of us.

Granted, they may be beautiful. But we still protest their unwelcome, parasitic presence. To no avail.

Here is a poem, by Jane Hirshfield, with a different point of view.

Burlap Sack

A person is full of sorrow
the way a burlap sack is full of stones or sand.
We say, "Hand me the sack,"
but we get the weight.
Heavier if left out in the rain.
To think that the sand or stones are the self is an error.
To think that grief is the self is an error.
Self carries grief as a pack mule carries the side bags,
being careful between the trees to leave extra room.
The mule is not the load of ropes and nails and axes.
The self is not the miner nor builder nor driver.
What would it be to take the bride
and leave behind the heavy dowry?
To let the thin-ribbed mule browse the tall grasses,
its long ears waggling like the tails of two happy dogs?

(In: Sieghart, 2019, p. 29)

Jane Hirshfield's poem, "Burlap Sack," paints a different picture of the relationship between our sorrows and our selves. They are luggage. They should be carefully carried, but eventually dropped, to reclaim our freedom to meander unencumbered. While in Clifton's standoff, I don't hear any possibility of a return to a pre-suffering self, for Hirshfield, that is exactly the desired, and accessible outcome.

Frost sees us on a pre-determined, one way path. In "Nothing Gold Can Stay" green can't go back to being gold. It is forever changed, by a force that brooks no opposition. Clifton's sorrows are also undeterred, no matter how hard she beseeches. There is no room for mercy. No one is tallying how much grief she has already endured, and commuting her sentence.

With Tolkien it is possible for us to go in reverse. Magic happens. Deep roots have just hibernated, but Spring brings them back to life. They hide from the frost, but are not permanently damaged by it. Similarly, in my understanding, Hirshfield sees us as able to emerge from grief, take up from where we left off, and reclaim our lives. Our selves are not irretrievably lost, or permanently damaged. They have had to shoulder a weighty burden, but, in time, they will be able to put it down.

Some of us see life through Frost's and Clifton's perspective. Others are more persuaded by the Tolkien/Hirshfield point of view. I don't think either is right or wrong, nor do I believe that we can entirely consciously choose to adhere to one or the other. Our lives tilt us, often predisposing us to confirm our underlying (generally non-conscious) beliefs. But I do think it is possible to recognize that both outlooks exist, and one way to achieve that recognition is by reading these poems, that themselves have been forged from differing life experiences.

4.

Let Be: Dialogues With Hamlet[*]

———∽∼∽———

I read Shakespeare's *Hamlet* as, among so many other things, a beautiful reflection on what it is like to be in mourning. Hamlet, that exquisitely self-reflective man, is ever curious about life, death, and, perhaps most of all, himself. He asks fundamental questions, about whether life is worth living; what we owe to parents; what happens after we die; how can we know a feeling, perception, or experience, is real; and above all, what are his own real motivations, absent of actions.

The question of what is real is a significant leitmotif in the play. Is Hamlet's madness real or feigned for the purpose of disguise? Are the Player King's feelings real when he enacts a scene about Hecuba's grief for her husband? Is Hamlet's intense sorrow for his father real, even though he doesn't carry out the ghost's commands? Is the ghost a real ghost? Do the people really approve of Claudius's marriage to Gertrude, and joyfully celebrate his coronation?

Hamlet raises questions each one of us confronts. Whoever we are, whatever our situation, we likely face losses, crises of faith, questions about our purpose, and doubts about our perceptions. No one has "solutions," but, like Shakespeare, there are poets who have found evocative ways to comment on the dilemmas facing human beings. I think there is a form of clarity

---

[*]   All line references are to Arden Shakespeare, "Hamlet," London: Bloomsbury, 2016.

that can come from "cross pollinating" some of these reflections. I believe that putting lines from *Hamlet* next to lines from Rainer Marie Rilke, or Emily Dickinson, can bring out aspects of what each is, and is not saying. Dialogue and contrast are fundamental to self—understanding. For example, as adolescents we find out who we are partly by discovering who we are not. As parents when we "set an example" we can hope that our children will use it as a model, but also differ with it in their own ways, as they evolve. My shorthand for this process is that contrast teaches. What might we hear when we listen to both Shakespeare and Mary Oliver, as they reflect on loss? How might the thoughts of each highlight the insights of the other?

"I Have That Within Which Passeth Show"

In the first scene of the play we see the guards at Elsinore confronting the ghost of the dead King Hamlet. Hamlet's friend, Horatio, at first skeptical about the ghost's existence, encounters the ghost and, with the guards, determines to tell the young Hamlet about this strange occurrence.

The second scene opens with the dead King Hamlet's brother, Claudius, and widow, Gertrude, celebrating their marriage, within a month of the old King's death. In this scene Hamlet's ongoing mourning over the death of his father is challenged by Gertrude and Claudius. They question his "show" of grief. Hamlet answers that it is not a show, but genuine feeling.[†]

> Queen: Good Hamlet, cast thy nighted colour off,
> And let thine eye look like a friend on Denmark.
> Do not for ever with thy vailed lids
> Seek for thy noble father in the dust:

---

† * All line references are to Arden Shakespeare, "Hamlet," London: Bloomsbury, 2016.

Thou know'st 'tis common,—all that live must die,
Passing through nature to eternity.
Hamlet: Ay, madam, it is common.
Queen: Why seems it so particular with thee?
Hamlet: Seems, madam! nay, it is; I know not 'seems.'
'Tis not alone my inky cloak, good mother,
Nor customary suits of solemn black,
Nor windy suspiration of forced breath,
No, nor the fruitful river in the eye,
Nor the dejected havior of the visage,
Together with all forms, moods, shows of grief,
That can denote me truly: these indeed, seem,
For they are actions that a man might play:
But I have that within which passeth show;
These but the trappings and the suits of woe.

Act I, Sc. 2, lines 68–86*

Of course, the queen's advice is monumentally self-serving. She and her new husband want her son, Hamlet, to move quickly past mourning his father's recent death. Their hasty marriage has made Claudius the new king, and they want this accession to be celebrated. The king and queen are eager for Hamlet to cease his "displays" of a grief that is inconvenient to them. Hamlet protests that this is not mere display. But, aside from the queen's ulterior motives, isn't she making the case for a time limited Stoic grief that was (and, to some extent, still is) a popular way of understanding the "healthiest" way to mourn? Gertrude's new husband states their position even more forcefully.

King: 'Tis sweet and commendable in your nature, Hamlet,
To give these mourning duties to your father:

But, you must know, your father lost a father
That father lost, lost his; and the survivor bound,
In filial obligation, for some term
To do obsequious sorrow; but to persevere
In obstinate condolement, is a course
Of impious stubbornness: 'tis unmanly grief:
It shows a will most incorrect to heaven;
A heart unfortified, a mind impatient;
An understanding simple and unschool'd:
For what we know must be, and is as common,
As any the most vulgar thing to sense...

(Act I, Sc. 2, lines 87–100)

Claudius has taken Gertrude's mild criticism of Hamlet's behavior much further, declaring it as stemming from stubbornness and flaws of mind and heart. But then he turns the knife even more, describing Hamlet's behavior as an affront to heaven, nature, and reason, and a "fault against the dead" (line 102). The king makes Hamlet's profound love and sense of loss into its opposite!

In several ways Shakespeare indicates Hamlet's profound isolation in his mourning. In Quarto 2 he enters the scene alone, separated from the king and queen. And, unlike them, he wears mourning clothes (Arden, 2016, p. 195, footnote). The scene confirms visually what his words express. He, alone, continues to mourn the sudden death of his father. The king implies that, since God ordained the death, it is impious for Hamlet to protest it. In time we will understand the self-serving nature of Claudius's position. But it introduces several of the play's central themes: the process of mourning, the question of what is ordained by God or fate, and, consequently, what is within our control, and, therefore, a matter of personal responsibility.

The idea that God ordains death, so it is impious to oppose his will by protesting it, is the subject of an interesting poem, written centuries later, by Ralph Waldo Emerson (In: S.A. Stuart, 1996, pp. 7–8). Appropriately enough, its title is "Terminus." I quoted it in Chapter Three. Please see the text there.

According to this thinking, it is our duty to accept death as God's will. Claudius accuses Hamlet of flouting God's authority by continuing to show sorrow. This isolates Hamlet in several senses. Not only is he alone in outwardly (and inwardly) expressing mourning, but, implicitly, he is branded as impious; as separating himself from proper religious observance. In the film of the play, directed by Kenneth Branaugh, Hamlet appeared in black, a stark contrast with the rest of the characters who were wearing bright colors and celebrating the union of Gertrude and Claudius. To me, Hamlet looked like an outcast and not just a solitary man. Immediately we see that Hamlet is not just in a state of mourning, but in a mourning colored by intense psychological isolation. I am reminded of how cultures shape rituals to give mourners connection with others who are also grieving. Elsewhere (2004, 2008, 2015) I have addressed how isolation can profoundly intensify sorrow. Normally, memorials bring us together with others who feel some of the same feelings we are enduring (even though the loss may have different meanings for each of us). But here, Hamlet is made aware that no one shares his state of mind. In her posthumously published paper, "On loneliness," the psychoanalyst, Frieda Fromm-Reichmann (1959) emphasized the lack of hope of connection as differentiating painful loneliness from potentially beneficial or benign states of aloneness.

This difference is highlighted in Act II, Sc. 2, line 484, just before Hamlet's soliloquy ("O, what a rogue and peasant slave am I!"). The Players and Rosencrantz and Guildenstern have exited, and Hamlet says, with evident relief, "Now I am alone." Hamlet, that most observed observer, is hardly ever alone, even when he might think he is. He is spied upon, plotted against, "sifted," in Claudius's term for it (Act II, Sc. 2, line 58). But, though rarely alone, he is emotionally virtually isolated. Horatio remains loyal but Ophelia, Rosencrantz, and Guildenstern join Claudius, Polonius, and even his mother, Gertrude, to trap him. In Hamlet we see the irony of a man unable to escape the company of others and, at the same time, almost entirely bereft of trustworthy human connection. I suggest that his acute isolation and sorrow exponentially augment each other.

Claudius added another argument against Hamlet's mourning: (Act I, Sc. 2, lines 106–108).

...We pray you throw to earth
This unprevailing woe, and think of us
As of a father....

I hear Claudius as implying that Hamlet's sorrow is useless, since it will have no constructive effect, so he should stop expressing it. This subtly conveys that feelings are only legitimate when they have practical consequences. Further, Hamlet should not be in grief, for he has gained a father, in Claudius, which makes up for the father he has lost. It is as though people can be replaced, like inanimate objects. One father is just as good as any other. Why grieve, when you now have a live father to take the place of the dead one? I return to this theme below.

In short, I think it is possible to view Hamlet as isolated in his grieving, and vilified for it, which would be likely to intensify its pain, and then accused of being profane, on the basis of that very intensity.

Even if Hamlet were not surrounded with spies and schemers, grief is inherently isolating. We are alone in our moments of greatest sorrow because we bring our whole history of suffering to each new grief. Thus, when someone says "I feel your pain" they may be trying to comfort, but it is not true, at least as I see it. No one can feel my pain as I do, because no one has experienced all the previous hurts that (consciously or non-consciously) accompany my present sorrow. Each of us has a personal history of loss, an internal relationship with it, built over all the years of our lives, just as we have a personal history of love, and other human feelings. While I am not going to attempt to write the story of Hamlet's childhood, (and my field, psychoanalysis, has been justly criticized for such attempts, as Levin, 2002, reminds us) I do presume that Hamlet, who is thirty years old when the play begins, has known some moments of acute and painful loss before this point. I believe they are still alive in him, in some form, and color the impact of the events that take place in the play. In that sense we are all "haunted" by our previous life experience.

So Hamlet is isolated in several senses. Many around him are plotting against him. He can't trust that a conversation is private, or that he is not being "sifted." His emotional state is described in castigating terms. And, internally, his grief is, itself isolating, since no one, not even the most sympathetic friend, can fully know what it feels like to Hamlet to lose his father, and to suffer all the other losses of hopes (of the crown) and beliefs (about his mother, and others) that set the action of the play in motion. Severe loss can carry any of us to an emotionally remote "island," that is, in some psychological sense, unreachable by even the most empathic other. The isolation of extreme suffering is expressed in W.H. Auden's unforgettable poem, "Musee des Beaux Arts" (in W. H. Auden, *Collected Poems*, Ed E. Mendelson, 1991, p. 179). I have thought about this poem for years. To me, it captures a truth about life more clearly than any other work of art I know. (Please see the text of the poem in Chapter Two).

The tragedy that abruptly ends life as we have known it may not be an important failure to anyone else. Within a month of the old king's death, Claudius and Gertrude have created a new covenant with Denmark and with each other. Claudius cleverly positions this compact as already ratified by the people (Act I, Sc.2) and commands, entices, bullies, shames Hamlet to join the party. He proclaims Hamlet the heir apparent, (line 109) making it clear that his "son" has only to get on board to have every ambition fulfilled in the future. We can imagine that he has used similar seductive tactics with Gertrude.

The interplay in Act I, Sc. 2 raises age-old questions about mourning. Is there a "normal" duration for inwardly accepting loss and outwardly expressing grief? Can there be any standards for "appropriate" sorrow? Are there any (timeless, cross cultural) generalizations that hold? Or should we say every loss is its own country, so to speak?

We can expand this issue to raise the broader question of the relationship between all intense emotions and health. Hamlet, himself, has something to say on the matter, in his praise for his friend Horatio's equanimity.

> Hamlet: ...For thou hast been
> As one in suffering all that suffers nothing—
> A man that Fortune's buffets and rewards
> Hast ta'en with equal thanks. And blest are those
> Whose blood and judgement are so well co-meddled
> That they are not a pipe for Fortune's finger
> To sound what stop she please. Give me that man
> That is not passion's slave and I will wear him
> In my heart's core—ay, in my heart of heart—
> As I do thee...
>
> (Act III, Sc.2, lines 61–70)

Hamlet's appreciation of Horatio's even keeled acceptance of all emotional visitations is echoed in a poem by Rumi, translated by Coleman Barks.

The Guest House

This being human is a guest house.
Every morning a new arrival.

A joy, a depression, a meanness,
some momentary awareness comes
as an unexpected visitor.

Welcome and entertain them all!
Even if they're a crowd of sorrows,
who violently sweep your house
empty of its furniture,
still, treat each guest honorably.
He may be clearing you out
for some new delight.

The dark thought, the shame, the malice,
meet them at the door laughing,
and invite them in.

Be grateful for whoever comes,
because each has been sent
as a guide from beyond.

(In: Sieghart, 2019, p. 93)

This poem reminds me of the (emotion theory, Izard, 1977) idea that all feelings carry potentially valuable information. When Rumi says that, no matter how badly behaved, each visiting feeling, "...may be clearing you out/ for some new delight," the poet suggests that the functions an emotion can serve are not always immediately evident, but we should assume they may exist. This anticipates the thrust of much of emotion theory (Izard, 1977; Buechler, 1995). It is an attitude that privileges the curiosity that is championed by clinicians (Stern, 1990; Buechler, 2004). Curiosity about his reactions is also a hallmark of Hamlet's incessant self-scrutiny. Since Rumi assumes that feelings carry potential information, he proposes that we welcome them all, rather than discriminate between those that present pleasantly versus those that don't. Hamlet praises Horatio's ability to accommodate all his emotional experiences. Horatio's "guest house" has a strong foundation, capable of withstanding all of Nature's onslaughts. His heart and head retain (or ably regain) balance. Interestingly Horatio (but, I suggest, not Hamlet) can face *almost* any misery without being fatally "tainted." This is precisely what the Ghost will ask Hamlet to do, as we shall see. I believe that Hamlet is unable to remain "untainted," but Horatio is capable of it, at least until his "sweet prince" is about to die. Then, even Horatio is ready to capitulate to sorrow, until Hamlet's dying request stops him from committing suicide.

Among the things I treasure about *Hamlet* are its nuanced portraits of grief. Hamlet, Laertes, and Ophelia bear the sudden losses of their fathers in strikingly different ways. As Claudius remarks, (Act IV, Sc.5, line 75) Ophelia's madness expresses grief's "poison" (though we find out she grieves for more than just the loss of her father). She can't bear that, as she sings, he "never will come again." A footnote (Arden, 2016, p. 419) explains the subsequent lyric "And we cast away moan" as meaning we waste our mourning. Perhaps it expresses that Ophelia's grief is "too deep for tears," as Wordsworth wrote in his poem "Ode: Intimations of Immortality from Recollections of Early Childhood" (In: *A Treasury of Great Poems: English and American*, 1995, Ed. Louis Untermeyer, pp. 654–658). In any case, Ophelia is driven mad and takes her own life which, in Shakespeare's time, was prohibited (as discussed below). Thus, the "poison" of grief can tempt us to commit the "sin" of suicide.

When her brother, Laertes, learns of Ophelia's suicide, he forbids himself to cry, but is overcome with tears:

Laertes: Too much of water hast thou, poor Ophelia,
And therefore I forbid my tears. But yet
It is our trick; nature her custom holds,
Let shame say what it will. When these are gone,
The woman will be out.— (Act IV, Sc. 7, lines 183–188)

I am reminded of King Lear's self-reproaches, as he (Act II, Sc. 2) forbade himself women's weapons, water drops. Aside from the gendered assumptions about how grief should be expressed, it is also clear that there are dangers in how it is experienced. In Shakespeare's world religion, culture, and the law forbade and actually criminalized suicide, which makes it understandable that grief is viewed with trepidation. Tears signal having "given in" to a dangerous (and womanly) weakness.

While the current climate may be less judgmental and stereotyping about crying, I think there is still a basic value placed on bearing loss with restrained fortitude. Many still laud the contained response to sorrow. Elsewhere (2015) I have discussed short stories and other literature in this vein. For example, in a marvelous story whose title gives away its basic premise, "The Management of Grief," by Bharati Mukherjee, (1992) a mother is lauded for being "strong" as she reacts to the death of her husband and two sons in a plane crash. Internally she feels like a freak, because of her terrible, senseless calm.

Where are the lines separating a clearly judgmental prohibition against tearful expressions, vs. a glorifying approval of "well contained" grief, and vs. a compassionate effort to help the mourner access the strength to go on ? Along with Joan Didion ("The Year of Magical Thinking," 2005) I see our culture as especially judgmental when grief has an impact on cognitive functioning. In her memoir about the sudden death of her husband, Didion recounts how she couldn't get rid of his shoes, because she felt he might come back one day and need them. Didion is making the point that extreme grief can elicit "magical thinking" in someone who generally has a firm grip on reality.

While most of us don't forbid ourselves tears, or judge others who cry at funerals, I think we still expect our "reality testing" minds to be unaffected. Didion's decision to keep her dead husband's shoes would raise some eyebrows among my psychoanalytic colleagues, as well as outside these circles. Below, I take further the challenge of defining mourning without gendered or moralizing generalizations. Loss is woven into human experience. How can we approach it as part of our lives, without seeing it as an adversary to be conquered, a temptation to be overcome, or a test of our psychic strength or cognitive soundness, or moral fiber?

The poet Mary Oliver wrote a beautiful poem that I think models gracefully integrating loss into the fabric of our life experience. Her poem, "Blackwater Woods" (In: A. Holden and B. Holden, 2014, pp. 231–232) is discussed at length in chapter 3. Briefly, Oliver advises us that relinquishing is part of living. When the time comes, we must be able to "let go" of the beloved.

Mary Oliver tells us to "let it go." Hamlet tells Horatio to "let be." In my reading, neither is telling us what to value, or what we may, or may not feel as we let (it) go. Oliver explicitly frames the essential challenge: invest those you cherish with all the love that is within you, and let go of them when you must. I don't hear a loss of tenderness in the ending. Nor does she tell us to be meek, or fierce. She is not prescribing or proscribing our emotions as we let go. Hamlet's "let be" has other nuances, that I explore shortly.

While we may explain it in different ways, there are aspects of the pain of being human that are familiar to us all. I believe that some sorrows strip us of parts of ourselves. For example, if my dear friend Ben dies, an aspect of myself may also perish. Let's say Ben was the only person on earth who cherished a particular brand of my humor. Just a wink would be all we would need to burst into gales of laughter that left everyone else baffled. Maybe someday I will share this mirth with someone else. Maybe not. But, at least, not for now. That part of me is gone, along with my loss of his grin. How can we bear this heavy double loss?

More than once the poet Rilke has served as my guide when I have navigated losses. He recommends penetrating deep into their territory. One of his many prescriptions advises us that our instinct should not be to desire consolation over a loss but rather to develop the curiosity to explore our losses completely, and to experience the peculiarity, the singularity, and the effects on our lives of each specific loss (in Baer, 2005, p. 109). But, I wonder, does Rilke understand what he is asking of me? Has he fathomed what it can mean to "explore this loss completely"? How can I sufficiently believe I have the strength to come out of it alive? I am reminded of the many myths and stories that center on journeys to a netherworld and back. Perhaps what they can tell us is that penetrating the "singularity" of a profound loss requires great faith.

For Hamlet, life has become a "sterile promontory" (Act II, Sc. 2, line 265). His is a complicated, angry, *emotionally* isolated, (though *surrounded* by observers) grief that constantly examines itself. Laertes' grief for his father and sister is effusive, and full of rage and thirst for vengeance. All three sorrow, but in somewhat different ways. In depicting these differences, Shakespeare has held the mirror up to Nature, as Hamlet recommends to the Players (in Act III, Sc. 2). While sadness is central in mourning, we each add a personal stamp, or what I have elsewhere (2008) called a signature style of grief. And within an individual's life, every loss carries its own meaning, which (at some level) is colored by all previous losses.

Laertes and Ophelia didn't just lose "a" father. They lost Polonius, a particular father. And Hamlet lost a unique man he clearly loved and deeply respected. Claudius and Gertrude take away the *specificity* of loss when they reduce it to the commonality of fathers dying. I am very aware that in "Oedipal" and other theories, my psychoanalytic colleagues can sound a similar reductionistic note. I hope I am not committing the same error by saying that, from my point of view, the generations *do* face a built in challenge, but it is usually not that the offspring want to kill one parent and marry the other.

Rather, it is about sorrow. One generation is reaching the peak of active life, while the older generation is moving past that stage. Fortunately, most of us don't have fathers who are murdered, but we all have (or have had) fathers and mothers who are growing older. However well our parents negotiate aging, the press of time is felt. Shakespeare has "held the mirror up" to our varying attitudes. Some of us just can't bear life's inherent tragedies, while others bear them in a sorrow spiked with anger; and still others with a hyper-conscious, relentless, self-questioning grief. To my mind, what Hamlet and Oedipus have in common has nothing to do with sexual Oedipal interpretations. It is their dogged pursuit of consciousness and the truth, regardless of where it leads.

A poem by Sherman Alexie (In: Seiden, 2016, pp. 1–2, and discussed in full in chapter three above) pivots around a contest between remaining constantly consciously aware of loss versus, even briefly, letting go of that awareness. The persona in it wants to tell his father a funny story, so he conveniently "forgets" that his father died almost a year ago. The forces against forgetting mete out severe punishment for this infringement. This poem highlights how our willful "forgetting" may interfere in integrating loss into the fabric of our experience. It creates a picture of a clash. It is as though the wish

("if only he were still alive") evolves into a lapse in remembering he is dead. The persona's apologetic tone, in acknowledging the lapse, and the punishment that comes at the end of the poem, suggest that indulging in wishful thinking can have a severe price. In a similar fashion, has wanting to see his father slipped Hamlet into an illusion (or delusion) with tragic consequences?

We might see ourselves as needing to grieve in a way that feels real and commensurate with the depth of our love for the deceased. This need is movingly expressed in a long poem by C. K. Williams, entitled "Grief" (In: K. Young, 2010, pp. 123–126). I quote a small portion of it. After the poet describes the gruesome torture endured by "Dossie" at the hands of modern medicine, he asks (p. 124) himself:

But still, is this grief: waking too early, tiring too quickly, distracted, impatient abrupt, but still waking, still thinking and working; is this what grief is, is this pain enough? I go to the mirror: someone who might once have felt something merely regards me, eyes telling nothing, mouth saying nothing, nothing reflected but the things of the world, nothing told not of any week's, no, already ten days now, any ten days' normal doings. Shouldn't the face evidence anguish, shouldn't its loving sadness and loss be revealed? Ineffable, vague, elusive, uncertain, distracted: shouldn't grief have a form of its own, and shouldn't mind know past its moment of vague, uncertain distraction the sureness of sorrow; shouldn't soul flinch as we're taught proper souls are supposed to, in reverence and fear? Shouldn't grief be pure and complete, reshaping the world in itself, in grief for itself?

Like Hamlet, C. K. Williams separates the "trappings" from the part of grief that "passeth show." But he is focused on their *resonance* with each other. For him, grief is questionably real unless its *outward visage accurately mirrors the depth of the loss*. In a subtly ironic sense, this heart-wrenching poem can leave no doubt about how keenly the poet feels his grief.

The idea that the "outward visage" should match the depth of the loss is echoed by Hamlet himself, in the "gravedigger" scene (Act V, Sc. 1, lines 243–246) of Ophelia's burial. Hamlet is offended by Laertes' extreme expression of grief:

> What is he whose grief
> Bears such an emphasis, whose phrase of sorrow
> Conjures the wandering stars and makes them stand
> Like wonder-wounded hearers?...

It is as though the "quantity" of grief should equal the "quantity" of love, and the outward expression should accurately represent the felt experience. C.K. Williams and Shakespeare are reflecting time honored popular assumptions that don't conform to real life, at least as I know it. Profoundly felt mourning can look any number of ways, from frozen silence, to adolescent acting out, to isolation, and so on. But Shakespeare *is* holding the mirror up to life, in the sense that people *expect* themselves to look more distressed, the more society categorizes the loss they have had as major. This often leads to shame, guilt, regret, and confusion. As Williams so beautifully portrays, the mourner can feel their behavior, and even their inner emotions, don't adequately represent what they "should" feel. Grief for someone we have truly cherished should be "pure" and utterly shatter us, or else we are insufficient in some way. We didn't love the departed enough; we are cold and unfeeling. But, at the other extreme, those overwhelmed by grief may be accused of exaggeration, attention-seeking, hysteria, over-dramatization.

Hamlet suggests that Laertes' grief is a form of competition with *him*. It is almost a reversal of the first scene, in which Claudius accuses Hamlet of "unmanly grief." I think Shakespeare is accurately representing the very common assumption that for sorrow to be legitimate it must be deserved, by virtue of the loss being substantial. We are allowed and expected to grieve (up to a point) about the death of a close relative or life partner. We are supposed to get the proportions "right," as though our emotional life is a cake that could be marred by too much or too little flour.

The vital issue raised by C.K. Williams is the notion of "pure" grief. To be feeling "pure" enough grief, are we barred from feeling anything else? Marie Howe so beautifully counters that idea in her poem about the death of her brother, Johnny, who, in reality, died of AIDS. Its title is "What the Living Do," and I quoted it in Chapters One and Two. Please see the text there.

Is Howe's grief not "pure" enough, because she also exults in being alive? I think *Hamlet* comments on this question in fascinating ways. At the beginning of the play, Claudius excuses his hasty marriage with Gertrude, less than two months after the death of her husband. He says that they have married

...as 'twere with a defeated joy,
With one auspicious and one dropping eye,
With mirth in funeral and with dirge in marriage,
In equal scale weighing delight and dole...
(Act I, Sc. 2, lines 9–13)

Of course, we learn that his position is self-serving, and there are many reasons why his grief would not qualify as "pure," in any sense. But Shakespeare, Howe, C.K. Williams, and so many others, reflect a fundamental dilemma that touches us all: is there anything we can know about how a human being can bear genuine grief as part, but not the whole, of an experience? We know (or come to know) that Claudius is merely being glib. He is trying to paper over the rush to marry Gertrude and establish his own right to the king's crown, lest Hamlet try to assert a claim to it. Hamlet is morally offended by the speed. He sees it as calling into question how much his father was truly venerated by the people and loved and respected by his mother. In this situation we know (or come to know) that Claudius is using words to manipulate opinions and achieve his self-interested goals. But, for me, it raises a very real question: can we genuinely have "one auspicious and one dropping eye"? Should we be suspicious of Howe's grief for her brother, or C.K. Williams' grief for Dossie, because that is not the only thing they feel? Isn't that actually how we all have to survive, at times, cherishing the laughter of a two year old child (for example) as we also genuinely grieve the death of her grandmother? Personally, I don't accept that the "auspicious" eye belies the "dropping eye." I think both can be heartfelt.

We could say that the more the "auspicious" eye dominates over the "dropping" eye, the more suspicious we become that the grief is not heartfelt. If self -interest is the strongest motive, how genuine was the love of the deceased? The footnote (Arden, 2016, p. 196) to the line (above) "In equal scale weighing delight and dole" reads "balancing joy against an equivalent quantity of sorrow." I think this could sound reasonable at this early point in the drama (if the reader/viewer didn't already know that Claudius murdered the old king, to steal his crown and queen). But, especially in emotionally trying times, it can be hard to feel clear when the balance is acceptable, and when it tilts too much toward a self-centeredness that belies the presence of true love and grief.

To illustrate the self-centered end of the continuum, nothing could be clearer than a delicious poem by Wendy Cope, titled "My Funeral" (in Sieghart, 2019, p. 167). Its sing-song beat is matched by its frank tone and irrepressible humor. Cope satirizes displays of sorrow that are not only marred by obvious self—interest, but actually motivated more by vanity than genuine love and pain. In her poem Cope is orchestrating her own funeral in advance, since she won't be there to control the actual event. She exhorts her friends to restrain themselves from preening at the service. In their remembrances, no one should exceed their time limit. No one should use the occasion as an opportunity to show off. Cope jabs at exaggerated displays of ostentatious grief.

As already noted, later in the play, Hamlet criticizes Laertes for what he sees as his extravagant display of grief over Ophelia's death. It can be hard to express grief in a way that adequately, but not excessively, communicates genuine love and loss. Perhaps Wendy Cope exaggerated her point, but it is true that too much concern for oneself can make mourning, and the love that underlies it, feel like a performance. Should the mourner cease to care how they *look* to others, to prove that their love and grief are genuine? Is it acceptable to still care about the quality of one's ongoing life, but not about one's appearance? Or, to be a genuine expression of love and loss, should the "dropping" eye stand out much more than the "auspicious" one (though, of course, this can't seem, or be contrived)? We are, in a sense, back to the distinction Hamlet makes in Act I Sc. 2, where he claims that one can "show" grief in many outward forms, but his is a grief "passing show." And, presumably, when grief "passeth show" it is an expression of true, pure love.

Hamlet objects to both extremes: Laertes' *intense* grief, and Claudius's and Gertrude's *insufficient* response to the old king's death. He is never more vitriolic than in his rebukes of his mother's all too brief mourning of the death of his father. To him, the speed of her marriage (and the possibility that she was having an affair even before old Hamlet died) call into question the sincerity of her love. Caustically, in scene after scene, he portrays her as a faithless hypocrite.

> Hamlet: O God, a beast that wants discourse of reason
> Would have mourned longer-married with my uncle,

My father's brother (but no more like my father
Than I to Hercules). Within a month,
Ere yet the salt of most unrighteous tears
Had left the flushing in her galled eyes,
She married. O most wicked speed!...
(Act I, Sc. 2, lines 150–156)

Hamlet's condemnations of his mother only get harsher in the "closet"
scene (Act III, Sc. 4) where he catalogues the evidence of her faithlessness
and asks (line 79) "O shame, where is thy blush?" It is interesting to reflect
on portrayals of the mourning process in this play. At the start, Hamlet's
lingering grief is called into question by his duplicitous uncle. And Hamlet
rages against Laertes' dramatic display of his grief for his sister in the
"gravedigger" scene. I imagine an audience forming its own conclusions
about "appropriate" and "inappropriate" mourning, while watching each
of these scenes. No matter how much we may believe in refraining from
judging, no matter how deeply we feel that each loss is unique, and the level
of pain of the bereaved can't be measured or prescribed, I think most people
do form judgments, even while watching a play. However vague "standards"
may be, most will have a sense that a month *is* a short period to grieve the
loss of a husband. Hamlet's questioning of the depth of his mother's love for
his father, given the speed of her re-marriage, probably would make sense to
most and, I think, allows us to empathize with him (whatever else we feel
about the many instances of his outrageous behavior).

Clearly, there can't be an "objective" standard for the expression of loss.
No specifiable "outward show" proves that the departed was truly loved. But
mourners are often judged, and often do judge themselves, as to whether
their grief is commensurate with the love they profess they had for the
departed. I come back to this issue several times, but here I just want to
mention the poet Elizabeth Jennings who (bravely) declares that she is not

being a traitor when, despite her loss, she still wants to celebrate life. Her poem, titled "Into the Hour," (In: Sieghart, 2019, p. 169) takes us to the point when grieving is giving way to a "white" healing. Jennings lets grief's ghosts inhabit corners, while her room fills with sunlight and budding life. There is no self-recrimination in this poem, but, perhaps, a concern that her lightening spirit might be misunderstood by others.

The wisdom, self-acceptance, and sheer kindness in this poem are stunning. Like Marie Howe, in the poem "What the Living Do," (mentioned above) Jennings can conceive of herself as mourning but not *just* mourning. She doesn't have to ask the meaning of this. It does not have to call the validity of her love into question. Grief is not gone, but it has changed. It is a scar, not an open wound. Jennings is able to watch sunlight scare ghosts into corners, without having to follow them there. She accepts that her understanding may lag behind her feelings. I think it takes faith in herself to do that. We have to believe that hearing the singing of the summer grass should not be taken as evidence of a betrayal of the departed. Words might distort, so it is better to trust holding hands. This is a mourning more commensurate with Hamlet's late expression "let be" than his state throughout most of the play. It shows an acceptance of rhythms that are beyond cognitive comprehension until well after the emotional "hour of white healing." Hamlet can no more offer this loving acceptance to his mother than he can extend it to himself, until he comes to the realization that, at most junctures of life, "the readiness is all" (Act V, Sc. 2, line 200). At that point Hamlet has the capacity to follow Rilke's advice when he tells the young poet to "let life happen to you. Believe me: life is right, in any case" (1934, p. 74).

Aside from the question of the meaning of Gertrude's behavior, Shakespeare's conception of true love in this play would make a fascinating study. In the "gravedigger" scene (Act V, Sc.1) Hamlet declares that his love for Ophelia was many times the love her brother, Laertes, could have had for her. How are we to hear this declaration? And what are we to make of Claudius's question to Laertes (Act IV, Sc. 7, lines 105–107):

> Laertes, was your father dear to you?
> Or are you like the painting of a sorrow,
> A face without a heart?

Ironically, Claudius is echoing Hamlet's comments (Act I, Sc. 2) that contrasted the outward show of grief with genuinely felt emotions. And then, (Act IV, Sc. 7, lines 109–111) Claudius makes some striking comments about love:

> ...love is begun by time
> And that I see in passages of proof
> Time qualifies the spark and fire of it.

This strikes me as so unlike the view of love that Shakespeare expressed in his sonnets, notably Sonnet 116, in which he declared "Love's not Time's fool" and "Love alters not with his brief hours and weeks,/ But bears it out even to the edge of doom" (Vendler, 1997, p. 487). Are we to hear Claudius's lines as commentary on his cynicism, or as an expression of the failure of his own love to last over time, or, merely, as words designed to have a desired effect on Laertes?

While I don't differ with Levin's (2002) point that Laertes is Hamlet's central foil, in that he functions to bring out Hamlet's character by contrasting with it, I would also argue that Claudius plays a similar role, at some points in the play, such as this point, in Act IV, Sc. 7, when Claudius is bent on gaining Laertes' collaboration in Hamlet's murder. I am not suggesting that this is Claudius's formal role in the play, but only that he clarifies Hamlet's character by being so different from it. Claudius is a schemer, a manipulator, using words as tools whereas, by Claudius's own admission, Hamlet is "remiss,/ Most generous and free from all contriving..." (Act IV, Sc. 7, lines 132–133) Claudius's actions are ruled by expediency. He does and says whatever he thinks will yield him the results he wants. In contrast, Hamlet is searching for conviction about what is right. When he says (Act II, Sc. 2, lines 538–540):

> ...I'll have grounds
> more relative than this. The play's the thing
> Wherein I'll catch the conscience of the King.

he is acknowledging his need for proof of the Ghost's account. He wants his actions to be right, whereas Claudius only wants them to be successful. The moral difference is telling. For Claudius words are interpersonal tools, to get the other person to fulfill his wishes. He is not looking for the word that best expresses the truth, or reality, but, rather, the word that will accomplish his ends. In this, he is like Richard III, another glib aggressor. Claudius even tries to shape his prayers into successful entreaties, but fails in that attempt. He concedes that bribery, seduction, verbal manipulation, don't work with God.

The conception of guilt in Hamlet is intriguing. Gertrude (Act IV, Sc. 5, line 22) speaks as though our efforts to hide our sins themselves bring on their disclosure. Guilty behavior backfires. Claudius's guilt blocks his "successful" praying. It is as though his guilt, or, perhaps, his conscience, has a different agenda from his efforts and obstructs them. Similarly ,when Laertes is about to kill Hamlet he says it is "almost against my conscience" (Act V, Sc. 2, line 279). In each of these examples guilt appears as an inner rebel, an obstacle to an action, opposing the character's will. It is a saboteur. In this I don't hear the idea of guilt, or, more specifically, a fear of guilt, as a potentially helpful internal guide, which is the perspective with which I am most familiar (Buechler, 1995). In fact I am not sure Gertrude and Claudius are actually talking about guilt, since they seem to be referring to a *fear* of consequences, rather than the feeling that what they have done is *counter to their values*. Once again, in this, I think the clearest contrast is between Hamlet and Claudius. As the king himself says, as he tries to pray, how genuine could his repentance be, since he still enjoys the fruits of the murder?

In the course of the play, besides the recent death of his father, Hamlet loses the throne, (when Claudius is crowned after marrying the queen) loses faith in his mother and Ophelia, loses any sense of security, (since he is spied upon and plotted against) loses belief in himself, (since he cannot act on his beloved father's command) loses Ophelia, (when she commits suicide), gives up his studies, loses Rosencrantz and Guildenstern as friends, (since they join Claudius in his scheming against Hamlet) almost loses his life, (when Claudius tries to have him killed) and, arguably, loses his mind. Since he is ever self-observant, and his creator is brilliantly holding the mirror up to nature, what does he tell us about bearing such diverse losses?

Defining "healthy," "reasonable," "manly," grieving as time limited has a long history. "Moving on" was the advice of philosophy, psychiatry, and psychoanalysis, as well as various "self-help" movements. *The Loss of Sadness: How Psychiatry Transformed Normal Sorrow into Depressive Disorder*, by Horowitz and Wakefield, 2007, tells the story of how sorrow, a normal response to loss, was turned into a medical disorder. For centuries clinicians judged sorrow as normal grief or pathological depression, depending largely on its duration. They, and most of the public, came to believe that grieving should proceed through a normal sequence of stages, from protest through acceptance. Although most clinicians in today's climate would not ascribe to such a formulaic schema, I think duration still remains a factor in their judgments, and in the thinking of the general public. Grief should be a time limited, reasonable phase, leading to the resumption of ordinary life. It is like a tunnel, a necessary passage, to be traversed on the way to something else.

Mourning is of great personal and professional interest to me. In my understanding of it, I include other losses, besides the loss of a person. I think we can mourn the loss of a hope, a dream, a loving feeling, faith, purpose, dignity, self-respect, security, and so much else. To me any and all of these losses can occasion a disillusioned sorrow. There may be particular stages of life where disillusionment is more frequent. I certainly have known many pre-adolescents who have suffered greatly when their heroes and heroines have been shown to be flawed. Serious suicidal gestures or attempts can result. But the pain of these losses can occur at any point in a life.

Mental health professionals have not been alone in prescribing "right" or "appropriate" and "inappropriate" forms of mourning. Constantine P. Cavafy wrote a beautiful poem that does something similar. It mentions Marcus Antonius, Cleopatra's lover, and the protagonist of another of Shakespeare's tragedies (*Antony and Cleopatra*). This poem is extremely direct and prescriptive in its advice to the bereaved. To Cavefy there is a right, dignified way to bear loss.

The God Abandons Anthony

When suddenly, at midnight, you hear
an invisible procession going by
with exquisite music, voices,
don't mourn your luck that's failing now,
work gone wrong, your plans
all proving deceptive—don't mourn them uselessly.
As one long prepared, and graced with courage,
say goodbye to her, the Alexandria that is leaving.
Above all, don't fool yourself, don't say

it was a dream, your ears deceived you:
don't degrade yourself with empty hopes like these.
As one long prepared, and graced with courage,
as is right for you who were given this kind of city,
go firmly to the window
and listen with deep emotion, but not
with the whining, the pleas of a coward;
listen-your final delectation-to the voices,
to the exquisite music of that strange procession,
and say goodbye to her, to the Alexandria you are losing.

(translated by Edmund Keeley and Philip Sherrard,
in E. Hirsch, 1999, p. 136)

This poem exhorts Mark Antony to bear his losses with the courage and dignity for which he is renowned. It is as though Mark Antony is being told to be, in his grief, who he has been, in the rest of his life. Don't let grief change you into a less "worthy" person.

In discussing the poem, Hirsch (1999, p. 137) points out that Cavefy took his title from Plutarch's "Life of Antony," where Plutarch "...describes a bacchanalia winding past Antony's house just before the fall of Alexandria and reads this as a sign of Antony's abandonment by Dionysus." This poem is a complex interplay, weaving together the poet's personal grief, the historical narrative of Mark Antony, and Shakespeare's *Antony and Cleopatra*. But the basic message about the proper way for a worthy man to mourn is unambiguous and stated with great conviction.

As I read it, the poem counsels Antony to:

1. Believe your experience, even if its basis is invisible to others.
2. Avoid "useless" mourning that won't change anything.
3. Avoid comparing reality with what should be, and what you expected.

4. Use your courage and life experience to fully confront losses. Be who you have always been. Don't seek the comfort of fantasies that counter the reality.
5. Feel the loss deeply, but without begging for it not to be true.

For a wonderful companion piece (in many senses of the word "companion") I turn to Deborah Paredez's "Wife's Disaster Manual."

> When the forsaken city starts to burn,
> after the men and children have fled,
> stand still, silent as prey, and slowly turn
>
> back. Behold the curse. Stay and mourn
> the collapsing doorways, the unbroken bread
> in the forsaken city starting to burn.
>
> Don't flinch. Don't join in.
> Resist the righteous scurry and instead
> stand still, silent as prey. Slowly turn
>
> your thoughts away from escape: the iron
> gates unlashed, the responsibilities shed.
> When the forsaken city starts to burn,
>
> surrender to your calling, show concern
> for those who remain. Come to a dead
> standstill. Silent as prey, slowly turn
>
> into something essential. Learn
> the names of the fallen. Refuse to run ahead

when the forsaken city starts to burn.
Stand still and silent. Pray. Return.

(In: Sieghart, 2019, p. 133)

This poem is itself a merry go round, turning back to its own recurring words, phrases, and ideas. It manifests, as it advises, slowly turning back to face disaster. Interestingly, it issues a challenge to "surrender to your calling," and "turn into something essential." This seems to me not unlike Cavefy's charge to "...go firmly to the window" and to "...say goodbye to her, to the Alexandria you are losing." Both poems exhort us to stand up to disaster, look it squarely in the eye, resist the urge to flee. Implicitly I think Paradez, like Cavefy, believes it is important to remain committed to our long standing values and standards of behavior as we face up to catastrophe.

I think about Hamlet, keeping in mind these standards. Some of them, like the counsel to avoid "useless mourning," sound like Claudius's moralistic exhortations. But it is interesting to ask what it would mean for Hamlet to grieve in a way that is consonant with his previous style of behavior. What might that signify for any of us? What can it mean, to remain oneself while grieving? More specifically, when loss alters our lives, in what sense can we remain the same (cognitively, emotionally, spiritually)? How would a courageous and dignified grief look? How does a "well-functioning" person bear loss? Is that a question worth asking, or is *any* judgment of someone's grief inappropriate and non-empathic?

> "Oh God, a beast that wants discourse of reason
> Would have mourned longer"
>
> (Act I, Sc. 2, lines 150–151)

At the opposite end of the spectrum from extreme expressions of grief might be the speedy resumption of normal life, that Hamlet despises in

288

his mother and her new husband. What does their attitude imply? In most respects Hamlet is ready to question his own perceptions and behavior. But there is one issue he approaches with consistent conviction. He is clear that it is an affront to his father's memory to have speedily "moved on," as his mother, uncle, and everyone else seem to do. As we see in the unforgettable scene between Hamlet and his mother in her chamber (Act III, Sc. 4)) he focuses on her willingness to replace his father in her bed. The early psychoanalytic literature paid a good deal of attention to Hamlet's focus, raising questions about his own incestuous motives. But, earlier on, Hamlet (wittily and bitterly) remarks on the sheer speed with which everyone (and not just his mother and uncle) took up business as usual after his father's sudden death. In Act I, Sc. 2, line 178, Horatio comments that the wedding of the king and queen followed "hard upon" Hamlet's father's death and in the next lines, Hamlet sarcastically answers:

Thrift, thrift Horatio! the funeral baked meats
Did coldly furnish forth the marriage tables. (lines 179–180)

Aside from the sexual aspects, Hamlet is offended by Gertrude's willingness (or is it eagerness?) to resume normal court life, with a new partner, seemingly unruffled by grief. What does this mean about her love for her former husband, Hamlet's father? Again, what is real and what is show? The new royal couples' speed is offensive to Hamlet, just as his slower pace outrages them (we later learn more about Claudius's need to bury, as it were, grief for his late brother).

The affront to a mourner of the world's indifference is a theme that has inspired some of my favorite poems. I single out just two here. I have written about each of them previously. Here I highlight their attention to the disparity between the grieving sufferer and all those who turn away and resume business as usual. But (to varying degrees, in various circumstances) doesn't that include us all? Don't we fail to register most of the world's suffering, especially if it is inconvenient? And, even if we notice it at all, don't we try to get away as quickly as we can, and back to ordinary life? For me, no one has expressed this with more poignancy than W.H. Auden in his poem, "Musee des Beaux Arts" (In: Auden, 1991, p. 179). I have already discussed this poem in chapter two, for its reflection on the isolation of suffering, so I will not repeat the poem itself here, but I will briefly comment on its expression of how we avoid facing sufferers. Please see chapter two for the text of the poem.

What could Auden mean when he refers to suffering's "position"? if we hear it as personifying suffering, it is as though suffering knows it has to be content to reside in a corner, taking up little space, not the main event for most of the scene's inhabitants. The main event is ordinary, ongoing living. Unending repetitive movements that are not conscious, or hardly conscious, make up most of life. Because of their very bulk they take up most of the stage. For Icarus his "failure" is all that is happening, but for everyone else it is barely noticed, if at all. When Icarus drowns the splash may not be heard by the ploughman, or, if it is, it is too unimportant to receive much attention. He barely registers it, if he registers it at all. Does he even turn to look? What I find particularly striking about Auden's insight is that it is not, necessarily, that the ploughman doesn't register the tragedy because he *needs* to look away from it. That would imply a conflict, a need to defend against seeing the tragedy. This seems to me akin to the usual psychoanalytic view. But Auden is saying something else that, I think, is more in line with current thinking in the Interpersonal school and in other quarters (though it actually has a longer history than that). Auden, like the analyst H.S. Sullivan (1953) is highlighting how we *focus*. Something can be too unimportant to us to focus on, *without our necessarily having a conflict about it*. To me, this is the brilliance of Auden's word "position." Rarely do we achieve in prose the economy of that word.

290

And what of the "expensive delicate ship" that "had somewhere to get to and sailed calmly on"? Here I think Auden's tone reaches the peak of resignation. Unlike in "Funeral Blues" (see below) he is not loudly protesting. He is merely observing the world's indifference. Presumably the ship is cared for. It is important enough to merit attention. We lavish attention on countless inanimate objects that are precious to us, but ignore the fall of the unfortunate. I can't help thinking there is a biting, bitter, but coldly calculating quality to Auden's observations. To say that Icarus' s "failure" was too "unimportant" for the ploughman to notice is to point out just how hollow the world becomes when we are oblivious of others' suffering. And Auden wrote the poem in December, 1938, in an ominous Europe he felt he had to leave. He never returned.

Hamlet is increasingly alone with his suffering over the course of the play, as seeming friends (Rosencrantz and Guildenstern, Ophelia) betray him. Eventually his only confidante is Horatio. As I suggested above, I think his isolation reflects the truth that each of us is alone with our grief. Even well—meaning friends don't really feel our pain, no matter what they might intend. We are the only ones who knew the departed as we did, and we bring our whole history of loss to each new grief. When the world keeps spinning, when it turns away "quite leisurely from the disaster," we may be enraged, on top of our sorrow. How dare it!

Auden expresses this with incredible precision and passion in another great poem (sometimes called "Funeral Blues" but part of a longer poem, "Autumn Song," Auden, 1991, p. 141). It can be read as a challenge to anyone who would go on with ordinary routines despite others' pain. Please see the text of this poem in Chapter Two.

It can seem absurd, even disrespectful, for anyone's life to go on as usual in the vicinity of supreme loss. When life will never be the same for one person, how does anyone else plan lunch? But, then, once again, isn't that just what we do, most of the time? We know about the suffering around the corner, and around the globe, and we go on with our lives.

In the last line of the poem, ("For nothing now can ever come to any good") Auden lets us see the fate of the anger that can accompany the sufferer's sorrow. Is the anger at the loss itself? At its arbitrariness? At the indifference of the rest of the world? Regardless, we can see how the anger works on the sufferer to poison life (just as it did Hamlet's). Nothing now can ever come to any good. I hear the line being spit out. In fact, in the face of devastating loss, the beauty of the world can seem like a taunt to the bereaved. I have heard so many in pain wish that the sun wouldn't shine so bright, as though the sun were showing them up. The more brilliant the stars, the more sufferers are aware that they shine for others but not for them. In the kind of depression where sorrow and anger mingle, people often wish for gray, cloudy days.

For the bereaved the world has been transformed, and will never be the same. Hamlet seems to be baffled, as well as enraged, by the world's willingness to rush past grieving. He is especially disheartened that his mother glides into her new life so easily. From my Interpersonal Psychoanalytic vantage point, Hamlet's extreme mourning answers the indifference of the others. The meaning of each is affected by the context of the other. That is, Hamlet's response looks more extreme because of the swift shift of the others, and their shift looks more extreme because of his fierce, transfixing grief. There are no absolutes here, as is always true. Everything human gains some of its meaning from its interpersonal context.

As indicated above, I do believe that sometimes we "look away" from tragedy simply because our focus is elsewhere. But sometimes it is true that we more actively defend against seeing it. We may feel that letting ourselves consciously absorb the sorrow all around (and, on some level, within) us would threaten our wellbeing. Personally, as I age, I have grown more forgiving toward this defensiveness. Experiencing how very hard life can be has acclimated me to the idea that whatever gets us through the night may be worth it. But this attitude is anathema to the character, Hamlet, and, perhaps, to his author. Shakespeare was in his thirties when he wrote the play and, while I don't want to indulge in psychoanalyzing him, I think an unbending stance on this subject is most often the position of someone who is relatively young. For example, in the first stages of Freud's career he believed that if he could convince his patients of the truth of the Oedipal origin of their neuroses, this "truth" would help to set them free. In my experience, most clinicians start our careers with a similar outlook, wanting to cut through swaths of defenses, as if we were mowing the grass, and get to a freeing kernel of truth. I think this perspective is usually quite well intentioned. But it also can be quite dangerous, as we find out when our patients either leave in a huff (as did Freud's patient, Dora) or, worse, suffer psychological damage.

"Taint Not Thy Mind"

The Ghost charges Hamlet with "remembering" him by revealing and revenging his murder. Hamlet expresses regret that he has to be the agent of that revelation:

> The time is out of joint; O cursed spite
> That ever I was born to set it right.   (Act I, Sc. 5, lines 186–187)

But the Ghost also gives Hamlet another responsibility:

> Taint not thy mind nor let thy soul contrive
> Against thy mother aught; ...   (Act I, Sc. 5, lines 84–85)

I have always found this puzzling. How could Hamlet live with the knowledge of his uncle's deeds (and his mother's questionable complicity) without it "tainting" his mind? I can only wonder what Shakespeare meant us to hear in this. In my dictionary "taint" can mean "an infecting touch, influence, or tinge." How is Hamlet to live with this new knowledge and carry out the revenge without being "tainted"? It is fascinating to me that, on the theory that Hamlet puts on an "antic disposition" as a strategic cover-up, he pretends to be exactly what the Ghost prohibited! Hamlet certainly behaves as if he were "tainted" by melancholy, by a fervent desire to unsettle and expose pretensions, and by his driven antics.

In the "Gravedigger" scene, Horatio counsels Hamlet not to stare too much at the decomposition that is our eventual fate.

> Hamlet: Dost thou think Alexander looked o'this fashion i'th' earth?
> Horatio: E'en so.
> Hamlet: And smelt so? Pah!
> Horatio: E'en so, my lord.
> Hamlet: To what base uses we may return, Horatio!
> Why may not imagination trace the noble dust of
> Alexander till 'a find it stopping a bung-hole?
> Horatio: 'Twere to consider too curiously to consider so.
> (Act V, Sc. 1, lines 187–194)

If Horatio is meant to represent a moderating aspect of Hamlet's mind (Garber, 2004, p. 469) as well as a separate person and friend, I take the message to be that there is no way to stare into some devastating truths without being "tainted." Horatio is making a plea for looking away, at least enough to bear life. Given my own beliefs it is no surprise that I hear this as a defense of the human need for defenses. Just as no one can know what

Hamlet knows without it tainting his mind, I don't think anyone can stare into skulls without paying a price.

In her imaginative fictionalized account of the relationship between actual events in Shakespeare's life and the play, *Hamlet,* Maggie O'Farrell (*Hamnet: A Novel of the Plague,* 2020) centers on the death of Shakespeare's son, Hamnet, when the child was eleven. O'Farrell names Shakespeare's wife Agnes (though in reality her name was Anne Hathaway). The description of Agnes's mourning, when her son succumbs to the plague, is as graphic and vivid as any account of a mother's grief that I can remember. O'Farrell inserts many interesting ideas about the relationship between Shakespeare's grievous loss and his creative process. She pictures Agnes's intense grief as like a fierce current, that her husband fears could carry him away from the writing career he has carefully nourished. In this fictional account, Shakespeare avoids visiting Agnes and their two remaining children for many months after Hamnet dies. When Shakespeare mounts the play, "Hamlet," Agnes goes to see it in London. She had approached the idea of it with rage, feeling her husband had usurped their personal tragedy, so that he could have a professional success. But, when she sees the play, she feels she understands why it had to be written. Agnes believes that Shakespeare has taken the real events and, with a kind of creative alchemy, turned them around, so that it is the father who dies. The actor who plays young Hamlet has many of their real son's quirks. Agnes believes her husband has, in a sense, resurrected Hamnet in the only way he could. O'Farrell's prose brims with compassion for both husband and wife. We understand Agnes's feelings of abandonment and betrayal, and her husband's desperate desire to hold onto his own life, in the face of intense grief for the shocking loss of his only son. We could stand apart from this fictionalized Shakespeare, and from all who are driven to look away from suffering, and, perhaps, along with Auden, we can decry "how everything turns away/ Quite leisurely from the disaster…" (of Icarus's fall, or Hamnet's death, or the grievous losses occurring somewhere in the world every minute). We can pass judgment on those who turn away from tragedy, or empathize, or (as I think we would if we follow Shakespeare's lead) both.

Turning away from sorrow has its price, but Hamlet is more than just unwilling to close his eyes. He is relentless in his quest for the truth of what happened to his father, in his frontal attacks on all hypocrisy and evasion, and in his insistence that his mother face her participation. He wants to rip away his mother's blinders, not just remove them. His is a missionary zeal. In my experience it is easy to fall into this zeal, once one views others' blinders as antithetical to one's objectives. Horatio's advice is useless. I think Hamlet's adversarial stance toward his mother's blinders is multi-determined, but, I would suggest, some of it is an inevitable result of "taint."

The line between a necessary confrontation and a destructive sadism is nowhere more problematic than in the scene in the Queen's bedchamber (Act III, Sc.4). This is a triangular scene, in that the Ghost makes an appearance (at least, to Hamlet). The Ghost reiterates that Hamlet should take care of his mother's state of mind: "O step between her and her fighting soul" (line 109). But Hamlet needs to *make* her see the error of her ways. His is a frenzied confrontation of her willingness to be seduced by Claudius. From Hamlet's point of view, she has *tainted* the sanctity of her first marriage by consenting to the second. His views are concisely expressed in lines in the play within the play:

Player Queen: A second time I kill my husband dead
When second husband kisses me in bed.
(Act III, Sc. 2, lines 178–179)

Hamlet drives his points home with frantic zeal, until the Ghost reminds him of his responsibility to preserve his mother's equanimity. But can we ever confront someone with a horrendous reality (in our own view) without damaging them? After the Ghost's appearance, Hamlet continues to pursue his point though, perhaps, with a bit less ardor:

> Hamlet: I must be cruel only to be kind
>
> (Act III, Sc. 4, line 176)

And he softens his message:

> Hamlet: And when you are desirous to be blessed
> I'll blessing beg of you....
>
> Act III, Sc. 4, lines 169–170)

Emily Dickinson has a fascinating description of how we can tell our truth caringly. Please revisit her Poem 1263, quoted in Chapter Two, "Tell all the truth but tell it slant-." Dickinson's truth telling requires self-control. It would be hard to achieve if one is feeling Hamlet's incensed, passionate repudiation of his mother's behavior. Hamlet is aware that his mother will try to find an escape clause. That is, she will be tempted to write off Hamlet's accusations as the product of his madness.

> Hamlet: ....Mother, for love of grace
> Lay not that flattering unction to your soul
> That not your trespass but my madness speaks.
>
> (Act III, Sc. 4, lines 142–144)

He tries to head off her effort to dodge his accusations. Perhaps he feels he has to shake her up, in order to have any chance of penetrating her defenses. But isn't that what we always tell ourselves? That we had to be cruel only to be kind? And, of course, sometimes it may be true. But with what *tone* did we tell our "truth"? Was there, perhaps an equally effective way to "tell it slant"?

A Sterile Promontory

What can we imagine happened to Hamlet when the Ghost described his father's death and bade him to "remember" him, and seek revenge? I think it is not an exaggeration to say that Hamlet lost his mind, not, necessarily, in the sense that he became "mad," but in that he lost the capacity for a simple relationship between his mind and the world around him. From that point forward everything that happened took its meaning from its impact on The Mission. Hamlet lost his capacity for the simple, direct interchange of a carefree mind. Already in mourning for his father, this loss of a kind of innocence clouded every event. University friends (Rosencrantz and Guildenstern) come for a "visit." But are they really spies? Ophelia waits for him, to return mementos. Is her father hiding and listening to their conversation? His favorite troupe of actors have arrived. Can they be used to catch the conscience of the King? Nothing is straightforward any more. Perhaps he lost simple pleasures, straightforward relating, and degrees of freedom he didn't even realize he had.

In the clinical (psychological and psychoanalytic) literature, this change would be described as the effect of trauma. The whole world is irreparably altered. Life is not the same, and one senses that it never will revert back to the way it was. We have been thrust out of paradise, never to return. Elsewhere (2008) I have described what I call the "loss of the unharmed self," when someone has been traumatized. Many who have been deeply harmed imagine how life could have felt, had the horror not occurred. Hamlet has been described (not convincingly, for me) as "melancholic," and he was already suffering grief about the loss of his father, but before the Ghost unfolds his story, Hamlet was a "scholar, soldier..." Without getting into the quagmire of diagnosis, I think it is safe to say that he is a changed man. The King (Act II, Sc. 2, line 5) refers to Hamlet's "transformation," and the Queen speaks of her "too much changed son." (Act II, Sc. 2, line 36).

298

In a cryptic but brilliant poem, Emily Dickinson describes subtle atmospheric changes, when summer gives way to autumn, and a warm intimacy gives way to a colder, intermittent connection.

Poem 1142 (In Vendler, 2010, p. 411)

The murmuring of Bees, has ceased
But murmuring of some
Posterior, prophetic,
Has simultaneously come.
The lower metres of the Year
When Nature's laugh is done
The Revelations of the Book
Whose Genesis was June.
Appropriate Creatures to her change
The Typic Mother sends
As Accent fades to interval
With separating Friends
Till what we speculate, has been
And thoughts we will not show
More intimate with us become
Than Persons, that we know.

Vendler notes (p. 413) the poem's sorrow over changes that necessitate concealment as a way of life: "We exist henceforth in a double consciousness that forever destroys simplicity of response toward other persons, including any other potential Friend." I think that accurately describes Hamlet's altered relationships, but for him the change invades perception itself. As Schachtel wrote so long ago (1959) there is a vast difference between "looking" at the world versus "looking for" something predetermined.

Post-revelation Hamlet, having heard the Ghost's story, is relieved only when he is alone. He nervously scans for spies and evidence of what really happened. Remarkably, Vendler (p. 414) has this to say about Dickinson's use of the word "speculate" in her poem: "The word 'speculate' shows us a mind constantly nervous, anxiously wondering, always suspecting, relentlessly doubting, covertly denying." She goes on to say that "In this poem, the mirror (speculum) held up to Nature gives no constant image to the agitated mind." Hamlet, the character, advises the Players to keep in mind the task of holding the mirror up to Nature. I think the play, *Hamlet* and Dickinson's Poem 1142 both hold up mirrors to a saddened, diminished, profoundly disappointed human being.

After the Ghost's revelations, Hamlet looks at everything with a purpose in mind. He is driven by a need for certainty, as though it will return some kind of peace. I will discuss this further below, but here suggest that I think that peace does come to Hamlet, at the end of the play, not out of certainty about the murder, or, even, out of having exacted vengeance, but, rather, out of submission to forces greater than his own. "Let be."

Hamlet describes his own dark mood to Rosencrantz and Guildenstern, just after they admit that they are spying on him for Claudius. (Act II, Sc.2, lines 261–276).

...I have of late-but wherefore I know not-lost all my mirth, forgot all custom of exercises; and, indeed, it goes heavily with my disposition that this goodly frame, the earth, seems to me a sterile promontory, this most excellent canopy, the air, look you, this brave, o'erhanging firmament, this majestical roof fretted with golden fire,—why it appears no other thing to me than a foul and pestilent congregation of vapours...man delights not me; no, nor woman neither, though by your smiling you seem to say so.

In these beautiful lines we can hear a superb description of some of sorrow's effects. For Hamlet all pleasure has been drained out of life. Shakespeare has understood the impact of one emotion on the experience of other feelings, in a way that is similar to the thinking of emotion theorists (Izard, 1977) hundreds of years later. When we sorrow, it affects our ability to be affected by other feelings. We can't take delight in Nature's majesty. The beauty that adds color to life has no impact on us. Usually, life's joys balance its pain, and strengthen us to bear our burdens. But in sorrow we are immune to the joys. I am reminded of a short story by Nathaniel Hawthorne, "The Minister's Black Veil" (1952). The protagonist feels as though a piece of crepe hangs between him and the world, and it "...separated him from cheerful brotherhood and woman's love, and kept him in that saddest of all prisons, his own heart, and still it lay upon his face, as if to deepen the gloom of his darksome chamber, and shade him from the sunshine of eternity" (p. 498)

The stultifying effect of grief was also stunningly portrayed by Emily Dickinson, in her well known Poem 372 (In Vendler, 2010, p. 168). "After great pain, a formal feeling comes-." I quoted it above, in Chapter Two. In that poem, mechanical feet, a stiff heart, a deadened will, render the sufferer practically inert. It doesn't matter to us whether we "outlive" this moment or succumb to it. There is no joy, no animation. Aliveness mutes and life fades.

There is an exchange, insignificant as it might at first appear, that I think expresses the depth of Shakespeare's understanding of grief. It comes when Gertrude tells Laertes that his sister, Ophelia, has drowned. It can seem awkward, as Laertes woodenly asks "Where?" and later repeats "Drowned." But, in its simplicity, I think it reflects the speechless shock with which we receive some unacceptable news. It is, in Dickinson's language, an "Hour of Lead." The mind stiffens, unable to wrap around the words. It reminds me of a heart breaking passage in James Agee's (2009) *A Death in the Family.*

At first, Mary is unable to comprehend her husband's tragic, fatal accident. She can't take it in. Then, slowly, she does:

And as she rocked and groaned, the realization gradually lost its fullest, most impaling concentration: there took shape, from its utter darkness, like the slow emergence of the countryside into first daylight, all those separate realizations which could be resolved into images, emotions, thought, words, obligations (p. 280).

To my mind the greatest writers hold a mirror to nature by accurately reflecting our stunned inability to take in vast sorrows. It taxes us to simply go on breathing, trying to make sense of the words or images. We stare, uncomprehending, at pictures of human beings flinging themselves off buildings on September 11. As in Dickenson's poem, there is chill, then stupor, then the letting go.

Alas, Poor Yorick

Hamlet: (taking the skull) (Let me see.) Alas, poor Yorick! I knew him, Horatio—a fellow of infinite jest, of most excellent fancy. He hath bore me on his back a thousand times., and now how abhorred in my imagination it is! My gorge rises at it. Here hung those lips that I have kissed I know not how oft. Where be your gibes now? your gambols? your songs? your flashes of merriment that were wont to set the table on a roar? Not one now to mock your own grinning? Quite chapfallen?
.... (Act V, Sc. 1, lines 174–182)

With these lines Hamlet expresses his horror as he looks at the skull that is all that remains of the jester Yorick, a beloved figure from his childhood. Can it be that this desiccated, lifeless object was once a supremely alive and unique individual? Is the dust that remains of Alexander the Great and Julius Caesar indistinguishable from the clay that patches a wall? It is one thing to know, in theory, that a corpse decays, and quite another to see the bizarre object that used to be a person.

In the "gravedigger" scene, (Act V, Sc. 1) Hamlet faces himself with some uncomfortable truths. He is clearly fascinated with decay, and how democratically death reduces us all to sediment. Rich and poor are stripped of pretensions. Roles that seemed inseparable from a person's essence have left no mark. The dust of the great Alexander might be comingled with other remains and used to stop a beer barrel. Hamlet is an equal opportunity leveler too, in a sense. His witty scorn cuts through hypocritical self-delusions wherever he finds them. But when he sees the skull of Yorick, the entertaining jester he remembered from childhood, his gore rises. He feels disgust, our body's inborn signal to extrude possibly dangerous matter. While Hamlet never misses a chance to strip away conceits, he finds death's physical demolishment hard to confront.

Centuries separate Hamlet's rising gorge from Philip Larkin's twentieth century poem, "Aubade" (In: A. Holden and B. Holden, 2014, pp. 214–217). Named for a musical composition that is meant to be played or sung at dawn, or in the early morning, this poem expresses profound and disturbing reflections. Waking at four, the poet finds all thought impossible, other than contemplation of death. It is not regret about the past that consumes him, but, rather, imagining death's endless, featureless realm. The dead cannot locate themselves because all sensation has ceased. Although death's vast void is unfathomable, the poet remains transfixed. In the "dead" of night there is no escape from these thoughts. Neither courage nor complaint tames them. As morning dawns ordinary life takes its usual shape. But the knowledge that he can neither escape death nor accept it accompanies the poet into the new day.

Larkin admits that his interrogation of death is, itself arid, and yet he cannot think about anything else. He is both held and horrified by his thoughts of endless emptiness. Like Hamlet, questioning whether to be or not to be and trying to fathom the "undiscovered country," Larkin imagines death as an anaesthetized state barren of thought, love, or linkage.

The skulls Hamlet ponders, like Larson's persona, have nothing to think with and nothing to love or link with. Hamlet focuses on the dust we become. Larkin emphasizes what is absent. Interestingly, he calls his feeling a chill that slows impulses, turning them into indecisions.

We might look at the mystery of Hamlet's difficulty fulfilling his vengeful impulses in this light. Does horror stultify impulse? In any case, the hundreds of years that separate Shakespeare and Larkin don't matter, as both stop in their tracks and ponder the reality of death. Larkin's "standing chill" brings to mind (above, Poem 372, in Vendler 2010, p. 168) Dickinson's "First Chill-then Stupor-then the letting go."

In his witty, clever play (1967/2017) *Rosencrantz and Guildenstern Are Dead,* Tom Stoppard makes dark humor out of conjectures about death. His characters speculate about what it would be like to be shut up in a box. Rosencrantz suggests that when we think about death, we imagine what it would be like to be confined to a casket while still alive. But then, he reflects (p. 64)that being dead in a box might be even worse than being alive:

Because you'd be helpless, wouldn't you? Stuffed in a box like that, I mean you'd be in there for ever. Even taking into account the fact that you're dead, it isn't a pleasant thought. Especially if you're dead, really...ask yourself, if I asked you straight off—I'm going to stuff you in this box now, would you rather be alive or dead? Naturally, you'd prefer to be alive...

But, a few lines later, Rosencrantz echoes the point Horatio makes in *Hamlet*: "I wouldn't think about it, if I were you. You'd only get depressed. (Pause.) Eternity is a terrible thought, I mean, where's it going to end..."

I think what Stoppard does so brilliantly is to take reality and nudge it just a bit further, toward the absurd, which can leave the viewer suspended between tragedy and comedy.

Like Stoppard's matter of fact commentators and Auden, in "Musee des Beaux Arts," Larkin remarks on the world's "uncaring" routines, that simply unroll while he is in the grip of terror. His early morning aubade sings to him, as the rest of the world carries on with ordinary life. I find Larkin's poem astonishing, in the clarity of its language, in the range of ideas that it covers, in its way of combining an intimate tone with reflections on the human condition, and in its sheer emotional power.

Similar in sensibility to Stoppard's caustic wit, the "gravedigger" scene (Act V, Sc.1) is often referred to as "comic relief" (for example, in the discussion of the film version of the play directed by Kenneth Branaugh, "Hamlet," Castle Rock Entertainment DVD, 2007). I would question that way of describing it, since to me it implies a break from the tragedy. I think its "comedy" is really another form of lament, and not a break at all. Hamlet comments on the first Gravedigger's ability to sing while he shovels skulls:

> Hamlet: Has this fellow no feeling of his business?
> 'A sings in grave-making. (lines 61–62)

Horatio answers that the Gravedigger's long experience of his trade has inured him to it, and Hamlet agrees. But when, for example, Tom Stoppard has Rosencrantz say "Eternity is a terrible thought, I mean, where is it going to end..." I think the playwright is showing us that with a little nudge tragedy becomes comedy. Similarly, I don't think it is an accident that the skull Hamlet contemplates once belonged to the king's jester. Comedy can be tragedy's furthest edge. In his "antics," Hamlet plays with grief shading into mockery; absurdity just a notch away from the unbearable. He pushes boundaries until they collapse, and the unthinkable is said. Mischief? Madness? Sadism? Horror? Uncontainable grief? Of course the work of Samuel Beckett comes to mind.

I see some of Hamlet's jesting as a form of grieving, in the sense that steam is water, although it has a different appearance. Another poet, Edna St. Vincent Millay, contemplates our journey from "dust to dust," but her reaction has a somewhat different tone.

Dirge Without Music (In: K. Young, 2010, p. 103)

I am not resigned to the shutting away of loving hearts in the
    hard ground.
So it is, and so it will be, for so it has been, time out of mind:
Into the darkness they go, the wise and the lovely. Crowned
With lilies and with laurel they go, but I am not resigned.

Lovers and thinkers, into the earth with you.
Be one with the dull, the indiscriminate dust.
A fragment of what you felt, of what you knew,
A formula, a phrase remains,—but the best is lost.

The answers quick and keen, the honest look, the laughter, the
    love,—
They are gone. They are gone to feed the roses. Elegant and curled
Is the blossom. Fragrant is the blossom. I know. But I do not
    approve.

More precious was the light in your eyes than all the roses in the
world.

Down, down, down into the darkness of the grave
Gently they go, the beautiful, the tender, the kind;
Quietly they go, the intelligent, the witty, the brave.
I know. But I do not approve. And I am not resigned.

Like Hamlet, and like Larkin, Edna St. Vincent Millay stares straight at the
grim reality of becoming the "remains" of a human being. Nothing about
how we have lived our lives counts for or against us in that transformation.
While religion's heaven and hell promise justice, dust is "indiscriminate."
Looking directly at these facts can be terrifying and heartbreaking. Along
with Hamlet's our "gorge" may rise at these thoughts. Some of us still look,
perhaps unable to look away, and others avoid thoughts of death for as long
as possible.

Emily Dickinson brings what can sound like a clinical detachment to her
study of death's leveling effect. (Poem 124, in: Vendler, 2010, p. 38).

Safe in their Alabaster Chambers—
Untouched by Morning—
And untouched by noon—
Sleep the meek members of the Resurrection,
Rafter of Satin and Roof of Stone—

Grand go the Years,
In the Crescent above them—
Worlds scoop their Arcs—
And Firmaments—row—
Diadems—drop—

And Doges—surrender—
Soundless as Dots,
On a Disc of Snow.

Vendler (pp. 38–42) comments on several versions of this poem. In each, the powerful, royalty, the wealthy, surrender to death. One version has a particularly interesting line:

Light laughs the breeze
In her Castle above them—
Babbles the Bee in a stolid Ear,
Pipe the sweet Birds in ignorant cadence—
Ah, what sagacity perished here!

Vendler (p. 39) points out that Dickinson is contrasting happy, innocent Nature, which is everlasting, with that which perishes. It seems to me that Dickinson finds some comfort in Nature's survival, even though the dead are sequestered away from Nature's pleasant sounds. In Dickinson life itself is ongoing, even though the dead are separated from it. Society's distinctions between Doges and subjects are erased, as Hamlet also observes. But, for Dickinson, there is still beauty and laughter. When I read this poem, I hear Dickinson as still able to enjoy the beauty of the sparkling firmament, unlike Hamlet, for whom, "...this most excellent canopy, the air, look you, this brave o'erhanging firmament, this majestical roof fretted with golden fire—why, it appears no other thing to me than a foul and pestilent congregation of vapors." (Act II, Sc. 2, line 265).

Wondrous Strange

One constant in Hamlet is his relentless self-questioning and curiosity. So, with Cavafy, we could see him as unchanged in this respect, asking questions and seeking their answers, as he (presumably) lived before his father died. Ophelia (Act III, Sc. 1) describes him as the consummate scholar, among other attributes. In that respect he doesn't change. In mourning, he is the same curious, questioning Hamlet he always was. Early on (Act I, Sc. 5, line 163) Horatio comments that the Ghost's appearance and Hamlet's behavior are "wondrous strange." Hamlet responds:

And therefore as a stranger give it welcome.
There are more things in heaven and earth, Horatio,
Than are dreamt of in your philosophy...   (lines 164–166)

The idea that unexplainable events should be welcomed, just as strangers should be given welcome, has tremendous appeal, and continued relevance. To mention yet another line from the play, sadly, it is very often honored in the breach, in our twenty first century public lives.

In a fascinating parallel, attitudes about curiosity in the *content* of the play have been enacted by its critics and commentators. That is, in *Hamlet*, some characters (e.g. Polonius) seek only to confirm their theories, rather than to open mindedly explore and discover the truth. Polonius believes Hamlet's "lunacy" is caused by thwarted love for Ophelia, and, regardless of evidence, looks only for confirmation of this belief. Elsewhere (2004) I have suggested that curiosity/willingness to be surprised exists on a continuum, the furthest opposite end of which is closed minded certainty (or, in clinical terms, paranoia). We are all, always, somewhere on that continuum, from avid curiosity to absolute certainty. Some of us live most of our lives open to "news," and willing to revise our most cherished hypotheses. Others live life looking for evidence for preformed, rigidly held "truths." One way I read the play, *Hamlet,* is as (in part) an exploration of this continuum. From its first line, "Who's there?" it asks anxious questions. In the first act (scene 1) Horatio brings his skepticism with him, but is willing to examine whether or not the Ghost exists, as Marcellus and Barnardo attest. Then, seeing the Ghost, he (lines 55–57) declares, "Before my God, I might not this believe/ Without the sensible and true avouch/ Of mine own eyes." Evidence convinces him to change his mind, and believe the Ghost is real, not a product of fantasy.

Several characters express a clear attitude on the open minded to closed minded continuum at some point in the play. For example, Hamlet continues to weigh evidence, well after he sees the Ghost.

> Hamlet: ...The spirit that I have seen
> May be a de'il, and the de'il hath power
> T' assume a pleasing shape. Yea, and perhaps
> Out of my weakness and my melancholy,
> As he is very potent with such spirits,
> Abuses me to damn me! I'll have grounds
> More relative than this...   (Act II, Sc. 2, lines 533–539)

Hamlet weighs alternative explanations, as does Claudius, who is willing to put Polonius's theory to the test (by listening in on the conversation between Hamlet and Ophelia) but drops this theory when what he hears doesn't conform to it. Gertrude is also willing to test Polonius's explanation by talking with Hamlet in the "closet" scene (Act III, Sc.4).

Interestingly, Horatio expresses concern when Hamlet examines the skulls in the "gravedigger" scene: (Act V, Sc. 1) "Twere to consider too curiously to consider so" (line 195). Horatio is worried about how Hamlet's unquenchable curiosity might unhinge his mind. This is not the first time

310

Horatio expresses anxiety about Hamlet's mental state. As early as Act I, Scene 4, when the Ghost beckons Hamlet to follow him, Horatio tries to hold Hamlet back, concerned that the spirit might

> Horatio:... assume some other horrible form
> Which might deprive your sovereignty of reason
> And draw you into madness...   (lines 72–74)

What is fascinating to me is that editors, critics, and commentators have paralleled the characters in their positions on the curiosity/certainty continuum. I find myself applauding Levin (in Kinney, 2002, p. 215) when he charges himself *not* to use the play to confirm his favorite hypotheses. In his conclusion he affirms his pluralism: "It does not follow, however, that this is the only correct way to interpret the play, because I am a pluralist and therefore believe that it is just one of several valid critical approaches, although I hope I have shown that it can illuminate aspects of the play that are neglected or obscured by many of the other of the approaches that now dominate academic criticism" (p. 227). Levin has a fully articulated point of view, but doesn't claim it as *the* truth. On the other side of the continuum, in my own opinion, there is an incredibly passionate controversy, over many decades, about which version of the play most conforms to Shakespeare's intentions, and why deviations among the versions exist. Werstine (in Kinney, 2002, pp. 115–135) gives us a good summary of the history of these positions. Suffice it to say that the arguments get heated, in the way academic opinions can tend to solidify. Certainty about the one "true" explanation attains the status of a holy grail. I hear a good deal of evidence seeking in the declarations about who *must* have made copying errors or cuts or changes to the script, resulting in the differences between the 1603 (Q1). 1604–1605 (Q2) and the 1623 (Folio) texts. Like the characters in the play, some critics doggedly cling to a theory, seeming only interested in finding ways to corroborate it. The search for "the truth" sometimes has the flavor of a detective story, as, of course, can much of the play itself.

Against this background, one character, Hamlet, doesn't easily adhere to a theory and, I think, by his shape shifting (an issue I will return to) unsettles other characters as well as his audiences. He welcomes surprises himself and visits shocking surprises on others, constantly stirring the pot. His attitude is likely to create an anxiety that perhaps can be quelled, by other characters and by audience members, critics, and all the rest of us, by seeing him as "mad." Can strange thoughts, unheard of ideas, spooky beliefs, be entertained without shaking foundations so much they crack? I think Ophelia can be seen as the character who simply couldn't hold together, under the strain of the sorrow and mystery of her father's death and its secretive aftermath. Sometimes, to allude to Yeats, under severe pressure, the center does not hold. In one of the most touching scenes (Act IV, Sc. 5) I have ever seen or read, the unhinged Ophelia offers her brother, Claudius, and Gertrude flowers symbolizing repentance, unrequited love, remembrances, thoughts, flattery, and fidelity. A discussion of this passage (Arden, 2016, pages 417–418, footnotes) emphasizes the question of which flowers are given to each character. I am struck by how thoughts and feelings are separated from each other.

Of course, I am plying my own theories, as I write this. I think there is no way to respond passionately to this play without developing and investing in a personally resonant point of view. But I hope I remain open to hearing others, even those that seem most "strange," or unsubstantiated to me.

I wonder if those who can more easily welcome "strange" ideas also have less trouble inviting actual strangers into their fold. I think this is a vital issue in the era in which we live. One of the most stirring expressions of welcoming the concrete, literal stranger is the poem inscribed at the base of the Statue of Liberty. It was written by Emma Lazarus. The text is quoted in Chapters Two and Three, above.

312

Just as some people strike us as strange, and we can rise to the challenge of welcoming them, ideas can also seem oddly divergent. The poet Rilke is my favorite spokesperson on behalf of their welcome. For example, in his *Letters to a Young Poet*, he exhorts the neophyte writer to bear his uncertainty about his professional future: "I want to beg you, as much as I can, dear sir, to be patient toward all that is unsolved in your heart and to try to love the questions themselves like locked rooms and like books that are written in a very foreign tongue" (1934, pp. 34–35).

Personally, I find it very moving that Shakespeare wrote about welcoming the stranger. In such a brief statement he encapsulated two of our greatest challenges. Can we open ourselves to curiosity about ideas, and people, that initially strike us as "strange"? Or must we see only confirmations of ourselves, and our accustomed ideas, everywhere we turn? Shakespeare's character, Hamlet, is confronted with a sight that shakes him to his very core. No stranger could be stranger than the ghost of his dead father. What the Ghost tells him re-writes a crucial event. Some suggest it even forces him to question whether his mother was adulterous before the death of the King. In any case, Hamlet responds by weighing the Ghost's story against other evidence, neither dismissing it nor immediately accepting it. For example, in the lead up to the play within the play, Hamlet is hoping that his uncle's response to the staged events will give him evidence that is "more relative," that is, more objective, than the Ghost's personal version. Hamlet is not closed off to the Ghost and his message, but neither is he blithely accepting. In a sense Hamlet acts like a scientist faced with an as yet unproved hypothesis. Ever curious, Hamlet responds to the Ghost, and to the skulls in the "gravedigger" scene, as a person open to experience, however jarring it may be.

Hamlet's curiosity can be given a different spin, depending on the interpretation of a line from near the end of the play. Osric, a courtier, bantering with Hamlet, (Act V, Sc.2) declares that Hamlet is not ignorant of Laertes' excellence. Hamlet replies:

I dare not confess that, lest I should compare
with him in excellence. But to know a man well were to
know himself. (lines 122–124)

How should we understand what Shakespeare means when he writes "...to know a man well were to know himself"? One translation (*Barnes and Noble Shakespeare*, 2007, Ed: Jeff Dolven, p. 362) suggests it means "In order to truly know another man's excellence, one must be capable of it himself." I prefer the Arden version, "...to know anyone else well one must first know oneself" (2006, p. 472). In this light Hamlet's self-exploration serves more than one need. It fulfills curiosity about himself, but it is also prerequisite to understanding the others who make up his interpersonal landscape.

Can Hamlet's curiosity be seen from yet another perspective? A poem by Emily Dickinson suggests one. Elsewhere (2004) I have discussed curiosity as a value, generally unequivocally embraced by clinicians. There I described a continuum, between open minded curiosity on one end, and paranoid certainty on the other (as mentioned above). We are all, always, somewhere on this continuum. I think of it as fluid. In an interpersonal interaction we affect each other's position, in many possible ways. So, for example, my tight certainty might bring out yours. To me, this is an extremely important dynamic in a treatment session, but I think it is equally applicable to a political debate, a marital discussion, or any other interchange of ideas. The paranoid extreme might be illustrated by the delusion that the cause of everything I feel is that "they" are poisoning my soup. This shows a tightly locked mind, unwilling to admit news. Emily Dickinson created a somewhat different, but related continuum.

Poem 1347 (in Vendler, 2010, p. 455)

Wonder—is not precisely knowing
And not precisely knowing not—
A beautiful but bleak condition
He has not lived who has not felt—

Suspense—is his maturer Sister—
Whether Adult Delight is Pain
Or of itself a new misgiving—
This is the Gnat that mangles men—

I can't imagine a better description of Hamlet's state, throughout much of the play, than to say he "is not precisely knowing, and not precisely knowing not." And he is not alone in that. Claudius doesn't precisely know what Hamlet does or doesn't intuit about the crime Claudius has committed. And we, as readers or audience members, don't precisely know what Gertrude knows or intuits. The play begins with a question, "Who's there?" As the action unfolds, we join in wondering about how that question should be answered.

Dickinson is quite convinced of the necessity of wonder. We have not lived if we have not felt it. But it brings with it its sister, suspense, with her misgivings. The poet creates a marvelously complex image of a gnat that can mangle a human being. We may imagine that a tiny misgiving bores its way into a person, wreaking havoc. Vendler (2010, p. 455) suggests that for Dickinson the continuum is between knowing, at one end, and not knowing, at the other, with various states in between, such as apprehension and doubt.

From this perspective, Hamlet could be seen as tortured by the gnat. He is supremely curious, which brings with it suspense and plaguing misgivings. This reading takes the moralizing out of an understanding of him. Rather than seeing his slow movement toward action as a fault, it sees it as a natural extension of a strength. I have always felt that our strengths come with price tags. Of course my view is just that, a perspective, shaped by my own values. I don't think there is a way to read or hear this play without some slant, that is itself a product of living in a particular time and place, and the personal experience we bring to it. Personally, I agree with Dickinson that wonder is a necessity. But it does incline us toward an intellectual restlessness. The profoundly curious person is driven never to rest content with pat answers, but rather to question received wisdom. Is that the "gnat" that Hamlet wrestles? For me, looking at it that way opens up a very interesting perspective on the last portion of the play, where he brushes off his own misgivings about engaging in the fencing match with Laertes. Horatio wants him to listen to these inner warnings, but Hamlet says

...We defy augury. There is a special providence in the fall of a sparrow. If it be, 'tis not to come. If it be not to come, it will be now. If it be not now, yet it will come. The readiness is all, since no man of aught he leaves knows what is't to leave betimes. Let be.

(Act V, Sc. 2, lines 197–202)

I return to these lines below, but for now, I wonder whether he is simply done with suspense. He knows he will die, if not now, then later, and he is ready for it. The "gnat" of uncertainty can torture him no more. Hamlet's last line in the play, "The rest is silence," also may be understood in this light. There is no more suspense and there are no more questions for inward and interpersonal debate. All that remains is silence. The gnat has lost its bite.

Many writers have (justifiably, I would say) been harshly critical of attempts to analyze Hamlet's character, or diagnose him, or interpret the time it takes for him to go from wanting to avenge his father's murder to acting on that desire. For a witty and succinct summary of the issues involved

I recommend Richard Levin's chapter in *Hamlet: New Critical Essays* (Ed. Arthur F. Kinney, Routledge, 2002, "Hamlet, Laertes, and the Dramatic Function of Foils" pp. 215–231). I will not add to the voluminous pile of attempts to analyze Hamlet's character, the play, or its author. But I want to suggest that those who see Hamlet's "over-thinking" as obstructing his action may not discriminate various types of thought. In my view, there are many common misconceptions about thought and, especially, introspective thought. For example, some people are afraid that self-examination will inhibit them creatively. I think they are mistakenly equating all thought with obsessive thought, which *can* obstruct functioning.

Hamlet engages in a particular *kind* of thinking, that searches for the motivations behind the actions of others, as well as his own motives. He is looking for what is behind observed reality, for what is "really" going on underneath the surface. And with good reason, since we know he is being spied upon and plotted against. But this makes him wary of everyone's "real" motives toward him. Why have Rosencrantz and Guildenstern come to visit? Where is Ophelia's father now? Who is listening in as he talks to his mother in her "closet"? Of course, once again, in each instance he is right to question Even if I wanted to "diagnose" his character, it would not be appropriate to use these instances. But the *focus* on figuring out the reality behind appearances leads him to look through people (including himself) rather than at them. In a sense he has lost the joy of open ended wonder. His curiosity has become a weapon. In Dickinson's language (above) it is more suspicion than wonder. I am distinguishing between wondering, or thinking, or curiosity itself versus suspicious scanning to uncover lies. In this sense, and in others (discussed above) Hamlet's mind is "tainted" by the encounter with the Ghost, regardless of the King's command ("Taint not thy mind" -Act I, Sc. 5, line 92). Perhaps we could say that a natural tendency to wonder has turned into a microscope for looking beneath the surfaces of his own and others' behaviors. For a playful, bracing poem about the dangers of certain kinds of thinking, I love Tony Hoagland's delightful poem, "I Have News For You" (In: Seiden, 2016, pp. 58–59).

There are people who do not see a broken playground swing
as a symbol of ruined childhood
and there are people who don't interpret the behavior
of a fly in a motel room as a mocking representation of their
    thought process.
There are people who don't walk past an empty swimming pool
and think about past pleasures unrecoverable
and then stand there blocking the sidewalk for other pedestrians.
I have read about a town somewhere in California where human
    beings
do not send their sinuous feeder roots
deep into the potting soil of others' emotional lives
as if they were greedy six—year—olds
sucking the last half-inch of milkshake up through a noisy straw;
and other persons in the Midwest who can kiss without
debating the imperialist baggage of heterosexuality.
Do you see that creamy lemon-yellow moon?
There are some people, unlike me and you,
who do not yearn after fame or love or quantities of money as
unattainable as that moon;
thus they do not later have to waste more time
defaming the object of their former ardor.
Or consequently run and crucify themselves
in some solitary midnight Starbucks Golgotha.
I have news for you—
there are people who get up in the morning and cross a room
and open a window to let the sweet breeze in
and let it touch them all over their faces and their bodies.

I find this poem biting and bracing, and I love its sarcastic lampoon of thought obsessed navel gazers. I would differentiate Hamlet from that group. He is forever questioning, but not out of ambition or pretension. He wants to solve mysteries. In that sense, Hamlet remains Hamlet. But the tenor of the questions does shift toward the suspicious end of the continuum.

What the Soul Seeks To Be

Some other characters, like Ophelia, seem utterly changed by the tragic events, and, in a sense, are robbed of who they were. The tragedy begins with the story of a robbery. From a Christian point of view, old King Hamlet was robbed of the chance to confess and repent his sins before his death, consigning him to a period of purgatory. From a secular point of view, I would suggest that he was robbed of the chance to die as he lived. There was nothing heroic about his death. He was stung while sleeping in his garden. Unlike his life, his last struggle was not exemplary in any way. This is (at least a part of) what Claudius did to him. This lack of symmetry between the life-style and the death—style is not uncommon in real life, but I think it always feels unjust. The brilliant Iris Murdoch ends life acting like a rebellious two year old, her mind destroyed by Alzheimers' disease (Bayley, 1999). A dignified life ends in countless indignities, as is so beautifully expressed in C. K. Williams' poem ("Grief" in Seiden, 2016, p. 125) about the death of his mother, Dossie. I quoted from it before, but here I note how desperately Dossie tried to remain Dossie at the end.

... "Eighty, dying, in bed, tubes in her chest, my mother puts on her morning makeup; the broad, deft strokes of foundation, the blended-in rouge, powder, eye shadow, lipstick; the concentration with which you must gaze at yourself, that ravenous, unfaltering focus. Grief for my mother, for whatever she thought her face had to be, to be made every morning; grief for my mother-in-law in her last declining, destroying dementia, getting it wrong, the thick ropes of rouge, garish green paint on her lips; mad, misplaced slash of mascara; grief for all women's faces, applied, created, trying to manifest what the soul seeks to be;...

Even strung between tubes, we still try to "manifest what the soul seeks to be..." When I think about the phrase, "what the soul seeks to be," one of Hamlet's soliloquies comes to mind. He is on his way to England, accompanied by Rosencrantz and Guildenstern (Act IV, Sc. 4). He encounters a Captain in the Norwegian army, and asks what is at stake in the battle against Poland. The Captain replies that the battle is over a very small and poor stretch of land. When Hamlet is alone, he marvels that the armies are willing to risk death for such a meager prize, while he is still unable to act to avenge his father's murder. What is worth doing with our lives? What makes a sacrifice or a courageous course of action worthwhile? Hamlet asks (line 32) "What is a man/ If his chief good and market of his time/ Be but to sleep and feed? A beast-no more." Then Hamlet goes on to answer his own question (lines 52–55):

> ...Rightly to be great
> Is not to stir without great argument
> But greatly to find quarrel in a straw
> When honour's at the stake...

The editor's note debates about the meaning of these lines (Arden, 2016, footnotes, p. 401). I take them to mean that engaging in a fight is worthwhile if we are standing up for values that give our lives meaning and purpose. In the chapter on *King Lear,* I write about the human need for an identity that defines us to ourselves. I explore how I think Lear lost that vision, and the tragic consequences that follow. I quote a poem, by William Stafford (In: Sieghart, 2019, p. 17) that firmly declares that a human life needs a unifying thread. The poem is titled "The Way It Is," and I quoted it in Chapter Two, above.

For the poet C.K. Williams' mother, Dossie, the thread was about how she needed to present herself to the world. Dossie wasn't Dossie to herself without makeup. She didn't let go of that thread. As a psychoanalyst, I often found that when people tell the story of their lives, threads emerge. Patterns give a life coherence.

I have always been attracted to paintings of the Annunciation. To me, it announces the meaning of Mary's life. It is a magical moment, when her purpose becomes clear to her. Throughout her Sorrows, even in the most intense grief, that thread remains.

In a sense, Hamlet's "annunciation" is in Act I, Sc. 4, when the Ghost tells him his mission. Even before he hears the Ghost's story, as he fights Horatio and Marcellus to let him follow the Ghost, he says (line 82) "My fate cries out..." This is the beginning of the thread's unraveling, but I think it is not until after the encounter with the Captain of Norway's forces in Act IV that Hamlet really understands his destiny.

Some of life's greatest tragedies involve mislaid or stolen threads. Those who die just as their lives are taking shape; promise struck down by disease, devastating accident, unrelenting addiction. Then there is the terrible pain when someone loses capacities cultivated over a lifetime. For me, personally, I find Sam Shepard's account (2017) of his steady deterioration almost unbearably sad. Shepard chronicles his descent into utter helplessness, as the disease, ALS, (amyotrophic lateral sclerosis) implacably progresses. In my mind's eye I watch this supremely creative, intellectually and physically adventuresome, highly self-sufficient man remember when he used to be able to wipe his own ass. It is heart breaking for someone to lose themselves before they lose their lives. In the manner of his death, the Old King Hamlet lost being who he had always been. To me, this is a particularly painful aspect of the tragedy. I suppose having that last chance to be ourselves is more meaningful to some people than others. In my imagination it would have been very meaningful to old King Hamlet and, for his watchful son, it would have had a good deal of meaning to see his father die a hero's death. In C.K Williams' language, that was what the old man's soul sought to be.

Hamlet, is an exercise in soulful introspection at many levels. It looks within, at theater itself, just as the character, Hamlet, is constantly examining himself. Garber (2004, p. 471) spells this out. "For one of the central tropes of Hamlet the play, (and indeed of Hamlet the prince and player) is what is called 'metatheater,' or 'metadrama,' the discussion of theater and drama within a play—the play talking about its own materials, and the self-referential gestures toward the world as a stage (or Globe)." This quality, of a process that looks at itself as part of its material, is very familiar to me as a psychoanalyst. For myself, but, I think, for many, part of the appeal of the play and the character is this translucence. Hamlet brings up the question of showing emotions appropriately, when instructing the players, at the same time as he engages in extravagant displays of emotions, as a character in a play called *Hamlet.* Method and content comment on each other, in ways we may hear only subliminally, which, I think, contributes to the play's impact.

Soliloquies give us access to Hamlet's thoughts, seemingly as he has them. We are his confidantes. The character is a mystery, but one we feel as though we should be able to penetrate, given our access to his mind. It reminds me of the genius of Velazquez, in his painting, "Las Meninas," letting us watch him paint the beautiful princess, while he also shows us her parents watching the process. Viewing the painting, we are put in the position Velazquez had to occupy, to paint the perspective as he did. We are in on it, in a way that is immediately captivating. Similarly, hearing the character, Hamlet, ask himself about himself involves us in his quandaries.

In Cavefy's poem, "The God Abandons Anthony," quoted earlier in this chapter, the poet's persona urges Antony to believe his losses are real. This seems to me to be a very interesting lens for looking at Hamlet's conflicts. As already stated, the question of what is real is a leitmotif in the play. Just as Cavafy's Antony is urged to believe his ears, Hamlet is challenged to believe his eyes when seeing the ghost in Act I, and believe his intuitive knowledge of his uncle's guilt. For much of the play, Hamlet tests his sense of reality, sometimes upbraiding himself for not acting faster, and sometimes blaming his melancholy for conspiring with the devil to create the ghost out of his own imagination. Is his "failure" to act really an inability to believe his own eyes, mind, and heart? From early in the play, Hamlet has grave misgivings and resentment about the speed of his mother's remarriage, and Claudius's assumption of the throne. Was he unable to glean enough from these feelings? I am reminded of William Blake's line "The tygers of wrath are wiser than the horses of instruction" (In "The Marriage of Heaven and Hell" and quoted in Seiden, 2016, p. 32).

In Act II, Sc. 2, lines 630–635, as he decides to have the players act out a version of his father's murder to test if Claudius has a guilty reaction, Hamlet also observes and questions his own experience:

...The spirit that I have seen
May be the devil: and the devil hath power
T'assume a pleasing shape; yea and perhaps
Out of my weakness and my melancholy,
As he is very potent with such spirits,
Abuses me to damn me...

We might say that what Hamlet's "soul seeks to be" is a man who always examines all the possibilities.

To Be or Not To Be

In arguably the most famous soliloquy in the English language, Hamlet weighs whether or not he should continue to live. Interestingly, this is framed as a question of whether living or dying is "nobler:"

> To be, or not to be—that is the question;
> Whether 'tis nobler in the mind to suffer
> The slings and arrows of outrageous fortune
> Or to take arms against a sea of toubles
> And by opposing end them...   (Act III, Sc. 1, lines 55–59)

To pose suicide as, perhaps, the more courageous choice was a courageous choice for the playwright, in his time and place. Suicide was sacrilegious. The First Gravedigger comments ironically that only the well born can get away with killing themselves and still be buried in hallowed ground:

> Gravedigger:
> ...the more pity
> that great folk should have countenance in this world to
> drown or hang themselves more than their even—
> Christen...   (Act V, Sc. 1, lines 26–29)

For Sylvia Plath, ("Tulips" In: Bialosky, 2017, pp. 165–167) suicide was not so much a matter of courage or class but rather, as I understand her, a confirmation of her existence on a different plane from the living. Plath writes about being watched by the tulips at her bedside. She imagines how she looks. Lying flat, her hands turned upward, she contrasts herself with the vividly alive flowers and the warm walls.

From someplace outside herself Plath sees herself observed by the tulips. Hamlet knows himself to be observed, and self-observant. Both live both inside themselves and, at the same time, imagine what observers see when they look at them. For Plath there is no distinction between tulips, persons, cats, and walls. Some are more peaceful than others, some disturb the air more. That is one way they can be distinguished. She longs for peace, and in that longing she identifies herself with the inanimate. Her heart may love her, beat for her, insist on life. But her heart is not her. Color, tulips, salt water, the beating of her heart, are reminders of the country of the healthy; a country so far away its existence can only be inferred. I imagine suicide would seem to her like a ratification of her state of mind.

For me, entering Plath's poem clarifies that Hamlet is thinking about *the concept* of suicide, rather than being in *a state of mind most cogently expressed by suicide*. Hamlet weights the pro's and con's. I think Plath might say that suicide is closer to the truth, for her, than living. She doesn't weigh it on a moral plane, judging whether the more courageous choice is to live or die. What I hear as similar is the yearning

> "...To die, to sleep—
> No more—and by a sleep to say we end
> The heartache and the thousand natural shocks
> That flesh is heir to—'tis a consummation
> Devoutly to be wished... (Act III, Sc. 1, lines 63–66)

Both yearn for peace, a peace that is unavailable in life. Or, perhaps, antithetical to life. There is no peace once there is a red pulsing heart (for Plath) and the heartache and natural shocks flesh is heir to (for Hamlet).

Hamlet raises the religious prohibition against suicide in his Act I, sc. 2 soliloquy:

O, that this too, too sallied flesh would melt,
Thaw, and resolve itself into a dew,
Or that the Everlasting had not fixed
His canon 'gainst (self slaughter!)...   (lines 129–132)

Here, it seems, Hamlet lacks only God's permission to kill himself. He is not cowed by fears about the "undiscovered country" as in the later soliloquy that questions whether "to be or not to be." He looks around, at "...Things rank and gross in nature..." and wishes for release, but God (and the law) forbid it.

Emily Dickinson sheds a different light on whether to be or not to be. Many of her poems imply thoughts and feelings about this subject. Here is just one example. (Poem 528, in Vendler, 2010, p. 243).

'Tis not that Dying hurts us so—
'Tis Living—hurts us more—
But Dying—is a different way—
A kind behind the Door—

The Southern Custom—of the Bird—
That ere the Frosts are due—
Accepts a better Latitude—
We—are the Birds—that stay.

The shiverers round Farmer's doors—
For whose reluctant Crumb—
We stipulate—till pitying Snows
Persuade our Feathers Home

Vendler (2010, p. 243) writes that this poem begins with a contrast between the hurt inflicted by dying and the hurt inflicted by living. Thus, the poet

326

starts by comparing one painful state with another, as Hamlet did in his "to be or not to be" soliloquy. But Dickinson clearly positions dying as preferable to the pain of being alive. ('Tis Living—hurts us more—). So, why are we the Birds that stay? Are we afraid of what awaits us when we are dead, as Hamlet implies? Dickinson pictures us as frozen in place, not so much cowards afraid to die, but "shiverers" who have to await the "pitying Snows." Only their intervention releases us to our deaths. Whereas in Dickinson's poem, we have to await the "pitying snows," in Hamlet's "too, too sallied flesh" soliloquy we would need God's permission to commit suicide. There it is God's decree that stands in the way of our relief from life. As I hear it, for Dickinson life is less an active choice than a state of immobility. We who are alive have not been able to be proactive and seek the better "Latitude" of death. Those able to commit suicide have accepted dying early, thus avoiding the more protracted process of shivering to death. Of course this poem speaks of spiritual "food," and not literally breadcrumbs. For Hamlet, in both soliloquies, and for Dickinson, in this poem, the world is a place of suffering, but they focus on different obstacles to our ending our pain.

Vendler (p. 244) connects this poem with Dickinson's Poem 372, "After great pain." As in that poem, the dying are anaesthetized and death is gradual. It is a mercy to die. And yet, we have to be "persuaded." As I hear the poem, we who stay frozen, rather than seeking a premature death, are acting on instinct, like birds migrating or staying put, depending on their inborn proclivities. Like Plath, Dickinson takes the choice completely out of the moral realm. After opening her poem by noting the tulips, Plath writes about it being winter, and that all is white, quiet, covered by snow.

I think both Dickinson and Plath see us as suspended, in a cold and impersonal world. Unlike Shakespeare I don't hear them saying we make a choice to live that reflects either courage or cowardice, or weighing of options, or anything deliberate. We just go on until we float into some kind

327

of merciful oblivion. I am reminded of Ophelia, in "Hamlet," who actually floats to her death. The scene is so beautifully and powerfully described:

> Gertrude: ...Her clothes spread wide
> And mermaid-like awhile they bore her up,
> Which time she chanted snatches of old lauds
> As one incapable of her own distress,
> Or like a creature native and endued
> Unto that element. But long it could not be
> Till that her garments, heavy with their drink,
> Pulled the poor wretch from her melodious lay
> To muddy death.
>
> (Act IV, Sc. 7, lines 173–181)

In Hamlet's soliloquy, and these poems, life's potential joys do not seem to figure in the decision whether to commit suicide. It is as though trials and tribulations so outweigh any joys that they are too fleeting, or too slight to be mentioned. Or, perhaps, life's joys are shadowed by the knowledge of the sorrows to come. Dickinson expresses this forcefully in her oft quoted Poem 1773.

> My life closed twice before its close;
> It yet remains to see
> If Immortality unveil
> A third event to me,
>
> So huge, so hopeless to conceive
> As these that twice befell.
> Parting is all we know of heaven,
> And all we need of hell.   (In: Vendler, 2010, pp. 520–521)

Vendler (2010, p. 520) sums up this forthright poem's message: "Dickinson, conceiving of Immortality as a hellish continuation of life, with further deadly closings lying in wait, expects 'A third event,' more 'hopeless' than the first two, bringing the final loss of everyone she has loved." As in Hamlet's soliloquy, for Dickinson the "undiscovered country" of the afterlife holds no promise of joy, or comfort, or the presence of loved ones. Like our existence here on earth, it consists of inconceivably huge blows that must be sustained. As in Hamlet's dark speech no joys, pleasures, loves, temper life's bleakness or the horrors that await us in the afterlife. Hamlet's soliloquy and Dickinson's poem negate any expectation of heavenly rewards.

So, why live at all? At the very end of the play, Hamlet gives perhaps the most definitive answer to the question of whether or not to be. He begs Horatio not to commit suicide:

If thou didst ever hold me in thy heart
Absent thee from felicity awhile
And in this harsh world draw thy breath in pain
To tell my story.   (Act V, Sc. 2, lines 330–333)

I hear a profound truth in this final passage. Whether or not life is more painful than dying, whether or not it is more courageous to go on with life or end it, the choice to persevere is made meaningful by *purpose*. In this situation (and, I would suggest, in much of life) we live on for each other. Hamlet calls on Horatio to withstand the temptation of suicide out of love. Horatio gives Hamlet this precious, final gift. He will live to tell the tale. He will make sure history records what actually happened. Horatio isn't choosing life because he is too frightened of what may be waiting for him in the "undiscovered country." He lives on out of love for his "sweet prince." It is not only the angels that sing Hamlet to his rest. It is also his dear friend, Horatio, who chooses to serve Hamlet's peace of mind rather than his own.

Hamlet was betrayed, spied upon, profoundly disappointed, disillusioned, endangered by many but he dies loved by his one true friend.

The last exchange between Hamlet and Horatio provides a sterling example of how we can't help bringing our own values to our vision of the play and its characters. For example, Bloom is persuaded that Hamlet has never loved anyone, with the exception of his image of his dead father (1998, p. 408).

Bloom goes on (p. 409) to characterize Hamlet's farewell to his dead mother as heartless, his assertion that he loved Ophelia as unbelievable, and his request that Horatio live to tell his story as the need of a charismatic man to be saved from having a wounded name. While I can understand this perspective, I don't think it is the only one that is possible. The whole play resounds with the importance of how the dead are remembered. Last rites, funeral arrangements, are central to the story. Laertes is incensed that his father and sister have not been buried with honor. In a sense, many characters in this play might cry "remember me," because how we are mourned, how our story is told, is part of our legacy. The Ghost says that Denmark has been abused by hearing a false story of how he died. He wants history to reflect the truth. Horatio tells Fortinbras that he must inform the people about what really happened to forestall dangerous conjectures. To see Hamlet's last wish as the product of a kind of pride about his name is not the only way to read it. To me, the interchange between Hamlet and Horatio is the culmination of a story of love that will go to any lengths for the other. For whom, and for what purpose, does Hamlet save Horatio from suicide? We can't possibly know, but I think we have to look at our conjectures about the motives of characters in a play, and, for that matter, about the motives of others, and interpretations of our own motives as *hypotheses* that, in part, mirror our own values, our life experience, and our inevitable subjectivity.

In that (unforgettable, sublime) ending, I am reminded of a poem by Robert Frost. It is "Stopping By Woods on a Snowy Evening," which I quoted in Chapter Two, above.

Kendall (2012, p. 320) sides with those who have heard Frost's poem as an expression of a death wish. The persona in the poem lives on because of the promises he has to keep. I think the same may be true for Horatio.

Frost's woods represent the temptation to "sleep" with which Hamlet struggles in Act III.

> ...To die, to sleep—
> No more—and by a sleep to say we end
> The heartache and the thousand natural shocks
> That flesh is heir to—'tis a consummation
> Devoutly to be wished...   (Act III, Sc. 1, lines 63–67)

While describing "Stopping by Woods" as expressing a conflict between life and death (even though Frost objected to such interpretations) Kendall emphasizes the poem's ambiguities. He asks whether, at its end, the poem's speaker finds the woods irresistible, or forces himself onward.

The peaceful, snowy woods bring Plath's poem, "Tulips," (discussed above) to mind again:

> ...it is winter here.
> Look how white everything is, how quiet, how snowed-in...
>
> In: Bialosky, 2017, pp. 165–167

For Plath, Dickinson, and Frost, snow's blanket offers the comfort of swaddling. Death is snug. It takes firm determination to turn away from this comfort and go on with our journey's many miles. Perhaps the motivation to turn away from the inviting woods would take different forms, for each of us. But I believe the strength to resist this particular temptation often stems from having a purpose. However burdensome it may be, it is often purpose that persuades us to traverse miles before we sleep. And many of the powerful enough purposes I can envision serve love.

O! What a Rogue and Peasant Slave Am I!

In addition to his grief, for most of the play, Hamlet suffers from self-recriminations about being unable to avenge his father's murder. When he sees the Player King reduced to tears over lines in a play, he is merciless in his self-condemnation. Hamlet wonders what his inaction says about who he really is, and what he genuinely feels. Is he a "rogue and peasant slave"? A "dull and muddy-mettled rascal" (line 502)? "...pigeon-liver'd" (line 512)? Added to his loss of his father is his loss of a good opinion of himself. Guilt, shame, and regret haunt him for most of the rest of the play. In the scene in his mother's chamber, when Hamlet sees the ghost again, he asks him whether he has appeared to chide him for not yet avenging his father's murder:

> Do you not come your tardy son to chide,
> That, lapsed in time and passion, let go by
> Th 'important acting of your dread command?
> O, say! (Act III, Sc. 4, lines 103–105)

Hamlet's painful regret reminds me of a poem by W.S. Merwin (1973) that captures what it is like to be haunted by that emotion. The poem is titled "Something I've Not Done." It is quoted in full in Chapter Three, above.

Hamlet's failure to act on his father's command and Merwin's elusive lost chances both speak of our "sins" of omission. They add an everlasting silence to all our compasses.

In her Poem 407, Emily Dickinson expresses how we can haunt ourselves. I hear shame, guilt, and regret as possible internal specters:

> One need not be a Chamber—to be Haunted—
> One need not be a House—
> The Brain has Corridors—surpassing
> Material Place—
>
> Far safer, of a midnight meeting
> External Ghost
> Than its interior confronting—
> That cooler Host—
>
> Far safer, through an Abbey gallop,
> The Stones a'chase—
> Than unarmed, one's a'self encounter—
> In lonesome Place—
>
> Ourself behind ourself, concealed—
> Should startle most—
> Assassin hid in our Apartment
> Be Horror's least—
>
> The Body—borrows a Revolver—
> He bolts the Door—
> O'erlooking a superior spectre—
> Or More—   In: Vendler, 2010, p. 184

Thinking of this poem, we can turn Hamlet's story inside out. The appearance of the Ghost makes manifest the ghosts that were already lurking in Hamlet's internal corridors. We can imagine that the Ghost's appearance shakes foundations in Hamlet that were already under siege from within. Aside from Freud's (1900) speculations about Hamlet's incestuous desire for his mother, and patricidal impulses, we can think of less dramatic "sins" that could haunt the young prince's mind. Hamlet spends a good deal of the dialogue unsettling someone, whether it is Polonius, Rosencrantz, Guildenstern, his mother, or Claudius. Even the loyal and mild Horatio receives his share of shocks. Hamlet may have racked up many years of outrageous behaviors, that have undermined the equanimity of those around him. He is practiced in seeing through pretensions and, possibly, frequently tempted to call them out, much to the discomfort of others. He has already harbored dark suspicions about Claudius and may have intuited an erotic connection between Claudius and his mother even while his father was alive. In this sense, his mind is ready for what the Ghost implants. Dickinson (above) says "The Brain has Corridors..." Might not some of Hamlet's inner corridors housed guilt/shame/regret inducing ghosts even before he encounters the Ghost in Act I? Vendler (2010 p. 186) interprets the phrase "Ourself behind ourself" as implying a self divided into two selves; one disturbing the other. This strikes me as an apt description of just what Hamlet does *to others*, as well as to himself. As he listens to Osric's vain posturing or Polonius's pompous phrases, he springs into contemptuous action. But he also has a habit of treating himself the same way. He exercises his expertise at spotting hypocrisy against himself. Being constantly subjected to his own razor sharp, witty scorn could be haunting indeed!

Sometimes our "sins of omission" appear to us, to haunt us when it is too late for redress. This is how I hear the self-recrimination in Robert Hayden's unforgettable poem, "Those Winter Sundays." I quoted it in Chapter Two, above.

For Hamlet's father, remembering him means avenging his murder. It is a demand, an injunction. So long as the young Hamlet has not yet killed Claudius, it is "something he's not done," in Merwin's words, and it certainly haunts him. Hayden's unsaid appreciation of his father haunts him, too, but Hayden's father's love, humbly expressed in caretaking gestures, didn't insist on being acknowledged. Hayden's regret touches on what I take to be our most frequent sin of omission: the failure to recognize and respond to each other.

It is inevitable that our regrets of omission and commission take on personal meanings, to some extent dictated by our culture, and to some extent by personal experiences. More generally, the effect of various feelings on our ability to take action can be seen from different angles. For example, Claudius articulates a belief about the relationship between our actions and heated emotions. Claudius (no doubt as a way to maneuver Laertes) spells out that when our passions cool we may desist from previously planned actions.

> Claudius:
> ...That we would do
> We should do when we would, for this 'would' changes
> And hath abatements and delays as many
> As there are tongues, are hands, are accidents,
> And then this 'should' is like a spendthrift's sigh
> That hurts by easing. (Act IV, Sc. 7, lines 116–121)

Claudius counts on the heat of passion to prompt Laertes to action. Hamlet believes that the conviction he needs to spur him into action can come from certainty about the king's crime. He isn't looking for immediate, or intense feeling to inspire action. He already has that. What he needs is proof.

> Hamlet: ...I'll have grounds
> More relative than this. The play's the thing
> Wherein I'll catch the conscience of the King.
>
> (Act II, Sc. 2, lines 538–540)

Hamlet gets his "relative" (convincing) evidence, but still doesn't act. Interestingly, part of the subject matter of the play within the play is the relationship between actions we expect ourselves to do and the actions we actually perform.

> Player King:
> Our wills and fates do so contrary run
> That our devices still are overthrown.
> Our thoughts are ours, their ends none of our own:
> So think thou wilt no second husband wed
> But die thy thoughts when thy first lord is dead.
>
> (Act III, Sc. 2, lines 205–209)

But it takes one more encounter to fully convince Hamlet. The chance meeting with the soldier (on the way to Poland) tells him that actions should be shaped, not by certainties, but by *values*.

> Hamlet:...Rightly to be great
> Is not to stir without great argument
> But greatly to find quarrel in a straw
> When honour's at stake...
>
> (Act IV, Sc. 4, lines 52–55)

We "deserve" to act on the basis of *who we want to be in the world*. We don't have to know our actions are merited, in any legal or literal sense, so long as they are consonant with our ideals. The Norwegian and Polish soldiers are not fighting because the little plot of land is so valuable. They are upholding honor, as they understand it. Hamlet has gone beyond relying on "proof positive" of Claudius's actions, in order to make up his mind about his own course. Now he asks himself, who do I want to be? How can my actions express my priorities?

It seems worth reflecting on the emphasis on forms of evidence in much of Shakespeare's plays. What can convince Hamlet of Claudius's guilt? What moves Othello to believe Iago's accusations about Desdemona's infidelity? What suffices as enough evidence to derail Leontes in "The Winter's Tale"? What does Edmund offer up to convince Gloucester of Edgar's treachery in "King Lear"? What does Polonius suggest to Claudius should convince him that Hamlet is suffering from rejected love? At least in these instances, conviction is largely a matter of the eyes and ears, not just the heart. If Hamlet were content to believe his heart, he would have known of Claudius's guilt from page one. Belief relies on the power of actual perceptions. Hearing the words, seeing the letter or handkerchief, is what moves the mind from uncertainty to certainty.

As I discussed above, Hamlet wants certainty. And, often, commentators want certainty about him. Was he a (reluctant, and/or ambivalent, and/or conflicted) hero, or a villain? A coward, shirking his duty, or a man of conscience, figuring out what was right? Was he mad or shrewd, playing or earnest? Was he, as he tells his mother, "cruel only to be kind" (Act III, Sc. 4, line 176) or was he cruel to be cruel? We want greater clarity than we can have, just as Hamlet did. Ophelia (Act III, Sc. 1, lines 150–153) described him as a renaissance man, wide ranging in his interests. I hear him as just as wide ranging in his motives, emotions, and styles of relating. The psychoanalyst H.S. Sullivan had (1953) a concept called "me-you patterns."

He described us all as having different behavior patterns in different roles. I hear Hamlet as a portrayal of an extreme of that concept. Contrary to H. Bloom, (1998) who declared Hamlet unable to love, except for his ennobled father, I hear him as quite able to love Ophelia, until she spurns his affections, and Horatio, throughout the play. But he could be decidedly unloving, once he felt betrayed. One can have very varying "me-you patterns" toward the same person, in different circumstances. I think it is part of Shakespeare's genius to give us different "Hamlets," thereby putting *us* in the position of wishing for more certainty than we can have. I believe that it is possible to be certain about some things but not others. Claudius either did or did not poison King Hamlet. But motives, characters, role-related behaviors can't be pinned down in the same way. They waver, which can make the flickering language of poetry especially apt to capture their essence. Is Hamlet "mad," or strategically putting on the "antic disposition" he predicted he would "think meet" in Act I, Sc. 5, lines 169–170? Without attempting a definitive answer, I would just mention that his behavior is vastly different from Ophelia's, which is clearly meant to represent true madness. We might consider separately what Hamlet says, what he seems to perceive, and his moods. That he sees the Ghost tells us nothing, since Horatio, that paragon of normality, saw the Ghost too in Act I, Sc. 1. Hamlet's emotions fluctuate wildly but, I would suggest, the hilarity is reserved for social situations, and seems to disappear when he is alone. As for the content of what he says, there is an interesting interchange when Polonius asks Hamlet what he is reading. Hamlet answers in a witty but disparaging and provocative way, acting as though he is reading about old men with Polonius's unpleasant appearance and behavior. Polonius concludes, "Though this be madness yet there is method in't." (Act II, Sc. 2, line 202).

Hamlet: Shape-Shifter

Hamlet's cruelty and violence contend with his heartrending sorrow as the basis for our feelings about him. Perhaps in some eras it has been easier to think him mad than to try to integrate our own reactions. Then, as Hamlet himself maintains toward the end of the play:

> Was't Hamlet wronged Laertes? Never Hamlet
> If Hamlet from himself be ta'en away
> And when he is not himself does wrong Laertes,
> Then Hamlet does it not; hamlet denies it.
> Who does it then? His madness...
> (Act V, Sc. 2, lines 211–215)

Like Gertrude, who "explains" Hamlet's murder of Polonius as the product of his madness, and offers a similar explanation of his behavior toward Laertes in the "gravedigger" scene, we can "write off" his violence as not reflecting his "true" character. But I think that robs the character, and the play itself, of one of the qualities that has made it so enduring. Hamlet stirs us so much because every way we describe him can be legitimately contradicted. Terence Hawkes ("The Old Bill" in Kinney, 2002, pp. 177–193) puts it succinctly:

If Hamlet's "policing" interventions serve ultimately to cloud the differences between hero and villain, they do so as part of a broader function which not only muddies the distinction between play-world and real world, but disturbingly reduces the distance between right and wrong. In the end, this hugely complicates the play, making its dilemmas to some extent unresolvable, and perhaps constituting the basis of the enigma from which its capacity to arrest and disturb derives (pp. 183–184).

The feelings Hamlet evokes in us captivate us. We are outraged by his treatment of Gertrude and Ophelia and his blithe absence of responsibility for her suicide in the "gravedigger" scene. But we are moved by his agonized responses to the Ghost, his sorrowful description of his melancholy (to Rosencrantz and Guildenstern in Act II, Scene 2) and his tender appreciation of Horatio (for example, when he says that he wears him in his "heart's core" in Act III, Sc. 2, line 69). I think we are also affected by Ophelia's and Horatio's sincere adoration of him. For myself, I can say that it is fascinating to have such extreme, and extremely varied responses to one character. There are, indeed, many Hamlets, as I have already suggested in a previous section.

The mystery of such disparate qualities in one person has been beautifully captured by a series of poems Lucille Clifton called her "shape-shifter poems" (In Moyers, 1995, pp. 81–93). These poems convey the complexity of her feelings about her father, who sexually abused her when she was a child. I have explored her work in previous chapters, so will not go into great detail about it. But, to me, it stands out as exemplifying the capacity to hold onto what Keats called "negative capability." To truly perceive another human being, as well as ourselves, we have to be able to hold contradictory truths simultaneously, without trying to reduce them to one, simple, storyline. Resisting a one-dimensional condemnation of her father, she said in Moyer's interview of her (p. 93) "...I am one of the people I want to see wholly, and my father is another person I want to see wholly..."

If we try to see Hamlet "wholly," he is profoundly unsettling. Like King Lear, out in the storm, he punctures the self-delusions of the "proper" members of society, and doesn't miss an opportunity to call out hypocrisy. It is very interesting to me that both of these possibly mad characters have no patience with those who "put on airs." Lear makes crystal clear how the law is tilted in favor of the upper classes. Hamlet is ruthless in his scorn for high class female coquetry. For example, in Act III, Sc. 1, lines 141–145:

> Hamlet: I have heard of your paintings well enough.
> God hath given you one face and you make yourselves
> another. You jig and amble and you lisp, you
> nickname God's creatures and make your wantonness
> ignorance....

With pitiless sarcasm he skewers Rosencrantz, Guildenstern, Polonius, Ophelia, Claudius, Osric, and even (or, perhaps, especially) his mother. I think the issue of dressing up the truth to fawn, or please, or fool, or satisfy the other is at the heart of this play, but is also expressive of the dilemma of a playwright who has to cater to producers, actors, and an audience. I wrote about this in an earlier chapter, in the section on love, but I think it has special relevance here. For example, in Shakespeare's Sonnet 138, quoted in Chapter Two, ("When my love swears that she is made of truth...") he explicitly deals with the hypocrisy we go along with, to get along.

I hear much of what in *Hamlet* has an overtly misogynous meaning as *also* about having to be two faced to get along in society. Hamlet excoriates Ophelia and his mother for painting their faces, and, in effect, selling themselves. The vitriolic misogyny in these lines is unmistakable. But there is *also* a more general theme of words used to cover over inconvenient or socially unacceptable truths. For example, Polonius admits to sugaring his designs with pious words.

> Polonius:...We are oft to blame in this—
> 'Tis too much proved that with devotion's visage
> And pious action we do sugar o'er

The devil himself.

(Act III, Sc. 1, lines 45–48)

And Claudius recognizes how much he has similarly sinned.

Claudius: O, 'tis too true.
(aside) How smart a lash that speech doth give my conscience!
The harlot's cheek beautified with plastering art
Is not more ugly to the thing that helps it
Than is my deed to my most painted word.

From his first lines in the play, Hamlet compares how one "seems" with the internal truth. Hamlet, and his author, are pointing out how much we cover the truth, even to ourselves. In some of the sonnets I heard Shakespeare as saying truth and tact must modulate each other, and we need to strive for a balance between them. But the character, Hamlet, tips the balance, ruthlessly exposing poseurs like Osric, liars, like Rosencrantz and Guildenstern, adept schemers like Claudius, and women who " ...jig and amble " (Act III, Sc.1, line 143). He has a fierce hatred for cover up of any kind. Of course we know he is surrounded by those who would betray and even kill him, but there is also something in his violent self-confrontation that begets equally stringent standards for truthfulness in others.

Some confrontations can unbalance our minds. In Act I, Sc. 4, Horatio introduces the topic of dangers to Hamlet's sanity, by cautioning him about following the Ghost.

Horatio: What if it tempt you toward the flood, my lord,
Or to the dreadful summit of the cliff
That beetles o'er his base into the sea,
And there assume some other horrible form

Which might deprive your sovereignty of reason
And draw you into madness?

(Act I, Sc. 4, lines 69–74)

In the "gravedigger" scene, (as already noted above) Horatio's voices concern for Hamlet's sanity, lest he become unbalanced by staring too hard at death's consequences. When Hamlet muses that the noble dust of Alexander might serve to stop a bung hole, Horatio cautions, "'Twere to consider too curiously to consider so" (Act V, Sc. 1, line 194). But that doesn't stop Hamlet, who goes on to speculate further about the fate of Alexander's remains.

Meaningfully, Horatio is afraid for Hamlet's sanity. Is he right? If we see Hamlet as (at some point) mad, does he succumb to staring too hard at life's terms? Is this a warning that to get along (in any relationship and in society) we can't shoulder too much truth? Interestingly, Hamlet orders himself to hypocritically separate his words from his actions when he goes to confront his mother in Act III, Sc. 2, lines 385–387.

Hamlet: Let me be cruel, not unnatural:
I will speak daggers to her but use none.
My tongue and soul in this be hypocrites.

When I read this, I assume Hamlet is following the Ghost's injunction against harming the Queen, but, in the scene that follows, Hamlet's words certainly "speak daggers" to his mother and, in a blind rage, he strikes out and kills Polonius (thinking him to be Claudius). When Gertrude reports these events to Claudius, she positions them as the outpourings of madness. Is that a prevaricating attempt to excuse them? To throw Claudius off the track of seeing that Hamlet meant to kill him? Is she deliberately using the notion of Hamlet's "lunacy," as documented by his insistently unseemly behavior, as a cover for his committing murder? Or, is she simply saying what she believes to be true? In this play, the line between postures and veridical expressions is often unclear.

The connection between what may seem mad and what challenges society is pithily summarized by Emily Dickinson in her Poem 620 (In: Vendler, 2010, p. 272).

> Much Madness is divinest Sense—
> To a discerning Eye—
> Much Sense—the starkest Madness—
> 'Tis the Majority
> In this, as all, prevail—
> Assent—and you are sane—
> Demur—you're straightway dangerous—
> And handled with a Chain—

But Hamlet does more than just poke fun at society. In a way, his actions are equal parts rashly impulsive and overly encumbered by thought. Because Shakespeare so deeply understood human variability, Hamlet is not a "type." He challenges all classification.

Let Be

Hamlet believes in fate, and yet he defies augury:

> Hamlet: ...There's a divinity that shapes our ends,
>   Rough-hew them how we will.
>
> (Act V, Sc. 2, lines 10–11)

And:

Hamlet: We defy augury. There is a special
    providence in the fall of a sparrow. If it be, 'tis not to
    come. If it be not to come, it will be now. If it be not
    now, yet it will come. The readiness is all, since no man
    of aught he leaves knows what is't to leave betimes. Let be.
    (Act V, Sc. 2, lines 197–202)

Let be. Other phrases from the play are quoted more frequently. But, for me, these two words end the most poignant lines. With patience, peace, and, perhaps, resignation, Hamlet faces whatever will come next. However our lives end, they will end sometime. Even if we can control some outcomes, there are so many significant aspects of life that are out of our hands.

I keep coming back to the words "let be." Perhaps their philosophy is so very striking partly because of the simplicity of its expression. It is poetry, in its succinctness. Sometimes we "let be" as a conscious decision but, I believe, most of the time it is less than conscious. I hear this idea in a poem by Leonard Nathan (Quoted in Hirshfield, 2015, p. 152).

Falling
Wherever you choose to stand in this world,
that place, firm as it feels,
is a place for falling.

In my own house I fell. A dark thing,
forgotten, struck my ankle
and I fell.

Some falls are so slow, you don't know
you're falling till years later. And may be
falling still.

Some of us are more inclined toward letting falling happen, in a gradual, and, perhaps graceful version of "let be." Others, more vigilant, are forever braced for the fall. I think that most often this is not a product of conscious choice. The difference is thorough, affecting every muscle. We can choose whether or not to fight climate change, or income inequality, but how much can we choose whether or not to accede to the shifting gravity of the body?

Is it our place to fight for justice, or on behalf of past or future generations, or in the name of life itself? Or are we meant to submit to life as it comes, not comparing it to what should be, but adopting the attitude "let be"?

This issue is at the heart of *King Lear,* and I write about it in my chapter on that play. Clearly, it also plays a central role in *Hamlet.* One way to hear the text is that it seesaws, between viewing Hamlet as gradually becoming able to carry out a plan to avenge his father's murder, vs. seeing him as gradually letting go of planning, and simply reacting to events as they happen. When the Ghost begins to tell him about the murder, Hamlet says,

> Haste me to know't, that I, with wings as swift
> As meditation or the thoughts of love,
> May sweep to my revenge. (Act I, Sc. 5, lines 29–31)

He sees the right course as sweeping into action, to assure that the outcome is just. We can view Hamlet as gradually developing sufficient conviction to carry out a plan. But I think we can also view him as becoming capable of simply reacting to each moment as it happens. Shakespeare is too subtle to let us settle into one or the other reading. I think each is a valid reading, which contributes to the play's complexity and enduring relevance.

We can hear another aspect of this complexity in the line "...the readiness is all." Perhaps readiness is all that (conceivably) can be within our control. Each of us struggles with what "readiness" can mean. I would suggest that King Lear was "ready" to die, which made dying welcome. Thinking he saw the breath of life in Cordelia was all he needed to release him. Is Hamlet "ready" in that sense? His dying words (Act V, Sc. 2, line 342) are "...the rest is silence." Hamlet has left Horatio in charge of words. Horatio will tell the story of what happened, and rescue Hamlet's name. Persuading Horatio not to drink the poison, Hamlet cries, "O God, Horatio, what a wounded name,/ Things standing thus unknown, shall I leave behind me!" (Act V, Sc. 2, lines 328–330). Perhaps for Hamlet, his life's work is complete if the story is accurately told, and he knows his legacy is in safe hands with Horatio. Personally, I have always heard "the rest is silence" in several ways. Aside from the most obvious meaning, that silence is all that is left, I also hear that silence and rest are synonymous. Hamlet has spent himself in "words, words, words" (Act II, Sc. 2, line 189). His job is done. Like Lear, he is ready to leave the rest (what remains) to be done by others.

Hamlet's "readiness" can be compared to his father's state, when he was murdered. The old king was decidedly *not* ready, in religious and other senses. As the Ghost states (Act I, Sc. 5, lines 74–79):

> Ghost: Thus was I sleeping by a brother's hand
> Of life, of crown, of queen at once dispatched,
> Cut off even in the blossoms of my sin,
> Unhouseled, disappointed, unaneled,
> No reckoning made but sent to my account
> With all my imperfections on my head.

As the footnote (Arden, 2016, p. 247) expresses it, the king was deprived of the last rites that are due to a dying Christian. This religious version of not being "ready" is only one sense of it. In a lovely short poem, Donald Hall conveys a related thought, also based on a religious outlook, but with a different tone. Hall's poem, titled "A Grace," (In: Moyers, 1995, p. 152) gives thanks for some boons (sexual love, food, books, birch trees) but then goes on to note his grief and dread in response to premature deaths. He terms those early deaths "unripe."

The phrase "the unripe dead" seems so full of meaning. It is written in the context of a prayer, but I hear it as expressing so many aspects of being "unready" to die. In an interview (same page) Hall explained the phrase:

> They are the dead whose deaths I particularly regret, who seem to have died before their time. We talked about my father earlier, and surely he would be one, but there are more recent examples. People rarely seem to me to have lived out their lives and to be finished when they die. When someone I love dies before that time, I regret it—and this is something I reproach myself for. If I accept God's control of the universe I should accept these deaths, and yet I don't. I don't believe that God oversees the fall of the tiniest sparrow in the sky.

Interestingly, Hamlet remarks (Act V, Sc. 2, line 197–198) "There is a special/ providence in the fall of a sparrow." Hall seems to feel he *should* believe God is directing events, and, therefore, he *shouldn't* have the feelings he has when the dead are "unripe." But Hamlet, told by the Ghost that his father was murdered without his reckoning, is horrified. What would Hall say? Does it follow that if we believe in fate, or God, or the stars, or Nature's control, then our role is to find a way to accede to death with grace? Elsewhere (chapter 3) I have written about Dylan Thomas's rejection of this attitude as well as the opposite point of view, that objecting to death is blasphemous. I can't imagine anyone, even Shakespeare, resolving these questions. At best, we may each find our own articulation of them. I can only express that I think the way we approach "readiness" needs to be consonant with the values that have shaped the rest of our lives.

For Hamlet, a guiding principle has always been profound curiosity and thorough self-reflection. When Polonius advises his son, Laertes "To thine own self be true..." (Act I, Sc. 3, line 77) I hear that as more than just a moral precept. I think we can also take it as the wisdom that bids us fashion every aspect of our lives according to consistent values. In other words, we need to maintain integrity, for the sake of good citizenship in the world, but, also, for our own mental health. Finding a personally resonant way to die is as imperative as finding a personal way to live any other of life's passages.

In my own imagination, I picture Hamlet hungrily exploring the "undiscovered country" of death, just as he has insatiably explored his own soul. From my point of view, no one captured this sensibility better than Mary Oliver (In: K. Young, 2010, p. 269). Her poem, "When Death Comes," is quoted in full in Chapter Three.

As I see it, both Lear and Hamlet made of their lives "something particular, and real" by the time of their deaths. We can see Lear's life as a long road toward being able to love another person. Cordelia is that person. His genuine love for her gives him the "readiness" to let go of life, at the end of the play. Hamlet's "mission" can be understood as being about what will be remembered. His father commands him, *"Remember me."* At his own life's end, Hamlet begs Horatio to tell his story, so *he* can be accurately *remembered.* Having avenged his father's murder, the story is complete, so long as there is someone left to tell it. Horatio, ("...as just a man/ As e'er my conversation coped withal" Act III, Sc. 2, lines 50–51) has both the facility and the will to do the job. He is the perfect chronicler, because he has been with Hamlet every step of the way. In him is joined fair mindedness and compassion. I think Hamlet has found the "readiness" to die once he has passed the full story to Horatio; once, like his father, he recruits the man who loves him best to set the record straight. Both the elder and younger Hamlet can "let be" once someone heeds their plea, "remember me," and promises that the truth will be told.

I don't believe it is merely pride about his name that drives Hamlet to beg
Horatio to live to tell his story (see Bloom, 1998, for another perspective). I
hear it as the human need to be witnessed, a need that may have a prideful
element, but is more complex. To me, it is about wanting to take part in
the future. We need impact, partly for our own sense of self, but also as
our final gift. Bequeathing our story truthfully can be a way to help future
generations avoid our misfortunes or, at least, understand their own better.
I think the multitude of Holocaust memoirs attest to this need. Here is an
apt expression of it, by Anna Ornstein (Ornstein and Goldman, 2004) from
her poignant Holocaust memoir, *My Mother's Eyes: Holocaust Memories of
a Young Girl.*

> To survivors, the permanent cording off of memory would mean
>   an ultimate tragic alienation
> from their history, an excision of part of their identity, even if that
>   is an ineradicably hurtful part.
>
> (p. 160)

I have suggested (above) that the Ghost's command to be remembered
without tainting Hamlet's mind is unrealistic. We have to be "tainted" by the
memory of what previous generations have suffered. Otherwise we couldn't
understand their missions or our own. In a discussion of a poem by Emily
Dickinson (2010, p. 486) Vendler likens the Ghost in Hamlet to the Angel
Gabriel in the Annunciation. I think the analogy is apt. The "news" both
bring conveys purpose. Mary is told the ultimate purpose of her life, and
Hamlet is told the mission that will govern and inspire the rest of his.

Conclusions

In a way, all "news" is old. The past imprints the present, though its etchings are often understood only in retrospect. In that sense we are all haunted by ghosts. As I see it, many of the characters in the play, "Hamlet," are haunted by spirits that have emerged out of the past to point out the direction they should, or should not take in the present and future.

From the play's famous first line, "Who's there?" we scan for who is present. We soon find out that it is not a simple question. Those keeping watch, Barnardo, Marcellus, and Horatio, fail in their effort to capture a fleeting spirit, and decide they must report this to Prince Hamlet. Thus begins the tragedy. Even before he sees the Ghost, Hamlet lets us know he is haunted by his father's death. It has turned his previous, scholarly life, into a new exercise. Whereas before this, (presumably) he has pursued philosophical ideas in the abstract, his father's death and his mother's hasty re-marriage have added a new dimension to his thinking. We don't know exactly what he studied at university, but we know how preoccupied he becomes with ultimate questions of life's purpose, death's meaning, the debt we owe to our parents, the value of correspondence between who we seem on the surface and who we are in our inmost depths, the nature of convincing evidence, the proper place of revenge, the appropriateness of being cruel to be kind, (or, in other words, whether the ends justify the means) the limits and extent of the loyalty owed to husbands, lovers, and friends, and the impact of the loss of those we cherish. Hamlet may have encountered some of these issues in his philosophical studies, but the events in the play transform them from "words, words, words" (as he sardonically jests to Polonius about what he reads, in Act II, Sc. 2, line 189) to living realities.

Hamlet is haunted by questions (including the question of who is and isn't "there"). In the "closet" scene, with his mother, when he sees the Ghost, he expects to be reprimanded. Exactly what he was charged to do is a matter of controversy among critics (for an apt summary, see Foakes, in Kinney, 2002, pp. 85–100). Did the Ghost expect him merely to remember him, or to take specific actions against his uncle? Whatever the playwright intended us to think, it is clear to me that he tells us that Hamlet eventually feels both guilt and shame. In my own (2008) emotion theory terms, the part that is guilt would be the sense that he has failed to live up to standards he himself espouses. The shame is the judgment that, as a human being, he has fallen short. In some sense he has proved himself insufficient. Both guilt and shame will haunt him for the rest of the play, sometimes in the entreaties and reminders of the Ghost, but most often expressed in Hamlet's own self-reflective soliloquies.

Claudius is also clearly haunted by guilt, most vividly expressed when he tries, and fails, to pray for mercy (In Act III, Sc.3). As he declares, (line 40) "My stronger guilt defeats my strong intent..." The queen is haunted too. In the "closet" scene, as Hamlet strives to force her to face her treacheries, Gertrude cries,

> O Hamlet, speak no more.
> Thou turn'st my very eyes into my soul
> And there I see such black and grieved spots
> As will leave there their tinct.   (Act III, Sc. 4, lines 87–90)

Just a bit later, Gertrude expresses how her guilt hounds her in Act IV, Sc. 5, lines 17–20:

> Queen (aside)
>   To my sick soul, as sin's true nature is,
>   Each toy seems prologue to some great amiss,
>   So full of artless jealousy is guilt
>   It spills itself in fearing to be spilt.

The footnote (Arden, 2016, p. 405) to these lines reads "Guilt produces such paranoia that it betrays itself by its very own fear of betrayal."

Polonius also has moments of reckoning with his behavior and its impact. In Act II, Sc. 1, Ophelia is terribly distressed as she describes to her father what has just occurred between her and Hamlet. Polonius realizes (lines 107–113) that he erred in jumping to the conclusion that she should bar Hamlet from all communication.

> Polonius: I am sorry that with better heed and judgement
> I had not quoted him. I feared he did but trifle
> And meant to wrack thee—but beshrew my jealousy—
> By heaven it is as proper to our age
> To cast beyond ourselves in our opinions
> As it is common for the younger sort
> To lack discretion...

In Act III, Sc. 1, lines 45–48, Polonius is similarly contrite, as he confides in Claudius:

> ...We are oft too blame in this—
> 'Tis too much proved that with devotion's visage
> And pious action we do sugar o'er
> The devil himself.

Polonius's confession provokes Claudius to confront his own similar, but far more egregious behavior.

Ophelia is haunted by memories of being loved by Hamlet, when he spurns her, and by her father, after he has died. Sorrow seems to be her prevailing emotion, rather than guilt or shame, but her feelings are hard to read in the "mad" scene. Like King Lear, who has to repeat the word "never" over and over, in his attempt to integrate the reality of Cordelia's death, Ophelia repeats that that her father will "never come again" (in the song she sings in Act IV, Sc 5, lines 182–186).

Interestingly, Horatio describes the Ghost as starting "like a guilty thing/ Upon a fearful summons" (Act I, Sc. 1, lines 147–148). Shortly, we learn that he died without the benefit of confession, and so is doomed to "fast in fires/ Till the foul crimes done in my days of nature/ Are burnt and purged away" (Act I, Sc. 5, lines 11–13).

Horatio is a major figure who does not seem to suffer from guilt or shame. Hamlet characterizes him as "A man that Fortune's buffets and rewards/ Hast ta'en with equal thanks" (Act III, Sc. 2, lines 63–64). Hamlet further characterizes him as not being a slave to passion, but, rather, as having a healthy balance between "blood and judgement" (line 65). Perhaps we are meant to think this quality insulates him from the rash behavior that might occasion shame or guilt. Fortinbras is also unencumbered by these emotions, seemingly because his being is entirely taken up by action, leaving no room for contemplative self-judgment.

Under what circumstances should the guilty be shown mercy? Claudius accepts that he doesn't deserve pardon, because he will not part with the fruits of his sins. But Hamlet begs his mother to abstain from going to Claudius's bed, implying that if she could refrain from further sinning she might redeem herself. Some sinners recognize they have forfeited their souls, while others believe in the possibility of redemption. Even Laertes, not the most soulful character, has a moment of reckoning when he says that going through with killing Hamlet is almost against his conscience (Act V, Sc. 2, line 279).

But for Ophelia and Hamlet there is no way back. Ophelia's death is labeled doubtful by the churlish priest, and it *is*, though, perhaps, not quite in the way he means. As the first Gravedigger so humorously points out, it is suicide if it was intentional. But we can never know her state of mind, as she sang her way to the bottom of the brook.

Hamlet declares his readiness for death, whenever fate decrees it. Unlike his father, he has had time to prepare. One meaning of his oblique last words (" The rest is silence") could be that, unlike his father, he will not have to haunt from the grave. He will have nothing to impart, since he trusts Horatio to tell the story accurately. After his death there will be no need for his ghost to persuade Horatio to act on his behalf. He won't need to walk the night, imposing duties on guilty survivors. Horatio will gladly carry out his mandate, so that the past is fully known. As Freud discovered so many years ago, when the past is not remembered we may be doomed to repeat it. Horatio cautions that the play's events must be told to prevent further "mischance" (Act V, Sc. 2, line 378). Hundreds of years before Freud, Shakespeare understood how undigested memories are those most likely to haunt us.

5.

"I Shall Go Mad:"

———～～———

Poets in Dialogue With "King Lear"

At the start of the play King Lear, imperious, announces his plan to give up the cares of ruling, and divide his kingdom into thirds, with a portion going to each of his three daughters. But first, they must undergo a test. Each is to declare their love for their father. The elder two have no trouble passing, showering their father with hypocritical hyperbole. But Cordelia, the youngest, with strict (and, perhaps, ungenerous) honesty fails and is hastily banished. Lear comes to regret his poor judgment, as he learns the bitter truth that his elder daughters have only selfish cunning in their hearts, and no real love for him. Each vies to accommodate his needs less, until he feels he has no choice but to leave everything behind and brave the elements. Lear wanders, lost in a terrible, engulfing storm that signifies his disordered mind, as well as his desperate circumstances. Meanwhile, in a subplot, the Earl of Gloucester similarly misjudges his two sons, hoodwinked by his conniving, bastard son into turning against his other, innocent, legitimate son. Gloucester is blinded by Lear's vicious daughter and her husband, for attempting to save the king. Lear, deranged and distraught, comes to feel pity for his fool, for a poor beggar he meets (Gloucester's innocent son in disguise). and all those who face life "unaccommodated." At the play's end Lear regains his senses and briefly reunites with Cordelia before she is murdered by his enemies. His heart breaks for Cordelia, his one true daughter, whose love for her father survived undiminished.

This is a play I love dearly. It raises some of life's most fundamental questions. How can intense grief drive us mad? Is giving in to sorrow a weakness? What are the inevitable and avoidable losses in aging? What can make it hard to recognize the powerful role of regret in our lives? For those not prone to suicide what can, nevertheless, make death acceptable, and even desirable? Can anger mobilize failing resources? When does its excess become a danger? What are some of the ways pride "goeth before a fall"? Can extremely self-preoccupied human beings develop a capacity for empathy? What is the nature of genuine love?

Remarkably, I do not think this is an exhaustive list. I find this play endlessly fascinating. Hamlet (Act III, Sc. 2, line 22) suggests theater should "hold, as twere, the mirror up to nature." Both *Hamlet* and *King Lear* hold up thrillingly accurate and devastating mirrors. In a letter, Keats captured the intensely moving experience of seeing or reading *King Lear*: "The excellence of every art is in its intensity, capable of making all disagreeables evaporate from their being in close relationship with Beauty and Truth. Examine "King Lear," and you will find this exemplified throughout." (Quoted in Muir, 1975, p. xiii)

As I have in the past (2008, 2017, 2019) in this essay I look at *any* intense emotion, even the most positive feeling, as potentially unbalancing. For example (to anticipate a later discussion) both Lear and Gloucester have been seen as dying from excessive joy. More about that later, but, for now, I look at the more "usual suspects," intense sorrow and rage, as endangering the stability of the mind.

Poets have addressed the same questions Shakespeare's plays raise, bringing to them their own tones, values, associations, imagery, and creative imagination. I have a belief that dialogue can be fruitful, so I am juxtaposing lines from the play with lines from other plays and a number of poets, to see what emerges. I am trusting that although these authors differ in very many respects, they share the fundamental experience of being human, so their work will reflect that commonality, which will make "dialogue" possible.

Intense Sorrow

In the course of the play, Lear suffers many losses, some self-inflicted, some imposed by other characters or circumstances. In a sense the loss that drives the plot is his voluntary abdication of the crown:

> '...tis our fast intent
> To shake all cares and business from our age,
> Conferring them on younger strengths, while we
> Unburdened crawl toward death... (Act I, Sc.1, lines 37–39)*

In one stroke he cedes control of his life and, arguably, his identity. As he himself asks later (Act I, Sc. 4, line 221) "Who is it that can tell me who I am?" His knowing Fool answers (line 222) "Lear's shadow." While the question might be asked in jest, over the course of the play it becomes an urgent and sincere inquiry. Who is Lear, without his crown, authority, status, full retinue? Who is anyone, without accustomed status, purpose, recognition, accouterments? Lear gives an answer, as he observes the half—naked, wild beggar "Poor Tom." He calls him "unaccommodated man." Although concretely this refers to "Tom's" nakedness, the phrase could be applied (in a different sense) to the king himself. Through a series of grave losses Lear, used to wielding automatic accommodation from everyone,

---

* Unless otherwise indicated, all quotes are from Arden Shakespeare, *King Lear*, Ed. R.A. Foakes, 1997.

finds out what beggars feel. The Fool and Kent argue with Lear's decision, but, as he says at one point, he is "firm" (Act I, Sc. 1, line 247). By the play's end we can look back at this line and hear a bitter irony, as Lear descends into *infirm* madness.

Some critics find Lear's decision unrealistic, and feel this mars the play. A literary figure no less than Tolstoy (in Bloom, 2008, pp. 156–162) said that Lear's behavior makes no sense, since he has no need to resign. More generally, says Tolstoy, the conflicts in the play do not arise from natural events, so *King Lear* is not art (!). Tolstoy goes on to declare that the speeches do not fit the characters. For Tolstoy, the older drama, upon which the play is partially based, is superior to Shakespeare's version. We can only speculate that Tolstoy was offended by some aspect of the play, such as its non-religious tenor, or its intense emotionality, or, perhaps, its irrational elements. Not surprisingly Freud is not put off by these qualities (Bloom, 2008, pp. 163–164). Freud suggests that perhaps Lear divides up his kingdom because he knows he is dying.

No doubt there are many reasons that I find the decision less puzzling than some do. As I read it, Lear, at age eighty, is ready to shed the cares of state, but still wants to command respect, and retain his one hundred followers. To me that desire does not sound mysterious, as *a wish* (for an understanding of its meaning in 17th century England see Foakes, 1997). But, believing himself to be a beloved monarch and father, he (mistakenly) assumes that all three of his daughters, and their husbands, will lovingly *accede* to his wishes. That sets in motion a great chain of disorienting losses.

Over the course of the play, through his own miscalculations and the cruelty of his eldest daughters, Lear loses his beloved Cordelia, his faithful follower Kent, his fool, his eldest daughters, his realm, his identity, his faith in justice, his image of himself as a kind father and good king, and his wits, to name just a few of the heavier forfeits. He comes to question his judgment quite early on (Act I, Sc. 4, lines 262–264).

...O Lear, Lear, Lear!
(striking his head) Beat at this gate that let thy folly in
And thy dear judgement out...

Sorrow braids with regret in these reflections. I find a poem by James Fenton almost uncanny in how it could fit Lear's backward glances. To me, this correspondence illustrates how aspects of the human condition do not really change:

The Mistake

With the mistake your life goes in reverse.
Now you can see exactly what you did
Wrong yesterday and wrong the day before
And each mistake leads back to something worse

And every nuance of your hypocrisy
Towards yourself and every excuse
Stands solidly on the perspective lines
And there is perfect visibility.

What an enlightenment. The colonnade
Rolls past on either side. You needn't move.
The statues of your errors brush your sleeve.
You watch the tale turn back—and you're dismayed.

And this dismay at this, this big mistake
Is made worse by the sight of all those who
Knew all along where these mistakes would lead—
Those frozen friends who watched the crisis break.

Why didn't they say? Oh, but they did indeed—
Said with a murmur when the time was wrong
Or by a mild refusal to assent
Or told you plainly but you would not heed.

Yes, you can hear them now. It hurts. It's worse
Than any sneer from an enemy.
Take this dismay. Lay claim to this mistake.
Look straight along the lines of this reverse. (In Sieghart, 2019)

It is loyal Kent, above all, who tried to warn Lear about his mistake, but the stubborn king would not heed and banished the "messenger" rather than listen to the message. Lear is left with only his fool to confide to, as he begins to sense he could go mad. Is it intense sorrow about his catalogue of losses that drives Lear mad? Or searing regret? Or the severity of his rage? Or, mainly, the loss of his identity, self-esteem, and sense of being known and respected? All of these? Something else? Whether it is in his nature to be rash, and this gets exacerbated, or his aging fundamentally changes him, or he has fits of hysteria, or loses his sanity altogether, are questions threaded through the play, and I think they elicit extremely interesting debates among critics. No less than the nature of sanity and madness is at stake.

What role does Shakespeare assign to Lear's advanced age? Commenting on Lear's banishment of Kent and Cordelia, Regan says (Act I, Sc. 1, lines 294–300):

'Tis the infirmity of his age, yet he hath ever but slenderly known himself.
(Goneril) The best and soundest of his time hath been but rash;
then must we look from his

age to receive not alone the imperfections of long-engrafted
condition, but therewith all the
unruly waywardness that infirm and choleric years bring with them.

Shakespeare embraces complexity. Lear's temperament, ever tending toward
rashness, is exacerbated by the toll of aging. I would find it very difficult to
sort out the role of aging in Lear's evolving disaster. His devastating losses
leave him vulnerable and virtually alone, except for a few loyal subjects.
When he loses the illusion that his eldest daughters will love and care for
him, he appeals to the heavens as a man as full of age as grief. They weigh
on him equally. Lear's internal world becomes as unreliable as the external
world. He loses the loyal companionship of his retinue at the same time as
he loses his inner sense of being a beloved father, and his faith in his mind's
capacity for sound judgments. He becomes aware that his wits begin to
turn, and, even after he wakes, wonders if he is in his right mind. To have,
in a sense, lost *oneself* along with most everyone else is the unfathomable
aloneness that accompanies aging more frequently than other stages of life.
It is hard to find words for the loneliness of losing one's past along with
one's orientation and sense of being what I call a "going concern." For Lear
the loss of place, position, retinue, sits beside the loss of faith in his own
mind as an effective protector. The inner "guardian" disappears along with the
external defenders. Losing an unself-conscious memory and easy confidence
in one's mind must be one of life's most devastating blows. Robert Frost
wrote a touching poem about it.

An Old Man's Winter Night

All out of doors looked darkly in at him
Through the thin frost, almost in separate stars,
That gathers on the pane in empty rooms.

What kept his eyes from giving back the gaze
Was the lamp tilted near them in his hand.
What kept him from remembering the need
That brought him to that creaking room was age.
He stood with barrels round him—at a loss.
And having scared the cellar under him
In clomping there, he scared it once again
In clomping off; —and scared the outer night,
Which has its sounds, familiar, like the roar
Of trees and crack of branches, common things,
But nothing so like beating on a box.
A light he was to no one but himself
Where now he sat, concerned with he knew what
A quiet light, and then not even that.
He consigned to the moon, such as she was,
So late arising, to the broken moon
As better than the sun in any case
For such a charge, his snow upon the roof,
His icicles along the wall to keep;
And slept. The log that shifted with a jolt
Once in the stove, disturbed him and he shifted,
And eased his heavy breathing, but still slept.
One aged man—one man—can't keep a house,
A farm, a countryside, or if he can,
It's thus he does it of a winter night. (In: *Robert Frost's Poems*,
commentary by Louis Untermeyer, 1971, pp. 116–117).

In the play's parallel plot, the Duke of Gloucester also suffers devastating losses. Like Lear, he misjudges his children, believing his eldest, Edgar, plots against him, and the bastard, Edmund, is loyal, when the reality is the opposite. Blinded by Lear's second daughter and cruel son in law, Gloucester loses everything, including the will to live. The many parallels between Lear's and Gloucester's situations invite comparison. At one point Gloucester remarks that Lear is better off since he is mad:

> Gloucester: ...Better I were distract;
> So should my thoughts be severed from my griefs,
> And woes by wrong imaginations lose
> The knowledge of themselves. (Act IV, Sc.6, lines 276–279)

Shakespeare made the extremely interesting choice for Gloucester to attempt suicide. The culture's severe prohibitions against it form a backdrop to Gloucester's conflict about wanting to end his afflictions (the religiously based cultural attitudes are explained in Act IV, Sc. 6, footnote, p. 329). When his attempt fails, Gloucester says, in misery,

> Is wretchedness deprived that benefit
> To end itself by death?" 'Twas yet some comfort
> When misery could beguile the tyrant's rage
> And frustrate his proud will. (Act IV, Sc. 6, lines 61–64).

In this and other passages, Gloucester portrays a deadly battle, between himself and the "tyrant" gods. To continue to suffer is to let the tyrants win. Indeed, shortly before this point, Gloucester admits that if he could accept the gods' decrees, he could live.

> Gloucester: If I could bear it longer and not fall
> To quarrel with your great opposeless wills,
> My snuff and loathed part of nature should
> Burn itself out. (Act IV, Sc. 6, lines 37–40)

Gloucester and Lear differ in that, for Lear, the suffering that is unbearable is the pain caused by his daughters, and not the impersonal pain inflicted by Nature, or the gods (more on this below). But for Gloucester, in a sense, the pain fate inflicts *is* personal. In effect, then, living means submitting to torture. A similar sentiment is starkly conveyed by Dickinson's Poem 588 (In Vendler, 2010, p. 264).

> The Heart asks Pleasure–first—
> And then—excuse from Pain—
> And then—those little Anodynes
> That deaden suffering—
>
> And then—to go to sleep—
> And then—if it should be
> The will of its Inquisitor
> The privilege to die—

Many passages in Emily Dickinson's poems comment on what makes life unbearable and death desirable. I would say that one of her central themes echoes Hamlet's question, "to be or not to be." To her, pain that is time limited may be endured. For example, one of her poems (Poem 240, in Vendler, 2010, p. 78) begins with

> Bound a Trouble—and Lives will bear it —
> Circumscription—enables Wo—
> Still to anticipate—Were no limit—
> Who were sufficient to Misery?

By this reasoning it is unending pain that is unendurable, and might justify the decision not "to be." In many of her best known poems, Dickinson, like

Gloucester, personifies the "tyrant" who subjects her to torture. I wonder if this conception adds to the agony, in that suffering becomes more than just pain, but also evidence of being a target of the gods' enmity. Putting together the idea that the unending is unendurable, and pain deliberately inflicted is most agonizing, perhaps suicide is most inviting when we feel a sadistic fate will never tire of inflicting suffering on us. Something like this is conveyed in Dickinson's Poem 425 (In Vendler, 2010, p. 198):

'Twas like a Maelstrom, with a notch,
That nearer, every Day,
Kept narrowing its boiling Wheel
Until the Agony

Toyed coolly with the final inch
Of your delirious Hem—
And you dropt, lost,
When something broke—
And let you from a Dream—

As if a Goblin with a Gauge—
Kept measuring the Hours—
Until you felt your Second
Weigh, helpless, in his Paws—

And not a Sinew—stirred—could help,
And Sense was setting numb—
When God—remembered—and the Fiend
Let go, then, Overcome—

As if your Sentence stood—pronounced—
And you were frozen led
From Dungeon's luxury of Doubt
To Gibbets, and the Dead—

And when the Film had stitched your eyes
A Creature gasped "Reprieve"!
Which Anguish was the utterest—then—
To perish, or to live?

Gloucester's answer to this question shifts several times. He temporarily
accepts Poor Tom's (Edgar's) argument that he should not take his life before
the gods will it. However, only a few lines later (Act IV, Sc. 6, line 227) he
changes his mind, welcoming Oswald's attempt to kill him. That too fails,
but Gloucester turns a third time toward welcoming death in Act V, Sc. 2.
He is once again dissuaded by the disguised Edgar, who argues, " Men must
endure/ Their going hence even as their coming hither. Ripeness is all" (Act
V, sc. 1, lines 9–11). By this reasoning being overcome by suffering is not an
acceptable basis for preferring to die. And yet, when Lear is on the brink of
death, and Edgar tries to get him to look upward, the loving Kent says "O
let him pass. He hates him/ That would upon the rack of this tough world/
Stretch him out longer" (Act V, Sc. 3, lines 312–314). On this issue and so
many others, Shakespeare is too subtle and wise to simply accept society's
prohibitions, or see the situation from only one side.

   Gloucester's misjudged son, Edgar, saves his own life, and his distraught
father's life, by roaming, disguised as "Poor Tom," a beggar in rags. In the
storm he encounters the mad king, and feels great pity. In Act III, Sc. 6,
lines 100–107, Edgar observes how his own suffering seems lighter when
he compares it with the king's, and how fellowship modulates pain.

When we our betters see bearing our woes,
We scarcely think our miseries our foes.
Who alone suffers, suffers most i'th'mind,
Leaving free things and happy shows behind;
But then the mind much sufferance doth o'erskip,
When grief hath mates, and bearing fellowship.
How light and portable my pain seems now,
When that which makes me bend makes the king bow;

For Edgar, comparing his pain to Lear's makes his own seem more palatable, and situates him as a human being, bearing pain, as others do. To add to the discussion of bearable and unbearable suffering it is interesting to compare Edgar's attitude to Dickinson's. She wrote many poems describing her psychic pain but one, in particular (Poem 550) compares her suffering with the sorrows of others. Here are the opening lines from that well known poem. (In: Vendler, 2010, p. 250).

I measure every Grief I meet
With narrow, probing eyes—
I wonder if it weighs like Mine—
Or has an Easier size—

Although by the end of the poem Dickinson derives some comfort from comparing her suffering to those in the Calvary, it doesn't seem as though comparison makes Dickinson's pain "light and portable" as it does Edgar's. Discussing this poem, Vendler (2010, p. 253) describes Dickinson as seeing her own suffering as irremediable and superlative, not comparable to the pain of other ordinary people, but only to the Calvary. Putting the two expressions of compared sorrows side by side illuminates both, for me. At this point in the play Edgar has lost everything: family, home, possessions, position. But he has not lost his mind, as has the king. Comparing his misery to the king's enables him to see that Lear's loss of his mind is an even greater burden than the ones Edgar carries. In psychological language, we might say this "re-frames" his grief, making it much more bearable. But such amelioration is of limited value to Dickinson. Her "re-framing" groups her with the Calvary, and she derives little comfort from being in their company.

In the great tragicomic encounter between the mad Lear and the blind Gloucester, we see the spectacle of the old king trying to convince his friend to find patience:

> Lear: If thou wilt weep my fortunes, take my eyes.
> I know thee well enough, thy name is Gloucester.
> Thou must be patient. We came crying hither:
> Thou knowst the first time that we smell the air
> We wawl and cry... (Act IV, Sc. 6 , lines 171–175)

Lear himself begged the gods for the patience to bear his burdens (Act II, Sc. 2, line 460). Now he preaches this virtue to Gloucester. These five lines seem to me to be extremely meaningful. First, Lear acknowledges Gloucester's empathy for him, ironically suggesting his friend should have his eyes, or the means, to do the weeping. Then Lear gives Gloucester the precious gift of *recognizing* him. Moments of recognition recur, and are often drenched with feeling. For example (as discussed above) the disgruntled (and, perhaps, deteriorating) Lear asked (Act I, Sc. 4, line 221) "Who is it that can tell me who I am?" Much later when Lear awakens, Cordelia asks if he knows who she is:

> Cordelia: Sir, do you know me? (Act IV, Sc. 7, line 48)

Thus when Lear names Gloucester he is giving him something meaningful. The last gift extended by Lear in these five lines is a bit of philosophy. What can give us the needed balm of patience is remembering that we knew we were born into a vale of tears. As we breathed in the air, we intuited that we live in an inhospitable place. It should be no surprise. In other words, impatience is a product of prideful, useless protest against the terms by which we live. Patience is remembering what we have always known in our hearts.

Perhaps, the play's most intense expressions of pure pain belong to Lear. Many poignant moments epitomize his awareness of grievous losses. One that especially moves me is his plea to Cordelia's corpse, as he grapples with recognizing the *irreversibility* of her death.

> Cordelia, Cordelia! stay a little... (Act V, Sc. 3, line 270).

If only he could rewind the clock, reverse death, re-write the scene! Lear's grief, as he tries to integrate that Cordelia will "never" come again, is unfailingly moving. So many poets have raised their voices in yearning for more life for those they love. Take, for example, Mary Jo Bang's beautiful elegy, "No More" (in K. Young, pp. 22–23).

> Good bye to forever now.
> Hello to the empty present and.
> Goodbye to the orchids woven
> With something that looks like a seed weed.
>
> Hello to the day
> We looked out through
> The juniper smudge

Burned to remember the moment.

The doctoring moment is over.
A sheaf of paper drops like lead
From the tree of the table it came from.
The eye plays tricks.

The quilt edge clasped in the hand
Goes on and on and on.
Rumination is this. You
A child, then a man, now a feather

Passing through a furious fire
Called time. The cone of some plant
From a place I don't know
In the high flames.

Rumination is and won't stop
With the stoppered bottle, the pills
On the floor, the broken plate
On the floor, the sleeping face

In the bassinette of your birth month,
The dog bite, the difficulty,
The stairwell of a three-flat
Of your sixth year, the flood

Of farthering off this all takes you
As thought and object become

What you are. My stoppered mind.
A voice carried by machine,

Across a lifeless body. Across
A lacerating lapse in time.

"Goodbye to forever now..." "Across a lifeless body. Across/ A lacerating lapse in time." What a stunning expression of the chasms that open up when someone dies! There is a chasm of time, the vast distance between time when the beloved was alive and the everlasting time they will be dead. There is a chasm of alteration, between the life of the bereaved then and their life now. Then there is the unbridgeable chasm between the dead person and the alive mourner. As Auden says, (In Mendelson, 1991, p. 141, in his own incredible poem (IX in "Twelve Songs") "I thought that love would last forever: I was wrong." Usually without consciously knowing it, we live day by day as though what we have will endure. Everyone who loses someone essential to them has to say *goodbye to forever*. Just now, Lear was (at last!) reunited with Cordelia, and they went off to prison together, where he expected to

...live
And pray, and sing, and tell old tales, and laugh
at gilded butterflies, and hear poor rogues
Talk of court news; and we'll talk with them too—
Who loses and who wins, who's in, who's out—
And take upon's the mystery of things
As if we were God's spies. And we'll wear out
In a walled prison pacts and sects of great ones
That ebb and flow by the moon. (Act V, Sc. 3, lines 9–19)
Later in this scene, (lines 305–307) the hanged Cordelia in his
arms, Lear utters the unforgettable lines:

Why should a dog, a horse, a rat have life
And thou no breath at all? O, thou'lt come no more,
Never, never, never, never, never.

As I listen to the drum-roll of Lear's cries of "never," I also hear Mary Jo Bang's "goodbye to forever." I note the difference between "goodbye to forever" and "goodbye forever." "Goodbye *to* forever" expresses the reverberating losses of a person, a future with that person, and the prospect of luxuriating in seemingly endless time together, "laughing at gilded butterflies." There is no more forever. In this heart wrenching moment, Lear says goodbye to *all* that.

The word "never" implies a backward glance at what could have been but, now, will never be. I think it is the entrance to mourning. When we lose someone we love, we don't lose them all at once. Perhaps we lose having breakfasts with them first and, later, we lose having cocktails, or dancing waltzes, or Thanksgivings. Each "never" is a separate loss. Over time we have to stitch them together. To others we might say "he died," but those are just words. For me, the tragedy in *King Lear* is that Lear just understood how precious Cordelia was to him. It finally clicked in place that nothing else mattered.

Some use the word "regret" to signify what we feel about all those lost breakfasts. To me it sounds too formal, too solid and discrete. I regret a harsh word, or a party I won't attend. Regrets are about something definitive and have limits. But sorrow has none. As soon as I realize there will never be another breakfast, I remember something else that will never happen again. Nothing feels like the bottom of sorrow.

But a poem by Sebastian Barker (in: Holden and Holden, 2016, pp. 284–285) tells me that others feel differently about the word "regret." Here are its first lines.

The Ballad of True Regret

Never to look on the clouds again,
Never the flowers, nor seas.
Never to look on the sparkling rain,
Nor Easter in the trees.

Never to tread on the forest floor
Mottled with pools of light.
Never to open the kitchen door
To walk in the starry night.

Said from the point of view of the one who is dying, this poem piles "never" on top of "never." This is how Barker expresses what he will miss most. Whether we are in the position of Lear or of Cordelia, death opens up a chasm between what could happen yesterday, and won't tomorrow.

Some poets who have lost children have found especially poignant words for their stunned disbelief and searing grief. Perhaps inevitably, the first reaction can be denial that someone so young and full of life is dead. Lear movingly portrays his desperation for Cordelia to come back to life. (Act V, Sc3, lines 261–263).

This feather stirs, she lives: if it be so,
It is a chance which does redeem all sorrows
That ever I felt.

Sometimes we bargain, to get the child back, or find a silver lining, or, at least, find some way to make sense of it. To the parent, the child may have represented the future. How can the future be dead? Ben Jonson, a contemporary of Shakespeare, tries to come to terms with the loss of his son in his poem "On My First Son" (In Bialosky, 2017, pp. 179–180).

Farewell, thou child of my right hand, and joy;
My sin was too much hope of thee, loved boy.
Seven years thou' wert lend to me, and I thee pay,
Exacted by thy fate, on the just day.
Or could I lose all father now! for why
Will man lament the state he should envy?
To have so soon 'scaped the world's and flesh's rage,
And, if no other misery, yet age?
Rest in soft peace, and asked, say, "Here doth lie
Ben Jonson his best piece of poetry."
For whose sake henceforth all his vows be such
As what he loves may never like too much.

A bitter solution but, perhaps, one that allowed the bereaved father to accept his loss. But some of us don't accept goodbye as meekly as this. Other poets have expressed outrage about death's impartial choices, that give no special dispensations to the young and/ or the good.

Dirge Without Music
Edna St. Vincent Millay (In: K. Young, 2010, p. 103)

I am not resigned to the shutting away of loving hearts in the
    hard ground.
So it is, and so it will be, for so it has been, time out of mind:
Into the darkness they go, the wise and the lovely Crowned
With lilies and with laurel they go; but I am not resigned.

Lovers and thinkers, into the earth with you.
Be one with the dull, the indiscriminate dust.
A fragment of what you felt, of what you knew,
A formula, a phrase remains,—but the best is lost.

The answers quick and keen, the honest look, the laughter, the
    love,—
They are gone. They are gone to feed the roses. Elegant and curled
Is the blossom. Fragrant is the blossom. I know. But I do not
    approve.
More precious was the light in your eyes than all the roses in the
    world.
Down, down, down into the darkness of the grave
Gently they go, the beautiful, the tender, the kind;
Quietly they go, the intelligent, the witty, the brave,
I know. But I do not approve. And I am not resigned.

In a much more feisty version, Carolyn Forche (in: K. Young, 2010, p. 121)
refuses to let go. While Lear begs Cordelia to "stay a little," St. Vincent
Millay withholds her approval, and Johnson bids his son "farewell," Carolyn
Forche forcefully demands that her grandmother come back to life. *Now!*

The Morning Baking

Grandma, come back, I forgot
How much lard for these rolls

Think you can put yourself in the ground
Like plain potatoes and grow in Ohio?
I am damn sick of getting fat like you

Think you can lie through your Slovak?
Tell filthy stories about the blood sausage?
Pish-pish nights at the virgin in Detroit?

I blame your raising me up for my Slav tongue
You beat me up out back, taught me to dance

I'll tell you I don't remember any kind of bread
Your wavy loaves of flesh
Stink through my sleep
The stars on your silk robes

But I'm glad I'll look when I'm old
Like a gypsy dusha hauling milk.

"Noble Anger"

I hear rage, along with sorrow, in Forche's remonstrances. How dare you leave *me* only partially risen! Forche hasn't been blanched of outrage. Her senses of sight, taste, smell, her sleep, her memories, and her identity brim with grandma, and from her report, grandma was not mild. Judging by this poem, neither is Forche. I hear a wonderful mix of tender love, unfailing humor, and maddened affirmation in the line "Think you can put yourself in the ground..." With these few words, Forche captures the absurdity of death and how truly unacceptable to the mind are the rituals that mark it.

This poem marries rage and sorrow, as does *King Lear*. I think they join to engender Lear's madness. The doctor who attends the sleeping king, asked about Lear's condition by Cordelia, says, "Be comforted, good Madam; the great rage,/ You see, is killed in him..." (Act IV, Sc7, lines 78–79).

Interestingly, a footnote (Muir, 1975, p. 179) defines this "rage" as "a frenzy, delirium." Until he is awakened in this act, Lear's sorrow and rage are intermingled, like strands braided together. I don't think we can tell them apart. From the time he is profoundly hurt by Cordelia's answer in the first scene, until he is awakened in the fourth act, Lear's rage is a form of sorrow, in the sense that steam is a form of water. They have different appearances, but are the same substance.

There are several times when Lear begs the gods to spare him from tearful sorrow or helpless madness. Either one "un-mans" him, from his perspective. He threatens, sputters, curses, roams, begs the gods for patience, all to escape the inescapable. But Shakespeare is too accurate a "mirror" of human nature, to allow for an escape from the various forms of grief that are part of our condition.

In many passages Lear expresses his hope that some form of anger can help him manfully stand up to sorrow. Here is just a sample. (Act II Sc2, lines 461–467).

> King Lear: You see me here, you gods, a poor old man,
> As full of grief as age, wretched in both:
> If it be you that stirs these daughters' hearts
> Against their father; fool me not so much
> To bear it tamely; touch me with noble anger,
> And let not women's weapons, water-drops,
> Stain my man's cheeks...

Lear seems to see anger as a better alternative than sorrow. He looks to it for strength. A few lines later (Act II, Sc.2, lines 471–475) he calls upon anger as a bulwark against dissolving in tears and going mad.

> ...You think I'll weep,

No, I'll not weep. (*'Storm and tempest.'*)
I have full cause of weeping, but this heart
Shall break into a hundred thousand flaws
Or e'er I'll weep. O fool, I shall go mad.

Tamely bearing his losses and grief would be the product of being duped. Giving in to sorrow would be unmanly. Lear can bear the hurt ("...this heart/Shall break into a hundred thousand flaws...") so long as he doesn't let himself dissolve in tears. He says something in a similar vein later in the play, as he and Cordelia march off to prison.

...wipe thine eyes;
The good years shall devour them, flesh and fell,
Ere they shall make us weep!
We'll see 'em starved first: come.

(Act 5, scene 3, lines 22–25)

One way I can think about this is that sorrow is bearable so long as it isn't accompanied by a tremendous loss of pride. If Lear weeps he forfeits his manhood and his identity. He believes anger can save him from this. He is not alone in this assumption. Perhaps Lear counts on rage's *outer* display of coherence, and gives too little attention to its internal dimension. I raise this, knowing full well that I am writing about a character in a play, but I think the playwright has tapped into a common belief. We *look* like we are in better control when we are furious than when we weep. But are we?

The psychiatrist H.S. Sullivan believed (1943) that anger is a protective device we learn early from its expression by our parents. Many years ago an Interpersonal analyst (Spiegel 1980) wrote that some forms of anger cohere our focus and functioning, while others fracture us. There are times when we *look* powerful, pumped up with fury, and this may inform the pride of bullies and the poetry of great authors, but internally it doesn't always work that way.

Actually, Sullivan was suggesting that anger can be a defense against dissolution from anxiety, not sorrow, but the reliance on it as a defense is similar. But when is the "cure" worse than the "disease"? When does anger, itself, do more damage than its alternatives? Can fury protect us from the searing pain of loss? Lear loses his beloved Cordelia, his loyal Kent, his position, and, eventually, his mind. At many points in the play he tries to stave off melting sorrow with whipped up rage. Some writers, and analysts, have seen anger related emotions as protective against losses of coherence, as though it can center us. In losing his identity as king, Lear certainly has lost a viable center. Can rage replace it?

In previous chapters I contrasted how poems by Blake and Lamb deal with the internal impact of roiling anger. Here I refer to them again, to juxtapose them with words from Shakespeare's play. First, Charles Lamb's poem, "Anger." (In: Sampson, 2013, p. 71)

> Anger in its time and place
> May assume a kind of grace.
> It must have some reason in it,
> And not last beyond a minute.
> If to further lengths it go,
> It does into malice grow.
> 'Tis the difference that we see
> 'Twixt the serpent and the bee.
> If the latter you provoke,
> It inflicts a hasty stroke,
> Puts you to some little pain,
> But it never stings again.
> Close in tufted bush or brake

Lurks the poison-swelled snake
Nursing up his cherished wrath;
In the purlieux of his path,
In the cold, or in the warm,
Mean him good, or mean him harm,
Whensoever fate may bring you,
The vile snake will always sting you.

Lamb emphasizes anger's duration, rationality, and intensity, as factors differentiating poisonous from non-poisonous anger. I read this as an expression of the truth that anger can become an *obsessive* preoccupation. It can fill the mind so full that there is no respite. It seems to me that this is one way to read what actually happens to Lear. In his period of madness, he can't stop thinking of what fires up his rage. He imagines "arraigning" his daughters (Act III, Sc.6). Seeing Poor Tom in his "unaccommodated" state, he can only think that it is the result of the perfidy of Tom's daughters (Act 3, scene 4, lines 48–49). "Didst thou give all to thy two daughters? And art/ thou come to this?" There is just one escape from his preoccupation. Eventually, sleep interrupts the repetitions of enraged thoughts, and is restorative.

While some (e.g. Tolstoy,1906/2008) criticize the play, finding Lear's rage and other aspects unrealistic, I think that its "unrealistic" elements contain its most profound wisdom. Tolstoy (in Bloom, 2008, pp. 156–162) objects to the play on the grounds that there is no explanation for Lear's anger at Cordelia, and the "...unnatural banishment of Lear during the tempest, and his roaming about the heath..." (p. 161) doesn't make sense. But, for me, the play is even more affecting because of some characters' determined irrationality. Outraged anger so often doesn't make rational sense!

In Blake's "A Poison Tree," (in Raffel, 1984, pp. 64–65) he gives poetic form to varieties of anger.

> I was angry with my friend:
> I told my wrath, my wrath did end.
> I was angry with my foe:
> I told it not, my wrath did grow.
>
> And I watered it in fears,
> Night and morning with my tears;
> And I sunned it with smiles,
> And with soft deceitful wiles.
>
> And it grew both day and night,
> Till it bore an apple bright.
> And my foe beheld it shine,
> And he knew that it was mine,
>
> And into my garden stole,
> When the night had veiled the pole;
> In the morning glad I see
> My foe outstretched beneath the tree.

This anger bears poisonous fruit when it is nurtured by other feelings, such as fear. For Lear, I think the emotion that often revs up his rage is his pride. As is all too often true in life off-stage, Lear is vulnerable to the feeling that his worth can be measured by how he is treated. This leads him to quantify love. When he thinks Goneril will allow him 50 followers, and Regan only 25, he considers going back to Goneril, since .....(to Goneril) I'll go with thee;

Thy fifty yet doth double five and twenty,

And thou art twice her love.   (Act II, scene 2, lines 447–449)

For a voice about the advantages of anger as a defense, I quote Dylan
Thomas's plea to his father. ("Do Not Go Gentle Into That Good Night,"
in K. Young, 2010, p. 19). In this poem the persona begs not to be left with
memories of a meek father, passively passing from old age to death. I have
discussed this poem's paean to the power of rage in chapter two. Here I
juxtapose it with King Lear's fierce determination to stave off all his sorrow,
his losses, and his diminishing powers, with a furious stance. First, Dylan
Thomas's poem.

Do not go gentle into that good night
Old age should burn and rave at close of day;
Rage, rage against the dying of the light.

Though wise men at their end know dark is right,
Because their words had forked no lightening they
Do not go gentle into that good night.

Good men, the last wave by, crying how bright
Their frail deeds might have danced in a green bay,
Rage, rage against the dying of the light.

Wild men who caught and sang the sun in flight,
And learn, too late, they grieved it on its way,
Do not go gentle into that good night.

Grave men, near death, who see with blinding sight
Blind eyes could blaze like meteors and be gay,

Rage, rage against the dying of the light.
And you, my father, there on the sad height,
Curse, bless me now with your fierce tears, I pray.
Do not go gentle into that good night.
Rage, rage against the dying of the light.

For me this poem, together with the play, *King Lear*, raise the question of the legacy of rage in contrast to the legacy of sorrow. How would each of us like to be remembered? In this poem the identity of each person shapes what dying means to them. For example, the good see how limited their deeds have been, compared to what they could have done. Who we have been in life shapes the cost of our death, for ourselves and for others. Death takes away whatever we have most valued in life. Although it robs us differently, we are all robbed. For me the question becomes how can we remain ourselves, in our death, as in our lives. I think that is one way to answer Thomas's plea. If he had a fierce father, then the best legacy might be a father who rages against the dying of the light. If rage was part of the *meaning* of his life, rage should be part of the *manner* of his death.

"Lear's Shadow:" Integrity and Identity

Lear struggles to have an identity at all once he has lost his royal position. Perhaps in jest, but, not just in jest, he asks (Act I, Sc.4, line 217) if anyone can tell him who he is, and his knowing Fool (line 222) answers "Lear's shadow." What meaning can our lives have, without a sense of identity? Elsewhere (2004) I wrote about integrity, or self-cohesion, and asked what it can mean, in our era of proliferating "self-states." That is, if our personalities vary in each of our roles, what holds us together? More specifically, who is Lear if he is not King Lear? How can he remain himself, in the manner

385

of his death, if he has lost track of that self? My point about the need for wholeness had more adherents in previous eras. For example, the psychoanalyst, Erich Fromm (1955, p. 326) said that the way to sanity lies in unification of the self. Cushman and Gilford (1999, pp. 18–19) proclaimed that we have moved from valuing a self that is singular and unified, to a need for varied exteriors to present to the world. No doubt they are describing a change in what society rewards, but I believe that the need for a unifying sense of self is integral to us as human beings. Without a centered self we can't define the meaning and purpose of our lives. I think that, quite literally as well as figuratively, the lack of a center makes us hollow.

A poem by William Stafford (In Sieghart, 2019, p. 17) expresses this point unequivocally.

The Way It Is

There's a thread you follow. It goes among
things that change. But it doesn't change.
People wonder about what you are pursuing.
You have to explain about the thread.
But it is hard for others to see.
While you hold it you can't get lost.
Tragedies happen: people get hurt
or die; and you suffer and get old.
Nothing you can do can stop time's unfolding.
You don't ever let go of the thread.

I think we can read part of Lear's story from these lines. He did let go of the thread, and got lost, (in many senses) tragedies happened, people got hurt or died, and he, and others suffered.

None of the characters seem to understand why Lear "needs" his retinue, why it means so much to him, even though he explains:

> "O, reason not the need! Our basest beggars
> Are in the poorest thing superfluous;
> Allow not nature more than nature needs,
> Man's life is cheap as beast's. Thou art a lady;
> If only to go warm were gorgeous,
> Why, nature needs not what thou gorgeous wear'st,
> Which scarcely keeps thee warm... (Act II, Sc. 2, lines 453–459)

The retinue represents (what is left of) his majesty, or, in the language of the poet, William Stafford, (above) his "thread."

That, for some, the "thread" takes a form others may label as "superficial" or "prideful" is so poignantly expressed by the poet, C. K. Williams. Writing about the gruesome death of his mother, Dossie, he describes her steadfast dedication to her makeup routine. This is just a segment of his long poem, "Grief," to which I referred in Chapter Three.

> ... "Eighty, dying, in bed, tubes in her chest, my mother puts on her morning makeup; the broad, deft strokes of foundation, the blended-in rouge, powder, eye shadow, lipstick; the concentration with which you must gaze at yourself, that ravenous, unfaltering focus. Grief for my mother, for whatever she thought her face had to be, to be made every morning; grief for my mother-in-law in her last declining, destroying dementia, getting it wrong, the thick ropes of rouge, garish green paint on her lips; mad, misplaced slash of mascara; grief for all women's faces, applied, created, trying to manifest what the soul seeks to be;...
>
> (In: Seiden, 2016, p. 125)

Rage becomes Lear's badge of identity. His fiercest quarrel is not with Nature, but with his daughters. As he says to the elements, during the storm (Act III, Sc. 2, lines 15–19):

> Rumble thy bellyful! Spit fire, spout rain!
> Nor rain, wind, thunder, fire are my daughters;
> I tax not you, you elements, with unkindness.
> I never gave you kingdom, called you children;
> You owe me no subscription...

I am accustomed to thinking about Lear, until the final scenes, as a narcissistically entitled old man, commanding love and demanding his due. But then I stop to think about these lines. What *do* we owe our parents? As they age are we obligated to extend to them the patience, gifts, loving care they (hopefully) rendered to us when we needed it? Or are we to think what they gave should have no strings attached, so it does not obligate us to return the gifts in kind (with several senses of that word)? Of course cultures, periods in world history, and personal histories play roles in what parents and offspring expect from each other. But thinking in these terms sheds a somewhat different light on Lear's bitterness.

Filial Obligations

I am reminded of a train of thought I have referred to in other chapters. It is the idea that the inter-generational saga is usually not about the younger generation wanting to marry one parent and kill the other, as early analysts suggested. Rather, it is about sorrow. As we come into our peak functioning, our parents are declining. The speed and timing of these phases of life may differ, but the essential contrast holds most of the time. How does that shape our debt to them? For me, no poet has been clearer about the changing of the guard that is built into the human condition than Donald Hall, in his poem, "My Son, My Executioner" (in Moyers, 1995, p. 150). While cradling his infant, Hall reflects that this son will bestow immortality on him. But, at the same time, each measure of the child's growth is like a signpost of his parents' decay and descent toward death.

In an interview (Moyers, 1995, pp. 143–158) Hall says he wrote this poem when his first son was born, and he was shocked by the feeling that his replacement had arrived. Years later, when that son was a teenager, the youngster interpreted the poem as really about Hall and his own father, who died just a year and a half after the poem was written. Hall now muses that perhaps he was really worried about being the one who replaces his father. In any case, the succession is inescapable. The feelings attached to these inevitabilities certainly differ, and may shift over time. Sorrow could be a component for each of the participants who become aware that, as the child's strengths stir, their parents "start to die together."

The question that I think pertains to Lear is, how does this affect what we owe to parents? A poem by Seamus Heaney raises the same issue, at least for me.

Follower

My father worked with a horse-plough,
His shoulders globed like a full sail strung
Between the shafts and the furrow.
The horse strained at his clicking tongue.

An expert. He would set the wing
And fit the bright steel-pointed sock.
The sod rolled over without breaking.

At the headrig, with a single pluck

Of reins, the sweating team turned round
And back into the land. His eye
Narrowed and angled at the ground,
Mapping the furrow exactly.

I stumbled in his hob-nailed wake,
Fell sometimes on the polished sod;
Sometimes he rode me on his back
Dipping and rising to his plod.

I wanted to grow up and plough,
To close one eye, stiffen my arm.
All I ever did was follow
In his broad shadow round the farm.

I was a nuisance, tripping, falling,
Yapping always. But today
It is my father who keeps stumbling
Behind me, and will not go away.   (In: Sieghart, 2019, p. 119)

This once strong, huge, deft hero has entered second childhood (and, perhaps, dementia). Shakespeare so beautifully and powerfully portrayed the seasons of life in his "seven ages" speech in *As You Like It* (Act II, Sc. 7, lines 139–166). The portrait of our boisterous entry and diminished exit ends:

... Last scene of all,
That ends this strange eventful history,
Is second childishness and mere oblivion,

Sans teeth, sans eyes, sans taste, sans everything.

Lear's elder daughters withhold what would lend his last years grace: the retinue that marks him as still a king, at least to himself. Their motives are tremendously complex, and some critics have seen the "retinue" issue as a "cover" for their desire to further reduce his power. Bloom (1998, p. 493) says that Lear always demands more love than can be given. I would say that is true up until the end, where he doesn't feel he deserves Cordelia's love at all. Lear says, to Cordelia:

If you have poison for me, I will drink it.
I know you do not love me; for your sisters
Have, as I do remember, done me wrong.
You have some cause; they have not.   (Act IV, Sc.7, lines 72–75).

Cordelia and Edgar feel pity, sorrow, exquisite empathy for their suffering fathers. They are willing to do anything to be of comfort; an attitude we (hopefully) encounter in parents toward their vulnerable children. In other words, *parents* freely give their children what Lear expects *from his daughters* at the play's opening. Childishly, he demands his vanity should be catered to. Taking away his retinue is like taking a child's toys. He screams and, quite literally, tantrums at Cordelia and Kent. Lear is, of course, not a child, so we may deride him when he claims the entitlements of a child, who does not have to bear responsibility but still demands his full complement of playmates. But what "accommodation" *should* be made for a man who feels ready to "crawl toward death"? Lear sees his elder daughters as owing him "love," or, perhaps, consideration. He expects them to give back what he feels he has generously given them. It is his turn. I think how we see his claims is an extremely personal and complicated question. Heaney's poem multiplies the vantage points I bring to it. I can see how grief might predispose Heaney to want his father to stop following him, to spare the son the heart-wrenching sight of a hero fallen. In that sense, the son or daughter who potentially feels the keenest sorrow for the failing parent may be the one who most needs to *avoid* looking at them. But, then, "plowing" ahead of the uncertain father can be cruel, just as it would be cruel to pay no mind to the child struggling to keep up. More generally, what form of kindness is owed to the "follower"? If he, or she, has met our childhood vulnerability with caring (or, perhaps, even if they haven't) what is owed to them, when they become vulnerable?

Lear is unequivocal about the debt. He howls against what he sees as both *ingratitude and injustice:*

> ...I am a man
> More sinned against than sinning.   (Act III, Scene 2, lines 58–59).

It is the injustice of his daughters' behavior that challenges his identity as a "kind father." Lear is focused on who he truly was, rather than on how he will be remembered. How can it be that he gave his elder daughters all, and they treat him with cruelty? Is he mistaken in everything? Was he a bad king and an unkind father? Once he realizes the horrible mistake he made in condemning and banishing Cordelia all his other beliefs are in doubt. Who Lear is to Lear, and how Lear is treated at present, seems to matter more for him than how he will be seen by future generations.

The storm scene paints an indelible picture of a man in a paroxysm. Lear fully inhabits it, even claiming that the storm outside makes it easier to bear the one within.

> This tempest will not give me leave to ponder
> On things would hurt me more....   (Act III, Sc. 4, lines 23–24)

I find this subtle and interesting. It is as though one misery can take the foreground, pushing others to background. For whom might this be so? Does Lear stand for us all in this? The miserable storm is a storm without any particular targets, while Lear's betrayal by his eldest daughters is personal. Do we all feel personal hurts more keenly, and do they regularly eclipse pain from other causes? Can the body's suffering take precedence, relegating psychic suffering imperceptible?

The Storm of Time

Lear does frequently mention one of Nature's miseries: the frailties of old age. He tends to claim it entitles him to respect and solicitude. For example: (Act 2, Scene 2, lines 379–383).

> ...O heavens!
> If you do love old men, if your sweet sway
> Allow obedience, if you yourselves are old,
> Make it your cause. Send down, and take my part!
> (to Goneril) Art not ashamed to look upon this beard?

And later, as he leaves with Cordelia (Act 4, Sc. 7, lines 83–84):

> You must bear with me. Pray you now, forget and
> forgive; I am old and foolish.

As I read it, the changes in Lear's claims reflect one of his greatest transformations. (I spell out others below). At the beginning of the play, he demands to be loved above all others and to be obeyed absolutely. Now, just after he wakes, he does not *expect* love ("I know you do not love me") but *just asks* for consideration as an old man.

Several poets, (I have discussed previously, Buechler, 2019) who wrote about aging, differed in whether they recommended that we quietly adapt or fiercely fight against change. I don't hear Lear as objecting to aging, or railing against it as a personal enemy. I think it is a part of Nature that he is willing to accept, and use in his claims for compassion. Of course, by the end of the play he is a humbler Lear.

But, even in the very beginning we could see him as bowing to aging in dividing up his kingdom.

As I have already suggested, this action has mystified some commentators (see, for example, Muir, 1974, footnote, p. 215). I hear Lear as adapting and even embracing changes wrought by aging, in deciding to hand over the cares of state to the young. In his own words (Act I, Sc. 1, lines 43–44) he is trying to avoid future strife by settling the inheritance while he is still alive. In what I hear as a similar spirit, Joseph Campbell (2004) suggested that some cultures' myths help the elderly achieve the disengagement from life that is part of healthy adaptation. It is best to gently, peacefully adapt to the aging process. In his words (p. 14) as we age we begin to lose our grip, in many senses, and long for sleep. Faced with a vigorous younger generation, the wise elderly think "Well, let them have it." I would say that is exactly what Lear does, in the first scene.

What does unresisting adaptation to aging look like, for those of us who are not kings? In his poem, "Terminus," Ralph Waldo Emerson (in Stuart, 1996, pp. 7–8) expresses an extreme level of adaptation. We should *embrace* and not just accept, the aging process.

Terminus

It is time to be old,
To take in sail...
Fancy departs: no more invent,

Contract thy firmament
To compass of a tent.
There's not enough for this and that,
Make thy option which of two;
Economize the failing river,
Nor the less revere the Giver,
Leave the many and hold the few.
Timely wise accept the terms....
As the bird trims her to the gale,
I trim myself to the storm of time,
I man the rudder, reef the sail,
Obey the voice at eve obeyed at prime:
'Lowly faithful, banish fear,
Right onward drive unharmed;
The port well worth the cruise, is near,
And every wave is charmed.

Trimming ourselves to the storm of time takes on an interesting meaning in W.H. Auden's (2003) remarkable poem, "The Sea and the Mirror." This poem takes off where Shakespeare's *The Tempest* ended. I discuss the play and the poem below but, for now, I will just quote one section, where Prospero, packing to return to Milan, after the conclusion of *The Tempest*, speaks to Ariel, the sprite that served him during the events of the play. He is anticipating what it will be like to resume his life in Milan, having shorn himself of magical powers.

> Prospero: Over there, maybe, it won't seem quite so dreadful
> Not to be interesting any more, but an old man
>   Just like other old men, with eyes that water
> Easily in the wind, and a head that nods in the sunshine,

Forgetful, maladroit, a little grubby,
And to like it... (Auden, 2003, p. 11)

Prospero, former magus, resuming his position as Duke of Milan, is hardly the average citizen, and yet Auden's depiction brings out an essential truth: that aging levels the playing field. King and pauper, we all become more near sighted, at least in one sense, but often in many. We become less flexible, in our joints if not also in our minds. We don't hear as well. Accepting all of this can make trimming ourselves to the storm of time into a test of our ability to overcome the need to be special, to be an exception.

Interestingly, given his character, I think Lear does trim himself to the "storm of time" from the beginning of the play, just as he seems to accept, and even welcome, the tumultuous winds in the meteorological storm on the heath. Once again, Lear's quarrels are not with Nature, so much as with the injustice and ingratitude of human beings. He expects what he feels is due to him, whether it is his daughters' love, Kent's obedience, or his hundred followers, and when he does not get it, he is enraged. Even (or, perhaps, especially) in his "madness" Lear is an acute observer of injustices and inequities in society. For example, (Act IV, Sc. 6, lines 160–163):

Through tattered clothes great vices do appear;
Robes and furred gowns hide all. Plate sin with gold
And the strong lance of justice hurtless breaks;
Arm it in rags, a pigmy's straw does pierce it.

This is just a sample of many passages depicting the differences between how the poor are punished by the law and the rich get away with similar behavior. In these pages we don't have the fulminating Lear, so much as the philosophical social observer. His observations are still relevant.

Lear certainly does have fierce objections to the death of Cordelia but, once again, it is (at least partially) on the basis of its *injustice*. But rage gives way to sorrow as he searches Cordelia's face for signs of life.

Why should a dog, a horse, a rat have life
And thou no breath at all?...   Act V, Sc. 3, lines 304–305

Willfulness and Will Power

Lear has lost the props (crown, kingdom, retinue) that held his identity together. More than that, he has lost his own sense of being a good king and father. But I think his rage has helped him come through it. Throughout his trials, what Lear didn't lose is a willful sensibility. Even at his most "mad," he talked back to society and Nature and "prosecuted" his elder daughters. Elsewhere (2008) I have written about the saving grace of self-assertion, which I see as a "cousin" of the anger related emotions. A poem by Elizabeth Bishop (discussed in a previous chapter) gives us a prescription for remaining in charge, even in the midst of grievous losses.

One Art

The art of losing isn't hard to master;
so many things seem filled with the intent
to be lost that their loss is no disaster.

Lose something every day. Accept the fluster
of lost door keys, the hour badly spent.
The art of losing isn't hard to master.

Then practice losing farther, losing faster:
places, and names, and where it was you meant
to travel. None of these will bring disaster.
I lost my mother's watch. And look! my last, or
next-to-last of three loved houses went,
The art of losing isn't hard to master.

I lost two cities, lovely ones. And vaster,
some realms I owned, two rivers, a continent.
I miss them, but it wasn't a disaster.

—Even losing you (the joking voice, a gesture
I love) I shan't have lied. It's evident
the art of losing's not too hard to master
though it may look like (Write it!) like disaster.

(In: K. Young, 2010, p. 215)

Like the persona in Bishop's poem, Lear gave himself orders, even when
he could give them to no one else. He forbade his own tears, commanded
himself to hold "trials" of his daughters, faced his failures, and braved the
storm. Bishop tells us to take charge of loss, by willing it. Will is what never
died in Lear, and I believe it is what held him together enough to eventually
recover, given rest, forgiveness, and Cordelia's loving care.

How we feel about Lear's willfulness eloquently demonstrates the
subjectivity of our perceptions. Where some (like his elder daughters) see
only a bothersome flaw, others see a more complicated balance sheet. In the
first scene, when he has banished Kent he proclaims, perhaps to clarify or as
a boast, that this will not be revoked, that he is firm. I have elsewhere noted
the irony of this comment, since Lear will soon be "infirm," in the sense
of mentally unbalanced (unless we consider him already so). As a powerful

king, Lear can make his will a decree. At what points in the story do we see his fierce will as a flaw, and where might we see it as a strength? How are his disastrous willfulness and unflagging will power related? When married to rash impulse, his will erases years of Kent's loyal service and Lear's own love for his favorite daughter, as well as her love for him, in his perception. But his will can be seen as motoring his unwavering stance toward the storm. Even in madness, Lear's will plays a role in galvanizing his exploration of the human and non-human environment. Lear never backs down. He stands up to his daughters, to the pelting rain, to the cold, to the strangers from Cordelia's court who come for him, to the grief that threatens to dissolve him in tears, and to the henchman who hanged Cordelia. When mad, he furiously plans his assault on his treacherous son in laws (Act IV, Sc. 6, line 183, "...kill kill, kill, kill, kill!). He even bellies up to death itself, (as already quoted) calling it to task for its injustices (Act V, Sc. 3, lines 305–306):

> Lear: Why should a dog, a horse, a rat have life
> And thou no breath at all?...

Finally, in his last moments on earth, he *persists* in looking for signs of life in Cordelia which (arguably) transforms his own death. My own question is, can one have his deep reserves of iron will without the stubborn rigidity that contributed so much to his downfall?

I think of Robert Frost as a poet of quiet determination. In some senses, his poems sound very different from Lear's rants. And yet, both have steely frames. In verse, at least, (if not in life) Frost doesn't bellow, but he doesn't back down, either. Here are excerpts from his poem, "Two Tramps in Mud Time" (In: Kendall, 2012, pp. 343–345).

> Out of the mud two strangers came
> And caught me splitting wood in the yard.

And one of them put me off my aim
By hailing cheerily "Hit them hard!"
I knew pretty well why he dropped behind
And let the other go on a way.
I knew pretty well what he had in mind:
He wanted to take my job for pay.

Good blocks of beech it was I split,
As large around as the chopping block;
And every piece I squarely hit
Fell splinterless as a cloven rock.
The blows that a life of self-control
Spares to strike for the common good
That day, giving a loose to my soul,
I spent on the unimportant wood...

The time when most I loved my task
These two must make me love it more
By coming with what they came to ask.
You'd think I never had felt before
The weight of an axe-head poised aloft,
The grip on earth of outspread feet,
The life of muscles rocking soft
And smooth and moist in vernal heat....

Out of the woods two hulking tramps
(From sleeping God knows where last night,
But not long since in the lumber camps).
They thought all chopping was theirs of right.

Men of the woods and lumberjacks,
They judged me by their appropriate tool.
Except as a fellow handled an axe,
They had no way of knowing a fool.

Nothing on either side was said.
They knew they had but to stay their stay
And all their logic would fill my head:
As that I had no right to play
With what was another man's work for gain.
My right might be love but theirs was need.
And where the two exist in twain
Theirs was the better right-agreed.

But yield who will to their separation,
My object in living is to unite
My avocation and my vocation
As my two eyes make one in sight.
Only where love and need are one,
And the work is play for mortal stakes,
Is the deed ever really done
For Heaven and the future's sakes.

Unlike Lear, Frost's persona listens to the other's counterarguments, and concedes their logic. But, in the end, both Lear and Frost carry out what their wills intend. Do we see it as stubborn, unyielding, impervious, or, in a positive sense, as backbone?

Intense Joy

Alack, too weak the conflict to support!
'Twixt two extremes of passion, joy and grief,
Burst smilingly;   (Act V, Sc. 3, lines 196–198)

In his introduction to *King Lear*, Kenneth Muir states (1975, p. xxxv) that both Lear and Gloucester die partly from joy. Edgar, Gloucester's son, who has attended his blind father, while pretending to be a beggar, has just revealed his true identity to his father. Edgar had assumed a beggar's disguise because of the false accusations of his scheming brother, Edmund. Misled by Edmund, Gloucester had forced Edgar to flee and hide in tattered anonymity. As Edgar tells the story:

Into a madman's rags, t'assume a semblance
That very dogs disdain'd: and in this habit
Met I my father with his bleeding rings,
Their precious stones new lost; became his guide,
Led him, begg'd for him, sav'd him from despair;
Never—O fault!—revealed myself unto him,
Until some half-hour past, when I was arm'd;
Not sure, though hoping, of this good success,
I asked his blessing, and from first to last
Told him my pilgrimage: but his flaw'd heart,
Alack, too weak the conflict to support!
'Twixt two extremes of passion, joy and grief,
Burst smilingly.   (Act V, Sc. 3, lines 186–197)

My reading would be that Gloucester died of the *conflict* between the passions of joy and grief, rather than either one of these emotions. It is as though his heart fails at the task of encompassing them both at once.

Similarly, Lear is thought to have died of the joy of (incorrectly) believing his dear daughter, Cordelia, was still alive:

> Lear: Do you see this? Look on her, look, her lips,
>   Look there, look there!
> Edgar: He faints! My Lord, my Lord!
> Kent: Break heart; I prithee, break!
> Edgar: Look up, my Lord.
> Kent: Vex not his ghost: O! let him pass; he hates him
>   That would upon the rack of this tough world
>   Stretch him out longer.
> Edgar: He is gone, indeed.   (Act V, Sc.3, lines 309–314)

The deaths of Gloucester and Lear express that sorrow is not the only emotion that can break our hearts. Perhaps they say that intensity of feeling, rather than its quality, is at issue here. The subtlety of Shakespeare's understanding of the human heart can't be overstated. In fact we now know that a condition, takotsubo cardiomyopathy, describes dangerous changes in the shape of the heart's left ventricle, that can be caused by excesses of joy. But leaving aside this medical condition, it is interesting to think about Shakespeare's meaning. To me it seems he is saying something about excess itself. Too much of anything unbalances us, however good it may be in smaller portions. Gloucester is described as feeling both joy and sorrow but to an unendurable intensity. To me it is as though Shakespeare is describing a system that is overrun by emotion, and can't maintain the necessary balances between one feeling and another, or feeling and thought, or stimulation from the outer and inner worlds.

These highly dramatic moments, where life drowns in joy, are not the only expressions of the dangers of excess in the play. In fact I think much of it could be read with this issue in mind. As I do so, passages that can appear confusing or contradictory become clearer.

For example, there is a moment of exquisitely acute perception in Act III, Sc. 4, lines 4–14, when Lear is grappling with the storm on the heath. Kent pleads for the old king to seek shelter, but Lear welcomes doing battle with the contentious winds.

> Lear: Thou think'st 'tis much that this contentious storm
> Invades us to the skin: so 'tis to thee;
> But where the greater malady is fix'd
> The lesser is scarce felt. Thou'dst shun a bear;
> But if thy flight lay toward the roaring sea,
> Thou'dst meet the bear in the mouth. When the mind's free
> The body's delicate; this tempest in my mind
> Doth from my senses take all feeling else
> Save what beats there—filial ingratitude!

A brilliant insight here is that focus is always a matter of foreground and background. So when Lear is bearing the pelting of the storm, this challenge takes up the foreground. Muir's footnote (1975, footnote 4, p. 107) explains that Lear is banking on the storm *distracting* him from his sorrow about his daughters' abandonment of him, and their ingratitude and betrayal. I certainly can see that interpretation, but I am led to an additional way of hearing it from the dialogue that follows (lines 24–33).

> Lear: ....I'll pray and then I'll sleep
> Poor naked wretches, whereso'er you are,
> That bide the pelting of this pitiless storm,

How shall your houseless heads and unfed sides,
Your loop'd and window'd raggedness, defend you
From seasons such as these? O! I have ta'en
Too little care of this. Take physic, Pomp;
Expose thyself to feel what wretches feel,
That thou mayst shake the superflux to them,
And show the Heavens more just.

In the storm Lear accesses the ability to focus on more than just his own hurt and rage toward his daughters. Along with this wider psychological perspective he also gains a kind of physical release from his bellicose bellying up to the raging storm: "Rumble thy bellyful! Spit, fire! spout, rain! (Act III, Sc. 2, line 14). The storm is more than just a distraction (although it is that, too). It gives Lear an outlet to express his extreme outrage through his body, by standing firm while being pelted. And, as he says, the storm is not a personal enemy, and doesn't occasion the feelings of hurt his daughters have caused him. It is an external foe (though, of course, it has also been read as a personification of internal forces. More on this below). In that it is not interpersonal, it doesn't cause the old man to question whether or not he really was a kind father and good king. He meets the storm as a man encountering Nature, not as Lear encountering Goneril and Regan. Thus the encounter is on a cosmic plane, and he relishes that. Not just as a distraction from the more immediate, familial arena, but, also, as a dimension that allows him to strike out against a grand enemy. He can give rage full vent against the towering winds. The full power of unleashed outrage seems to rescue Lear from the tears of personal sorrow. The mighty storm brings water more mighty than his tears. A man can (nearly) drown with his dignity intact in such an overwhelming tide. Sometimes completely letting loose can bring us gleeful joy.

In *Shakespeare After All,* Marjorie Garber (2004, p. 671) describes the storm as a projection of Lear's mental condition on a larger screen. In Bloom's (1998, p. 493) dark reading, the play itself is a storm, with no clearing .So the storm can be seen as a mirror of Lear's inner state, an outlet, a distraction, or a statement of a nihilistic world view (amid, perhaps, other possibilities).

For me, it is fascinating to think of Lear in the storm as an expression of the interpenetration of outer and inner conditions. In effect, there is no skin between Lear and the storm. In losing his identity Lear has lost his shape, and is no longer a figure against a ground. Figure and ground are one. Perhaps this speaks to a dread we can all inhabit; the dread of truly becoming "nothing." This word pervades the story, from the first encounter between Lear and Cordelia through the Fool's use of it to taunt the king. To become one with the atmosphere, to de-differentiate, is truly to be nothing. It is the death Hamlet confronts in the "Gravedigger" scene, only there it is pictured as the body decaying into dust. Dust to dust.

> Hamlet: ...Alexander died, Alexander was buried,
> Alexander returneth to dust; the dust is earth:
> of earth we make loam; and why of that loam
> whereto he was converted might they not stop a
> beer-barrel?
>> (Arden Shakespeare, 2016, Ed.: Thompson and Taylor,
>> Act V, Sc1 , lines 198–202)

The merging of self and non-self is portrayed in a very different emotional key in Frost's poem, "Desert Places" (In Hirsch, 1999, p. 158).

> Snow falling and night falling fast, oh, fast
> In a field I looked into going past,

And the ground almost covered smooth in snow,
But a few weeds and stubble showing last.

The woods around it have it—it is theirs.
All animals are smothered in their lairs.
I am too absent-spirited to count;
The loneliness includes me unawares.

And lonely as it is, that loneliness
Will be more lonely ere it will be less—
A blanker whiteness of benighted snow
With no expression, nothing to express.

They cannot scare me with their empty spaces
Between stars—on stars where no human race is.
I have it in me so much nearer home
To scare myself with my own desert places.

Hirsch (p. 159) writes of the dialogue between inner and outer worlds, or inner and outer weather, in this poem and others by Frost. The scene can be understood as an emblem or manifestation of the persona's internal state. His is a vast loneliness devoid of meaning, as is this endless stretch of snow. Returning to the play, we could say that Lear prefers the neutral, impersonal storm to the turmoil of his daughters' ingratitude, which is full of personal meaning and intent. Both Frost and Lear seem to me to be bellying up to Nature, as if bragging "You don't terrify me, because I have that within which is much more terrible than you can ever be." But one can get lost in endless space, whether it is external or internal. While an impersonal adversary doesn't have the sting of a targeting daughter, it does present the danger of absorption into a meaningless void.

But *King Lear* is not an endless emotional descent. There are instances of quiet joy, alongside the tumultuous feelings. Hundreds of years before emotion theories (Izard, 1972, 1977) Lear tells us how a feeling can shape our experiences and fashion moments of appreciations from small blessings. He cogently observes the effect of necessity on our perceptions. When Kent begs Lear to enter a poor hovel, the king replies:

> Lear: ....Where is this straw, my fellow?
> The art of our necessities is strange,
> And can make vile things precious. Come your hovel.
> (Act III, Sc. 2, lines 69–71)

This is not the only time Shakespeare anticipated insights described years later by emotion theorists. For example, in *The Tempest*,[†] Gonzalo, a wise old man, articulates how one feeling can modulate the simultaneous experience of other emotions. Gonzalo is the voice of what I would call "emotional modulation." He advises the king, Alonso, to balance the sorrows of their situation with its joys. (Arden Shakespeare, 2011, Eds.: V. Vaughan and A. Vaughan, Act II, Sc. 1, lines 1–9):

> Beseech you, sir, be merry. You have cause
> (So have we all) of joy, for our escape
> Is much beyond our loss. Our hint of woe
> Is common: every day some sailor's wife,
> The masters of some merchant, and the merchant,
> Have just our theme of woe. But for the miracle,
> I mean our preservation, few in millions

---

† Unless otherwise indicated, all references to *The Tempest* refer to the Arden Shakespeare, Eds. V. Vaughan and A. Vaughan, 2011.

Can speak like us. Then wisely, good sir, weigh
Our sorrow with our comfort.

Truth Tellers in *King Lear*

Another reading of *King Lear* puts the issue of truth telling at the center. When does the truth set us free, as the saying goes? When should truth be softened, slanted, or even silenced, in the name of tact? Years ago a very interesting play, *Art*, by Yasmina Reza, explored this question. A man bought a painting. It was just a rectangular canvas covered with white paint. That was it. The proud owner asked two friends to look at the painting and give their assessments. One felt he should tell the unvarnished truth: that he thinks it is worthless. The other, although sharing this opinion privately, felt it would be unkind to voice it. The assumption in the play is that the owner of the painting can't get his money back, so the opinions have no practical consequences. The question becomes how much is telling the truth an end in itself.

This question reverberates throughout *King Lear*. It begins with the first scene, in which Lear's eldest daughters tell patent lies, outrageously flattering him to obtain his favor and bounty. Cordelia, his youngest and favorite daughter, refuses to play the game. She tells Lear she loves him according to their bond, no more or less than that. He is outraged.

> Lear: So young, and so untender?
> Cordelia: So young, my Lord, and true.
> Lear: Let it be so; thy truth then be thy dower...
> (Act I, Sc. 1, lines 106–108)

Earlier in this chapter I questioned whether we should hear her as being ungenerous, as well as truthful. When her father says, "Let pride, which she calls plainness, marry her" (Act I, Sc. 1, line 128) I think he has a point. While surely the old king has created an impossible situation, I wonder whether pride played a role in Cordelia's unbending stance. But that assumes she really *could* have found words for her feelings, and *chose* not to give them to Lear. That seems to be what Lear assumes, since he responds to her as a disobedient and ungrateful daughter. But what she says would suggest that she couldn't find the words.

> Cordelia: Unhappy that I am, I cannot heave
> My heart into my mouth... (Act I, Sc. 1, lines 90–91)

It is interesting to me to think about Cordelia as truly unable to find words for her love for Lear. Of course the line between being unable and unwilling is often unclear. But I think our assumption about Cordelia's statement makes a difference in how we hear the tragic standoff. Garber (2004, p. 655) has an empathic understanding:

> Some things cannot be said, cannot be given words. To abjure language in such cases
> is not a refusal of speech, like Iago's final words, but rather an acknowledgment of the
> limitations of language, and the place of the ineffable or unutterable.

In his poem "East Coker," T.S. Eliot eloquently articulated the limitations of language. His success at expressing this almost seems to belie his point.

.....Trying to learn to use words, and every attempt
Is a wholly new start, and a different kind of failure
Because one has only learnt to get the better of words
For the thing one no longer has to say, or the way in which
One is no longer disposed to say it. And so each venture
Is a new beginning, a raid on the inarticulate
With shabby equipment always deteriorating
In the general mess of imprecision of feeling,
Undisciplined squads of emotion. (Eliot, 1943)

One way of hearing the scene is that Cordelia is truthfully expressing her inability to perform that raid. Within that scene there is another instance of telling unvarnished truths. Kent begs Lear to reconsider his decree, that Cordelia will be banished forever, and Goneril and Regan, with their husbands, will share the kingdom. The noble Kent is absolutely direct, with no care for his own safety, with the result that he is banished, too. Afterwards Gloucester bluntly describes Kent as punished for the "fault" of honesty (Act I, Sc. 2, line 114).

Lear's behavior *is* rash, foolish, and, perhaps most consequential for him, totally lacking in self -understanding. As his eldest daughters correctly (and coldly) assess:

Regan:...he hath ever but slenderly known himself.
(Act I, Sc. 1, line 293)

The question of most interest to me, is, does Shakespeare (and do we) think it would have been wiser for both Kent and Cordelia to *shape* their truths so that they might be more palatable to the man receiving them? Or is anything but the straight, blunt truth a hypocritical evasion?

This issue also comes up in *The Tempest*, with the old man, Gonzalo, voicing the cautious approach. He chides another character (Sebastian) for being too direct with Alonso, the grieving King of Naples, who thinks he has lost his only son in the tempest. With a tact I would especially recommend to all clinicians, (and everyone else) he says:

> My lord Sebastian,
> The truth you speak doth lack some gentleness,
> And time to speak it in. You rub the sore
> When you should bring the plaster.   Act II, Sc. 1, lines 137–140

But Shakespeare also presents instances where total honesty seems to be the most honorable path. In another passage in *King Lear* Kent (Act II, Sc. 2) tells the absolute truth about Oswald, and gets himself put in the stocks. The evil Cornwall delivers a blistering rebuke to Kent. Since it comes from such a treacherous character, in this instance we are likely to incline toward siding with the truth teller:

> Cornwall: This is some fellow,
>   Who, having been prais'd for bluntness, doth affect
>   A saucy roughness, and constrains the garb
>   Quite from his nature: he cannot flatter, he,
>   An honest mind and plain, he must speak truth:
>   And they will take it, so; if not he's plain.
>   These kinds of knaves I know, which in this plainness
>   Harbor more craft and more corrupter ends
>   Than twenty silly-ducking observants,
>   That stretch their duties nicely.   (Act II, Sc. 2, lines 92–101)

When Lear finds (the disguised) Kent in the stocks he is infuriated, since Kent was serving as the king's messenger. Of course it is easy to see this scene from the point of view of the truth teller, especially since Cornwall is such a vile spokesperson, but, as usual with Shakespeare, we find ourselves considering more than one side of the issue.

The Fool has a role which requires him to tell the truth. I often think of him as occupying a position not unlike the psychoanalyst, in our day. In Shakespeare's time he is a character with license to speak about anything, but in rather convoluted terms. His "interpretations" take the form of stories, jests, analogies, riddles, songs, and challenges. Clearly, Lear and his Fool show warmth toward each other, and the Fool is the character in whom Lear confides his worries about losing his mind:

> O! Let me not be mad, not mad, sweet heaven;
> Keep me in temper; I would not be mad!
>
> (Act I, Sc. 5, line 42–43)

My question is whether the Fool (not unlike some practitioners of psychoanalysis, in my experience) went too far in confronting Lear, and helped to precipitate his breakdown. For example, just before the quote I just mentioned, when Lear begins to feel his wits turn, the Fool confronted him with, perhaps, the harshest truth uttered in the play.

> Fool: Thou should'st not have been old till thou had been wise.
>
> (Act I, Sc. 5, line 41)

True, but uttered just after Lear has begun to realize his tragic mistake in banishing Cordelia, and has lost all hope for comfort from Goneril. Of course, the role of the Fool is to tell truth disguised in merry witticisms, though even Fools sometimes get in trouble for their truth telling. As he, himself, complains: (Act I, Sc. 4, lines 176–180).

> Fool: I would fain learn to lie.
> Lear: An you lie, sirrah, we'll have you whipp'd.
> Fool: I marvel what kin thou and thy daughters are:
> they'll have me whipped for speaking true, thou'lt
> have me whipped for lying;....

When a chastened and gracious Cordelia meets Lear toward the end of the play, and they reconcile, he asks her forgiveness, stating that she had cause to be angry with him, but she says "No cause." Of course this is not literally true, since he publicly castigated her, banished her, and disowned her in the first scene. So what does Cordelia's clearly loving statement mean? I take it to express that the truth has many sides. Literal truth is not its only aspect. Caring about one's impact can persuade someone to "slant" truth, as Emily Dickinson advised: (Poem 1263 in Vendler, 2010, p. 431).

> Tell all the truth but tell it slant—
> Success in Circuit lies
> Too bright for our infirm Delight
> The Truth's superb surprise
> As Lightning to the Children eased
> With explanation kind
> The Truth must dazzle gradually
> Or every man be blind—

Jane Hirshfield's wise assessment (2015, p. 114) states that:

Perhaps one message to be taken from the many myths that speak of a broken concealment is the need for tact. In life, as in literature and myth, the desire to strip reality down to some bare and blunt truth reflects delusion, hubris, or reductionism's inedible dust. As there is a connection between modesty, the generative, and a clear-seeing compassion, there is one also between hubris and an ensuing blindness. *What is bared without sufficient respect may not be bearable, or bearable only at enormous cost.* (Italics mine).

There are other meaningful interplays about truth in *King Lear.* As already noted, Gloucester's loyal son, Edgar, disguises himself as "Poor Tom," a ragged beggar, and attends his blind father. Seeking to prevent him from suicide, Edgar tricks Gloucester into thinking he has survived a fall off a Dover cliff. Edgar explains that he is deceiving his father so as to convince him that he is *meant* to continue to live. It is true that Edgar's ruse saves Gloucester's life (for a while) but there is one aspect of it that he comes to regret:

> Edgar: Never—O fault! reveal'd myself unto him,
>   Until some half-hour past,... (Act V, Sc.3, lines 191–192)

I take this to mean Edgar wishes he had revealed himself to his father earlier, so they might have had more time to reconcile, or, perhaps, so the shock/joy/sorrow would not have killed the old man. Although I have described Edgar's efforts (above) I think it is worthwhile to review his actions to save himself and his father, because they raise so many highly significant and complex psychological issues. At first, as he inhabited the guise of "Poor Tom," Edgar seemed reconciled to his lot.

Edgar: ...To be worst,
The lowest and most dejected thing of fortune,
Stands still in Esperance, lives not in fear.
The lamentable change is from the best,
The worst returns to laughter...   (Act IV, Sc. 1, lines 2–6)

But this relative equanimity is shattered when he happens on his father, Gloucester, wandering, blind, after being cruelly attacked by the Duke of Cornwall. Gloucester has had his eyes plucked out, for supporting Lear against his villainous older daughters. Seeing his father's plight, he realizes that he is much more wretched than he could have imagined in the past:

Edgar: ...the worst is not
So long as we can say 'This is the worst.'
                    (Act IV, Sc. 1, lines 29–30)

Here is when Edgar achieves what I think of as his most remarkable transformation, *not* of appearance but of purpose. He takes on the role of caring for his father, Gloucester, leading, begging, consoling, and, most of all, countering his father's suicidal urges. Edgar employs tricks for this purpose. When the old man asks to be led to Dover's cliff, to commit suicide, Edgar pretends to comply.

Edgar: Give me your hand: you are now within a foot
Of th' extreme verge. For all beneath the moon
Would I not leap upright.
                    (Act IV, Sc. 6, lines 25–27)

Why does this work? How does it work? Upon first seeing his blind and bleeding father, escorted by an old servant, asking to be led to Dover cliff so he could kill himself, Edgar (Poor Tom) says to himself that he can't bear to answer his father's request. But a moment's thought tells him that he has no choice, for the old man is helpless. It must be about now that Edgar hatches the plot to pretend to lead Gloucester to the cliff, and make his father think he has actually jumped off of it. A footnote (p. 326) tells us that in leading Gloucester toward the place where he could kill himself, Edgar is playing the traditional role of the devil, although we in the audience know it is for a benign purpose.

Edgar pretends to describe the view from the top of the cliff, in beautifully poetic terms. ("The fishermen that walk upon the beach/ Appear like mice....Act IV, scene 6, lines 17–18). Gloucester repays him by giving him his purse, with a precious jewel. Edgar pretends to part and Gloucester jumps, thinking himself committing suicide by jumping off the cliff but, in reality, only leaping a short distance on the ground. There is a good deal of controversy about what Edgar is trying to do. Why does he fool his father in this way? And why doesn't he reveal his true identity to his father until later, shortly before Gloucester's death? Here is the interpretation given in a footnote on pages 328–329:

> Edgar may be seen as playing a game with his father, one that has an element of cruelty, since it Leads Gloucester to expect, and then denies him, the one thing he wants, death...No wonder that there has been much debate about the nature of this episode, which may be seen as grotesque, comic, absurd, tragic, or a combination of these...

As Gloucester "falls," ostensibly from a great height, he explains to the gods that if he could submit to their wills he would live out his life to its natural end, but he can't do it (lines 37–40).

Another footnote (p. 329) suggests that Edgar is deceiving his father in order to coax him to live again, which is the version that makes the most sense to me.

After Gloucester "lands" (a few feet from where he has leapt) Edgar creates another persona for himself. Now he pretends to be a poor man, who has happened on the fallen old man at the bottom of Dover's cliff. As though amazed by Gloucester's soundness of body upon "landing," Edgar declares that the old man's "life's a miracle" (line 55). Here is where philosophies, rather than bodies, collide. Upon realizing that he has not succeeded in killing himself, Gloucester complains (lines 60–63):

Is wretchedness deprived that benefit
To end itself by death? 'Twas yet some comfort
When misery could beguile the tyrant's rage
And frustrate his proud will.

A footnote (p. 331) suggests that Shakespeare had in mind the Stoic belief that power over oneself is the greatest good. It is always impossible to know what was in Shakespeare's mind, but I think another reading might be plausible. Gloucester has suffered unbelievable cruelty in the hands of Cornwall and Regan, lost his sight, learned that the son he thought was his protector (Edmund) betrayed him, and the son that he had maligned (Edgar) was blameless, but banished. Gloucester believed he would never see Edgar again, even "feelingly." So I think that one way to hear these lines is that Gloucester saw life as a losing battle with a nameless, uncaring, tyrannical god of fate. He wanted to die as a kind of "checkmate." It was an expression of pure rage, a retributive act. In a parallel to the rash rages of Lear, Gloucester was fuming, not so much to prove his power but rather to express his outrage. "As flies to wanton boys are we to the gods,/ They kill us for their sport" (Act IV, Sc, 1, lines 37–38).

His loving son persuades him to a different, more benevolent view.

Edgar....Therefore, thou happy father,
Think that the clearest gods, who make them honours
Of men's impossibilities, have preserved thee. (lines 72–74)

And, a moment later, Edgar asks his father to:

Edgar: Bear free and patient thoughts. (line 79)

What comes to my mind is the dramatic scene (Act III, Sc. 1) when Lear first encounters the storm.

For him, this is a much more bearable misery than the outrage he feels toward his eldest daughters. The storm's pelting is not personal. Suffering it causes does not lead Lear to question how those he loved and cared for could be so ungrateful. The misery is just discomfort, nothing more. What tears at his heart is the pain, rage, and shock of his daughters' hateful behavior.

As I read it, when Edgar frames our lives, with their entrances and exits, and their many forms of suffering, as ordained, he takes the pain, and the decision about whether to live, out of the personal realm. He tells his father that all he has to do is bear life, not fight it. Lear (Act IV, Sc. 6) also lectures Gloucester that we come crying into this world and leave it in similar fashion, and we must bear it all patiently (lines 174–179). We might take from this that sorrow that is just sorrow, sorrow that just exists, but is not being imposed on us because we have earned it, or because the gods are against us, or for any reason whatsoever, can be borne. But when we feel targeted, singled out, in some way, sorrow is mingled with hurt, rage, and other feelings that may make it beyond bearable.

The ruse is not a final victory for Edgar in his opposition to his father's suicidal intent. Finding out that Lear's side has lost the battle against

Goneril and Regan, Gloucester is, once again, ready to die. As Edgar extends his hand to help his father flee, the old man says, "No further, sir; a man may rot even here" (Act V, Sc. 2, line 8). Edgar replies, "What, in ill thoughts again? Men must endure/Their going hence even as their coming hither./ Ripeness is all. Come on." (Act V, Sc. 2, lines 9–11). Convinced, Gloucester replies "And that's true too" (line 12) and allows himself to be led away. A footnote (pp. 363–364) suggests both Stoical and Biblical references for this phrasing. What gives it its power?

Of course we can never know Shakespeare's intention. To me it seems plausible that Edgar wanted Gloucester to believe that the gods, and not his son, sought to keep him alive, that his survival was a miracle, a divine sign that it is Gloucester's duty to live until death overtakes him. Edgar reveals himself at the end, believing it might be his last chance to do so, since he might lose the fight with Edmund. He wanted each of them to take the experience of mutual forgiveness and reunion to their graves. These are my (admittedly thoroughly biased) conjectures.

Would it have been as convincing to Gloucester if Edgar had simply revealed himself from the start, and pleaded for his father not to take his life? If he had said something like, "Please live for my sake," rather than a version of "Your life is a miracle, ordained by the gods, so it is therefore your duty to live until they decide you should die." Although it is an *entirely* different situation, I am reminded of the "neutrality" prescribed to the psychoanalyst in the early days of classical Freudian analysis. In both, it is assumed that the power of a message comes (in part) from its unbiased source. The analyst "spoke" for the truth of the unconscious, and Edgar contrived to deliver the message of the impartial gods. Neither the analyst nor the disguised Edgar wants to appear as a messenger of their own subjectivity. They claim they represent a universal "truth." Their power to persuade is based on that premise.

Toward the play's end Edmund, a villainous character who betrays his father and brother, and is slain, tries to reverse his order to have Cordelia and Lear killed, but it is not in time to save Cordelia. He has one moment of truth, just before he dies. Edmund explains this uncharacteristic behavior, by saying he is moved by Edgar's story of attending their father. But within Edmund's last speech there is a curious detail. Before he attempts to save Cordelia and Lear he declares: (Act V, Sc. 3, lines 238–240)

> Edmund: Yet Edmund was belov'd:
> The one the other poison'd for my sake,
> And after slew herself.

I wonder if Shakespeare is telling us that the bastard, who felt cursed by a society that defined him as inferior from birth (like Richard III, among others in Shakespeare's panoply) was able to "reform" and deliver truth once he felt loved. Of course there is no way to know, but otherwise I find this speech puzzling.

In a sense I see Truth as a character in this play, weaving in and out of the drama, sometimes in a binary relationship with hypocrisy, sometimes in more nuanced forms. Is it Truth that drives Lear mad?

King Lear is "only" a play, a fiction, and yet I think it has much to tell us about fact and fiction, truth and dare, honesty and tact. I hear it as a study in loving truths; that is, in loving the truth and in telling truths lovingly. As I read it, eventually it is his obedience to truth that helps to save Lear, along with his capacity to become loving. Lear begins the play believing he has been a kind father and a good king, believing all his daughters love him, and believing it is safe to hand them his crown. Experience teaches him otherwise. But Lear faces the ensuing "storms." He doesn't flinch. He keeps going. He actually becomes the loving father and wise man he earlier falsely thought himself to be. By the end of the play, I think Lear becomes "every inch a king."

"Take Physic, Pomp:" Transformation in Lear and Prospero

To me, part of the brilliance of this play is in Lear's transformation. Before I describe it, as I see it, I want to explore how some see Lear as *unchanged*. Perhaps most noteworthy is the opinion of Harold Bloom (1998, p. 506–507) who wrote;

> Love redeems nothing—on that Shakespeare could not be clearer—but the powerful representation of love askew, thwarted, misunderstood, or turned to hatred or icy indifference (Goneril, Regan, Edmund) can become an uncanny aesthetic value. Lear, surging on through fury, madness, and clarifying though momentary epiphanies, is the largest figure of love desperately sought and blindly denied ever placed upon a stage or in print. He is the universal image of the unwisdom and destructiveness of paternal love at its most ineffectual, implacably persuaded of its own benignity, totally devoid of self-knowledge, and careening onward until it brings down the person it loves best, and its world as well.

Just a few paragraphs later (p. 509) Bloom concludes that the play is "...a drama in which everyone would have been better had they not been born. It is not so much that all is vanity; all is nothing, less than nothing." Bloom sees what looks like changes in Lear as "flashes of compassion and social insight" that essentially are "emanations of his wholeheartedness, rather than the transformations Bradley and most subsequent critics have judged them to be." While describing the play's nihilism (p. 493) Bloom declares that "Lear's suffering is neither redeemable nor redeemed."

Bloom is certainly not alone in this opinion. Swinburne (in Bloom, 2008, p. 134 "A Study of Shakespeare") said "Requital, redemption, amends, equity, explanation, pity and mercy, are words without meaning here." I have already mentioned comments by Tolstoy (above). Apparently Tolstoy's criticisms of the character extended to the whole play. In 1906 (in Bloom, 2008, pp. 156–164) in an essay entitled "On Shakespeare," Tolstoy wrote that "...far from being the height of perfection, it is a very bad, carelessly composed production, which, if it could have been of interest to a certain public at a certain time, can not evoke among us anything but aversion and weariness." Tolstoy saw the conflicts in the play as *not* flowing from the course of events or from the characters' natures but as created arbitrarily by Shakespeare. Tolstoy goes on to find many aspects of the dialogue impossible to believe. No one, he declares (p. 159) would say that "...it is easier to bear one's grief and the soul leaps over many sufferings when grief finds fellowship. .." (as Edgar declared in Act III, Sc. 6, lines 103–104). In brief, Tolstoy far preferred older versions of the play, that pre-dated Shakespeare's. Alexander Blok, who was a Russian poet, says (p. 167) about Lear's heart "...all is dry and bitter; there is none of that life-giving dew which washes away all sorrow, which softens suffering, smooths out sharp angles and draws together the edges of the fire-flaming wound." (essay entitled "Shakespeare's King Lear: An Address to the Actors," In Bloom, 2008, pp. 164–169).

I have a different reading. I think by the end of the play love, above all, as well as humility and a deeper appreciation of human vulnerability, have re-shaped Lear's character. He is still the Lear of old, in some respects. He can still show a pugilistic side. But I think Lear's heart wrenching pilgrimage moved him into a far greater intensity, to borrow from T.S. Eliot, who said:

Old men ought to be explorers
Here and there do not matter
We must be still and still moving
Into another intensity
For a further union, a deeper communion
Through the dark cold and empty desolation,
The wave cry, the wind cry, the vast waters
Of the petrol and the porpoise. In the end is my beginning.
"East Coker" In: "Four Quartets," 1943, p. 32

Lear certainly set forth into the dark cold and empty desolation, in the outer world and his own, inner life. As I read the play, he evolved into an entirely new intensity. In the beginning of the play Lear can only see how others reflect on him. He is flattered by those who mirror him back to himself in shining terms. He can see no further than that Cordelia has chosen her truth over stroking his ego. He doesn't seem to understand that "loving" her has to include seeing her for who she is. I think she made the same mistake. The apple didn't fall far from the tree, as the saying goes. His vision of "love" is, in several senses of the word, tribute. The daughter who would let him have 50 followers is twice as loving as the one who will only allow 25. Quantity, outward show, is all Lear knows of love. But that changes. Lear comes to fully inhabit a caring love for the Fool, Poor Tom, and, above all, for Cordelia. Hoping against hope to see a sign she is still alive he says, (Act V, Sc. 3, lines 232–234):

This feather stirs, she lives: if it be so,
It is a chance which does redeem all sorrows
That ever I have felt.

These lines resonate with the piteous cry of the other loving father, Gloucester, who, blinded, longs for one more chance to "see" his wronged son Edgar, through touch: (Act IV, Sc. 1, lines 23–26):

...O dear son Edgar,
The food of thy abused father's wrath
Might I but live to see thee in my touch,
I'd say I had eyes again.

Lear left everything familiar, and cast off into the world almost literally naked. He suffered immensely, lost enormously, but also gained a deepened curiosity, augmented compassion, and heightened capacity to love.

Love's power to transform also occupies center stage in the play *The Tempest*. Putting side by side Lear and Prospero, another controlling father, yields interesting similarities and differences, and sheds light on both characters. Here is a brief summary of the plot of *The Tempest*. Prospero, once the Duke of Milan, was cheated out of that position by his brother, Antonio, and set adrift in the sea, along with his three year old daughter, Miranda. The play begins twelve years later, on their isolated island refuge. Prospero is a magus, a magician with enormous powers, and rules the island's few inhabitants with an iron hand. Aside from Miranda there is Ariel, a magical sprite, and Caliban, an earthy slave that once tried to rape Miranda and, since that time, has been treated quite roughly by her father. By chance, Prospero's enemies are sailing near the island, so he is able to magically create a tempest that grounds their ship. This is the situation in which Prospero faces several moral dilemmas. Should he forgive his cruel brother and his co-conspirators? How should he treat the scheming Caliban? How can he let go of magical control and sacrifice his own needs as his daughter becomes ready for a separate life?

As the play opens, Prospero tells his daughter, Miranda, that just by existing she saved his life.

> Miranda: Alack, what trouble
> Was I then to you?

> Prospero: O, a cherubin
> Thou wast that did preserve me. Thou didst smile,
> Infused with a fortitude from heaven,
> When I have decked the sea, with drops full salt,
> Under my burden groaned, which raised in me
> An undergoing stomach to bear up
> Against what should ensue.
>
> Act I, Sc. 2, lines 151–159

Later on (Act III, Sc 4, lines 3–4) Prospero calls Miranda, "...that for which I live" and "one third my life." While Prospero is certainly controlling, arguably too possessive, and sometimes harsh, he is doubtlessly devoted to his daughter. She gave him a reason to keep on living.

I have always felt that in this play and in *King Lear,* Shakespeare really got to the essence of love, as I understand it. (In plays like *Romeo and Juliet* he got to the essence of passionate adoration, but, I would say, not love). In the beginning of both plays, Lear and Prospero are not really capable of loving or even really knowing their daughters. Miranda has a mischief in her (telling Ferdinand her name) that I think Prospero knows nothing about. And Lear certainly doesn't understand Cordelia. Both fathers are only capable of possessing their daughters at the start of each play. But I think both become capable of fully loving and knowing their daughters by the end. I am not referring to adoration, idealization, surrender, possession, or worship, but, rather, love (Buechler, 1995) that knows and accepts the other and puts their welfare ahead of other considerations. I like the psychiatrist H.S. Sullivan's definition of love. While cumbersome, like most of his language, in my opinion, it captured something vital. He said love exists when (1940, pp. 42–43) "...the satisfaction or the security of another person becomes as significant to one as is one's own satisfaction or security, then the state of love exists." Similarly, in his wildly popular book, *The Art of Loving*, (1956, p. 24) Erich Fromm defined love as the "active concern for the life and growth of that which we love." By these standards I feel that both Lear and Prospero become able to fully know and love their daughters by the end of the plays.

The Tempest expresses the usual (good vs. evil) binary, with some characters clearly representing goodness (e.g. Gonzalo) and some evil (e.g. Prospero's brother, Antonio) but, I believe, it surpasses such simplicity by its end. We see the mixture of scheming and redeeming penitence in Alonso, the King of Naples, who conspired to supplant Prospero, but asks forgiveness of Prospero and Miranda. Prospero himself has both the generosity of a loving father and the obsessive, punitive rage of a vengeful god. The "higher" values, that rise above blind justice and over simplified categories, that were a thread in *Measure for Measure* and *The Merchant of Venice* are more fully nuanced in *The Tempest*.

Prospero loved Miranda from the start but, as I see it, he grows into greater caring about her "satisfaction and security." By the end of *The Tempest* Prospero has made three significant sacrifices. He gave up his daughter to her beloved, Ferdinand, out of love for her. To restore harmony, he gave up his search for revenge against his brother, the conspirators, and Caliban. Finally he renounced his magical powers, and became fully human. Prospero began the play as a man literally and figuratively on an island. I believe that, in many senses, he left the island by the play's end. Love, compassion, and mercy won out.

In a similar movement, Lear journeys toward generosity. No longer protected by his position, out in the cold in every sense, Lear's suffering humanizes him, and teaches him to love. Forced to live among the "unaccommodated" he develops genuine interest in the living beings around him. For the first time, he lets his heart register their plight. At one point, struck by the helpless shivering of the beggar, he chastises himself for a lifetime oblivious to those in need. He recognizes that he has "taken too little care of this." (Act III, Sc. 4, line 33). His heart breaks, but it also breaks open, and he is able to experience empathy and the full power of love (for Cordelia) by the play's end.

Over the course of the play, Lear evolves from a man obsessed with getting his due, to a man who can see injustices everywhere he looks. Rather than centering only on proving he is "more sinned against than sinning," (Act III, Sc. 2, lines 58–59) he becomes able to see how unfair life is to those who are "unaccommodated." He comes to have empathy for the poor, who suffer much more harshly when they run afoul of the law. They are vulnerable to all the elements, both natural and societal. He can pity the beggar, "Poor Tom," whose body and mind seem totally defenseless. Both Lear and Gloucester dream of a more equitable society. Giving the "beggar" (Edgar in disguise) his purse, Gloucester says "...distribution should undo excess/ And each man have enough..." (Act IV, Sc. 1, lines 73–74). While "mad," Lear comes to recognize hypocrisies built into society. For example,

Thou rascal beadle, hold thy bloody hand;
Why dost thou lash that whore? Strip thine own back,
Thou hotly lusts to use her in that kind
For which thou whipp'st her. (Act IV, Sc. 6, lines 156–159).

And,

Through tattered clothes great vices do appear;
Robes and furred gowns hide all. 'Plate sin with gold,
And the strong lance of justice hurtless breaks;
Arm it in rags, a pigmy's straw does pierce it. (same scene, lines
    160–163)

The idea that the "mad," those on the outside of society, can see through
its hypocrisies was the witty subject of a poem by Emily Dickinson: (In:
Vendler, 2010, p. 272). In his madness, Lear comes to encompass insights
not unlike Dickinson's.

Much Madness is divinest Sense—
To a discerning Eye—
Much Sense—the starkest Madness—
'Tis the Majority
In this, as all, prevail—
Assent—and you are sane—
Demur—you're straightway dangerous—
And handled with a Chain—

Lear won't seek his own shelter until the Fool, at one point, and the beggar,
at another, are out of harm's way. He struggles (Act III, Sc.4) to take off his
own garments to share them with Poor Tom.

  Both Lear and Gloucester understand their situations too late to fully
savor their newly acquired wisdom. But I believe that before the play's end
Lear's most significant change is a total alteration in what most matters to
him. He becomes a man more centered on the plight of humanity than on
the tally sheet of wrongs against him. In a sense, he is more fully human.
With a more genuine caring for Cordelia comes a greater capacity for love
in all its forms. In the Bible, to love is sometimes expressed as "knowing"

("And Adam knew Eve, his wife, and she conceived" Genesis, 4:1, intro). Taking that word in a non-sexual sense, Lear becomes capable of *knowing* Cordelia, that is, of seeing and loving her. In his period of "madness" he develops an interest in mice, flies, adulterers, Gloucester, the world around him, and in justice for all, not just for himself. He realizes that his flatterers were liars. "...Go to. They are not men o' their words: they told me I was everything; 'tis a lie. I am not ague-proof" (Act IV, Sc. 6, lines 103–104). In a sense he understands what is false about all beliefs that one (a country, or an individual) is the exception. As a king or a madman he still has a body, subject to all the human vulnerabilities. He sees he is, in the words (1953) of the psychoanalyst, H.S. Sullivan, "more simply human than otherwise." For me the sheer poetry of the play makes it thrilling. But what makes it inspiring is that an emotionally limited, narrowly self-centered man becomes able to love others and to revere life itself.

When Love and Truth Collide

From its opening scene, this play can be understood as an exploration of love and truth. Lear asks his daughters to publicly declare their love for him. Supposedly, the one who loves him most will receive the largest third of the kingdom.

> Lear: Which of you shall we say doth love us most,
>   That we our largest bounty may extend
>   Where nature doth with merit challenge...
>   (Act I, Sc. 1, lines 51–53)

The words "nature" and "merit" have been understood in various ways (Muir, 1975, footnote, p. 6). They could mean that the king will give the largest portion to the daughter who adds affection for her father to the claims she already has because of her birth. Or, "nature" could mean a father's affection for his child, while "merit" could mean the child's affection for the father. In any case, love, here, is a kind of commodity. This slant will be carried forward in the negotiations about the size of Lear's retinue, with the old king initially holding out for a full complement, while his elder daughters bargain him down to nothing. It is as though love can be measured and quantified and compared with other valuables. Goneril claims to love her father "Beyond what can be valued, rich or rare" (Act I, Sc.2, line 57). Regan asks to be valued at the same rate as her elder sister ("prize me at her worth," line 70). When Cordelia responds that she gives only half her love to Lear, since half her love will go to her husband, she is also treating love as a measurable and limited commodity (as is suggested by Foakes, 1997, Act I, Sc. 1, footnote, p. 165). This treats love as if we have a finite store of love to give out, bestow an amount of it to someone, keep a tally, and expect to be fairly recompensed. Interestingly, Freud's (1917) early thinking was built around the idea that each of us have a limited amount of "cathexis," which meant that it was necessary to let go of one "object" in order to invest in another. But later Interpersonal theorists rejected the idea of a limited store of cathexis, believing instead that loving someone can expand our capacity to love (Buechler, 1995).

Another (though related) reading of the scene is that it is a public test of obedience. Lear has asked his daughters to flatter him, promising to pay them for complying. The eldest two accept the compromise, in several senses of that word. They settle for the deal he offers. They compromise their integrity in being willing to sell their words. They give concessions to obtain the settlement they want. Truth is compromised. On the other hand, Cordelia refuses to compromise at all, just like her father. She won't cater to his need for her obedience or tribute.

As I read it love, in this opening scene, is defined by Lear as a form of commerce, demanded out of pride and bestowed out of obedience and self-interest. Quite a different definition is enacted by Kent, whose love for Lear impels him, at all personal risk, to try to stop the king from making grave errors. Kent and Cordelia can be seen as representing the refusal to compromise, but for different reasons. Their love is married to their truth, but Kent has Lear's interests at heart, while Cordelia's heart is set on being true to herself.

But matters don't end here. By the end of the play, Cordelia learns that sometimes love and absolute truth point in different directions (as when she tells Lear she has "no cause" for retaliating against him, as discussed above). When love and truth conflict, what is the wisest course? For an answer, we can turn to Shakespeare himself. Although this sonnet may be written tongue in cheek, it does express the value of modulating truth with tact, out of loving consideration for the feelings of the beloved.

Sonnet 130

My mistress' eyes are nothing like the sun;
Coral is far more red than her lips' red;
If snow be white, why then her breasts are dun;
If hairs be wires, black wires grow on her head.
I have seen roses damasked, red and white,
But no such roses see I in her cheeks,
And in some perfumes is there more delight
Than in the breath that from my mistress reeks.
I love to hear her speak, yet well I know
That music hath a far more pleasing sound;
I grant I never saw a goddess go—
My mistress when she walks treads on the ground.

And yet by heaven I think my love as rare
As any she belied with false compare.

(In: H. Vendler, 1997, p. 555)

More generally, how should we decide the priority, when our values collide? This is a central theme in many of Shakespeare's plays. In *Measure for Measure*, Isabella must choose between her chastity and saving her brother's life. And her brother chooses to ask her to compromise herself, to save him. In *The Merchant of Venice*, exact justice and mercy point in different directions. In *Hamlet* the young prince (Act II, Sc. 2, lines 467–469) reprimands Polonius for offering to give the players just the welcome their station merits, chiding him: " ...Use every man/ after his desert and who shall scape whipping? Use/ them after your own honour and dignity—the less they/ deserve the more merit is in your bounty..." And Lear, confronted by his daughters with a logical argument that he doesn't really "need" a retinue, argues that the needs that should be met are not always those that are apparent on the surface: (Act II, Sc. 2, lines 453–472) "O, reason not the need!..." Sometimes love asks for more than what is owed, or what reason has a right to demand. Sometimes justice contends with mercy as to which value will prevail. Or self-interest conflicts with caring for others, or for the community. Conflicting impulses in childhood are usually posed as matters of right versus wrong, but adults (at least, in my experience) often must choose between wrong and even more wrong, or right and even more right. How do we decide what value should prevail?

I think this is at the heart of *King Lear*, in more than one sense of the word "heart." Lear's tragic mistake in the opening scene was not (in my judgment) that he wanted to be flattered, but, rather, that he valued being flattered *more* than he valued anything else. He was willing to sacrifice his beloved daughter on that altar. Cordelia's tragic mistake was adhering to her version of the truth without any attempt to understand her father's perspective or give an inch. The clash of these two unfortunately rigid positions resulted in the play's tragic consequences. In parallel fashion Gloucester allowed Edmund to persuade him that his faithful son, Edgar, was plotting to steal his father's wealth. He let this suspicion weigh more heavily than the love and understanding he had for his son up until that point. The villains of the piece, Edmund, Goneril, Regan, Cornwall, and Oswald, seemingly have no conflicting priorities. Self-interest alone guides them at every turn. In contrast Edgar (who I could see as a heroic figure) puts truth and all other considerations aside to pretend to lead Gloucester to Dover cliff and trick his father into continuing to live; an act that I can only understand as an act of love.

By the play's end, Gloucester and Lear have transformed into human beings who put reverence for life and love *ahead* of every other consideration. Gloucester does battle with his suicidal impulses, and lets himself be persuaded to go on living by his (disguised) loyal son Edgar: (Act IV, Sc.6, lines 72–77)

> Edgar...Therefore, thou happy father,
> Think that the clearest gods, who make them honours
> Of men's impossibilities, have preserved thee.
> Gloucester: I do remember now. Henceforth I'll bear
> Affliction till it do cry out itself
> 'Enough, enough' and die...

Lear cares only for Cordelia by the last scene (Act V, Sc. 3, lines 262–264):

> Lear: This feather stirs, she lives: if it be so,
> It is a chance which does redeem all sorrows
> That I ever felt.

I think the capacity to love allows Gloucester and Lear to have the best possible deaths. Both have come full circle and seen that the life of their beloved, faithful child is what matters most to them. In a sense, there are no more conflicting priorities, since one imperative stands out. Edgar is what matters to Gloucester, and Cordelia is Lear's only concern. Love has concentrated each father on his loyal child, and taken all other cares away. Gloucester dies off stage, but Lear dies concentrating on Cordelia, in the hope that from her lips he sees the breath of life.

> Lear: Do you see this? Look on her: look, her lips,
> Look there, look there! (He dies).

Critics differ in whether they believe that Lear dies, joyfully, thinking Cordelia is alive, or dies knowing that she is dead. Foakes (1997, pp. 390–391) has a succinct summary of the arguments. He says that the last lines made it possible to believe that "…Lear dies in joy, believing Cordelia to be breathing and alive. If Lear does think so he is deluded, or perhaps delirious, and others have insisted that the ending is painful. It is impossible to say what Lear sees, or thinks he sees, but these lines complicate the ending by their very ambiguity. Lear's death is at once painful and a welcome release, for who, as Kent says, would wish this decayed old figure to live longer with such grief when, even if he is deluded, he dies with all his attention focused on Cordelia, not any longer on himself."

As I read it Lear's emotional life is distilled, his love purified. All that matters is pared down to the one breath he longs to see.

I have had the thought that life often prepares us for death by piling on suffering, so that death can a relief. Of course I am not saying this is a thought out strategy, but I think it works that way for many. The more fortunate deaths afford relief, to end the pain, and generative love, to pass the torch.

Another perspective is that as we approach death we can find peace from truly embracing the cyclic nature of life. I find Tolkien's poem (in Sieghart, 2019, p. 13) "All That Is Gold Does Not Glitter," particularly apt for Lear. For a discussion of the poem, please see Chapter Three.

"The Younger Rises When the Old Doth Fall": Inter-Generational Conflict

I return to *The Tempest*, to further contrast its main character, Prospero, with Lear. Just as juxtaposing poems and lines of dialogue with other poetry brings out meanings, I believe that comparing these two magnificent characters yields thoughts about each. Lear and Prospero, two old men, powerful in their time, bent on controlling their daughters, expect unquestioning obedience to their wills. Both feel unjustly served, Lear by his daughters, Prospero by the brother who stole his position. Forgiveness becomes a central theme at the end of both their lives, but in different ways. Lear seeks forgiveness from his youngest daughter, Cordelia, while Prospero becomes able to forgive those who betrayed him. Lear retires and cedes his crown at the beginning of the play, while Prospero waits until near the end to let go of his magical powers.

> ...But this rough magic
> I here abjure; and when I have required
> Some heavenly music (which even now I do)
> To work mine end upon their senses that
> This airy charm is for, I'll break my staff,
> Bury it certain fathoms in the earth,
> And deeper than did ever plummet sound
> I'll drown my book.   (Act V, Sc. 1, lines 50–57)

Much can be said about the similarities and differences between Lear and Prospero, as their powers dim. So great a playwright as Shakespeare writes characters whose complexities invite varying interpretations. My perspective is that both plays present us with problematic features of the relationships between the generations as the aged decline. Some younger characters in both plays treat their elders as obstacles to be overcome ("The younger rises when the old doth fall" Edmund in Act III, Sc. 2, line 24 in *King Lear*). Edmund, Goneril, and Reagan treat Lear and Gloucester as encumbrances. Caliban, Stephano, Trinculo, Antonio, and Sebastian take a similar view in *The Tempest,* plotting to kill those in power for their own advancement. On the other hand, Cordelia, Kent, Edgar, and Gloucester (and, ambivalently, the Fool) treat Lear as a revered elder whose diminishment is lamented, and Ferdinand and Miranda play that role in *The Tempest*.

I would like to frame my comments about reactions to parental decline with a poem by W.H. Auden. Titled "Old People's Home," (In: Auden, 1991, p. 860) it vividly conveys the descent of the aged, and some of the dilemmas it raises for those in attendance. Auden's matter of fact, yet heart breaking language chronicles stages of increasing indignity, as the inhabitants wend their way to death. Their weigh stations remind me of the rings of hell. The best functioning can still read and play music. The next and most populous group can get around in wheelchairs and engage in some group or solo activities. Last come those whose conditions render them forevermore incompetent. Auden astutely questions whether the most able are best off since they may be most aware of their downward slide. But he notes that what they all have in common is that in their time older people had more relevance, as grandparents who often fulfilled some caretaking functions. Now they are like excess, "unpopular" baggage stored out of the way. As the poet prepares to endure paying a dutiful visit, he examines what it means that he wishes his elderly relative a painless, but speedy death. Does that mean that he is cold or is he being merciful and echoing the old woman's prayers for herself?

Auden's description of luggage that has become unpopular reminds me of Lear's (Act II, Sc. 2, line 344) bitter comment "Age is unnecessary." Is unpopular luggage best put away, with all the murderous connotations of that phrase? Auden pairs the aged's loss of a useful function in the rearing of children with their being put out of sight, in "homes" that heartlessly, impersonally classify them according to their functioning level. Auden asks whether his wish for his grandmother's speedy death means he is cold. It does vote for her elimination, but, at least to me, it doesn't seem cold. Perhaps some read it as a wish to *get rid of the conflict she evokes* in the poem's persona: to endure the pain of visiting her or to endure the guilt of not visiting her. I can certainly imagine this as a possibility, but it seems also to speak of compassion, and a wish to end the beloved old woman's suffering.

At the end of Lear's life, Kent expresses something similar, when Edgar tries to get the old king to revive.

> Kent: ...O, let him pass. He hates him
> That would upon the rack of this tough world
> Stretch him out longer.   (Act V, Sc. 3, lines 312–314)

It seems clear that Kent wants Lear to die not out of any motive other than love.

Both *King Lear* and *The Tempest* allude to the loss of power with aging (however voluntary or involuntary it may seem to be). Or is it really the *illusion* of power that is lost, or, rather, bequeathed to the younger generation? How much power does anyone (even a king) really have, when:

> Gloucester: As flies to wanton boys are we to the gods,
> They kill us for their sport.   (Act IV, Sc. 1, lines 37–38)

Prospero's power, his "rough magic," has been likened to Shakespeare's, in that both can conjure fantastic events. Since *The Tempest* was written very late in Shakespeare's career, and after writing it he left his London theater, critics have wondered about the autobiographical element. For example, in their footnote (2011, p. 307) the editors (V. Vaughan and A. Vaughan) suggest that the Epilogue "...relates Prospero's art to the dramatist's skill, and the conventional request for applause also relates to the play's themes of reconciliation and forgiveness." There certainly are some parallels between Prospero and his author. Like Prospero, Shakespeare channels powers beyond reason. Some (e.g. Edward Hirsch, 1999, p. 26) have even described the power of the poet as a kind of dark magic: "....poetry is dangerous. It is allied closely to madness and is not entirely at the dispensation of the poet's conscious will or intellect." Surely this would apply to Shakespeare the dramatist as much as Shakespeare the poet. Further, the dramatist controls the fate of his or her characters and creates, and can destroy, whole worlds. Similarly, Prospero looks back on his life of magic and describes (in Act V, Sc. 1, lines 48–50) and remembers "graves at my command/ Have waked their sleepers, ope'd and let 'em forth/ By my so potent art." Shakespeare has that ability too.

Regardless of one's view on that point, what is it like to lose (or pass on) what is experienced as such an integral part of one's identity? Since Shakespeare (as his character, Hamlet, advised the Players to do) held the mirror up to Nature, I believe that the great playwright (in dialogue with other poets) has much to teach us about the aged as their grip loosens, and the young, as they watch this happen.

Aging can be seen against the backdrop of a particular culture and era's values. What is held as most precious, the freshness of youth, the accumulated experience of age, or other qualities? Auden's poem (above) makes the cultural contribution clear. But I think it raises, rather than answers, other questions. I am reminded of Gloucester's comment: "Better

I were distract,?/ So should my thoughts be severed from my griefs,/ And woes by wrong imagination lose/ The knowledge of themselves." (Act IV, Sc. 6, lines 275–278). Might he be better off if, like Lear, he went mad and didn't fully comprehend his situation? In Auden's array, who suffers most, those "intelligent of what has happened" or the "terminally incompetent"? Regardless, Auden points out how in the past, the aged had a value to the family and a role, which could prompt joy, and not just guilt-ridden duty.

Lear's daughters can be seen as occupying extremes about the value of the old, from Regan's cold assessment ("O, sir, you are old: / Nature in you stands on the very verge/ Of her confine. You should be ruled and led/ By some discretion that discerns your state/ Better than you yourself..." Act II, Sc. 2, lines 335–339) to Cordelia's loving kindness ("Had you not been their father, these white flakes/ Did challenge pity of them. Was this a face/ To be opposed against the warring winds?" Act IV, Sc. 7, lines 30–32).

From the beginning of *King Lear*, the question of how the young feel toward the old, and how the old feel entitled to be treated, is central. Edmund is easily able to convince his father that Edgar wants to shove him aside, so he can enjoy his inheritance at the prime of his youth. Regan bitterly responds to Lear's protest that he gave his daughters all by implying he waited too long to hand over his kingdom ("And in good time you gave it" Act IV, Sc. 2, line 439). Youth's impatience to inherit is viciously expressed by Gloucester's bastard son Edmund in many passages. Lear sputters, as he curses Cordelia, and later his elder daughters, for their "filial ingratitude." Lear expects to be loved and given latitude to hold onto his retinue, in exchange for all he has given. His elder daughters see no need to fulfill a bargain they don't believe they agreed to. Perhaps each era, each culture, and each person frames the "deal" between the generations somewhat differently, but it is a powerful theme, and Shakespeare takes full advantage of that. I don't think we have to read this in classically psychoanalytic Oedipal terms, though we may. Not every intergenerational interchange is about sexual issues, parricide, or any of the conflict ridden themes the early analysts stressed. As already stated, *King Lear* is as much about the *sorrow* of the younger for the older as it is about anything else. Cordelia and Edgar feel the tragedy of Lear's and Gloucester's downfalls with great poignancy. As Edgar says, (Act IV, Sc. 6, lines 137–138) when the mad king meets his blind father, "I would not take this from report: it is,/ And my heart breaks at it."

What Lear Loses

Lear: O let me not be mad, not mad, sweet heaven! I would not be mad.
Keep me in temper, I would not be mad.

Some see this as Lear's first premonition that he could go mad, while others believe he was mad almost from the beginning of the play (see footnote, Foakes, p. 215). "Temper" is considered (same footnote) to mean "mental balance." If we use this definition it would be possible to say that Lear loses his temper throughout the play, in one sense or another. Or, we might even say that he regains his "temper" during the "mad" scene between him and the blind Gloucester. In that scene, when he counsels the Earl to have patience, Lear seems more emotionally balanced, in the sense that no strong emotion is overpowering him, though, in another sense, he is "unbalanced," in his relationship to reality. Not much later, the doctor comments that the rage in Lear is gone. It is not that he is without feelings. Indeed Bloom (2018) sees Lear's intense emotionality to be his great, in a sense tragic flaw. But, as we have already seen, his elder daughters have no regard for his feelings.

Regan: O, Sir, you are old:
Nature in you stands on the very verge
Of her confine. You should be ruled and led

By some discretion that discerns your state
Better than you yourself.... (Act II, Sc. 2, lines 335–341)

This argument (whether or not it is meant as genuine reasoning) seems to me to suggest that by virtue of being old and near to death, Lear can't be aware of his state, or condition, or status/position. Consequently, he should defer to the superior powers of judgment of those younger than himself. Again, taking it literally (which we may not be meant to do) does it suppose that discernment decreases with age, or with nearness to death? More specifically, since it argues that Lear lacks discernment of his own "state," does it imply that approaching death obliterates vision of all aspects of one's situation? That nearness to dying overpowers all self-awareness?

"Confine" is an interesting word here, as it can connote the period of childbirth, as well as an enclosure. I wonder whether it implicitly links infancy and old age as times when we must be governed by others. In any case, both *King Lear* and *The Tempest* invite us to examine our assumptions about those approaching death. *The Tempest* takes up the sorrowing of old and young from many causes, but there is ample evidence of the empathy of each generation for the losses incurred by the other. Hearing the story of Prospero's displacement by his brother, Miranda, Prospero's young daughter, clearly moved, (Act I, Sc. 2, lines 131–134) says:

Miranda: Alack, for pity.
I, not rememb'ring how I cried out then,
Will cry it o'er again. It is a hint
That wrings mine eyes to't.

Ferdinand, Alonso's son, is equally distressed by the thought of his father's suffering in the throes of the tempest. As for the distressed fathers, Prospero, unlike Lear, is not looking to be taken care of by Miranda. He bears a different grief. His problem is letting go of *taking care of her.* I think this perspective would be quite familiar to a modern audience. In this view of the dynamic between old and young there are not so much villains as human beings caught in inevitable conflicts. The young want to take their next steps. For example Miranda, disobeying her father by telling Ferdinand her name, movingly portrays her struggle between obeying Prospero and going forward, toward her own future. Miranda is never portrayed as wanting, or needing, to rid herself of Prospero, but merely to disobey him, in order to follow her heart. Prospero's motives are much more complex. He "provides" Miranda with Ferdinand, but then blocks their union (ostensibly to make sure Miranda is properly valued). Prospero has to become able to let go of Miranda and Ariel, his servant, who annoys Prospero by lobbying for his early release and freedom to be on his own. Young and old suffer, not out of hatred for each other, but because going forward means leaving each other behind. This is a play of affectionate leave takings. Even the non-human sprite, Ariel, needs to hear Prospero loves him before he can fly to his freedom. The shift toward the future comes with costs. It is a sorrow many twenty first century parents and offspring would find familiar.

In fact *The Tempest* can be understood as an exploration of letting go. Prospero lets go of his desire to avenge his brother's betrayal of him, his antipathy toward Caliban, his magic, his daughter, his sprite, and his island home. For her part Miranda lets go of childhood and magical protection by her all-powerful father. In a way, all the characters in this play let go of the past. Auden (as discussed earlier) wrote a fascinating work of his own, (" The Sea and the Mirror," 2003) about what could have come next.

The Meaning That Remains

If, along with Auden in his poem, "Old People's Home," (above) we believe that human beings wither without a useful function, we can cite several of Shakespeare's tragic characters as illustration. For example, when Lear gave up his crown, as the Fool so frequently reminds him, and as Kent warned him, he gave up something central to his meaning, in his own eyes. Prospero, although he will have a function when he returns home, will not have the function of taking care of Miranda, who he earlier (Act III, Sc. 3, line 4) called "that for which I live." As he hands her over to Ferdinand he tells them that "every third thought will be my grave." In unforgettable words, Shakespeare has Prospero comment on his art's (and his life's?) ephemeral quality in Act IV, Scene 1 (lines 147–158):

> Prospero: Our revels now are ended. These are actors,
>   As I foretold you, were all spirits and
>   Are melted into air, into thin air;
>   And—like the baseless fabric of this vision—
>   The cloud-capped towers, the gorgeous palaces,
>   The solemn temples, the great globe itself,
>   Yea, all which it inherit, shall dissolve,
>   And like this insubstantial pageant faded,
>   Leave not a rack behind. We are such stuff
>   As dreams are made on, and our little life
>   Is rounded with a sleep…

We know Shakespeare left London after writing *The Tempest*, returned to Stratford, wrote little, and died two years later at the age of 52, but we don't know what he felt he had accomplished. We can only speculate as to the "mark" or impact he had wanted to have, and how much he believed he had

444

achieved. Of course it would be deeply ironic if the man who, arguably, made more of a mark than any other playwright in the English language, felt he left "not a rack behind"!

What should follow from our awareness of being ephemeral? How do we retain some sense of meaning, once we no longer inhabit our roles, whatever they might be? Clearly these are questions humankind has approached throughout our history and no one play, not even a great one by Shakespeare, can fully answer them. What answer, however partial, does Shakespeare suggest in *The Tempest*? Even after making his pronouncement about giving up his magic, Prospero continues to purposefully shape events. Influenced by Ariel's description of his enemies' suffering, he brings them together and gives each pardon. The "insubstantial pageant" still seems to matter. I return to Prospero's final statement below.

Without expecting anything like a definitive answer, I turn to Mary Oliver for a response to the challenge of valuing the ephemeral. In her poem, "Blackwater Woods," (In: A. Holden and B. Holden, 2014, pp. 231–232) Oliver refers to a river of loss whose meaning we will never fully understand. Against that backdrop she juxtaposes three requirements that are crucial, to live in this world. We must be able to cherish what is mortal, holding it close to us. We must recognize that loving the ephemeral is a human necessity, vital to our lives. Finally, when it is time, we must let it all go. Can this prescription from Mary Oliver bolster me, as I face the vast array of potential losses described by Auden (in the poem "Old Peoples' Home" referred to above) and countless others?

The comfort I get from Oliver's gentle advice comes, at least in part, from poetry's freeing influence. Under its jurisdiction I can let go of needing things to make rational sense. I need this permission in order to value what happens in my "little life" despite (or, perhaps, because of) the "black river of loss." As I read it, though, Shakespeare needed something else, something (I describe below) that he asks for in the epilogue to *The Tempest*.

Auden's elderly lost all meaningful functions, at least in part, because society changed the role assigned to them. Lear gave away his title and, to a large extent, his identity. Prospero let go of his magus role after he had achieved the resolutions he sought. It seems like it should be a victory, and, yet, the epilogue tells us that although Prospero has freed the other characters he (and, perhaps the author) is not yet free. What more has to happen for Prospero (and Shakespeare?) to leave his magical island and go home?

At the end of *King Lear*, Edgar declares that the young will never live as long or suffer as much as their elders have. It is as though the play's epic struggles can't be repeated. But conflicts between the generations go on, if in altered form, as *The Tempest*, and so much else attests. Both young and old have to deal with life's seasons, which brings each sorrows. The past must be sacrificed for the sake of the future. While there are always those who would murder and steal, more frequently the generations play out their differences less violently. In *The Tempest*, as I read it, the principal conflict is really between Prospero and Prospero. Forgiving his brother and his brother's cohorts, relinquishing the power of magic, blessing the marriage of Ferdinand and Miranda, freeing Ariel, and even Caliban, and settling all the old scores, are (to me, at least) monumental achievements. And Prospero does all this without much help, or even encouragement. Only Ariel chides him, saying that, were he human, he would feel sorrow for the grief stricken old, tempest tossed Gonzalo, among others. For the most part Prospero evolves through contemplating what he thinks is right. I find the precise wording of the play's epilogue, that ends his journey, extremely moving. I understand it as a statement of what we all need:

> Prospero: Now my charms are all o'erthrown,
> And what strength I have's mine own,
> Which is most faint. Now, 'tis true

I must be here confined by you,
Or sent to Naples. Let me not,
Since I have my dukedom got
And pardoned the deceiver, dwell
In this bare island by your spell;
But release me from my bands
With the help of your good hands.
Gentle breath of yours my sails
Must fill or else my project fails,
Which was to please. Now I want
Spirits to enforce, art to enchant;
And my ending is despair,
Unless I be relieved by prayer,
Which pierces so that it assaults
Mercy itself, and frees all faults.
As you from crimes would pardoned be,
Let your indulgence set me free.

(Arden, 2011, "Epilogue," pp. 307–308)

Prospero opens up to the audience, embracing his need for our responsiveness, in order to free his spirit. No play, no poem, is complete without the partnership of the reader. Without that the author has no meaningful role and leaves no mark. As Hirsch (1999, p. 6) put it: "The poet is incited to create a work that can outdistance time and surmount distance, that can bridge the gulf—the chasm—between people otherwise unknown to each other."

But this magic can only happen through collaboration. Throughout his book about poetry's magic, Hirsch emphasizes how (p. 27) the writer and reader create meaning together. This is the hope, the plea, the dependence expressed in the epilogue of *The Tempest*, which ends with Prospero's rewording of the Golden Rule. He asks us to give him the response that we, ourselves, would want to receive.

I hear a meaningful parallel to the standoff and eventual resolution of the Lear/ Cordelia story. In the first scene their rigidity doesn't allow them to offer each other any "give." In that sense Lear is right that "nothing will come of nothing." All each of them can do is withhold, siding with prideful principle against loving understanding. But by the end, the penitent father gives his daughter recognition of her "cause" and the empathic daughter gives her father forgiveness from a full heart. Each character gives something the other needs, just as authors and readers/viewers complete each other. Their heartfelt compassion makes the brevity of Lear and Cordelia's embrace just bearable, at least for me.

The surface story of *The Tempest* reflects its other meanings, as the surface of the storm-tossed water reflects its churned depths. It is a magical play about magic, and it took some magic to put on, with its raging sea and flying characters, before the era of special effects. Perhaps the playwright is taking a last bow. (The Tempest is the last complete play he wrote on his own). We, the audience, can free him by partnering him. We "fill his sails" by doing our part in a mutual process of meaning making. Our "good hands" give applause which is (on one level) a form of approval. But it also signals that the author's words, communicated, have taken on meanings (partly) shaped by each recipient. We free him by indicating that we heard him, and now it is up to us to make of his message what we will. Shakespeare (and Prospero) have done their part and are free to leave. And by freeing them we earn similar consideration for ourselves, just as the character, Prospero, earned mercy by learning to be merciful to others. The epilogue (and the rest of the play as well) has the intricacy of poetry, making it very hard to render its meaning and beauty in prose. But we hear its frank admission of need, and the call to us to follow the golden rule and give others the consideration we would hope to receive.

Isaac Asimov (*Asimov's Guide to Shakespeare,* 1978, Avenel Books, NY, p. 668) sees the end of the play somewhat differently. In his words:

Many critics seem to think that this is Shakespeare's farewell to his art. He is saying he will write no more and will no longer practice the matchless magic of his literary genius. This is, in my opinion, too sentimental an interpretation and I doubt it. For one thing, a compulsive writer like Shakespeare couldn't deliberately plan to give up writing while he was capable of holding a pen—on this one point I claim to be an authority.

Asimov seems to believe the writer can't abandon his magic because the consequences would be too dire. Can any of us, writers or others, ever let go of our powers without sinking into despair? Can we meet the challenge of letting go, in Mary Oliver's great poem (quoted above)? Sometimes Shakespeare seems to equate relinquishing efforts to remain in control with a peaceful surrender to fate. For example, in *Hamlet,* the prince has the beautiful lines I quote in the chapter on this play:

...we defy augury: there's a special providence in the fall of a sparrow. If it be now, 'tis not to come; if it be not to come, it will be now; if it be not now, yet it will come: the readiness is all: since no man knows what aught of what he leaves, what is't to leave betimes? Let be.

Arden, 2016, Act V, Sc.2, lines 218–224

Hamlet accepts how little is in human control, and death's inevitability. I don't hear these lines as sorrowful so much as expressing a tender and peaceful melancholy, the sweet resignation of one who has accepted Mary Oliver's "black river of loss." When Prospero speaks of giving up his magic (Act V, Sc. 1, line 51) having accomplished all that he set out to do, with his daughter about to be wed and his former enemies penitent and forgiven, perhaps he, too, is ready to be at peace. Having given away his superhuman powers, this epilogue is not about a battle of titans, or a murderous clash between generations, but a plea for participation and affirmation. We, audience and author, (and, more generally, human beings) can free each other, by giving to others the willing collaboration, kind recognition, and mercy we would hope to receive. Unlike (in "King Lear") Edmund's "zero-sum" declaration of the young rising when the old falls, this is about all of us creating meaning by rising together. One perspective is that in the character of Lear we see love lend his life and death meaning, *through* (rather than despite) his suffering.

Before I "let go" of this book, I would like to mention some poignant poems that touch on how suffering can color the end of life. I feel they strike up an interesting dialogue with some passages in Shakespeare's plays. For example, when Edgar first sees his bleeding, blinded father he reflects on how suffering can affect the will to live.

> World, world, world
> But that thy strange mutations make us hate thee,
> Life would not yield to age.   (Act IV, Sc. 1, lines 11–13)

I am particularly aware of one version of Hamlet's (Act III, Sc. 1, lines 61–62) "thousand natural shocks/ That flesh is heir to" that can, I feel, make death " a consummation/ Devoutly to be wished" (lines 64–65). What I am envisioning is the contemporary situation of being strung up in-between tubes in a hospital bed, waiting to die. For me, this is the epitome of what can turn death into a relief, for the dying as well as everyone around them. Suffering, beyond some point, can, indeed, wipe out all awareness of anything else. We return to being merely vessels. The feel of this, as well as a contrary, primitive force that hangs on, merely to hang on, has been captured by C.K. Williams, in a poem he entitled "Grief" (in K. Young, pp. 123–126). I mentioned this poem in previous chapters and earlier in this one. It is a long poem, so I will quote passages from it.

> Gone now, after the days of desperate, unconscious gasping, the
>   reflexive staying alive,
> tumorous lungs, tumorous blood, ruined, tumorous liver
>   demanding
>   to live, to go on,
> even the innocent bladder, its tenuous, dull golden coin in the
>   slack
>   translucent bag;
> gone now, after months of scanning, medication, nausea, hair loss
>   and weight loss;
> remission, partial remission, gratitude, hope, lost hope, anxiety,
>   anger,
>   confusion,
> the hours and days of everyday life, something like life but only as
>   dying is like life;
> gone the quiet at the end of dying, the mouth caught agape on its
>   last
>   bite at a breath,
> bare skull with its babylike growth of new hair thrown back to
>   open
>   the terrified larynx;...
> under the earth, cold earth, cold grasses, cold winter wind,
>   freezing
>   eternity, cold, forever....
> pain for all human beings who know they will go and still go as
>   though they knew nothing,...

Stripped now of its raiment, the mouth, caught in its last labored
breath, finds last resolution;
all the flesh now, stripped of its guises, moves toward its place in
the
peace of the earth...

This poem is tender and savage, in equal measure. The nearly unbearable, exquisite horror of the terrified larynx and the mysterious, reflexive gasping for one last breath are two equal strands of the same experience. What Hamlet, C.K. Williams, and all the rest of us have in common is that we know we "..will go and still go as though" we knew nothing. Death is both anticipated and a shock. And at times it may be "a consummation" devoutly wished, but also, at the very same time, fiercely fought off. I hear in C.K. Williams' poem something about the animal nature of any living being caught in death's grip. Animals fight for last gasps not, necessarily, because life is so wonderful, but, because animals have to breath.

Personally, I don't think the surreal horror of death, where the human being becomes dust, or a corridor between tubes, has really changed much over the centuries. Regardless of what the modern version looks like, the idea of becoming a concentrated quiver will always terrify. The bridge from being myself to being interred will always loom as a bridge too far.

Gerald Stern's poem, "I Remember Galileo" portrays the pleading animal in all of us (in Seiden, 2016, p. 115):

I remember Galileo describing the mind
as a piece of paper blown around by the wind,
and I loved the sight of it sticking to a tree,
or jumping into the back seat of a car,
and for years I watched paper leap through my cities;
but yesterday I saw the mind was a squirrel caught crossing

Route 80 between the wheels of a giant truck,
dancing back and forth like a thin leaf,
or a frightened string, for only two seconds living
on the white concrete before he got away,
his life shortened by all that terror, his head
jerking, his yellow teeth ground down to dust.

It was the speed of the squirrel and his lowness to the ground,
his great purpose and the alertness of his dancing,
that showed me the difference between him and paper.
Paper will do in theory, when there is time
to sit back in a metal chair and study shadows;
but for this life I need a squirrel,
his clawed feet spread, his whole soul quivvering,
the loud noise shaking him from head to tail.
O philosophical mind, O mind of paper, I need a squirrel
finishing his wild dash across the highway,

rushing up his green ungoverned hillside.

C.K. Williams and Gerald Stern help me access the pleading animal in myself. In *The Tempest, King Lear,* and so much else, Shakespeare confronts me with ordinary and extraordinary suffering. Mary Oliver gently, wisely, tells me what I will need to do, to still "live in this world."

References

Agee, J. (2009). *A Death in the Family*. New York: Penguin Books.

Alexie, S. (2016). Grief calls us to the things of this world. In: H. Seiden, *The Motive for Metaphor: Brief Essays on Poetry and Psychoanalysis*. London: Karnac.

Amichai, Y. (2016). The precision of pain and the blurriness of joy. In: H. Seiden, *The Motive for Metaphor: Brief Essays on Poetry and Psychoanalysis*. London: Karnac.

Angelou, M. (2019). Still I rise. In: W. Sieghart, *The Poetry Remedy: Prescriptions for the Heart, Mind, and Soul*. New York: Viking.

Aristotle (fourth century B.C.). *The Nicomachean Ethics*, Trans. H. Rackham. Ware, Hertfordshire: Wordsworth Editions.

Asimov, I. (1978). *Asimov's Guide to Shakespeare*. New York: Avenel Books.

Auden, W.H. (1991. Old peoples' home. In: *A Treasury of Poems*, ed. S.A. Stuart. New York: Galahad Books.

——— (1991). In memory of W.B. Yeats. In: *W.H. Auden: Collected Poems*. ed. E. Mendelson. New York: Vintage Books.

——— (1991). Loneliness. In: *W.H. Auden: Collected Poems*. ed. E. Mendelson. New York: Vintage Books.

——— (2003). *The Sea and the Mirror: A Poem*. (Ed. A. Kirsch). Princeton: Princeton University Press.

——— (2016). Lullaby, In: H. Seiden, The Motive for Metaphor: Brief Essays on Poetry and Psychoanalysis. London: Karnac.

——— (2017). Musee des beaux arts, In: J. Bialosky, *Poetry Will Save Your Life: A Memoir*. New York: Atria Books. Also in W.H. Auden: Collected Poems. ed. E. Mendelson. 1991, New York: Vintage Books.

Baer, U. (2005). *The Poet's Guide to Life:* The Wisdom of Rilke. New York: Modern Library.

Bang, M.J. (2010). No more. In: K. Young, *The Art of Losing: Poems of Grief and Healing*. New York: Bloomsbury.

Barker, S. (2016). The ballad of true regret. In: A. Holden & B. Holden, *Poems that Make Grown Women Cry*. New York: Simon & Schuster.

Baum, F. L. (1900/2000). *Annotated Wizard of Oz*, ed.: M.P. Hearn. New York: W.W. Norton.

Bayley, J. (1999). *Elegy for Iris*. New York: Norton.

Berry, W. (2019). The peace of wild things. In: W. Sieghart, *The Poetry Remedy: Prescriptions for the Heart, Mind, and Soul*. New York: Viking.

Bialosky, J. (2017). *Poetry Will Save Your Life: A Memoir*. New York: Atria Books.

Bishop, E. (2010). One art. In K. Young, *The Art of Losing: Poems of Grief and Healing*. New York: Bloomsbury.

——— (2016). In the waiting room. In: H. Seiden, *The Motive for Metaphor: Brief Essays On Poetry and Psychoanalysis*, ed. H.M. Seiden. London: Karnac Books.

Blake, W. (1984). A poison tree. In: B. Raffel, *How to Read a Poem*. New York: Meridian.

Blok, A. (1920/2008). Shakespeare's King Lear: An address to the actors. In: *Bloom's Shakespeare Through the Ages: King Lear*. (ed. H. Bloom). New York: Checkmark Books

Brodsky, J. (2010). A song. In: K. Young, *The Art of Losing: Poems of Grief and Healing*. New York: Bloomsbury.

Brouwer, J. (2010). The spots. In: K. Young, *The Art of Losing: Poems of Grief and Healing*. New York: Bloomsbury.

Buechler, S. (1995). Emotion. In: *Handbook of Interpersonal Psychoanalysis*, ed.: M. Lionells, J. Fiscalini, C.H. Mann, & D.B. Stern. Hillsdale, N.J.: The Analytic Press.

———— (2004). *Clinical Values: Emotions that Guide Psychoanalytic Treatment*. Hillsdale, N.J.: The Analytic Press.

———— (2008). *Making a Difference in Patients' Lives: Emotional Experience in the Therapeutic Setting*. New York: Routledge.

———— (2012). *Still Practicing: The Heartaches and Joys of a Clinical Career*. New York: Routledge.

———— (2015). *Understanding and Treating Patients in Clinical Psychoanalysis: Lessons from Literature*. New York: Routledge.

———— (2017). *Psychoanalytic Reflections: Training and Practice*. New York: IPBooks.

———— (2019). *Psychoanalytic Approaches to Problems in Living: Addressing Life's Challenges in Clinical Practice*. New York: Routledge.

Bullen, A.H. (2015). Chronology of Shakespeare's Plays, Stratford Town Edition. In: *The Complete Works of William Shakespeare*, New York: Barnes and Noble.

Burt, S. & D. Mikics, (2010). *The Art of the Sonnet*. Cambridge, Mass: Harvard University Press.

Campbell, J. (2004). *Pathways to Bliss: Mythology and Personal Transformation*. Novato, California: New World Library.

Cavefy, C.P. (1999). The god abandons Anthony. In: E. Hirsch, *How to Read a Poem and Fall in Love with Poetry*. Translated by E. Keeley and P. Sherrard. New York: Harvest Books, Harcourt, Inc.

Clifton, L. (1995). At the cemetery, Walnut Grove Plantation, South Carolina, 1989. In: The Language of Life: A Festival of Poets, ed. B. Moyers. New York: Anchor Books.

———— (1995). Sam (poem and interview). In*: The Language of Life: A Festival of Poets*, ed. B. Moyers. New York: Anchor Books.

———— (1995). Shapeshifter poems. In: *The Language of Life: A Festival of Poets*, ed. B. Moyers. New York: Anchor Books.

———— (2020). Fury, In: *How to Carry Water: Selected Poems*. Rochester, N.Y.: BOA Editions.

———— (2020). Sorrows. In L. Clifton, *How to Carry Water: Selected Poems*. Rochester, N.Y.: BOA Editions.

Collins, B. (2012). Musee des beaux arts revisited. In: E. Fragos (ed.). *Art and Artists: Poems*. New York: Alfred A. Knopf.

Cope, W. (2019). Defining the problem. In: W. Sieghart, *The Poetry Remedy: Prescriptions for the Heart, Mind, and Soul*. New York: Viking.

———— (2019). My funeral. In: W. Sieghart, *The Poetry Remedy: Prescriptions for the Heart, Mind, and Soul*. New York: Viking.

Corbett, R. (2016). *You Must Change Your Life: The Story Of Rainer Maria Rilke and Auguste Rodin*. New York: W.W. Norton.

Crane, H. (2010). To Emily Dickinson, In: Burt, S. & D. Mikics, *The Art of the Sonnet*. Cambridge, Mass: Harvard University Press.

Cruz, V.H. (1995). In: *The Language of Life: A Festival of Poets*, ed. B. Moyers. New York: Anchor Books.

de Button, A. & J. Armstrong, (2013). *Art As Therapy*. New York: Phaidon Press.

Cushman, P. & P. Guilford, (1999). From emptiness to multiplicity: The self at the year 2000. *Psychohistory Review* 27:15–32.

Deutch, H. (1973). *Confrontations With Myself*. New York: W.W. Norton.

Dickinson, E. (1960). Poem 326, In: The Complete Poems of Emily Dickinson, ed. T.H. Johnson. Boston: Little, Brown, & Company.

———— (2010). In: H. Vendler, *Dickinson: Selected Poems and Commentaries*. Cambridge, Mass:Harvard University Press.

———— (2010). Poem 23, In: H. Vendler, *Dickinson: Selected Poems and Commentaries*. Cambridge, Mass: Harvard University Press.

—— (2010). Poem 124, H. Vendler, *Dickinson: Selected Poems and Commentaries.* Cambridge, Mass: Harvard University Press.

—— (2010). Poem 165, In: H. Vendler, *Dickinson: Selected Poems and Commentaries.* Cambridge, Mass: Harvard University Press.

—— (2010). Poem 240, In: H. Vendler, Dickinson: Selected Poems and Commentaries. Cambridge, Mass: Harvard University Press.

—— (2010). Poem 314, In: H. Vendler, *Dickinson: Selected Poems and Commentaries.* Cambridge, Mass: Harvard University Press.

—— (2010). Poem 326, In: H. Vendler, *Dickinson: Selected Poems and Commentaries.* Cambridge, Mass: Harvard University Press. Also in: The Complete Poems of Emily Dickinson, ed. Thomas H. Johnson, 1960, Boston: Little, Brown & Company.

—— (2010). Poem 372, In: H. Vendler, *Dickinson: Selected Poems and Commentaries.* Cambridge, Mass: Harvard University Press.

—— (2010). Poem 407, In: H. Vendler, *Dickinson: Selected Poems and Commentaries.* Cambridge, Mass: Harvard University Press.

—— (2010). Poem 425, In: H. Vendler, Dickinson: Selected Poems and Commentaries. Cambridge, Mass: Harvard University Press.

—— (2010). Poem 466, In: H. Vendler, *Dickinson: Selected Poems and Commentaries.* Cambridge, Mass: Harvard University Press.

—— (2010). Poem 519, In: H. Vendler, *Dickinson: Selected Poems and Commentaries.* Cambridge, Mass: Harvard University Press.

—— (2010). Poem 528, In: H. Vendler, *Dickinson: Selected Poems and Commentaries.* Cambridge, Mass: Harvard University Press.

—— (2010). Poem 550, In: H. Vendler, *Dickinson: Selected Poems and Commentaries.* Cambridge, Mass: Harvard University Press.

────── (2010). Poem 588, In: H. Vendler, Dickinson: Selected Poems and Commentaries. Cambridge, Mass: Harvard University Press.

────── (2010). Poem 591, In: H. Vendler, *Dickinson: Selected Poems and Commentaries*. Cambridge, Mass: Harvard University Press.

────── (2010). Poem 620, In: H. Vendler, *Dickinson: Selected Poems and Commentaries*. Cambridge, Mass: Harvard University Press.

────── (2010). Poem 1142, In: H. Vendler, *Dickinson: Selected Poems and Commentaries*. Cambridge, Mass: Harvard University Press.

────── (2010). Poem 1263, In: H. Vendler, *Dickinson: Selected Poems and Commentaries*. Cambridge, Mass: Harvard University Press

────── (2010). Poem 1347, In: H. Vendler, *Dickinson: Selected Poems and Commentaries*. Cambridge, Mass: Harvard University Press.

────── (2010). Poem 1429, In: H. Vendler, *Dickinson: Selected Poems and Commentaries*. Cambridge, Mass: Harvard University Press.

────── (2010). Poem 1773, In: H. Vendler, *Dickinson: Selected Poems and Commentaries*.. Cambridge, Mass: Harvard University Press.

────── (2015). Poem 419, In: J. Hirshfield, *Ten Windows: How Great Poems Transform the World*. New York: Alfred A. Knopf.

────── (2017). Poem 288. In: J. Bialosky, *Poetry Will Save Your Life: A Memoir*. New York: Atria Books.

Didion, J. (2005). *The Year of Magical Thinking*. New York: Alfred A. Knopf.

Douthat, R. (2017). The misery filter In: *New York Times Sunday Review*, October 29, p. 9.

Dove, R. (1995). Lady Freedom among us (Poem and interview). In: *The Language of Life: A Festival of Poets*, ed. B. Moyers. New York: Anchor Books.

────── (2010). Party dress for a first born. In: *The Art of the Sonnet*, eds, S. Burt & D. Mikics. Cambridge, Mass.: Harvard University Press.

Durcan, P. (2019). Maureen Durcan. In: W. Sieghart, *The Poetry Remedy: Prescriptions for the Heart, Mind, and Soul*. New York: Viking.

Edwards, P. (2002). The dyer's infected hand: The sonnets and the text of Hamlet. In: *Hamlet: New Critical Essays,* ed. A.F. Kinney, New York: Routledge.

Eliot, G. (Mary Ann Evans). 2010, Brother and sister, 7 and 8. In: *The Art of the Sonnet,* eds, S. Burt & D. Mikics. Cambridge, Mass.: Harvard University Press.

Eliot, T.S. (1930). The love song of J. Alfred Prufrock. In: *Selected Poems.* New York: Harcourt.

——— (1943). East Coker. In: *Four Quartets.* New York: Harcourt.

Emerson, R.W. (1996). Terminus. In: A Treasury of Poems, ed. S.A. Stuart. New York: Galahad Books.

Fenton, J. (2019). The mistake. In: W. Sieghart, *The Poetry Remedy: Prescriptions for the Heart, Mind, and Soul.* New York: Viking.

Flynn, N. (2010). Sudden. In: *The Art of Losing: Poems of Grief and Healing,* ed. K. Young. New York: Bloomsbury.

Foakes, R.A. (1997). Introduction: King Lear. Arden Shakespeare. London: Thomas Learning.

——— (2002). Hamlet's neglect of revenge. In: *Hamlet: New Critical Essays,* ed. A. F. Kinney, New York: Routledge.

Forche, C. (2010). The morning baking. In: K. Young, *The Art of Losing: Poems of Grief and Healing.* New York: Bloomsbury.

Freud, S. (1900). The Interpretation of Dreams. *Standard Edition* 4–5, London: Hogarth Press.

——— (1905/1953). Fragment of an analysis of a case of hysteria. *Standard Edition* 7, pp. 3–122. London: Hogarth Press.

——— (1913/2008). The theme of the three caskets. In: H. Bloom, *Bloom's Shakespeare Through the Ages: King Lear.* New York: Checkmark Books.

——— (1917/1957). Mourning and melancholia. *Standard Edition* 14, 237–258. London: Hogarth Press.

(1926/1959). Inhibitions, symptoms, and anxiety. *Standard Edition* 20, pp. 87–175. London: Hogarth Press.

(1930/1961). Civilization and its discontents. *Standard Edition* 21, pp. 59–145. London: Hogarth Press.

Fromm, E. (1955). *The Sane Society.* New York: Holt, Rinehart & Winston.

——— (1956). *The Art of Loving.* New York: Harper & Row.

——— (1962). *Beyond the Chains of Illusion.* New York: Trident Press.

——— (1968). *The Revolution of Hope.* New York: Harper & Row.

——— (1976). *To Have or To Be?* New York: Harper & Row.

Fromm-Reichmann, F. (1959/ 1990). Loneliness. *Contemporary Psychoanalysis* 26: 305–330.

Frost, R. (1970). Nothing gold can stay. In: *A book of Modern American Poetry.* ed.: J. McDermott & T. Lowry. New York: Harcourt Brace Jovanovich, Inc.

——— (1971). An old man's winter night. In: *Robert Frost's Poems.* L. Untermeyer. New York: St. Martin's Paperbacks.

——— (1991). The road not taken. In: T. Kendall, *The Art of Robert Frost.* New Haven: Yale University Press.

——— (1999). Desert places. In: E. Hirsch, *How to Read a Poem and Fall in Love with Poetry.* New York: Harvest Books, Harcourt, Inc.

——— (2012). Stopping by woods on a snowy evening. In: T. Kendall, *The Art of Robert Frost.* New Haven: Yale University Press.

——— (2012). Two tramps in mud time. In: T. Kendall, *The Art of Robert Frost.* New Haven: Yale University Press.

Frye, M.E. (2019). Do not stand at my grave and weep. In: W. Sieghart, *The Poetry Remedy: Prescriptions for the Heart, Mind, and Soul.* New York: Viking.

Funk, R. (1982). Erich Fromm: *The Courage To Be Human.* New York: Continuum.

Garber, M. (2004). *Shakespeare After All.* New York: Anchor Books.

Gilbert, J. (2019). Falling and flying. In: W. Sieghart, *The Poetry Remedy: Prescriptions for the Heart, Mind, and Soul.* New York: Viking.

Girmay, Aracelis, 2019, "Second estrangement," In: W. Sieghart, *The Poetry Remedy: Prescriptions for the Heart, Mind, and Soul.* New York: Viking.

Gluck, L. (1994). *Proofs & Theories: Essays on Poetry.* Hopewell, N.J.: The Ecco Press.

Grennan, E. (2016). Details. In: H. Seiden, *The Motive for Metaphor: Brief Essays On Poetry and Psychoanalysis,* ed. H.M. Seiden. London: Karnac Books.

Hall, D. (1995). A grace. In: *The Language of Life: A Festival of Poets,* ed. B. Moyers. New York: Anchor Books.

(1995). My son, my executioner. . In: T*he Language of Life: A Festival of Poets,* ed. B. Moyers. New York: Anchor Books.

Harjo, J. (1995). In: *The Language of Life: A Festival of Poets,* ed. B. Moyers. New York: Anchor Books.

Harper, M. (1995). In: *The Language of Life: A Festival of Poets,* ed. B. Moyers. New York: Anchor Books.

Hartwig, J. (2015). "Feeling the way" In: J. Hirshfield, (2015). *Ten Windows: How Great Poems Transform the World.* New York: Alfred A. Knopf.

Hass, R. (2016). Heroic Simile, In: *The Motive for Metaphor: Brief Essays On Poetry and Psychoanalysis,* ed. H.M. Seiden. London: Karnac Books.

Hawkes, T. (2002). The old Bill. In A.F. Kinney, *Hamlet: New Critical Essays.* New York: Routledge.

Hayden R. (2017). Those winter Sundays In: J. Bialosky, *Poetry Will Save Your Life: A Memoir.* New York: Atria Books.

Heaney, S. (2001). Clearances. In: T. Ogden, An elegy, a love song, and a lullaby. *Psychoanalytic Dialogues* 11(2): 293–311.

———— (2019). Follower. In: W. Sieghart, *The Poetry Remedy: Prescriptions for the Heart, Mind, and Soul.* New York: Viking.

Heisenkamp, G. (2001). Is psychoanalysis a cheerless (Freud-less) profession? Toward a psychoanalysis of joy. *The Psychoanalytic Quarterly* 70: 839–871.

Hettich, M. (1984). Lion. In: B. Raffel, *How to Read a Poem.* New York: Meridian.

Hirsch, E. (1999). *How to Read a Poem and Fall in Love with Poetry.* New York: Harvest Books, Harcourt, Inc.

———— (2011). Fast break. In: E. Hirsch, *The Living Fire: New and Selected Poems.* New York: Alfred A. Knopf.

Hirshfield, J.(2015). *Ten Windows: How Great Poems Transform the World.* New York: Alfred A. Knopf.

———— (2019). Burlap sack. In: W. Sieghart, *The Poetry Remedy: Prescriptions for the Heart, Mind, and Soul.* New York: Viking.

Hoagland, T. (2016). I have news for you. In: The Motive for Metaphor: Brief Essays On Poetry and Psychoanalysis, ed. H.M. Seiden. London: Karnac Books

Holden, A. & B. Holden, (2014). *Poems That Make Grown Men Cry.* New York: Simon & Schuster.

Horwitz, A.V. & J.C. Wakefield (2007). *The Loss of Sadness.* New York: Oxford University Press.

Howe, M. (2016). What the living do. In: T*he Motive for Metaphor: Brief Essays On Poetry and Psychoanalysis,* ed. H.M. Seiden. London: Karnac Books.

Hughes, L. (1995). Harlem/ Montage of a Dream Deferred. In: *The Collected Poems of Langston Hughes.* ed: A. Rampersad. New York: Alfred A. Knopf.

———— (2017). I, too. In: J. Bialosky, *Poetry Will Save Your Life:* A Memoir. New York: Atria Books.

—— (2017). *You and your whole race.* In: J. Bialosky, Poetry Will Save Your Life: A Memoir. New York: Atria Books.

Izard, C.E. (1972). *Patterns of Emotion.* New York: Academic Press.

—— (1977). *Human Emotions.* New York: Plenum Press.

Jackson, S. (1982). The lottery. In: *The Lottery and Other Stories.* New York: Farrar, Straus, and Giroux.

Jennings, E. (2019). Into the hour. In: W. Sieghart, *The Poetry Remedy: Prescriptions for the Heart, Mind, and Soul.* New York: Viking.

Jin, Ha. (2019). Ways of talking. In: W. Sieghart, *The Poetry Remedy: Prescriptions for the Heart, Mind, and Soul.* New York: Viking.

Jonson, B. (2017). On my first son. In: J. Bialosky, *Poetry Will Save Your Life: A Memoir.* New York: Atria Books.

Joseph, J. (2013). Warning. In: *Poems to Learn By Heart.* ed, A. Sampson. London: Michael O'Mara Books.

Kaminsky, I. (2019). We lived happily during the war. In: *Deaf Republic.* Minneapolis, Minn: Graywolf Press.

Keats, J. (1952). Ode on a Grecian urn. In: *Immortal Poems of the English Language*, ed.: O. Williams, New York: Simon and Schuster (Pocket Books).

Kohut, H. (1971). *The Analysis of the Self.* New York: International Universities Press.

Kunitz, S. (1995). In: *The Language of Life: A Festival of Poets*, ed. B. Moyers. New York: Anchor Books.

Lamb, C. (2013). Anger. In: *Poems to Learn By Heart.* ed, A. Sampson. London: Michael O'Mara Books.

Lansky, M. & Morrison, A. (eds.) (1997). *The Widening Scope of Shame.* Hillsdale, N.J.: The Analytic Press.

Lazarus, E. (2006). The new colossus. In: D. Lehman, ed. *The Oxford Book of American Poetry.* Oxford: Oxford University Press.

Levenson, E. (1991). *The Purloined Self: Interpersonal Perspectives in Psychoanalysis*. New York: Contemporary Psychoanalytic Books.

Levertov, D. (2019). Primary wonder. In: W. Sieghart, *The Poetry Remedy: Prescriptions for the Heart, Mind, and Soul*. New York: Viking.

Levin, R. (2002). Hamlet, Laertes, and the dramatic function of foils. In: *Hamlet: New Critical Essays*, ed. A. F. Kinney, New York: Routledge.

Logue, C. (2019). Come to the edge. In: W. Sieghart, *The Poetry Remedy: Prescriptions for the Heart, Mind, and Soul*. New York: Viking.

Longfellow, H.W. (2010). The cross of snow. In: Burt, S. & D. Mikics, *The Art of the Sonnet*. Cambridge, Mass: Harvard University Press.

McCarriston, L. A castle in Lynn. In: *The Language of Life: A Festival of Poets*, ed. B. Moyers. New York: Anchor Books.

——— Billy. In: *The Language of Life: A Festival of Poets*, ed. B. Moyers. New York: Anchor Books.

McKay, C. (2010). America. In: : Burt, S. & D. Mikics, *The Art of the Sonnet*. Cambridge, Mass: Harvard University Press.

Marshall, M. (2017). *Elizabeth Bishop: A Miracle for Breakfast*. NY: Houghton Mifflin Harcourt.

May, R. (1953). *Man's Search for Himself*. New York: W.W. Norton.

——— (1991). *The Cry for Myth*. New York: Dell Publishing.

Millay, E. St. V. (2010). Dirge without music. In: *The Art of Losing: Poems of Grief and Healing*, ed. K. Young. New York: Bloomsbury.

——— (2017). What my lips have kissed, and where, and why. In: J. Bialosky, *Poetry Will Save Your Life: A Memoir*. New York: Atria Books

Mitchell, S.A. (1993). *Hope and Dread in Psychoanalysis*. New York: Basic Books.

Morris, J.N. (2014). For Julia in the deep water. In: *Poems That Make Grown Men Cry*, ed. A. Holden and B. Holden. New York: Simon and Schuster.

Moyers, B. (1995). *The Language of Life: A Festival of Poets*, New York: Anchor Books.

Muir, K. (1975). *Introduction to King Lear.* New York: Methuen.

Mukherjee, B. (1992). The management of grief. In: J.C. Oates (ed.). *The Oxford Book of American Short Stories.* New York: Oxford University Press.

Nathan, L. (2015). Falling. In: J. Hirshfield, *Ten Windows: How Great Poems Transform the World.* New York: Alfred A. Knopf.

New, E. (2019). *Poetry in America,* tape, PBS.

Nye, N.S. (1995). The art of disappearing. In: *The Language of Life: A Festival of Poets,* ed. B. Moyers. New York: Anchor Books.

O'Farrell, M. (2020). *Hamnet: A Novel of the Plague.* New York: Alfred A. Knopf.

Olds, S. (2016). The race. In: *The Motive for Metaphor: Brief Essays On Poetry and Psychoanalysis,* ed. H.M. Seiden. London: Karnac Books.

Oliver, M. (2010). When death comes. In: *The Art of Losing: Poems of Grief and Healing,* ed. K. Young. New York: Bloomsbury.

(2014). In Blackwater woods. In: *Poems That Make Grown Men Cry.* ed. A. Holden & B. Holden, New York: Simon & Schuster.

Orange, D. (2010). *Thinking for clinicians.* New York: Routledge.

Ornstein, A. & S. Goldman, (2004). *My Mother's Eyes: Holocaust Memories of a Young Girl.* Cincinnati, OH: Emmis Books.

Paredez, D. (2019). Wife's disaster manual. In: W. Sieghart, *The Poetry Remedy: Prescriptions for the Heart, Mind, and Soul.* New York: Viking.

Pawlowski, R. (1984) My Maggie machine. In: B. Raffel, *How to Read a Poem.* New York: Meridian.

Paz, O. (1995). In: *The Language of Life: A Festival of Poets,* ed. B. Moyers. New York: Anchor Books.

Perry, J. (2019). The haunted. In: *New York Times Magazine,* Sunday, Nov. 3, pp. 32–43.

Plath, S. (2017). Tulips. In: In: J. Bialosky, *Poetry Will Save Your Life: A Memoir*. New York: Atria Books.

Pugh, S. (2019). What if this road. In: W. Sieghart, *The Poetry Remedy: Prescriptions for the Heart, Mind, and Soul*. New York: Viking.

Raffel, B. (1984). *How to Read a Poem*. New York: Meridian.

Rich, A. (1995). "Dedications," In: *The Language of Life: A Festival of Poets*, ed. B. Moyers. New York: Anchor Books.

(2014). Eastern war time," In *Poems That Make Grown Men Cry*, ed. A. Holden & B. Holden, New York: Simon & Schuster.

Rilke, R.M. (1934). *Letters to a Young Poet*. New York: Norton.

——— (2016). The archaic torso of Apollo. In: R. Corbett, *You Must Change Your Life: The Story Of Rainer Maria Rilke and Auguste Rodin*. New York: W.W. Norton.

Robinson, E.A. (2010). Firelight. In: The Art of the Sonnet, ed. S. Burt & D. Mikics. Cambridge, Mass: Harvard University Press.

Rossetti, C. (2010) Later life 17. In: *The Art of the Sonnet*, ed. S. Burt & D. Mikics. Cambridge, Mass: Harvard University Press.

Rumi (translated by Coleman Barks) The guest house. W. Sieghart, *The Poetry Remedy: Prescriptions for the Heart, Mind, and Soul*. New York: Viking.

Sappho (1984). In: B. Raffel, *How to Read a Poem*. New York: Meridian.

Sartre, J.P. (1956). *Being and Nothingness* (H.E. Barnes, Trans). New York: Philosophical Library.

Scannell, V. (2019). Nettles. In: W. Sieghart, *The Poetry Remedy: Prescriptions for the Heart, Mind, and Soul*. New York: Viking.

Schachtel, E.G. (1959). Metamorphosis: On the Conflict of Human Development and the Psychology of Creativity. Hillsdale, N.J.: The Analytic Press.

Schecter, D.E. (1979). The loving and persecuting superego. *Contemporary Psychoanalysis* 15: 361–379.

School of Life (2018). *What is culture for?* London: The School of Life Press.

Seiden, H. (2016). *The Motive for Metaphor: Brief Essays on Poetry and Psychoanalysis.* London: Karnac

Severson, E. (2011). *Scandalous Obligation: Rethinking Christian Responsibility.* Boston: Beacon Hill Press.

Shakespeare, W. (1972). *King Lear. Arden Shakespeare*, ed: K. Muir. New York: Methuen & Co.

——— (1997). *King Lear. Arden Shakespeare*, ed. R.A. Foakes. London: Thomas Learning.

——— (1997). Sonnet 73. In: H. Vendler, *The Art of Shakespeare's Sonnets.* Cambridge, Mass: Harvard University Press.

——— (1997). Sonnet 116. In: H. Vendler, *The Art of Shakespeare's Sonnets.* Cambridge, Mass: Harvard University Press.

——— (1997). Sonnet 130. In: H. Vendler, *The Art of Shakespeare's Sonnets.* Cambridge, Mass: Harvard University Press.

——— (1997). Sonnet 138. In: H. Vendler, *The Art of Shakespeare's Sonnets.* Cambridge, Mass: Harvard University Press.

——— (2008). *Measure for Measure. Arden Shakesp*eare (ed. J.W. Lever). London: Bloomsbury.

——— (2000). *The Merchant of Venice*, ed: A.R. Braunmuller. The Pelican Shakespeare, New York: Penguin Books.

——— (2011). *The Tempest*, ed: V.M. Vaughan & A.T. Vaughan. Arden Shakespeare. London: Bloomsbury.

——— (2015). As You Like It. In: *The Complete Works of William Shakespeare*, New York: Barnes and Noble.

——— (2015). Romeo and Juliet. In: *The Complete Works of William Shakespeare*, New York: Barnes and Noble.

——— (2015). *Twelfth Night; or, What You Will.* In: The Complete Works of William Shakespeare, New York: Barnes and Noble.

———— (2016). Hamlet. ed. A. Thompson & N. Taylor, *The Arden Shakespeare*. London: Bloomsbury. Also (2007). *Barnes & Noble Shakespeare*, ed. J. Dolven, New York: Barnes & Noble.

Shepard, S. (2017). *Spy of the First Person*. New York: Alfred A. Knopf.

Shinder, J. (2010). Coda. In: K. Young, *The Art of Losing: Poems of Grief and Healing*. New York: Bloomsbury.

Shikibu, I. (2019). Although the wind. In: W. Sieghart, *The Poetry Remedy: Prescriptions for the Heart, Mind, and Soul*. New York: Viking.

Skinner, B.F. (1968). *The Technology of Teaching*. New York: Appleton-Century-Crofts.

———— (1976). *About Behaviorism*. New York: Vintage Books.

Snyder, G. (1995). In: *The Language of Life: A Festival of Poets*, ed. B. Moyers. New York: Anchor Books.

Spiegel, R. (1980). Cognitive aspects of affects and other feeling states with clinical implications. *Journal of the American Academy of Psychoanalysis* 8: 591–614.

Stafford, W. (2019). The way it is. In: W. Sieghart, *The Poetry Remedy: Prescriptions for the Heart, Mind, and Soul*. New York: Viking.

Stern, D.B. (1990). Courting surprise. *Contemporary Psychoanalysis* 26: 425–478.

Stern, G. (2016). I remember Galileo. In: H. Seiden, *The Motive for Metaphor: Brief Essays on Poetry and Psychoanalysis*. London: Karnac.

Stevens, W. (1984). "The house was quiet and the world was calm," In: B. Raffel, B. Raffel, *How to Read a Poem*, New York: Meridian.

———— (1984). "The snow man," In: B. Raffel, *How to Read a Poem*, New York: Meridian.

Stoppard, T. (1967/2017). *Rosencrantz and Guildenstern Are Dead*. New York: Grove Press.

Sullivan, H.S. (1940). *Conceptions of Modern Psychiatry*. New York: Norton.

———— (1948/1964). *The Fusion of Psychiatry and Social Science*. New York: Norton.

———— (1953). *The Interpersonal Theory of Psychiatry*. New York: Norton.

———— (1954). *The Psychiatric Interview*. New York: Norton.

———— (1956). *Clinical Studies in Psychiatry*. New York: Norton.

Swinburne, A.C. (1880/2008). A study of Shakespeare. In: *Bloom's Shakespeare Through the Ages: King Lear*. (ed. H. Bloom). New York: Checkmark Books.

Thomas, D. (2010). Do not go gentle into that good night. In: *The Art of Losing: Poems of Grief and Healing*, ed. K. Young. New York: Bloomsbury, USA.

Timrod, H. (2010). "I know not why, but all this weary day," In: *The Art of the Sonnet*, ed. S. Burt & D. Mikics. Cambridge, Mass: Harvard University Press.

Tolkien, J.R.R. (2019). All that is gold does not glitter. In: . In: W. Sieghart, *The Poetry Remedy: Prescriptions for the Heart, Mind, and Soul*. New York: Viking.

Tolstoy, L. (1886/1982). The death of Ivan Ilych. In: *The Raid and Other Stories*, trans. A. Maude & L. Maud. New York: Oxford University Press.

———— (1906/2008). On Shakespeare. *Bloom's Shakespeare Through the Ages: King Lear.* (ed. H. Bloom). New York: Checkmark Books

Transtromer, T. (2012). Vermeer. In: *Art and Artists*, ed.: E. Fragos, London: Everyman's Library.

Trethewey, N. (2010). Myth. In: *The Art of Losing: Poems of Grief and Healing*, ed. K. Young. New York: Bloomsbury, USA.

Vendler, H. (1997). *The Art of Shakespeare's Sonnets*. Cambridge, Mass.: Harvard University Press.

———— (2010). *Dickinson: Selected Poems and Commentaries*. Cambridge, Mass: Harvard University Press.

Walcott, D. (2019). Love after love," In: W. Sieghart, *The Poetry Remedy: Prescriptions for the Heart, Mind, and Soul.* New York: Viking.

Waters, M.Y. (2003). Since my house burnt down. In: M.Y. Waters, *The Laws of Evening.* London: Simon & Schuster.

Werstine, P. (2002). "The causes of this defect": Hamlet's editors. . In: *Hamlet: New Critical Essays,* ed. A. F. Kinney, New York: Routledge.

Wilbur, R. (1989). The writer. In: L. Havens, *A Safe Place.* New York: Random House, p. 23.

(2009). A reckoning. The New Yorker, August 31, p. 55.

Williams, C.K. (2010). Grief. In: *The Art of Losing: Poems of Grief and Healing,* ed. K. Young. New York: Bloomsbury, USA.

Winnicott, D. (1949). Hate in the countertransference. *International Journal of Psychoanalysis* 30: 69–75.

——— (1971). *Playing and Reality.* London: Tavistock.

Wordsworth, W. (1805/1988). *Ode: Intimations of immortality from recollections of early childhood.* In: Wordsworth's Poetical Works. London: Moxon. Also in: (1995) *A Treasury of Great Poems: English and American,* ed. L. Untermeyer, New York: Simon & Schuster.

——— (1952). Daffodils. In: *Immortal Poems of the English Language.* ed: O. Williams. New York: Simon & Schuster.

——— 1984). The world is too much with us. In: B. Raffel, *How to Read a Poem,* New York: Meridian.

Yeats, W.B. (1996). When you are old. In: *A Treasury of Poems,* ed. S.A. Stuart. New York: Galahad Books.

——— (2016). Crazy Jane talks with the bishop. In: H. Seiden, *The Motive for Metaphor: Brief Essays on Poetry and Psychoanalysis.* London: Karnac.

Young Lee, L. (1995). In: *The Language of Life: A Festival of Poets,* ed. B. Moyers. New York: Anchor Books.

Permissions for Republication

Angelou, M. (2019). "Still I Rise" from AND STILL I RISE: A BOOK OF POEMS by Maya Angelou, copyright © 1978 by Maya Angelou. Used by permission of Random House, an imprint and division of Penguin Random House LLC. All rights reserved.

Auden, W.H. (1972)."Loneliness," copyright © 1972 by W. H. Auden; from COLLECTED POEMS by W. H. Auden, edited by Edward Mendelson. Used by permission of Random House, an imprint and division of Penguin Random House LLC. All rights reserved.

Auden, W.H. (2017). Musee des beaux arts, In: J. Bialosky, Poetry Will Save Your Life: A Memoir. New York: Atria Books. Also in W.H. Auden: Collected Poems. ed. E. Mendelson. 1991, New York: Vintage Books.

Bang, M.J. Mary Jo Bang, (2007)."The Role of Elegy" from *Elegy*. Copyright © 2007 by Mary Jo Bang. Reprinted with the permission of The Permissions Company, LLC on behalf of Graywolf Press, Minneapolis, Minnesota, graywolfpress.org.

Barker, S. (2016). The ballad of true regret. In The Land of Gold, 2013 London: Enitharmon Press

Berry, W. (1968). "The Peace of Wild Things" from *New Collected Poems*. Copyright © 1968, 2012 by Wendell Berry. Reprinted with the permission of The Permissions Company, LLC on behalf of Counterpoint Press, counterpointpress.com.

Bishop, E. (2001). "In the Waiting Room" and "One Art" from POEMS by Elizabeth Bishop. Copyright © 2011 by The Alice H. Methfessel

Dove, R. (1995). "Party Dress for a First Born", from MOTHER LOVE by Rita Dove. Copyright © 1995 by Rita Dove. Used by permission of W. W. Norton & Company, Inc

Durcan, P. (2012). "Maureen Durcan" from *Praise in Which I Live and Move and Have my Being* by Paul Durcan published by Harvill Secker. Copyright © Paul Durcan 2012. Reproduced by permission of The Random House Group Ltd.

Edwards, P. (2002). The dyer's infected hand: The sonnets and the text of Hamlet. In: Hamlet: New Critical Essays, ed. A.F. Kinney, New York: Routledge.

Fenton, J. (1994). "The Mistake" from OUT OF DANGER by James Fenton. Copyright © 1994 by James Fenton. Reprinted by permission of Farrar, Straus and Giroux. All Rights Reserved.

Flynn, N. (2000). "Sudden" from *Some Ether*. Copyright © 2000 by Nick Flynn. Reprinted with the permission of The Permissions Company, LLC on behalf of Graywolf Press, Minneapolis, Minnesota, graywolfpress.org.

Forché, C., (1974). "The Morning Backing.in "GATHERING THE TRIBES (1974) copyright. Yale University Press.

Girmay, A. (2016). "Second Estrangement" from *The Black Maria*. Copyright © 2016 by Aracelis Girmay. Reprinted with the permission of The Permissions Company, LLC on behalf of BOA Editions Ltd., www. boaeditions.org.Hass, R. (2016), Heroic Simile, In: The Motive for Metaphor: Brief Essays On Poetry and Psychoanalysis, ed. H.M. Seiden. London: Karnac Books.

Hall, D. (1990). "A Grace" from OLD AND NEW POEMS by Donald Hall. Copyright © 1990 by Donald Hall. Reprinted by permission of Mariner Books, an imprint of HarperCollins Publishers. All rights reserved.

Hall, D. (1990). " My Son, My Executioner" from OLD AND NEW POEMS by Donald Hall. Copyright © 1990 by Donald Hall. Reprinted by permission of Mariner Books, an imprint of HarperCollins Publishers. All rights reserved.

Hass, R. (1979). "Heroic Simile" from *Praise.* Copyright © 1979 by Robert Hass, published by HarperCollins Publishers Inc. Reprinted by permission of Robert Hass. Emailed HarperCollins

Hartwig, J. (2015). " Feeling the way" translated by John and Bogdana Carpenter, translation copyright © 2008 by John Carpenter and Bogdana Carpenter. Used by permission of Alfred A. Knopf, an imprint of the Knopf Doubleday Publishing Group, a division of Penguin Random House LLC. All rights reserved.

Heanys, S. (1998). "Follower"; excerpt from "Clearances" from OPENED GROUND: SELECTED POEMS 1966–1996 by Seamus Heaney. Copyright © 1998 by Seamus Heaney. Reprinted by permission of Farrar, Straus and Giroux. All Rights Reserved.

Hirsch, E. (1981). "Fast Break" from WILD GRATITUDE by Edward Hirsch, copyright © 1981 by Edward Hirsch. Used by permission of Alfred A. Knopf, an imprint of the Knopf Doubleday Publishing Group, a division of Penguin Random House LLC. All rights reserved.

Hirshfield, J (2006). "Burlap Sack" from After: Poems by Jane Hirshfield. Copyright (c) 2006 by Jane Hirshfield. Used by permission of HarperCollins Publishers.

Hoagland, T (2020). "I Have News for You" from *Unincorporated Persons in the Late Honda Dynasty*. Copyright © 2010 by Tony Hoagland. Reprinted with the permission of The Permissions Company, LLC on behalf of Graywolf Press, Minneapolis, Minnesota, www. graywolfpress.org.

Index

Asimov, Isaac, 449

attention seeking as strength vs. sin, 239–45

attentiveness, 142. *See also* focus

"Aubade" (Larkin), 303–5, 307

Auden, W.H.

on aging, 229, 396, 437, 440

"Funeral Blues," 74–75, 291, 292

"Loneliness," 55–57

"Lullaby," 104–6, 120

"Musee des Beaux Arts," 50–52, 192–95, 267, 290, 291, 295, 305

"Old People's Home," 228–29, 437–40, 444–46

"Twelve Songs," 373

Baer, Ulrich, 155

Baldwin, James, 4

Berry, Wendell, 98–99

"Beyond the Chains of Illusion" (Fromm), 61

Bialosky, Jill, 51, 61–62, 174

"Billy" (McCarriston), 28–31

birds, 125, 158–59, 326, 327

Bishop, Elizabeth

"In the Waiting Room," 95–98, 101, 250–52, 397, 398

"One Art," 171–76, 181

"Blackwater Woods" (Oliver). *See* "In Blackwater Woods"

Blake, William, 323

"A Poison Tree," 110–11, 113, 224, 381, 383

blindness. *See under* Gloucester

Bloom, Harold, 391, 406, 422–23, 441

Bosch, Hieronymus, 192–93

Brodsky, Joseph, 213–15

Rilke and, 28, 65, 155–57, 273 (*see also* inseeing)
vs. security, 211

"Daffodils" (Wordsworth), 148
darkness, 84, 85, 162
"Day of the Dead" (Harjo), 25
de Botton, Alain, 26
"dead Silencer," 240, 245
death and dying
    Dickinson on, 307–8, 326–29, 331, 366
    "Do not go gentle into that good night" (Thomas), 114, 226, 228–29, 348, 384, 385
    "Do Not Stand At My Grave and Weep" (Frye), 83–84
    humor and, 273, 304, 354–55
    internal efforts to maintain relationships with the deceased, 82–83
    letting go of life, 226–33
    "to be or not to be" (Hamlet), 73, 203, 304, 324–32, 366
    "Tulips" (Plath) and, 324, 325, 327, 331
    "When Death Comes" (Oliver), 199–204, 349
    See also afterlife; "Dirge Without Music"; funerals; grief/mourning; suicidality; "What the Living Do"
Death in the Family, A (Agee), 301–2
Death of Ivan Ilych, The (Tolstoy), 88, 233
"Dedications" (Rich), 44–45
defensive and non-defensive postures, oscillating between, 31
"Defining the Problem" (Cope), 122
depression/melancholy, 19, 39–40, 53, 54, 218, 219, 292
    Freud on, 173, 216, 217
    in *Hamlet*, 294, 298, 310, 323, 340, 449
    vs. normal grief/sadness, 40, 82, 216, 217, 284–85

Howe, Marie
grief/mourning and, 5–7, 75, 82, 88, 277, 278, 281
Seiden on, 72
"What the Living Do," 5–7, 70–75, 81–82, 205–7, 277, 281
Hughes, Langston, 247–49
humor, 218
death and, 273, 304, 354–55
Dickinson and, 154–55, 308
in Shakespeare's tragedies, 31, 305, 354–55, 370
sorrow and, 77, 273

"I am living, I remember you" (Howe), 7, 71, 72, 205
"I Have News for You" (Hoagland), 318–19
"I Know Not Why, But All This Weary Day" (Timrod), 38–41
"I Remember Galileo" (Stern), 199, 201–6, 452–53
Icarus
fall/failure of, 194, 196, 209, 290, 291, 295
myth of, 51–53
identity and integrity, 385. *See also under* King Lear
illuminating what is hidden, 19–21
immortality
Dickinson on, 328–29
See also "Ode"
"imprisoned lightening" (Lazarus), 165, 167, 236
imprisonment
John McCain's, 45, 169
"To prisoners" (Brooks), 161–62
"In Blackwater Woods" (Oliver), 118, 171, 172, 174–76, 181, 272, 445, 449, 453
"In the Waiting Room" (Bishop), 95–98, 101, 250–52, 397, 398

life force, 72, 73, 123, 125, 135, 162, 199, 201, 249
life purpose, 350
"Lion" (Hettich), 90–95, 145, 150
Logue, Christopher, 190
loneliness, 26, 57, 58
    vs. benign aloneness, 57
    emotions and, 21, 44
    "love's austere and lonely offices" (Hayden), 16, 132, 140–43, 145
    in *The Merchant of Venice* (Shakespeare), 64
    "On Loneliness" (Fromm-Reichmann), 27, 47, 265
    overview and nature of, 45–64
    poetry assuaging, xi, 19, 21, 27, 44, 47, 48, 53, 60, 61, 64
    in Robert Frost poems, 407
    Wordsworth on, 137
"Loneliness" (Auden), 55–57
Longfellow, Henry Wadsworth, 80–82, 215–16
losing. *See* art of losing
loss
    bearing, 171–75
    courage and, 285–87
    inevitable loss and inevitable renewal, 255–59
    inherent in aging, 65, 89, 175–81, 255, 438
    Rilke and, 28, 65, 78, 81, 155, 273
    See also under power; *specific characters in King Lear*
love, 105, 117–22, 447
    careful, 182–91
    Cordelia and, 349, 357, 358, 374, 391, 398, 409–10, 424–25, 428–32, 434–35, 440
    definitions, 427
    power to transform, 425

self-love, 57–58
when truth collides with, 430–36
See also specific characters in Hamlet and King Lear
"Love After Love" (Walcott), 57
"Lullaby" (Auden), 104–6, 120

"mad" scene (*Hamlet*), 353–54, 441
madness
    Dickinson on, 344, 429
    in *Hamlet*, 261, 270, 297, 298, 306, 309, 311, 312, 337–39, 342–43,
        353
    infirm, 360, 362–63, 398
    of King Lear, 115, 353, 358, 360, 362, 365, 368, 370, 378–80, 382,
        396, 397, 399, 413, 421, 422, 428–30, 440, 441
    poetry and, 439
    Polonius and, 309, 338, 339
magic, 439. *See also under* Prospero
magical thinking, 272
"Management of Grief, The" (Mukherjee), 271
Marshall, Megan, 98
"Maureen Durcan" (Durcan), 229–30
May, Rollo, 212–13
McCain, John, 45, 169
McCarriston, Linda
    "Billy," 28–31
    "A Castle in Lynn," 4–5
meaning making process, 3, 60, 142, 448
Measure for Measure (Shakespeare), 223, 427, 433
melancholy. *See* depression/melancholy
Merchant of Venice, The (Shakespeare), 63–64, 220, 223, 427, 433

"Those Winter Sundays" (Hayden), 16, 131–32, 140–43, 145, 234, 235, 334–35

time

    storm of, 393–99

    transformation of, 87–88

Timrod, Henry, 38–41

"to be or not to be" (Hamlet), 73, 203, 304, 324–32, 366

"To prisoners" (Brooks), 161–62

"To You" (Whitman), 25

tolerance, in praise of, 253–55

Tolkien, J.R.R., 255–56, 259, 436

Tolstoy, Leo, 88

    The Death of Ivan Ilych, 88, 233

    King Lear and, 360, 382, 423

Tom o' Bedlam, Edgar (in *King Lear*) disguised as. *See* "Poor Tom"

transformation, 25, 416

    of Hamlet, 298–300

    of King Lear, 127–28, 393, 422–30, 434

    of Prospero (*The Tempest*), 425–27, 442–43, 446–50

    of time, 87–88

transformative power of poetry, 44

transitional object, 141–42

transitional space, 56, 141–42

trauma, 100, 101, 298

Trethewey, Natasha, 212, 213, 215

Trinity, Dickinson's version of the, 18

truth, 211

    Dickinson and, 100, 101, 152, 207, 222, 297, 414

    Jill Bialosky on, 174

    and madness, 421

psychoanalysis and, 100–101
Shakespeare and, 122 (*see also under* truth telling)
tact triumphing over, 122
"To thine own self be true," 349
when love collides with, 430–36
See also certainty
truth telling, 409
    Cordelia's, 121, 357
    Earl of Kent's, 411–13, 432
    by poets, 4
    by Shakespearean Fool, 107–8, 222, 413–14 (*see also* Shakespearean Fool)
    "Tell all the truth but tell it slant" (Dickinson), 100, 207, 297, 414
    truth tellers in *King Lear*, 222, 409–22, 432
    See also honesty; truth
"Tulips" (Plath), 324–25, 327, 331
Turner, Dennis, 69, 77
Twelfth Night (Shakespeare), 223–24
"Twelve Songs" (Auden), 373
"Two Tramps in Mud Time" (Frost), 399–401
"tyrant" gods, Gloucester and, 365, 367, 418. *See also* gods

uncanny, 95
uncertainty, 337
    "gnat" of, 315, 316
    "Lion" (Hettich) and, 93, 95
    See also certainty
unconscious. *See* hidden; repression
unharmed self, loss of the, 298
United States. *See* America